Learning Activities
for Reading

Learning Activities for Reading

Fourth Edition

Selma E. Herr
Formerly Director of Reading Laboratory
Tulane University/New Orleans

wcb
Wm. C. Brown Company Publishers
Dubuque, Iowa

Library of Congress Catalog Card Number: 76-44125

ISBN 0–697–06191–4

Printed in the United States of America

Contents

List of Figures

Preface

A sound and effective reading program is dependent on many factors. The most important would be teaching, methodology, materials and the curriculum. These may be called the teaching-learning climate.

Regard the classroom as your office and the curriculum as the business to be transacted. You are the salesperson and the pupils are your buyers. You must make sure your wares are attractive so that the buyers will be interested and more of your goods will leave the classroom.

True, your wares must be attractive but the place where they are displayed must also be attractive and inviting. Today the precept is to return to the basics in our school programs and rather than thinking that this will make learning less enticing for the learner, it should make the acquisition of knowledge more acceptable.

In recent years teachers have often placed much faith in the efficacy of materials per se. Often they are considered as panaceas and breakthroughs in reading instruction. Improved instruction emerges only as the result of teacher behavior.

This book has attempted to provide the teacher with ideas that can motivate the acqusition of the basic skills which are essential for the development of the successful and achieving individual.

The activities will help the teacher discover procedures in which the basic skills can be presented in a motivated situation. Mental activities, concentration, and insight are a part of the general pattern of procedures which will help the children learn more readily and effectively.

The first chapter of the book presents the developmental sequence involved in learning to read and discusss the classroom situation and the skills that will be developed.

Prereading and beginning reading instruction includes activities that will be helpful in enriching the children's reading and learning processes.

Since comprehension is considered one of the important facets in any subject, and especially in reading, many suggestions for improving the comprehension skills are included in the third chapter. The fourth chapter continues with critical reading, recognition of fact or opinion, drawing conclusions, predicting outcomes, making inferences, perceiving relationships, and problem solving.

The next chapter continues with locational skills and the development of organizational patterns. Vocabulary development is discussed in the sixth chapter. This includes phonics, dictionary usage, syllabication, prefixes and suffixes, and Latin and Greek roots and stems.

Chapter seven involves the child that must learn English as the second language. In order to help the bilingual child, it is necessary to understand his environmental background and to be able to help the child adjust to his new situation.

Perceptual awareness is an important facet in learning, and the training in sensory acuity and emotional reactions is discussed in chapter eight. Listening and remembering are also a part of this chapter.

Chapters on the diagnosis and the remediation of reading problems and the use of instruments as teaching aids conclude the book.

1 Introduction

Reading is everywhere. One reads people's faces, their hands, their attitudes, their behavior, their intentions. One reads instruments such as gauges, meters, and clocks. One reads the clouds, the sunsets, terrains, and all of nature about us. One reads pictures, music, and the printed page. How well one reads and remembers is usually the result of elementary school training.

The teacher must bear in mind that learning to read is a long-term developmental process extending over a period of many years, and that the child's early attitude towards reading is very important and can influence a child's learning and reading habits for life.

Teaching is more than telling and there is a difference between lesson hearing and real teaching. There are three ingredients of reading progress—an understanding teacher, a variety of reading techniques, and a wide range of interesting reading materials. It should be added that the willing and ready student is an important factor also but the child's behavior is dependent upon the first three ingredients to a large extent.

A variety of approaches in reading instruction are essential because children learn by different methods. If there are significant individual differences in the way children learn to read, it follows that different approaches must be used. Children grow and mature at varying rates and therefore reading instruction must be adjusted to meet the physical, social, emotional, and developmental needs of all the children. They learn to read at a level commensurate with their ability. Every child sees reading as a meaning-making process, but he must experience a motivational satisfaction from the procedure. Reading competence is the result of developing varied interests which differ in the rate of growth of each child.

If the teacher fully understood how the pupil learns to read, the teaching of reading would be rather simple. Unfortunately, this is not the case. The teacher thus is faced with the task of constantly checking his teaching practices against theory and experimentation. He needs to know *why* certain methods work and why some do not.

To be effective, teachers must know the pupil's individualness. Without this knowledge they cannot provide meaningful learning experiences. Without this knowledge all the rules and generalizations are empty for these are modified and changed in and by every individual. Without this knowledge, the teacher cannot adapt his responses, his rules, and generalizations to the individual.

Carefully selected and well-directed learning activities should meet the following criteria:

1. The activity should be directed at some important reading technique or skill.
2. The work should be educationally sound.
3. The contents should be related to materials in other subjects in the curriculum as well as to the reading assignment.
4. The material should be properly prepared.
5. The work should be interesting and stimulate curiosity. Opportunity for initiative and originality should be provided.
6. The directions should be clear and easily followed.
7. Printed material should be neat and legible, and contain only known words.
8. The pupils should have the purpose clearly in mind.
9. The activity should permit the child to think through the problem.
10. The exercise should provide for repetition. The skill should have been taught previously.
11. The activity should hold the child's interest and attention comparable to his attention span and mental maturity.
12. The work should be adapted to the age and developmental level of the child.
13. The activity should be self-checking whenever possible.
14. The material should be relatively inexpensive.
15. The activity should provide for evaluation.
16. The work should be within the child's current experience, real or vicarious.
17. If the activity is supposed to be an independent one, it should be just that.
18. The experiences should be varied in order to carry out a well-balanced reading program.
19. Emphasis should be placed on building understandings and critical thinking.
20. Self-control, resourcefulness, independence, and good work habits should be developed.
21. The individual needs of each child must be met.

The easiest way for children to learn is through activities in which they can discover through trial and error. Situations in which there is too much reliance on rote memory rather than on understanding and experiencing is not the best learning situation.

Sufficient and varied reading experiences and materials at the appropriate instructional levels should be easily accessible for the children's use. The room environment and choice of activities provided should be such that an element of curiosity will stimulate further reading in all areas of the curriculum.

Activities should be experiences in learning and motivating—not testing. However, the activities should have a diagnostic and prognostic value to the teachers. Through the children's work, the teacher should be able to determine their needs and evaluate their growth. If work is assigned and then forgotten or relegated to the wastebasket, the children are quick to notice, and they may attempt to get by with as little work as possible. If work is assigned to the pupils, they are expected to complete it to the best of their abilities, and the teacher is expected to check the work. If the child is unable to complete the work, the teacher should examine the situation and make proper adjustments.

All pupils in the classroom cannot be under the teacher's guidance at all times. Therefore, it is necessary to provide quiet instructional and creative activities. Such periods should allow for initiative and provide practice in the needed skills.

GROUPING

Cooperative group work is essential to democratic living. Group planning is an important factor in the children's growth and as the children plan together, they learn the processes of thinking in concrete terms and also of democratic leadership. It instills the feeling of responsibility and develops a group climate important to each member's personality.

Better relations prevail if the grouping is so flexible that the child does not feel that he belongs to one group only. A child may be able to work in one group in reading and another group in mathematics. There are several types of grouping and the ones most frequently referred to are the homogeneous and heterogeneous, but there are also friendship, interest, age, physical, and community groups. In some subject fields, such as mathematics and reading, the homogeneous or ability grouping usually seems most satisfactory.

The purpose of grouping is to meet the individual needs of the children and to develop responsibility. Group standards should be set up. These should include neatness or housekeeping duties, courtesy toward others, discipline, and satisfactory execution of the assignments. The teacher must provide activities and materials for the needs of the various groups.

The teacher should discover the different achievement levels of each child through the accumulative records, tests, the child's choice of books, and his reading ability. Many teachers provide constant regrouping of the children as they develop in their abilities. A child might be in one group in social studies, another group in arithmetic, and in another group in reading.

Children should not feel that there is a stigma attached to being in a lower group, but rather that they are in the group wherein they can achieve most successfully without frustration. No longer do we have the Bluebirds, Chickades, and Brownies. Many a disturbed mother used to visit the teacher to inquire why Johnny was a Brownie. The children knew which was the highest and the lowest achieving group without being given discriminating names.

Some children know how to disguise their inefficiency in a group because they are good listeners and have good memories. Individual follow-up activtiies help the teacher in discovering the children's capacities.

There are several workable groupings of children. Achievement grouping is one of the most frequently used procedures. Usually three groups in the classroom are the most easily handled. The children work at a level where the material is comfortable for them. They can feel a degree of success in their activities. The material must have a high interest level, and the instructional level should be considered in planning the material.

When the tutorial grouping is used, the children work in pairs. The children should be on friendly terms, and each child should know what to do and have a definite task to perform. These pairs are changed frequently for best results.

Interest groupings are developed so that children interested in similar projects may work together. Research groupings are also used successfully when the children have reports or certain projects to prepare. The teacher must understand the purpose of the groupings and be aware of the danger of a fixed-type grouping. The children may be members of various committees, such as research for finding certain information in science or social studies, or vocabulary-study committees which work on certain words needed for a topic which is being studied. The children should feel the responsibility of belonging to groups and should know that when their work is of a superior nature, they may be permitted to go on into a higher group. For this reason a mobility-type grouping is usually more successful.

Children like to know what is expected of them, and they like to follow some definite schedule. The daily schedule may be written on the blackboard or printed on a chart. Some teachers use a wall-pocket chart with removable strips of cardboard containing assignments. These may be removed, filed, and used again if the need arises.

For the reading hour, the chart below is one of the easiest to follow.

Group	1st 20 Minutes	2d 20 Minutes	3d 20 Minutes
1	Developmental reading with teacher	Follow-up work	Independent activities
2	Independent activities	Developmental reading with teacher	Follow-up work
3	Follow-up work	Independent activities	Developmental reading with teacher

The first group is the slowest, and because these children have difficulty in remembering the assignment from the previous day, they begin with developmental reading with the teacher, who gives them the complete assignment for the hour. The second group of children is at the next level of learning. The third, or highest group, is able to remember the directions from the previous day and consequently can do the follow-up work first.

Two other forms of charts are shown (figs. 1.1, 1.2). The center wheel is made movable by being fastened to the chart with a paper fastener. The pockets at the bottom hold the children's names and are the same color or design as the part of the wheel designating their group. The names, printed on cards, can be moved from one group to the next. (A child may be delegated to to the responsibility of moving the wheel after each twenty-minute period.) In the second chart, the activity period may be either for the entire day or whatever time is needed. Group leaders may be assigned, and it should be their responsibility to see that the groups work at the projects assigned and use the keys provided to check their results. It is well for the teacher to stop at each table with suggestions and help with group analysis and evaluation.

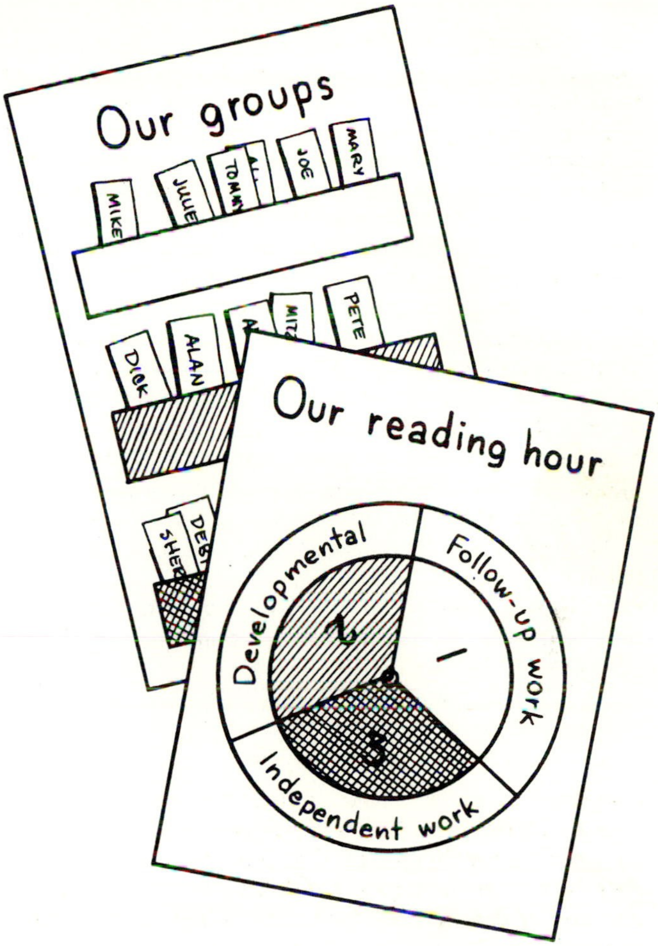

Figure 1.2 Group Chart

The work should be planned with the children. If plans for the following day are made just before dismissal time, the children have something to look forward to for the next day and to talk over with their parents. The day's work should be prepared before the school day begins. Books and materials should be on hand so there will be no delay when the children come into the classroom. The childern should be trained in good work habits and to become self-reliant. They should learn to listen to directions, begin work promptly, complete their work and check it. Supplies, books, games, and activities should be returned to their proper places by the children after a check has been made to see that all the parts are together. Shelves should bear the proper labels so the children will know where to put the materials they have used.

The suggestions that follow may be modified for use at various grade levels. Teachers may use the follow-up work and learning activities from year to year. When duplicating follow-up work, the teacher may make extra copies for use in the groups that will follow; or she may save the master copy. She should use a key to tell her what pages of the readers the material was taken from. The material may be filed in manila folders or envelopes after it has been properly labeled. Writ-

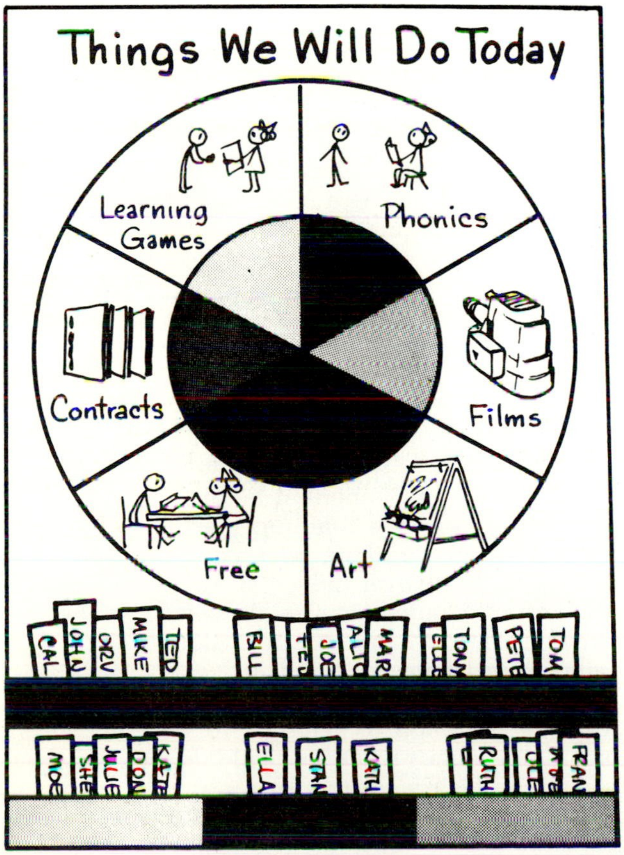

Figure 1.1 Grouping Chart

ing the date used and the group using the material aids the teacher. Some teachers include pictures, poems, and stories that will enrich the lesson.

It is not possible to know exactly when a child learns to read, when he reads to learn, or when he develops an appreciation and curiosity in reading. Skill development does not come in capsule form like time-release medical pills. Each ingredient is released in its own structured time. It is the teacher, in the case of reading, who can influence the unfoldment of these many skills. All teachers in the elementary grades should be familiar with the total program and recognize its continuity.

The introduction of reading skills is useless unless the child's subsequent reading experiences serve to maintain them. The reading program must provide the opportunity for the child to move beyond the basal materials. The child should be given the opportunity to experience enjoyable literary material. He needs to acquaint himself with animal stories, fiction, fairy tales, folk tales, and scientific and cultural materials.

Good teachers, even when they use a basal reading approach, do not use only basal materials exclusively. Neither do they require each child to read the same books. The children's supplementary reading is not restricted and the teacher does not discriminately ignore children's readiness and abilities by grouping them into reading groups where each child takes his turn at orally reading the same book.

If a child is to succeed in school, the emotional and physical factors must be given proper consideration. A child who is happy and is well motivated can concentrate and learn more easily. Some children have a deep sense of guilt and atone for it by receiving the scoldings and reprimands that accompany failure, and some children will use failure as a means for punishing the adult.

Poor readers may be adjusted or maladjusted. They do not have identifiable personalities. An enthusiastic teacher is more likely to motivate students than one who is not motivated or interested herself. The students reactions are contagious and if they are even unconsciously aware of the teacher's lackadaisical attitude they will react much in the same way. The teacher needs to let the pupil know that the instructor believes in him and will guide him. It is important that the teacher is able to communicate with the home and to have rapport with the parents.

Since there is no one best way to approach reading improvement, the best procedure is through the combining of effective instructional techniques that will result in good reading habits. There must be an intrinsic need for reading on the part of the pupil.

To provide for the needs of all the pupils, the program must be kept flexible. The success of the reading program is dependent upon the technique and materials used, the enthusiasm of the teacher, and the motivation and desire of the student.

The reading program must be purposeful, and comprehension must be the primary objective. The soil and climate for growth are success and security, and the pupils must progress along a well-defined road to maturity in reading according to their own ability rather than to a set time schedule.

When homework is assigned, discuss home study facilities with the pupil. Good study habits and satisfactory work headquarters are important to the satisfactory execution of homework assignments. Be certain that the pupil knows what is expected of him and that he understands the directions. A pupil is not always fortunately enough to have a room all to himself, and if he does not have his own room, a study area should be set aside for him. It must be agreed that this is his own corner and he must not be disturbed and distractions must be eliminated. It is difficult to don one's best work if there is no special time or place for study. Trying to work in a room with the family assembled and talking is not conducive to concentration. Noise and talking can be very distracting.

When discussing the homework with the parents, let them know the purpose and the importance of assigning the work to the pupil. Explain that constructive help is good, but doing the work for the child has little value for the learning process. Doing the work for the child defeats its purpose. Sometimes the parents do not realize that there are environmental factors important to good home study habits.

The room should be well ventilated, and the temperature should be not over 70 degrees. A room that is too cold can hamper the pupil's progress as much as an overheated room. A stuffy room will make for sleepiness and he will not be alert.

The desk should be cleared of all distractions; paper, pens, pencils, dictionary, and books should be the only things on it. If the student has a typewriter, a small typewriting table makes a better height for typing than the desk, and will prevent tiredness, too.

A comfortable, straight-backed chair is needed. Sitting on the bed or in a soft chair can be too relaxing. The chair should be the proper height so that the pupil can sit comfortably at the desk. A chair that is too low or too high will cause the shoulders to be out of their correct position.

There should be a good light. The light should be placed so that there will be no shadows or glare on the paper. This is very important because headaches and fatigue can result from improper lighting. Explain to the pupils that for those who are right-handed, the light should come over the left shoulder, and for those who are left-handed, it should come over the right shoulder. This will prevent a shadow over the page while he is writing.

A special time should be set aside for study. It is easier for the pupil to get right to work in this way than if he wonders what he should do first. He should then inform his friends that he is not to be telephoned during this period. By following this regimen he can get his work done much faster. Pencils should be sharpened and ready for use before the student starts work. If there are little chores or things that need to be done before sitting down to work, they should be attended to. He should get his drink of water before getting to work, so he won't have to get up during study period. There are little distractions that have a way of worming into one's mind during the study period, and these habits must be broken without delay.

A dictionary is a must. When one comes to a word he doesn't know, he can read the entire sentence or paragraph and try to get the meaning from the context clues, or he can use the dictionary if he can't get the meaning from the context clues.

It is believed that taking a five-minute rest period after every twenty-five minutes of study is better than trying to study right straight through for several hours without a break. After the five-minute break, the student should study another twenty-five minutes and take another five-minute break until the work is completed. During the break he should get up and move about and get that drink of water if he wishes, but care must be taken to not stretch out the break into long periods. He must discipline himself to get back to work immediately after his five minutes are up.

The radio, record player, or television set have no place at the pupil's study headquarters during study time. Some students claim that they can study better if there is soft music in the background. They claim it shuts out the household talk and noise. This could be true, providing one doesn't become too enthusiastic about the music and forget about the work.

VISION: THE PRICELESS INGREDIENT

Reading is a sensory process. It requires the use of the senses—especially vision. Good eyesight is extremely important to good reading. If the printed page seems blurry and the student complains about headaches, the parents or the school nurse should be consulted.

If the student cannot focus well, it takes much longer to read the material, or all the words may not be interpreted accurately. He can become tense and uncomfortable and he is apt-to tire more easily.

In becoming a good reader, the student must learn how to use his eyes correctly and also how to care for them properly. It is suggested that a reader not look continually at the printed page but that looking up from one's work and looking into the distance can rest the eyes. This of course does not mean long continued gazes but small rest periods at reasonable intervals.

It must be remembered that the young child has a much shorter attention span and a much narrower perceptual span than a more mature individual. His fixation span is usually not more than a three-letter word when he first begins to read. As he matures he should see several words at a fixation instead of looking at and reading one word at a time.

The eyes can learn to move very swiftly along the printed line. A great mistake made by some teachers is that of pointing to the first letter of a word, especially in reading experience charts or chalkboard materials. The teacher, if she must point, should either use her hand or a ruler and hold it under the entire word.

As the pupil becomes older, show him how to look or fixate on the fourth, fifth, or sixth letter at the beginning of a line or sentence, rather than fixating on the first letter of the word.

The students in the intermediate and upper grades are interested in how they use their eyes. Explain to them that as they read, the eyes move swiftly along the printed line. The eyes make a quick jerky movement, fixate on several words, then swiftly move on to the next group of words. This is called *eye movement.* The individual can see only while the eye is fixating on the words. The movement of the eye is so very rapid that there is only a blur as they jump from one group of words to another. It is possible to see 2¼ inches of printed material when the book is held sixteen inches from the eyes.

Sometimes people make quick backward movements on the line of print. These backward movements are called *regressions.* When the individual makes these regressions, he is wasting his time because he is rereading material already read. It takes practice to overcome this habit, but it is important that one does not make regressions. If the pupil does not understand what he has read, he should continue reading to the end of the paragraph. He may then be able to get the meaning. If he does not, he may then skim through the paragraph to find the information he wants. If the material is too difficult, it may result in making many regressions. Simpler material should be provided.

Ask the students to avoid vocalizing or moving the lips or the tongue. Holding a finger over the lips will help. If the students wish to read faster than they can speak, they must overcome the habit of lip movement. The head should be held still while reading. Only the eyes should move. Pointing with a finger or pencil is also a hindrance to reading improvement.

The pupils enjoy class discussion regarding ways to improve their reading. They may wish to make small books and list suggestions for improving reading.

TYPES OF READING

All material cannot be read at the same rate of speed or with the same degree of comprehension because the individual will be reading for different reasons. Some material will prove to be much more difficult to read than other material, due perhaps to the fact that the reader will have a more meager background in some areas than in others. And of course, the direct opposite may be the case. Therefore the rate and comprehension will vary from day to day and from subject to subject.

There are numerous types of reading, which include the following:

I. **Developmental Reading**

   A. Vocabulary development
      ....through context
      ....structural analysis
      ....phonetic analysis
      ....dictionary

B. Comprehension and interpretation
....grasping inferred ideas
....recognizing fact or opinion
....interpretation of ideas
....visualizing content
C. Evaluating and organization
....drawing and proving conclusion
....classifying
....choosing main idea and supporting details
....relating associated ideas
....summarizing
....outlining
D. Retention
E. Oral reading abilities
....enunciation and pronunciation
....fluency
....interpretation
F. Mechanical makeup of book
G. Appreciation

II. Work-Type Reading

A. Interpretation
B. Locating information
C. Following directions
D. Use of workbooks; exercise sheets; contracts
E. Read to find the answer
F. Read to help solve problems

III. Functional Reading

A. Development of ability in content fields
B. Technical vocabulary
C. Graphs, charts, maps, etc.
D. Development of units of work
E. Finds answers—solves problems

IV. Assimilative Reading

A. Children make their own
....charts, posters, scrapbooks, stories, etc.

V. Recreative or Independent Reading

A. Read for pleasure and enjoyment
B. Extension of experiences
C. Escape or fantasy
D. Materials easy and well illustrated
E. Bulletin boards
F. Contract reading
G. Library experience

VI. Critical Reading

A. Evaluation
B. Selection
C. Find specific purpose
D. Formulation of opinions
E. Organization of ideas

VII. Locational Reading

A. Ability to locate information
B. Skimming for certain facts

VIII. Selective Reading

A. Children read graded material at instructional level
B. Teacher evaluates reading

These types of reading encompass a wide variance in reading rate—the words-per-minute count ranging from a hundred to perhaps a thousand, depending on the individual, the material, the environment, and the interest. Just as a person does not drive a car at the same speed in traffic as on a smooth, paved highway, similarly, the rate and comprehension in reading must vary. Unfortunately, however, many people plod through the sports section or other light reading as if it were the fine print in a mortgage. It is important that the student learn to adjust his reading pace to his specific needs—to discriminate between that which is truly important to him, and that which really is not.

For example, in study- or work-type reading, the student learns to read in low gear, just as a person must watch the road carefully when he is going over difficult or unfamiliar highways.

The recreative or informational type of reading is at a more rapid pace, but the student must be able to understand what he is reading, whether it is for pleasure and enjoyment, or for assimilating facts for assignments. When people refer to reading rates, it is usually the recreative type of reading that is used as the general measure for determining the words per minute. To be more specific, the student should really keep two charts, one for recording his rate on the work-type reading, and the other for his recreational reading.

Functional reading involves the perusal of material for the subjects the student is taking. The rate will vary greatly in this type of reading, but the comprehension should be constantly good.

Developmental reading includes the gaining of the various skills in reading. The student must learn to apply his newly developed habits derived from this developmental reading to all phases and types of reading. Developing word power is extremely essential in this form of reading, and he must learn how to attack new words with accuracy and ease.

Critical reading is of utmost importance, because today, more than ever, our citizenry must be informed and concerned with world events. It is through knowledge that society can grow, and the well-informed reader, who can read between the lines, will be the one who will understand what the author is trying to say. Students must read reflectively and think while they read, instead of merely accepting everything that is printed as the complete truth. Too many people think that if it is in the paper or in a book, it must be true. Such persons have not learned to evaluate and read critically.

Finally, as a corollary to all of the above, we come to skimming, which is reading of a high-gear type wherein the reader is only seeking out certain pertinent facts and does not need to read the entire selection. He skims rapidly over the material and picks out only those bits of information that he is searching for, or that will lead him to what he is searching for.

SKILLS IN READING

It is important that children learn to develop the various reading skills in order to read effectively. The skills listed below can be developed through the suggested activities given in this book.

A. Skills in Word Recognition

1. Context clues (meaning from sentence)

2. Configuration (look at shape of word)
3. Structural analysis (roots, prefixes, syllables, base words, compounds)
4. Phonetic analysis (sound elements)
5. Dictionary usage (final answer)

B. Skills of Meaning (Comprehension and Interpretation)

1. Getting central idea of selection
2. Studying organization
3. Using mental imagery (wire for sound—color)
4. Relating ideas in own words
5. Characterizing
6. Judging
7. Inferring
8. Generalizing
9. Predicting
10. Skills of oral interpretation
11. Making conclusions
12. Proving conclusions
13. Reflective thinking
14. Seeing relationships
15. Listing ideas in sequence
16. Application—solving and constructing
17. Organizing facts to support a conclusion
18. Associating related ideas
19. Identifying important and unimportant details
20. Relating to own experiences
21. Reading between the lines

C. Study Skills

1. Finding and selecting information for specific questions or problem
2. Organizing (topic sentence, main and subpoints)
3. Locating information
   a. Different types of books
      ....textbooks, encyclopedias, atlases, yearbooks, bound volumes
   b. Library
      ....card catalog
      ....Reader's Guide
   c. Parts of book
      ....table of contents
      ....index and glossary
      ....maps, charts, graphs
      ....topical headings
      ....copyright page to determine recency
      ....footnotes
   d. Dictionary
      ....using guide words at tops of dictionary page
      ....abridged and unabridged
4. Following directions
5. Retaining and remembering
6. Skimming to find the answer

D. Skills of Appreciation

1. Appreciating types—poetry-prose, new, old, factual, political, humorous, argumentative, fictional
2. Style-manner of speech, period written, rhythm, visual clarity, words used
3. Quality—truth of life, author's purpose, fundamental honesty, factuality

E. Retention of Ideas

1. Choosing ideas to remember
2. Expressing accurately
3. Summarizing
4. Outlining

F. Evaluation

1. Judging statements of importance
2. Evaluating for completeness, organization, clarity, style
3. Studying guide words
4. Checking printed statement
5. Difference between fact and opinion
   Use of clue words: "It has been reported," "Many people believe"
6. Examining one's impression as a whole
7. Evaluating accuracy of author's logic

SEQUENTIAL DEVELOPMENT IN READING

FIRST GRADE

Readiness

1. *Centers of Interest:*
   Home, play, pets, toys
2. *Auditory perception:*
   a. Identifying sounds from surroundings
   b. Identifying initial consonant sounds
   c. Identifying words that rhyme
   d. Listening to rhymes and songs
3. *Visual discrimination:*
   a. Recognizing likeness and differences in shapes, color, size
   b. Recognizing word symbols
4. *Kinesthetic development:*
   a. Development of muscular co-ordination
   b. Development of eye, motor, and voice coordination
   c. Left to right progression
   d. Holding book
5. *Comprehension and interpretation:*
   a. Reading pictures
   b. Story sequence
   c. Making comparisons
   d. Noticing details
   e. Following directions
   f. Classifying ideas
   g. Anticipating what happens (What do you think will happen?)
   h. Making inferences (What did the boys do to the ball?)

Preprimer

1. *Centers of Interest:*
   Pets, toys, home, play
2. *Vocabulary growth:*
   a. Concept of printed symbols
   b. Extension of word meanings
   c. Use of picture, context, and configuration clues
   d. Capital and lowercase letters in words
   e. Recognition of words in isolation
   f. Using *s* plural forms of nouns and verbs

   Phonetic skills:

   Auditory and visual perception of initial consonants and rhyming words
3. *Kinesthetic development:*
   a. Muscular coordination
   b. Eye, motor, voice coordination
   c. Left to right progression
   d. Coloring, painting, drawing, clay
   e. Handling books

4. *Comprehension and interpretation:*
   a. Picture reading
      What is in the picture?
      What are they doing?
      Why is the little girl excited, or sad?
      What do you think the man is saying?
      Color of clothing, hair, eyes, surroundings
      What time of year is it? How do you know? etc.
   b. Following directions
      Draw a house ....
      Print directions on strips as "Go to the door"
   c. Sentence comprehension (match picture and sentence)
      "Read the sentence that says ...."
   d. Paragraph comprehension
      Children find and read the phrase or paragraph that tells, for example, the size of the ball.
   e. Finding the main idea
   f. Perceiving story sequence
      What was the first thing that happened? What happened next?
   g. Noting and remembering details.
      Compare pictures on right and left side of book.
      Close book and think of the things Mary saw., etc.
   h. Clarification and enrichment of meaning
      Use pictures and dramatization to develop concepts.
      Real and vicarious experiences
      What have you seen or felt that is like this?
   i. Making inferences
      This is so because ....
   j. Identifying the characters.
      What word tells the name of the girl in the story?
      What kind of a girl is she? Why does she do this?
      How old?
   k. Recall of events.
      Who ran to meet Mary? What do you think they planned to do?
   l. Recognizing relationships
      Place first sentence in chart. Children find one of remaining three sentences that go with first.
      Relationships of time, cause and effect, etc.
   m. Classification
      Put similar objects in same classifications.
      Lists on board or worksheets, classify pictures
   n. Anticipating outcomes
      Do you think Jack will find the dog? etc.
   o. Making comparisons
      How are these the same? Different?
      Comparison of phrases, e.g. a ball—the ball
   p. Locating phrases, sentences or words
      Child reads sentence. Show sentence card for each sentence read. Another child reads the sentence on the strip and tells if it is the same as the one read by child from the book.

      Write sentences on the blackboard. Read aloud a phrase in one of them. A child finds the phrase, frames it and underlines it.

      Show the word *ball.* The children find the word in a sentence in the book. A child reads the sentence in the book. A child reads the sentence he finds. Children use words in their own sentences.
   q. Evaluating the story
      What did you like about the story?
      Could anything like this happen to you?
   r. Making judgments
      What are the reasons?
   s. Identifying words in context.
   t. Dictionary chart
      (to be read orally.)

      Children choose parts of story they will prepare to read orally

      Title.
      Read the part that tells what Jack wanted to do.
      Read the part that tells what Mary said.
      Read the part that tells what Mary did.
      Read the two pages about Spot.

Primer

1. *Centers of interest:*
   a. Work and play at home, play with friends
   b. Experiences with store, zoo, farm, park, airport, etc.
2. *Vocabulary:*
   a. Developing structural analysis skills
   b. Plural ending *s*
   c. Compound words as *snowball, sunshine,* etc.

   Phonetic skills:

   a. Initial consonants, *b, c, d, g, h, l, m, n, p, r, t, w*
   b. Final consonants, *d, l, s, t*
   c. Digraphs, *ch, th, wh*
3. *Comprehension and interpretation:*
   a. Phrase and sentence comprehension
   b. Finding the main idea
   c. Perceiving story sequence
   d. Reading for details
   e. Recall of story facts
      Who did the following things:
      ....went up the hill. ....came to the door, etc.
   f. Perceiving relationships
   g. Classifying ideas
   h. Forming judgments
   i. Making inferences
   j. Interpretation of pictures
   k. Using context clues
   l. Reading for information
      Who put out the fire? Where did Jack go? etc.
   m. Mental imagery
   n. Purposes for rereading
      Suggest another title for the story.
      Find answers to specific questions.
      Select sentences that describe pictures.
      Describe the character.
      Locate certain information.
      Find sequence of events.
      Prepare for dramatization.
      Compare two episodes.
      Reading aloud
4. *Rules for an audience:*
   a. Listen closely.
   b. Look at the person reading.
   c. Sit quietly, etc.

First Grade

1. *Centers of interest:*
   Neighborhood, school activities, park, stores, bus, etc.
2. *Vocabulary:*
   a. Ending of *d* and *ed* for verbs.
   b. Verbs with *ing* forms.
   c. Compound words, possessives.

Phonetic skills:
a. Initial consonant, *dr, b, pr, st, tr*
b. Final consonant, *nd, nk, nt, st*
c. Recognize vowel letter forms, *a, e, i, o, u*

3. *Comprehension and interpretation:*
a. Interpreting use of punctuation marks.
b. Making inferences.
Can you think of something else they should do?
c. Anticipating what will happen.
d. Making comparisons.
e. Finding answers.
f. Using the contents page.
g. Locating phrases, sentences
Finding phrases or sentences to answer the questions
h. Reading to evaluate
i. Reading to verify answers
j. Association of ideas
Words that belong together: ate....bread, hear.... sound, etc.
k. Retelling stories
l. Opposites
Using words in reader, e.g. cats, cow, ducks, apple, berries, etc.
m. Classifying words
n. Reading to dramatize
o. Learning that words have different meanings
well, rock, run, box, trip, kind, etc.
p. Locating story details
q. Grouping of related ideas
r. Verifying facts
s. Anticipating what will happen

SECOND GRADE

1. *Vocabulary:*
a. Clarifying and extending word meanings
b. Using picture and context clues
c. Recognizing words of similar and opposite meanings
d. Recognizing variant meanings of words
e. Recognizing root forms
f. Using *es* forms of nouns and verbs
g. Using *er* and *est* forms of words
h. Changing *y* to *i* before adding endings
i. Possessives and contractions

Phonetic skills:
a. Initial consonants, final consonants
b. Changing *y* to *i* before adding endings
c. Consonant blends
d. Long and short sounds of vowels
e. Diphthongs
f. Identifying silent consonants

2. *Comprehension and interpretation:*
a. Phrase and sentence comprehension
b. Paragraph and story comprehension
c. Finding the main idea
d. Reading for details
e. Perceiving story sequence
f. Following directions
g. Perceiving relevant ideas
h. Classifying and summarizing ideas
i. Perceiving cause-effect relationships
j. Forming judgments
k. Making inferences and drawing conclusions
l. Predicting outcomes
m. Evaluating literary characteristics
n. Discriminating between conversation and narrative
o. Discriminating between fact and opinion, realism and fancy
p. Locating answers to questions, locating information
q. Finding proof
r. Locating sentences
Children read aloud from their books the sentences that answer questions listed on blackboard or paper.
s. Using the contents page
t. Descriptive words
List words. Children give the name of the person or thing each one describes, such as quiet, loud, brave, etc.
u. Recall of story detail
v. Classifying words
w. Context clues
x. Anticipating what will happen
y. Locating quotations, such as
"I see a light in the window."
z. Association

The sun is shining.
The rain is falling. etc.

THIRD GRADE

1. *Vocabulary:*
a. Using meaning clues
b. Recognizing words of similar and opposite meanings
c. Recognizing variant meanings of words
d. Recognizing shades of meaning of words
e. Recognizing homonyms, synonyms, antonyms, root word forms
f. Using apostrophes
g. Using hyphenated words
h. Using prefixes *a, be, un*
i. Using suffixes *en, er, est, ful, ish, ly, y*
j. Recognize syllables in words

Phonetic Skills:
a. Recognize hard and soft sound of *c* and *g*
b. Final and initial digraphs and blends
c. Long and short vowel sounds
d. Diphthongs
e. Determining vowel sounds by position in words
f. Identifying silent consonants and vowels in words

2. *Comprehension and interpretation:*
a. Phrase, sentence, paragraph and story comprehension
b. Finding main idea
c. Reading for details
d. Perceiving sequence
e. Recalling story facts
f. Following directions
g. Forming opinions, making judgments
h. Making generalizations
i. Noting variety in literary thinking
j. Critical thinking, creative thinking
k. Characteristics of folk tales, fables
l. Perceiving relevant ideas. Checking comprehension and memory.
m. Classifying and summarizing ideas
n. Verifying conclusions
o. Visual imagery
p. Clarifying and expanding concepts, clarifying meaning
q. Unusual expressions
r. Making inferences and drawing conclusions
s. Perceiving cause-effect relationships

t. Predicting outcomes
u. Discrimination between realism—fancy; fact—opinion
v. Recognizing contradictory statements
w. Recognizing organization of content materials
x. Reference material, locating information in books, card catalog
y. Integrating new ideas with past experience. Extending interpretation.
z. Alphabetizing
a′. Research
b′. Noting the use of figurative speech
c′. Impersonations
d′. Noting emotional aspects, noting mood
e′. Author

FOURTH GRADE

1. *Vocabulary:*
   Continue with suggestions in previous grades.
2. *Interpretation and comprehension:*
   a. Sensing broader meanings
   b. Selecting relevant ideas
   c. Skimming
   d. Alphabetizing
   e. Using diacritical marks
   f. Developing concepts of time
   g. Establishing authenticity of material
   h. Using the glossary
   i. Reading to find the general idea
   j. Making critical interpretation
   k. Locating the setting
   l. Finding proof
   m. Reading to locate information
   n. Synonyms, homonyms, antonyms
   o. Interpreting idiomatic expressions, colloquialisms, figurative speech
   p. Seeing deeper implications
   q. Clarifying ideas
   r. Applying understandings. Comparing differences between present and past.
   s. Summarizing
   t. Reading to identify evidence
   u. Visualization, forming sensory images
   v. Predicting outcomes
   w. Recalling details
   x. Following directions
   y. Appreciating artistry of style
   z. Integrating new ideas with past experiences
   a′. Classifying ideas
   b′. Forming opinions
   c′. Analyzing conclusions
   d′. Interpreting colorful expressions
   e′. Understanding abstract terms
   f′. Cause and effect
   g′. Fusing ideas gained through reading
   h′. Identifying good words, prefixes, and suffixes
   i′. Using the glossary
   j′. Summarizing sequence of events
   k′. Sensing implied meaning
   l′. Making critical interpretations
   m′. Knowing compound words
   n′. Deriving meaning from context
   o′. Using syllabication principles
   p′. Judging validity of material
   q′. Outlining
   r′. Finding informational details

FIFTH AND SIXTH GRADE

1. *Comprehension and interpretation:*
   a. Finding the main idea
   b. Making comparisons
   c. Outlining
   d. Learning about the author
   e. Classifying terms
   f. Distinguishing syllables
   g. Fusing ideas gained through reading
   h. Using table of contents, section title
   i. Indexing
   j. Matching words with meaning
   k. Heteronyms: a tame dove—dove into woods.
   l. Forming opinions
   m. Association of ideas, such as:
      charm—something worn to keep away ill fortune.
   n. Appreciation of style
   o. Alliteration: as, for example, each word in sentence beginning with same letter
   p. Figurative speech
   q. Critical thinking
   r. Making comparisons
   s. Seeing deeper implications
   t. Reading to answer specific questions
   u. Analyzing conclusions
   v. Knowing about authors
   w. Matching ideas and paragraphs
   x. Skimming to find details
   y. Drawing conclusions
   z. Noting character traits
   a′. Drawing inferences
   b′. Verifying statements
   c′. Finding the climax; determining the plot
   d′. Summarizing

EVALUATIONS IN READING

While working with children, a teacher must evaluate not only their changing behavior patterns, but also the knowledge they have gained. There must be emotional and intellectual growth. However, besides teacher evaluation, there must also be pupil participation in evaluation of their own work and attitudes. It is through cooperative evaluation that children can understand and appreciate their problems. Some questions for the teacher to ask herself are:

Are the children growing in respect for one another?

Are they able to talk over their ideas?

Is their interest continuing from day to day?

Do they wish to extend their interests beyond school and home?

Do they show resourcefulness?

In reading:

Does the child have an adequate meaning vocabulary?

Does he make the best possible use of his mental maturity?

Is he accustomed to using phonetic abilities?

Does he have good health and energy?

Is he emotionally and socially adjusted?

Is he absorbed in the content of what he is reading?
Does he have a good imagination?
Can he constructively appraise his own work and the work of the group?

For the older child:

Can he select main ideas?
Can he recall details?
Does he know how to locate information?
Can he draw conclusions?
Can he distinguish between fact and opinion?

In developing skills in reading, the child should learn to evaluate what he has read. In primary grades simple *yes* and *no* exercises are helpful. He should be able to look at pictures and evaluate the action that is taking place.

For older children, giving statements which they can look up in the reference books is a helpful activity. Questions pertaining to the reason the character in the story reacted as he did and evaluating this reaction will help in more critical reading.

AN EVALUATION

The reading instruction should develop many new skills without the student becoming aware of them. These new skills become interwoven with the older ones to make a more effective reader who will enjoy reading. The following points should be stressed:

1. Old habits, though difficult to break, must be replaced by correct procedures.
2. The pupil's attitude toward himself and his reading must be good. A good reader knows that he has the ability to succeed and that he can succeed.
3. Reading improvement means reading. If a reading skill is once established, other skills develop from it.
4. Pupils should learn to look for the main ideas and supporting details. They should learn to visualize what they have read. This helps them remember much more easily.
5. Encourage pupils to always have on hand a book to be read at home. They will then get into the habit of picking up such a book and reading it in spare moments.
6. The pupils in the third grade and on up should set a goal of the number of books they would like to read each month.
7. Concentration is very important. Help the pupils develop this ability.
8. Reading should be for enjoyment. In reading, the individual should relax and become a part of the action in the story. He should become acquainted with the characters in the story and actually see and hear them.
9. One of the reasons for not understanding the reading materials, or oral discussions, is not knowing the meaning of words. It is possible to get the meaning of some words from the context, that is by reading the entire sentence or paragraph. Using the dictionary should become a habit, from the second grade on for getting the meaning of other words.
10. Lip movement, vocalization, and finger pointing should be eliminated. Any physical movement can be tiring and slow down a reader.

EVALUATION TEST

The teacher should take this evaluative test to see how he scores. This test may be given to students in fourth grade and on up.

Do You Know the Answers?

Read the statements given below. Some are true and some are not. Answer *yes* or *no* for each statement.

1. Sitting in a straight-backed chair is conducive to efficient reading.
2. The attitude of the individual toward his reading will often determine the success he will have in his reading.
3. If a pupil approaches his reading with the determination to learn, he is less likely to succeed than if he does not try to force himself.
4. It is a waste of time to try to decide what questions might be answered in any material before beginning to read it.
5. Some pupils need a warm-up period when they start to read.
6. It is important to attempt to concentrate in spite of distractions.
7. It is usually very easy to overcome habits of inattention while reading.
8. Movement of the vocal chords can take place without movement of lips.
9. Lip movement tends to make the reader's silent reading rate low.
10. It is a poor plan to push the pupil to read at more than his usual rate of speed.
11. The length of the sentence is not likely to cause a problem in comprehension.
12. The topic of a paragraph is always stated in the first sentence.
13. For increasing one's vocabulary it is important to use the new words.
14. Good readers always maintain the same reading speed.
15. Pupils should be urged to have a specific study area at home.
16. They should learn to put distracting things away.
17. A slow reader gets the ideas better than the rapid reader.
18. A fast reader makes many pauses on a line of print.
19. A good reader points to the words.
20. A reader should move his lips when he reads silently.
21. The eyes should see a group of words at one glance.
22. Moving the lips while reading silently helps to get the thought.
23. Everyone should know how to read at several reading rates.
24. One's reading efficiency can be improved by the spending of fifteen minutes a day on reading.
25. With some effort, reading can be improved within a week.
26. A reader can expect to have some feelings of discomfort if he reads with a poor light.
27. Active thinking means fully understanding what an author is saying.
28. If a man can get his ideas into print, those ideas must be correct and therefore must be true.

29. There is no point in a reader agreeing or disagreeing with an author.
30. Occasionally expressing your thoughts in writing will sharpen your thinking process.
31. To become a well-rounded reader, one should explore unknown fields and read many kinds of articles.
32. Any person of normal intelligence can learn to concentrate.
33. Personal interest and background are important to good concentration.
34. All books should be read in the same way.
35. Careful perusal of the table of contents can heighten interest in the book.
36. A reader should be more concerned with eye movements than of getting the thought.
37. Reading is not directly concerned with words, but only with ideas.
38. Main ideas are more important than minor details.
39. There is no law against reading slowly, provided you are able to read rapidly also.
40. In any learning process, there are plateaus.
41. A skillful reader unconsciously directs his eye movements.
42. A good reader reads one word at a time.
43. A limited vocabulary may be a cause of regressions.
44. The ability to read responsively is an art over which one can gain mastery only through persistent practice.
45. Rapid readers generally have better overall comprehension than slow readers do.
46. A reader should learn to read about as fast as he can pronounce the words to himself.
47. Effective reading is an active process which involves thinking.
48. If the eyes move rhythmically across the page, good comprehension will result automatically.
49. It is necessary to push oneself beyond the point of comfort to improve one's reading.
50. Visualizing what has been read is detrimental to good reading.

* * *

This is a helpful test for the teacher. Check the answers and give yourself two points for each correct answer. A score of eighty is excellent. Pupils in the fourth, fifth, and sixth grade enjoy this test. A discussion period should follow so they will understand the points they didn't know.

Key for the Evaluation Test

1. yes; 2. yes; 3. no; 4. no; 5. yes; 6. yes; 7. no; 8. yes; 9. yes; 10. no; 11. no; 12. no; 13. yes; 14. no; 15. yes; 16. yes; 17. no; 18. no; 19. no; 20. no; 21. yes; 22. no; 23. yes; 24. yes; 25. yes; 26. yes; 27. no; 28. no; 29. no; 30. yes; 31. yes; 32. yes; 33. yes; 34. no; 35. yes; 36, no; 37. yes; 38. yes; 39. yes; 40. yes; 41. yes; 42. no; 43. yes; 44. yes; 45. yes; 46. no; 47. yes; 48. no; 49. yes; 50. no.

REPORTING PRACTICES

Reporting practices vary according to the school systems and the needs of the individual pupil. In many reading courses the student is given the regular school grade, which may or may not also carry credit. At other times, the parents may be brought in for a conference. This is particularly true if the student is having a great deal of difficulty in his work.

If a group conference is called for, the teacher will discuss the plans that have been carried out in the reading course. He should explain the educational principles involved and the procedures that were followed. He must remember that the parents should be given a simple explanation if they are to understand what he is doing. The equipment and materials should be demonstrated to the group. Some teachers have found that the parents enjoy taking reading tests and doing some of the work that has been presented in the class. The charts, graphs, and workbooks should be on display.

Parent Conferences

In a parent conference, the daily and weekly outline of the work should be discussed. The good qualities and strength should be discussed first, and then the parent should be encouraged to discuss the student in relation to outside interests and his reaction to school life. A wise teacher avoids recording weaknesses for which there are no apparent solutions. Speak the language of the parents and avoid technical terms they do not understand.

At the close of the meeting, summarize the conference for the parents. It helps the parents to be understood, too. Such comments as, "You have given me a great deal of help in understanding" or "It is important to us that we remember these things about your child" will bring appreciation and understanding from the parents.

In counseling with parents, the following outline may help the teacher.

1. Get the facts of the case.
2. Work on rapport. People respond to your interest in them.
3. Know the limitations.
4. Avoid giving advice, admonishing or becoming emotionally affected.
5. Avoid lecturing, preaching, or moralizing.
6. Avoid eliciting more anxiety than you can handle.
7. Never attempt to teach a person something when he is emotionally upset.
8. Show that you respect confidences.
9. Be attentive.
10. Be sympathetic but firm.

Discussing Problems with Parents

The teacher must remember that parents are either ill at ease and apologetic, or they are hostile. Those who are ill at ease need reassurance and understanding. Frequently they blame themselves for their child's predicament. The hostile parent is more difficult to deal with, but the wise teacher will be careful not to further aggravate the situation. At times it is well to have a third party sit in on the conference. Whether the conference has been called, or the parents have walked in unannounced, the teacher is at an advantage if she has definite questions in mind to ask the parents and to guide the discussion. Questions that should be directed to the parents include the following:

1. What seems to be the nature of the student's difficulty? What do you think might be the cause? Are you doing anything to remedy the situation?
2. In what way would you like him to improve?
3. What disciplinary measures are used in the home? Who administers the punishment? Is the discipline consistent?
4. What kind of a disposition does he have? (quarrelsome, cheerful, sympathetic, normally agreeable)
5. Does he manifest any unusual behavioral responses? (overly-aggressive, rejected by group, rejects group, upset by changes in routine, unduly annoyed by noise, extremely irritable, hyperactive, on verge of tears, destructive, stutters or stammers, complains of health, does not always tell truth, bites nails, has headaches, daydreams, steals, strives to gain recognition, worries, etc.)
6. What does he do that makes you most proud of him?
7. What would you like him to be as an adult?
8. Who are his friends? With whom does he play after school? Are they his age?
9. Does he get along with his friends? Is he a leader or a follower? Do his friends come to the home?
10. Does he get along with other members of the family?
11. Does he show independence or does he depend on others?
12. Are there any unusual mannerisms which might indicate physical or emotional problems?
13. Does he need constant prodding, or does he go ahead, using his own initiative?
14. How does he go about getting what he wants?
15. Is he self-confident or does his self-confidence need to be bolstered?
16. What are his work habits?
17. Does he talk about school at home?
18. Does he feel insecure in some school subjects?
19. How does he react to group participation?

* * *

It is well to remember, while reporting or counseling with parents, that they may not always feel they should tell everything about the child or the home, and the teacher must learn to piece bits of information together and try to come up with an analysis of the situation.

The teacher should remember that, in the treatment of students, relapses are the rule rather than the exception and improvement is very slow and gradual. Maladjustments did not come all at once but were the outgrowth of an evolutionary development. A disturbed child means that one will usually find a parent almost as disturbed. An emotional turmoil in the home may distract the student so completely that he is unable to concentrate on his schoolwork. If the teacher is able to alleviate the stress in the home, the progress in school will go forward in an orderly manner.

Report Forms

When report forms are sent to the parents, the teacher should be certain that they will know how to interpret the information. Most parents are unfamiliar with R. A., E. A., and so on. They will probably have to be told something about the skills that are being presented and the purpose for developing them. An informed parent will usually be a more cooperative one also.

When the report card serves as a means of conveying the student's progress, an additional note may help clarify certain points.

Some clinics send progress reports at regular intervals. These give information on the student's progress in the various skills. Too much stress is frequently placed on reading rate. Rate alone is not the answer. If the material is not understood, reading (if it can be called that) at three or four hundred words a minute is a complete waste of time.

A simple report form follows.

Progress Report for Reading

Name .... Date ....
Progress has been shown in the following skills:
Comprehension ....
Word Analysis ....
(Other skills, depending upon grade level) ....
....
Suggestions: ....
....
....
(Teacher's name)

Summary

School systems vary in their reporting practices. In some instances the student may be given a regular school grade for his reading, whereas in other instances parents and students are brought in for conferences.

Parent conferences can be very helpful for all parties concerned, and they should be encouraged whenever possible. The teacher should have her plans for questioning well in mind before calling the parents in. The students frequently resent having the teacher discuss their problems with their parents, and they must learn to understand that it is to help them that the teacher is having the meeting. Some teachers find it helpful to have the student as well as the parents attend the conference.

INDIVIDUALIZED INSTRUCTION

THE CONTRACT PLAN OF READING

No single reading procedure can serve the needs of all the children in a given classroom. Yet, too frequently, we try to teach every child in the same way, forgetting that the home environments, the experiences, and the physical factors of the children differ greatly. Since each child will have a different background, the approach to the task of reading must also differ. No one specific method will apply to every child in the classroom.

Instruction cannot be dominated by the grade-level system. It is erroneous to believe that each child must be taught to read at the same level as the others regardless of whether or not we can teach him, and whether or not he is interested. Seldom are two children ready to be taught reading from the same material at the same time. Individualized reading focuses on the child, and reading becomes personal involvement.

The range of differences in the level of mental development within the first grade may be as much as five years, and the individual differences in reading ability will increase for each year of the pupil's life. At the first grade there are differences, but when these same children get into sixth grade, there is a wide range of differences.

A popular approach to helping the child who has problems in reading is through individualized instruction. However, the above-average reader is sometimes bored with the assigned reading program. There are avid readers who are interested in almost every type of book, and the teacher should be able to keep him busy with as much reading material as possible. By using the *Contract Plan* of reading, each child can work at his own level of achievement and achieve a feeling of success.

There are some children who have met with continual failure and frustration in reading, and may have never read a book to completion. By using the Contract Plan of reading, as described, these children have a feeling of success and achievement. They are competing with no one but themselves.

In an individualized reading program, some schools use many books at various levels of interest and difficulty. There may be little or no reliance on the basal readers as instructional tools, and the emphasis is placed on the children's selection of the reading material. In such a situation the reading skills may not be presented systematically, or they may not be introduced at all. It is suggested that by using the basal reader approach and supplementing it with the Contract Plan, the teacher will have control of the necessary skills that must be taught to the class.

If definite periods are set aside each week for this type of individualized instruction, all students can work happily and busily, with the teacher giving help wherever it is needed. Some teachers like to have the contracts available at all times, and permit the children to work on them whenever they wish. There are the above-average readers who enjoy reading the stories and articles because they love to read, and then there are the children who feel a great sense of achievement because they can see what they have accomplished.

In using the Contract Plan, children are able to help each other in the work. The classroom should contain an ample supply of library books, basal readers of lower grade levels, magazines, and booklets that the children have made. Suitable auditory-visual equipment and activities should be available.

THE CONTRACT PLAN OF READING IN PRACTICE

This method of reading can be used for recreatory, supplementary, or corrective reading. If the teacher can secure the assistance of mothers of pupils and some of her friends in preparing the materials, it will create much interest among the parents, while saving time for the teacher.

Readers that are not used as the basal or supplementary textbooks in the classroom are torn apart by taking off the backs, loosening the staples that hold the pages together, and removing the pages in sections from the back first. Each book is divided into

Figure 1.3 Contracts

twelve or sixteen units. Even more units may be made, but it is well to keep the same number of units for all the contracts. Several stories can be put together into one unit but too many pages in a unit or booklet should be avoided. After the book has been divided into units, the pages are stapled into covers made from tagboard, old manila folders, or heavy wrapping paper.

Comprehension exercises consisting of multiple-choice or true and false questions are made for each unit. These are typed on a sheet of paper the size of the booklet, or on cards. Some teachers prefer to have the questions on cards placed in a small envelope at the back of the booklet, and others prefer to staple or paste the questions in the booklet. Again, some teachers have the key in the booklet while others prefer to keep it in a small card file.

The units should be in proper sequence. A strip of colored paper pasted on the back of all booklets will help indicate the grade level and help keep the booklets together. Some teachers use a certain color to designate the grade level. For example, blue might mean second-grade level. The twelve booklets would each have a similar shade of blue pasted on the back. Another contract of twelve booklets that is a little more difficult would have a darker shade of blue, and each contract of succeeding difficulty would be designated by a still darker shade of blue. Green could designate third grade, and so on. It is well to write in code on the back of each booklet the publishing company, title of the book, grade level, and the pages in the booklet.

The contracts, consisting of twelve or sixteen booklets, are placed in a box with backs up to show the color of the contracts. In this way the children can go to the box and get the right unit to read. It is not necessary that the child read the units in sequence, so as many as ten children can be working on the same contract. After any child has read his booklet, he may either write the answers to the test on paper and check the answers himself, or he may have the teacher ask him the questions orally. Gradually the child learns to understand that if he does not copy the answers from the key, he will learn much more and that he is only harming himself by being dishonest in copying the answers.

The child signs his "contract" promising to complete his work within a reasonable period of time. As he finishes each unit or booklet, the teacher checks off that unit on his contract and records his progress on a card or small booklet made for him, or that he has made. When he has completed the entire unit of his contract he may go on to the next contract. The children show much interest and seriousness in their contract reading. They enjoy this type of reading because they feel satisfaction at the completion of each unit.

It is important that the teacher develop her contracts at the lowest levels that her pupils read, so that they can feel success in their work. A list of words may be used in phrases at the beginning of each unit, if the teacher wishes. These words can be obtained from the back of the book. When the teacher first begins to build her set of contracts, it is well to start with a reader at each level, and then later she and the parents can develop more contracts at each grade level.

These assignments seem so much smaller and less formidable to the child, and the plan is excellent where materials are limited, or there are reluctant readers.

1. Contract may be made by using books containing short stories. There should be at least one book available for each student in the group. The pupil need not complete the entire book, but rather do a required number of stories.
2. Reference readings can be assigned in contract form. The student is required to read the number of pages or articles.
3. Select countries or states and have the students read and report on the required number. Science and mathematics can be correlated in the same way.

2 Early Reading Activities

For many years educators have been defining reading readiness. They realize that readiness is something that just doesn't happen and that it must end with the calendar year. There is no magic, either for the teacher or for the child. Although maturational changes usually are orderly and sequential, the teacher has teaching to do through every sequence of the child's learning. If reading satisfies the needs of the child, the child is more likely to read if he has the capacity to learn.

Children today differ from those of a few decades ago. They have seen more of the world, have had more out-of-home experiences, and have had closer association with other people. There are many significant differences among children as they begin learning to read. Since our society places a high premium on reading ability, it is important that every child must have the privilege of reading effectively.

READINESS DEFINED

Readiness is the teachable moment for reading. Preparing for reading implies the careful structuring of experiences by the teacher and the active participation on the part of the child. The readiness moment varies with each child. Readiness means a preparing for action and an attitude or mind set. The readiness period is a unique and precious period of opportunity for both the teacher and the child.

Entering the first grade is a very wonderful and a very important time. It is a time of new adjustments, learning to make decisions and learning to read. The child learns to organize his experiences and thinking and to become a member of a group. But on the child's sixth birthday, he does not magically or automatically gain all those complex skills which will open for him the doors to successful reading.

Children should not be forced into readiness training until there is an adequate maturational development. Premature training may actually be harmful. The more mature that child is, the less readiness training is required to develop reading proficiency.

The shy child should be provided with opportunities in which he becomes involved in activities in which he can achieve successfully. Self-confidence is very important for the beginning reader and if this is lacking, there is apt to be an over-reaction when there is difficulty in performance in learning to read. The teacher must structure the experiences so that the classroom will not be a threat but rather one of safety.

The over-assertive child may be a more serious problem than the shy and retiring child. The over-aggressive child needs to find himself by acting as a helper and a teacher for those who are less confident.

Fortunately, children are quite pliable. They may have an initial desire to learn to read but sometimes standards and our set goals can be interpreted as threatening rather than as rewarding. A child who fails to meet arbitrary group standards may find the reading experience as frustrating and unsatisfactory. There is always an element of ego-involvement and it is important in learning to read. Even when failure is not present, ego-involvement may divert the child away from the structured activity and disrupt the child's learning as well as that of others.

Failure in reading in later grades is undoubtedly due, at least in part, to an inadequate program for the child's first year in school. When we realize that so many children read below their norms, it makes us realize that we must help the child get the best start possible in reading. We must realize that this reading incompetency can create unhappy children that may develop into emotional conflicts. Children are eager to learn and most children anticipate starting to school so that they can learn to read. At no other age do we have the enthusiasm expressed as by this age-group. This is the time for teachers to make the most of their opportunities.

PARENTS AS PARTNERS

Parents have an interest in their children's education and well-being, and most of them are only too anxious to be helpful. The fortunate parent learns to know the school as a partner in the child's development.

Some parents do not realize that school practices have changed since they themselves attended school. Most schools inform the parents of the school policies and the school curriculum. This is done through conferences, PTA, school newsletters, and the media.

Parents can be very useful to the school by enlisting their help as room mothers, teacher aids, librarians, and in developing learning activities.

A good-working relationship between teacher and parents will provide a more secure atmosphere for the child. The child who is just entering school needs especially to feel this harmonious understanding between parent and teacher.

TEACHER AND PUPIL RELATIONSHIP

All children pass through a succession of stages in an orderly growth pattern. Each stage is dependent upon the preceding ones, and no two children progress at the same rate. There are children who learn slowly and those who learn quickly. Some carry heavier emotional loads than others. These need to develop faith in themselves and in their teacher. Some feel that you are an impediment to their freedom and happiness. They must learn to know that the teacher wants to give them her love, understanding, and encouragement.

Children are eager to learn and the teacher has willing subjects to guide into the exciting realm of reading. Very few children come to school who do not want to learn to read. Unhappy and frustrating experiences at the outset of learning to read can change all that. Some children are easily discouraged and have marked feelings of insecurity and inferiority. Some give up too easily. Social and emotional immaturity makes for unhappy children, and inhibits their learning. It may result in adults who cannot live effectively with benefit to themselves and others.

The school should be a social laboratory wherein children experience living and learning together. The teacher must have sensitivity to children. They are her publicity agents, her critics, and her fans.

There is no fixed readiness period of three weeks or three months. There is no "right time" to begin to read, and there is no sharp line between readiness and reading. The transition will take place almost unnoticed.

Language development is an important part of the preparatory period. A command of oral English is essential to the mastery of reading. Correct pronunciation and enunciation are an essential part of this period.

When correctly used, readiness workbooks can be helpful, but they are not self-directive. Merely coloring the pictures will not instill the desire to learn to read.

Through experience and training the teacher learns to recognize that particular phase of a child's development which indicates his readiness for reading. Sometimes the child will ask, "Aren't we almost reading?" Usually, the child knows when he is ready to read and when this enlightenment has come to him, he will not want to stop reading.

ENRICHMENT FOR LEARNING

There are many suggestions in this book for developing reading readiness and for first-grade experiences. These should be modified for the individual's specific needs. Parents should be enlisted to help prepare these games and activities. If the parents know that you can use magazines, cardboard, bright scraps of yarn and cloth, plastic containers, cardboard boxes, and many other items that would otherwise be discarded, they will be delighted to save them for you.

When the games and activities have been prepared, they should be stored and housed in boxes and labeled with the directions.

Factors that influence reading readiness are:

A. Physical Readiness

1. Visual readiness
2. Auditory acuity
3. Motor coordination
4. General good health

B. Social Readiness

1. Self-reliance
2. Ability to cooperate and share with others
3. Good habits of listening
4. Ability to assume responsibility

C. Mental Maturity

1. Mental age of six-and-one-half years
2. Good memory span
3. Good speech
4. Emotional security

D. Environmental Factors

1. Good instruction
2. Enrichment of experiences
3. Satisfactory home conditions
4. Satisfactory school conditions

READING READINESS

There is no such magic as a quick-change "ready to read." It is something that the teacher must develop. A few suggestions are given below.

1. Listening Activities

Listening to stories, rhymes, various classroom-made sounds, tapping of rhythms, records, and so on—all play an important part in the development of the child's auditory acuity. A sheet of cardboard is placed between the teacher and the children. The children are to listen to what the teacher is doing. The teacher may for example, wrinkle a sheet of typing paper, ring a small bell, or sharpen a pencil. Oral directions may be given and the children try to follow them. A good game to play is "Hide the Thimble." When the child is far from the object, the others are to clap softly; when he is near, they may clap loudly. Another listening game is to have the children close their eyes and listen to sounds about them. They may tell about things they heard. Children may also tell about the happiest, the pleasantest, or the saddest sounds they have heard.

2. Art Expression

Easels are placed in convenient places about the room. The children are shown how to use the paints and brushes. If finger paint is to be used, only a few children work with it at one time. Clay is very helpful in giving the children an opportunity to express themselves. If crayolas are used, the large kindergarten variety should be provided because the children have not yet developed their small muscles, and they become fatigued holding small crayons.

3. Muscular Co-ordination

Many activities, such as bouncing a ball and counting the bounces, building with blocks, dramatic play, rhythms, clapping, cutting out pictures, and the like, are helpful in developing good muscular coordination.

4. Looking at Books

Colorful books are placed about the room. The children are encouraged to look at these and to learn how to hold them correctly. The children may wish to make scrapbooks about pets, animals, birds, babies, flowers, home, food, etc.

5. Use of Pictures

Large attractive pictures that do not have too much detail are used. These pictures are discussed with the children. The children are to tell what they think will happen, what they see, what they think is in the box, and so on.

A picture file is very helpful for the teacher. The pictures may be mounted on tagboard or cardboard of uniform size and filed alphabetically. Small pictures may be mounted on 5-by-8-inch cardboard for the children's near-point examination.

6. Picture Race

Pictures may be cut from magazines or workbooks and pasted on uniform size cards. There should be about six houses, six boys, six dogs, six girls, six balls, and so on. The picture cards are shuffled and each child is given the same number of picture cards. The children try to get six pictures of the same kind by asking each other such questions as, "John, do you have a picture of a dog?"

7. Flannel Board

Flannel boards are very useful for illustrating stories. The children enjoy using them when they tell their stories or tell about some experience. The little flannel boards, about 9 × 12 inches, may be made by covering cardboard with pieces of flannel. A pocket on the back holds the small scraps of colored felt which the children use in making pictures. These pictures may be set up on the chalkboard ledge for a few days for the children to admire. Words, pictures, shapes, and figures from old readers may be cut out for use in storytelling. A piece of felt, glued to the back of the pictures, will help make them stick to the flannel board.

8. Color Games

Objects of various colors are placed on a table or desk. The children are asked to find the color that tells about a bright day, a red apple, someone's dress, or the like.

9. Learning Color

Colored cars may be cut from magazines and pasted on pages of a booklet. A different colored car is pasted on each page. In the first grade, the name of the color is printed under the car. The children may match color words with the color of the car. The cars may be pasted on a large poster if the teacher wishes. The teacher may ask the children to name objects in the room that are the same color as the car she has pointed to. They may also match strips of cloth or paper with the color of the car. Children will become aware of the various shades and tints of the color.

10. Pantomime

The teacher may ask a child to pretend he is a certain animal. The other children are to guess what animal the child is imitating. Community helpers, toys, and so on may also be imitated.

11. Guessing Game

A child or the teacher says, "I am thinking of a milkman. How many things can you name that go with the milkman?" The children name milk, truck, bottles, and so on.

12. Lost Baby Animals

Pictures of mother animals are on the chalkboard ledge. The children are given pictures of the babies. They take turns in placing them with the mother and naming the animal.

13. Who Is Playing?

Several children put their heads down on the table while the children in the other group hold rhythm band instruments. One child plays his instrument and those with their heads down guess what instrument was played.

14. How Many Jumps?

The children put their heads on the desk, while one child makes a certain number of jumps. The children tell how many jumps they heard. A rubber ball may be bounced instead of anyone's jumping.

15. Add a Word

Each child selects a picture of an animal. (Vegetables, flowers, etc., may be used also.) The first child shows his picture and says, "I went to the zoo and saw an elephant." The next child shows his picture and says, "I went to the zoo and saw an elephant and a tiger," while the third sees three animals, and so on. The children may display their pictures to help the others remember at first. This is good for memory training.

16. A Visit to the Zoo

Each child selects a picture of an animal and then shows his picture, giving one fact about it.
Example: An elephant has a long trunk.

17. Following Directions

Children are told to do things that involve two directions, then three, then four and five directions.
Example: Go to the table and pick up a book.

18. Left to Right

Count or name objects or pictures, going from left to right.

19. The Mouse Game

The children are given sheets of paper with paths marked off in little squares. Each child is given a button, which he pretends is a mouse, a dog, or any animal. The teacher bounces a ball on the floor two or three times. The children move their mouse, or dog, that many spaces on their sheets. She then bounces the ball several times again, and the children move until the mouse gets to his cheese or mousehole at the other end of the path. The mouse must always return to the left-hand side of the path, and always move from left to right (see fig. 2.1)

20. Guessing Game

The teacher places several objects, pictures, or toys on her desk. The children are told to look at them and try to remember what they see. Then they close their eyes and the teacher removes one object. The children tell what has been removed. The teacher may shift the objects about and the children may place them in their original order.

21. Remembering

Several small objects that are in a box are exposed for a few moments, after which the children are asked to name as many things as they can remember. This game may be varied by having the children close their eyes while one object is removed and then telling what is missing.

22. Noting Similarities in Shapes

On sets of 6-by-10-inch cards, two-inch squares are marked off. In these squares, smaller circles, triangles, and squares of red, green, and blue paper are pasted. Two-inch squares with similar designs and color are made. These are to be laid over those on the larger card (fig. 2.2).

23. Matching Circles

Circles cut from red and green paper, with the designs cut from red, green, brown, and yellow paper, are pasted on folders as shown in figure 2.3. The children are to place the second set of circles under the matching

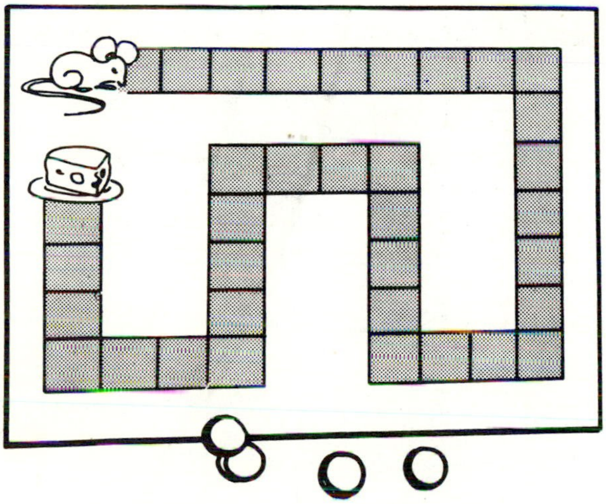

Figure 2.1 The Mouse Game

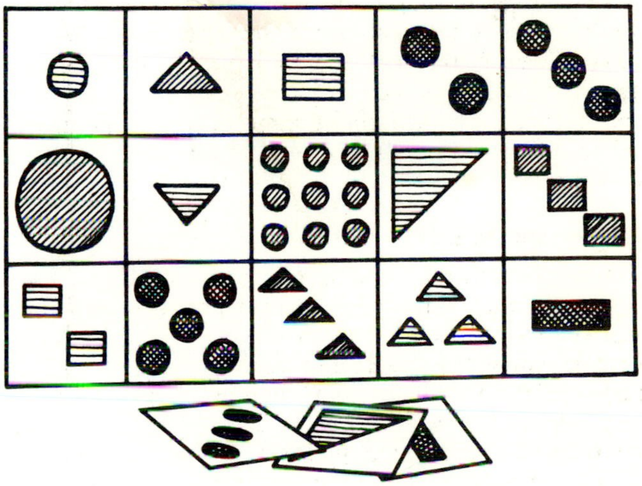

Figure 2.2 Noting Similarities in Shapes

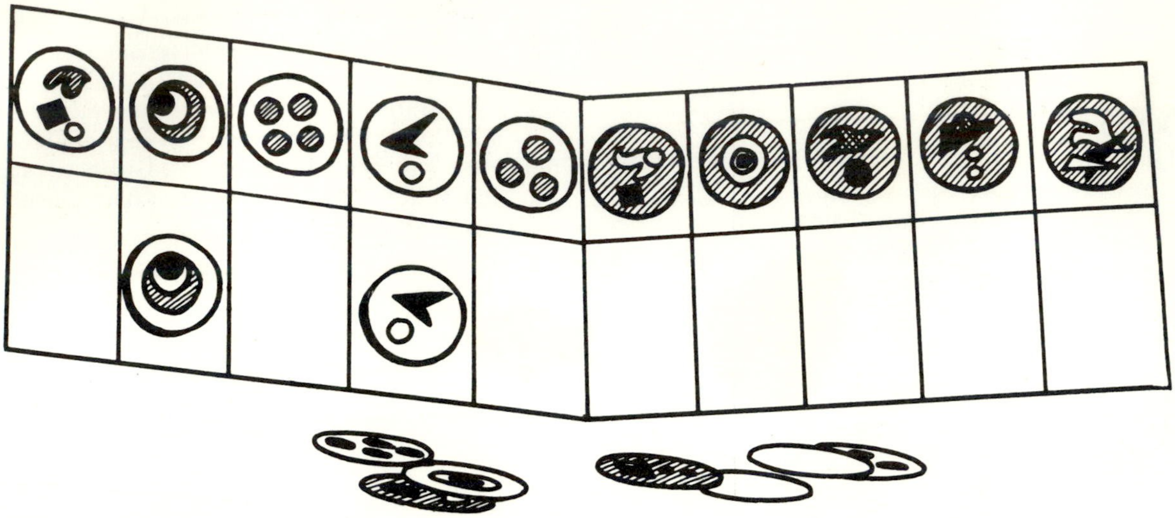

Figure 2.3 Matching Circles

circles. An envelope is needed on the back of the folder for holding the loose circles. This activity is excellent for detecting color blindness (fig. 2.3).

24. Which Are Alike?

Folders and smaller pieces similar to the illustrations in figure 2.4 are prepared. The children match the pictures in answer to the following questions:

a. Which belong together?
b. Which are almost the same?
c. Which are alike?
d. Where do they live?
e. Where are the babies? mothers?
f. What do they eat?

25. Picture Dominoes

With two pictures on each 2-by-4-inch card, the children are to match pictures similar to the game of dominoes. Some cards have matching pictures and others have pictures that are not alike. Each child draws six cards and proceeds as in dominoes (fig. 2.5).

26. Feel Book

Cardboard pages are fastened together with metal rings. Samples of velvet, sandpaper, rough fabrics, plastics, corrugated paper, fur, and so on, are pasted on different pages. Under each sample a short description is written as, "This feels very smooth. Other things that feel like this are........." The children enjoy feeling these samples (fig. 2.6).

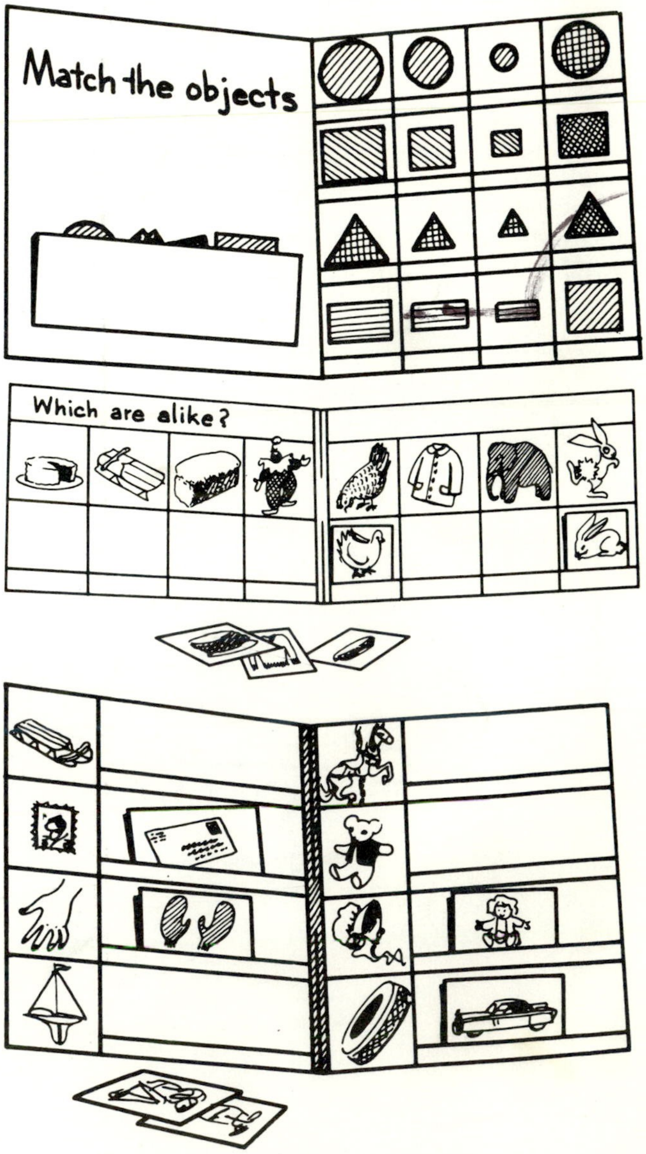

Figure 2.4 Which Are Alike?

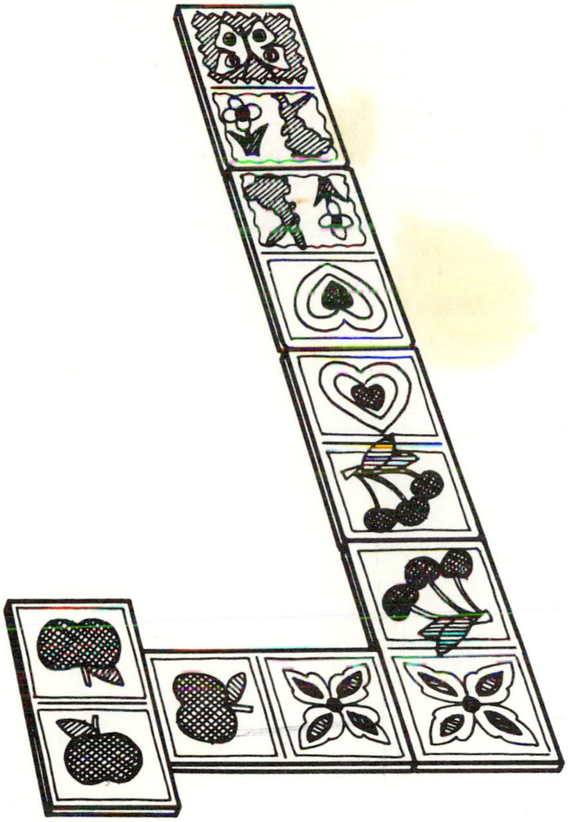

Figure 2.5 Picture Dominoes

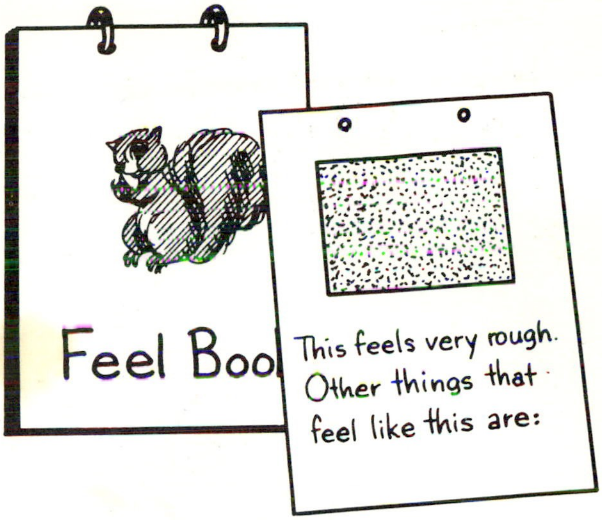

Figure 2.6 Feel Book

27. Matching

Folders similar to the illustration below are prepared, using cloth or wallpaper on the pockets. Similar pieces are pasted on the upper half of 2-by-4-inch cards. The child is to place the cards in the correct pockets (fig. 2.7).

28. Noting Similarities and Differences

Four letters are cut for each letter of the alphabet, using different colors for each letter. One letter is pasted on

Figure 2.7 Matching

the 6-by-9-inch card, as in figure 2.8, and the other three letters are pasted on 1¾-inch-square cards. The children are to match the letters.

For additional suggestions refer to both the table of contents and the index.

Figure 2.8 Similarities and Differences

FIRST GRADE READING EXPERIENCES

A. **Objectives**

1. To develop an interest in reading
2. To develop the awareness that printed symbols convey meaning
3. To stimulate oral language development
4. To foster group participation
5. To develop concepts
6. To develop a sight vocabulary
7. To develop left-to-right progression
8. To learn to read silently before reading orally
9. To learn to use picture, oral, and context clues
10. To develop the ability to follow directions

B. **Materials**

1. Chalkboard and chalk
2. Motivating materials, such as a child's pet rabbit puppet, rabbit pictures, stories, books, and poems about rabbits, music and records, finger plays, rhythms, filmstrips, and flannel board.
3. Chart materials: ruler, poster paper or newsprint, lettering pen and India ink or Flo-master, scissors, picture.

C. **Motivation**

The motivating materials listed above may be used. Children's questions may be listed, if the teacher wishes.

D. **Procedures for Reading and Preparing the Story**

(Groups of eight or nine children are with the teacher, while the other children will be working with clay, coloring, painting, or using learning activities at tables.) The children have discussed the rabbit and have told some of the things they know about it. It is possible that a child may say, "We could write a story about our rabbit." Or the teacher may say, "I thought it would be fun to write a story about some of the things we learned about our bunny." The teacher stimulates interest and response through such questions as are listed below.

Who can think what we might call our new story? (Several responses)

Which title do you like better (or best)? (Children decide)

Where shall I write the title of the story? (The teacher uses manuscript on the board.)

What shall we write next? (Contributions from the group)

What else can we say?
The story should be no more than four or five lines. The vocabulary in the back of the preprimer should be kept in mind, and these words should be used whenever possible.

After the story has been written on the board, the teacher holds a yardstick under the entire sentence. Standing on the left-hand side in order to promote left-to-right progression, she reminds children that we always read to ourselves before we read to others. In calling on the children, directions are given first, then the child's name is used. This helps hold attention. The teacher may say, "Will you read the name of the story, Mary? Will you read the sentence you gave us, Henry?"

After the chart has been read through, some teachers have the children read it again in unison.

On the following day, the teacher has had two charts printed, one to be kept whole and the other to be cut up for matching. The following statements by the teacher are suggested:

"Today we will read our new story. First we will look at the picture and talk about it. Then we will read the title of the story, and you may then read the entire story to yourselves. Now let us listen quietly while Jack reads the story to us."

After this, the teacher directs the children as follows:

"Remember we always read to ourselves before we read to others."

"Who can read the sentence that tells us what we see?"

"Who can read the sentence that tells about the bunny's nose?"

"Who can read the sentence that tells about bunny's ears?"

"Who can tell us what the *last* sentence says?"

(The teacher is giving oral clues to the children as well as helping them develop the use of context clues.)

"Now we will take our *second* chart." (Teacher cuts off the title. A child takes the strip, matches it with the first chart, reads it silently and then orally. He places the strip in the wall-pocket chart.)

"Who knows what this sentence says?" (The strip is cut and the children repeat the matching.)

(The teacher cuts off each sentence and after matching and reading the strips are placed in proper sequence in the wall-pocket chart.)

"Who will find the sentence in the wall-pocket chart that tells about bunny's nose?" (It is matched with the first chart.) (This is repeated until all sentences are removed.)

On the second day the sentences may be cut into phrases. The chart is reread similarly to suggestions given above. On the second or third day, the teacher asks: "What words rhyme with bunny? Can you find the word?" Auditory training in phonics may be given by asking questions like: "What words can you think of that rhyme with *hop? nose?* Which words begin alike: *nose, not, bunny?*"

"How many times can you find the word *bunny, funny, has, our?*"

After the second or third day, the chart is placed on the bulletin board and after several days it is removed and filed, or it may be put into book form with large rings. Children enjoy the large books and will reread the charts many times.

These correlated activities are suggested:

Number concepts: long, longer, longest; second, first, last, how many?

Language development: stories, oral expression.

Music: songs, rhythms, listening to records.

Art: clay carrots, rabbits; drawing and painting rabbits; paper bag puppets.

A dramatic play could be presented.

The children can develop their own books. They can draw pictures of the family, pets, friends, or experiences. They can illustrate these with their own drawings or they can use magazine pictures.

EXPERIENCE CHARTS

A. Scope

1. For beginning reading
2. For language organization
3. For cooperative group work
4. For information
5. For reminders
6. For learning experiences, not drill purposes

B. Purpose

1. Contributes to growth in reading
2. Makes reading functional
3. Integrates with other subjects
4. Helps children learn to work together
5. Causes problematic thinking
6. Provides parallel reading enrichment
7. Prepares pupils for reading
8. Helps children learn to summarize
9. Broadens pupil interest

C. Types of Charts and Posters

1. First-grade experience charts
2. Information charts
3. Room standards
4. Daily experiences
5. Weather charts
6. List for room helpers
7. Posters, charts, graphs
8. What-to-do charts
9. Library book lists
10. Narratives
11. Record of plans
12. Record of experiments
13. Questions
14. Vocabulary
15. Directions
16. News records
17. Special days
18. Riddles
19. Color
20. Poems
21. Numbers
22. Calendar
23. Health
24. Directions for playing games

D. Materials

1. Oak tag or tagboard
2. Poster paper
3. Newsprint (for posters not to be saved)
4. Wrapping and shelf paper (for posters not to be saved)
5. Old posters from stores (cover these with paper)
6. Cardboard
7. Cardboard boxes (cover with paper)

E. Principles

1. The chart should be attractive.
2. It should be interesting and have a measure of literary quality.
3. It should use perceptual clues.
4. Phrasing should be considered.
5. It should be accurate and neat.

F. Printing Materials

1. India ink, speed ball pen for permanent charts
2. Flowmaster (comes in colors)
3. Crayolas for quick, temporary work
4. China-marking pencil

G. Physical Makeup of Charts

1. Use sufficiently large sheet, 24-by-36 inches, for first grade.
2. Mark lines (chart liners can be made or purchased).
3. Allow for margins and space for picture at top.
4. For first grade use 1½-inch letters.
5. For third grade use 1-inch letters.
6. Smaller letters used for near-point charts, only.
7. Mark in letters with a pencil first.
8. Leave same space between lines as height of tall letters.
9. Round letters must be round and close together.
10. Tall letters must be vertical and spread out more than round letters.
11. Leave space of two round letters between the words.

H. Composition of Chart

1. There must be a motive for composing the chart.
2. The teacher asks meaningful questions.
3. The teacher prints the children's sentences on the board.
4. After the chart is printed on the board, the children read it.
5. On the following day, two charts should be printed. One is to be cut up.

I. **Reading of the Chart**

The teacher should:

1. Ask a child to read the sentence that "tells us ...."
2. Cut the duplicate chart into sentences. The child reads the sentence and matches it with the one on the chart.
3. Put the sentences in the wall-pocket chart and reread.
4. Cut the sentences into phrases when the children know the sentences.
5. Write half of the sentence on the board; a child supplies the other half.
6. Ask a child to frame the line or phrase that "tells us ...."
7. Write the phrases on the board; children draw lines to the matching parts.
8. Always read silently before reading orally.
9. Read for understanding.
10. Charts are reread for several days, then put on the bulletin board for a few more days. Then they are put in book form or stored.

A WALL CHART

This wall chart (fig. 2.9) is made from wrapping paper and cardboard and is used for the purpose of holding flash cards or daily assignments. (It is especially useful in primary reading and number work.) A piece of cardboard, of the size you need for the chart, and a large piece of wrapping paper are collected. The wrapping paper should be several inches wider than the cardboard and about twice as long as the finished chart is to be. A convenient size for the pocket is 1 inch deep with a back 3 inches high.

Allowing extra space at each end, the paper is marked off at intervals of 3 inches and 1 inch, alternating. Using accordion-type folds, the first 1-inch section is creased and folded forward over the second 3-inch section. The second 1-inch section is folded over the 3-inch section, and so on. The folding is continued throughout the length of the paper. The folded paper is placed face downward on a flat surface and the cardboard laid on it. The edges of the paper are folded over and pasted over the back to cover the edges. The back may be covered with a plain sheet of paper if desired.

By running strips of transparent gummed tape lengthwise over the pockets, sections for individual pupils may be made. The size of the chart may be varied.

FINGER PLAYS

This is an old activity, the popularity of which is being renewed substantially and rapidly. Several very good finger-play books were copyrighted in 1890, and have become very popular in kindergarten, first, and second grades. Even in upper grades, the children enjoy finger plays for relaxation. Finger plays are invaluable for small children because they give an opportunity for expression and movement.

Finger plays are valuable in lower grades for relaxation and for developing various skills in listening, following directions, appreciation, and working in groups. Some of the finger plays are given below. However, the teacher can use poems that lend themselves to finger plays.

Purpose

Relieves tensions and provides relaxation
Aids in appreciation of poetry
Encourages reserved children to express themselves
Develops grasp of concepts and verbal meaning
Encourages better speaking
Satisfies need for physical expression
Expands powers of imagination
Develops ability to memorize
Develops social attitudes and adjustment through participation

Procedures

The teacher says the rhyme and gives the exercises with her fingers.
The children watch and listen.
The teacher discusses the poem with the children and shows pictures.
A record pertaining to the rhyme is played, if available.
Children act out the plays while the teacher speaks the verses.

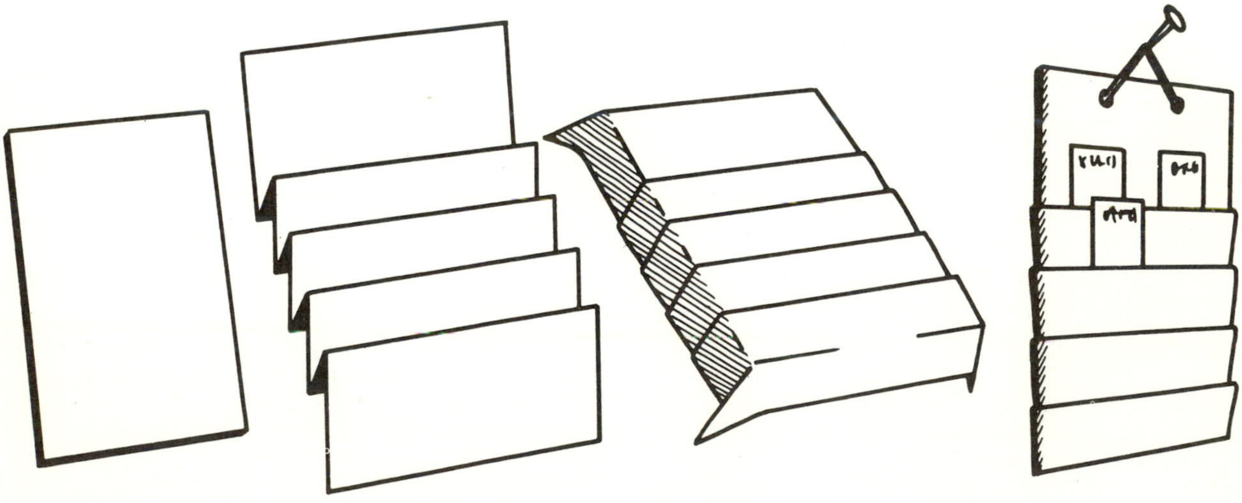

Figure 2.9 Wall Chart

The children are encouraged to say the rhymes with the teacher.
As they become acquainted with the rhymes, the children begin to say them themselves.

Evaluation

Do the children enjoy the plays?
Do they understand them?
Do they ask for new finger plays?
Are provisions made for individual differences?
Are good listening habits formed?
Do children learn to follow directions?
Are behavior patterns developed?

What Shall We Do?

Oh, little Red Hen, what shall we do?
Let's scratch, scratch, scratch all day. (*scratch*)
Oh, Cock-a-doodle-doo, what shall we do?
Let's flap our wings all day. (*flap arms*)
Oh, Donald Duck, what shall we do?
Let's swim, swim, swim all day. (*move arms in swimming movement*)
Oh, Porky Pig, what shall we do?
Let's eat, eat, eat all day. (*pretend to eat*)
Oh, Pussy dear, what shall we do?
Let's sleep, sleep, sleep all day. (*head on arms*)

—from *Instructor Magazine*

One, two, What shall we do?
Three, four, We'll sit on the floor.
Five, six, Hear the clock tick.
Seven, eight, We'll sit up straight.
Nine, ten, Our hands are in our lap again.

The Lambs

This is the meadow where all the long day,
Ten little frolicsome lambs are at play (*wiggle fingers*)
These are the measures in which the farmer brings (*cup hands*)
Corn and meal and so many other good things
This is the lambkins' own big water trough (*make trough with hands*)
Drink little lambkins and then scamper off (*wiggle fingers*)
This is the rack where in winter they feed (*cross fingers to form rack*)
These are the big shears to shear the old sheep (*make shears with fingers*)
Dear little lambkins their soft wool may keep.
Here, with its big double doors shut so tight (*hold clenched hands together*)
This is the barn where they all sleep at night.

The Hen and Chickens

Good Mother Hen sits here on her nest,
Keeps the eggs warm beneath her soft breast
Waiting, waiting day after day
Hark! there's a sound she knows so well
Some little chickens are breaking the shell
Now they're all out, Oh see what a crowd
Good Mother Hen is happy and proud
Cluck-cluck, cluck-cluck, clucking away.
Into the coop the mother must go
But all the chickens run to and fro
Peep-Peep, peep-peep, peeping away.
Here is some corn in my little dish;
Eat, Mother Hen, eat all that you wish,
Picking, picking, picking away.
Happy we'll be to see you again,
Dear little chicks and good Mother Hen!
Now, good-by, good-by for to-day.

The Little Plant

In my little garden bed
Raked so nicely over (*fingers for rake*)
First the tiny seeds I sow (*sow seeds*)
Then with soft earth cover. (*cover over*)
Shining down, the great round sun (*make sun*)
Smiles upon it often
Little raindrops, pattering down (*make pattering sound*)
Help the seeds to soften.
Then the little plant awakes! (*stretch*)
Down the roots go creeping (*wiggle fingers*)
Up it lifts its little head (*thumb up*)
Through the brown earth peeping.
High and higher still it grows (*move thumb up*)
Through the summer hours,
Till some happy day the buds
Open into flowers. (*open hand*)

India Rubber Man

I am an India rubber man.
I stretch and stretch as far as I can.
I stretch my neck, I stretch my hands,
I stretch my legs like rubber bands.
And then the stretch goes out of me,
And I'm as limp as I can be. (*excellent for relaxing*)

Ten Little Finger People

Two little houses all closed up tight (*fists closed—thumbs in*)
Open up the windows and let in the light (*stretch out fingers*)
Ten little finger people tall and straight
Ready for school at half past eight.

Making a Jack-O-Lantern

Cut into a pumpkin (*pretend to cut off top*)
Scoop it with a spoon.
Carve a little mouth that turns
Endwise like a moon.
Cut two eyes to twinkle (*make two circles with fingers*)
And a big three-cornered nose. (*make triangle*)

Use for teeth ten shiny seeds
Placed in grinning rows. (*hold ten fingers in a row*)
Light a little candle, (*hold up finger and pretend to light*)
And when the shadows fall,
Set the jolly fellow in the darkest hall. (*pretend to set on shelf*)
Listen for the laughter (*hand behind ear*)
As folks spy the elf, Grinning down at all of us
From the darkest shelf.

Five Little Squirrels

Five little squirrels sitting on a tree. (*hold up left hand*)
This one says, "What do I see?" (*point to thumb*)
This one says, "I smell a gun."
This one says, "Oooh, let's run."
This one says, "I'm not afraid."
This one says, "Let's hide in the shade."
Then bang went the gun (*clap hands*)
And away they ran, everyone. (*hand behind back*)

The Pigs

Two mother pigs (*hold up thumbs*) lived in a pen (*make pen with arms*)
Each had four babies (*hold up fingers*)
And then there were ten.
These four babies (*hold up four fingers*) were black as night.
These four babies (*hold up other four*) were black and white.
Now all eight babies loved to play
And they rolled and rolled in the mud each day (*roll hands over*)
And at night, with their mothers, they curled in a heap, (*make fists*)
And squealed and squealed till they went to sleep (*head on hands and go to sleep*)

The Sparrows

"Little brown sparrows flying around,
Up in the tree-tops, down on the ground,
Come to my window, dear sparrows, come!
See! I will give you many a crumb.
Here is some water, sparkling and clear:
Come, little sparrows, drink without fear.
If you are tired, here is a nest;
Wouldn't you like to come here to rest?"
All the brown sparrows flutter away,
Chirping and singing, "We cannot stay;
For in the tree-tops, Among the gray boughs,
There is the sparrows' snug little house."

Counting Lesson

(*Right hand*)
Here is the beehive (*close fist, thumb inside*)
Where are the bees?
Hidden away where nobody sees.
Soon they come creeping out of the hive—
One—two—three—four—five. (*show each finger as you say number*)

(*Left hand*)
Once I saw an anthill with no ants about; (*clinch fist as before*)
So I said, "Dear little ants, Won't you please come out?"
Then as if the little ants had heard my call
One—two—three—four—five came out.
And that was all.

Itsy-Bitsy Spider

The itsy-bitsy spider
Went up the water spout,
Down came the rain,
And washed the spider out
Out came the sun,
And dried up all the rain,
And the itsy-bitsy, spider, went up the spout again.

Mrs. Pussy Cat

Mrs. Pussy, sleek and fat,
With her kittens four,
Went to sleep upon the mat,
By the kitchen door.

Mrs. Pussy heard a noise—
Up she jumped in glee:
"Kittens, maybe that's a mouse!
Let us go and see!"

Creeping, creeping, creeping on,
Silently they stole;
But the little mouse had gone
Back into his hole.

"Well," said Mrs. Pussy then,
"To the barn we'll go;
We shall find the swallow there
Flying to and fro."

So the cat and kittens four
Tried their very best;
But the swallows flying fast
Safely reached their nest.

Home went hungry Mrs. Pussy
And her kittens four;
Found their dinner on a plate
By the kitchen door.

The Caterpillar

Fuzzy little caterpillar,
Crawling, crawling on the ground!
Fuzzy little caterpillar,
Nowhere, nowhere to be found,
Though we've looked and looked and hunted
Everywhere around!

When the little caterpillar
Found his furry coat too tight,
Then a snug cocoon he made him
Spun of silk so soft and light;
Rolled himself away within it—(*twirl thumb*)
Slept there day and night.

See how this cocoon is stirring! (*wiggle thumb*)
Now a head we spy—
What! Is *this* our caterpillar
Spreading gorgeous wings to dry? (*place tops of hands together, fingers for wings*)
Soon the free and happy creature
Flutters gayly by.

The Mice

Five little mice on the pantry floor, (*five fingers*)
Seeking the bread crumbs or something more:
Five little mice on the shelf up high, (*five fingers on top of hand*)
Feasting so daintily on a pie—
But the big round eyes of the wise old cat (*makes eyes by curling fingers*)
See the five little mice are so fat.
Quickly she jumps! but the mice run away,
And hide in their snug little holes all day.
"Feasting in pantries may be very nice:
But home is best!" (*make home of two hands*)
Say the five little mice.

The Squirrel

"Little squirrel, living there (*use of one hand to represent tail*)
In the hollow tree,
I've a pretty cage for you! (*cage from hands*)
Come and live with me!
You may turn the little wheel—(*make turning motion*)
That will be great fun
Slowly round, or very fast, if you faster run.

Little Squirrel, I will bring in my basket here (*make basket*)
Every day a feast of nuts!
Come, then, squirrel dear."
But the little squirrel said from his hollow tree:
"Oh, no, no! I'd rather far live here and be free."

The Church

This is the church,
This is the steeple,
Open the door and see all the people.
Close the door and let them pray.
Open the door and they all go away.

Fishes

Five little fishes
Swimming in a pool.
This one says: "The pool is cool."
This one says: "The pool is deep."
This one says: "I'd like to sleep."
This one says: "I'll float and dip."
This one says: "I see a ship."
Fisherman's boat comes, line goes—Splash (*clap hands*)
Away our five little fishes dash.

The Ball

Here's a ball (*make ball with fingers*)
And here's a ball (*larger circle with both hands*)
And a great big ball I see (*use both arms*)
Shall we count them? Are you ready? One! Two! Three!
(*Make each circle as counted*)

Hands

My hands on my hips I place
On my shoulders, on my face,
On my knees and at my side,
Then behind me they would hide.
Then I raise them up so high,
Swiftly let my fingers fly.
Quickly count one, two, three
And see how quiet they can be. (*bring hands down and fold in lap*)

Open—Shut

Open, shut them,
Shake them very lightly
Open, shut them, open, shut them,
Clasp them very tightly.
Open, shut them—open, shut them
Now give a little clap,
Open, shut them, open, shut them,
Put them in your lap.

Five Little Rabbits

Five little rabbits went out to walk,
They liked to boast as well as talk,
The first one said, "I have a gun."
The second one said, "I will not run."
Two little ones said, "Let's sit in the shade."
The big one said, "I'm not afraid."
Bang, bang went the gun.
And the five little rabbits ran, every one.

The Cat, by Mary Britton Miller

The black cat yawns,
Opens her jaws,
Stretches her legs,
And shows her claws.

Then she gets up
And stands on all four
Long stiff legs
And yawns some more.

She shows her sharp teeth,
She stretches her lip,
Her slice of a tongue
Turns up at the tip.

Lifting herself
On her delicate toes,
She arches her back
As high as it goes.

She lets herself down
With particular care,
And pads away
With her tail in the air.

The Squirrel

Whisky, frisky, hippity hop,
Up he goes to the tree top!

Whirly, twirly, round and round,
Down he scampers to the ground

Furly, curly, what a tail!
Tall as a feather, broad as a sail!

Where's his supper? In the shell,
Snappity, crackity, out it fell.

The Seals, by Dorothy Aldis

The seals all flap
Their shining flips
And bounce balls on
Their nosey tips,
And beat a drum,
And catch a bar,
And wriggle with
How pleased they are.

The Pigs

Piggie Wig and Piggie Wee (*show thumbs*)
Hungry pigs as pigs could be,
For their dinner had to wait
Down behind the barnyard gate. (*hold fingers to make gate*)
Piggie Wig and Piggie Wee
Climbed the barnyard gate so high, (*move thumbs up as if peeping through fingers*)
But no dinner could they spy.
Piggie Wig and Piggie Wee
Got down sad as pigs could be: (*move thumbs back down*)
But the gates soon opened wide (*spread hands apart to open gate*)
And they scampered forth outside. (*move thumbs on table*)
Piggie Wig and Piggie Wee
What was their delight to see
Dinner ready not far off—
Such a full and tempting trough! (*make trough with hands*)
Piggie Wig and Piggie Wee,
Greedy pigs as pigs could be,

For their dinner ran pell-mell;
In the trough both piggies fell. (*thumbs inside trough*)

A Little Boy's Walk

A little boy went walking (*move two fingers as if walking*)
One lovely summer's day;
He saw a little rabbit (*hold two fingers up for rabbit's ears*)
That quickly ran away; (*move away*)

He saw a shining river
Go winding in and out, (*dramatize*)
And little fishes in it (*move hands sidewise to represent fish*)
Were swimming all about:

And, slowly, slowly turning (*moving hands over each other in large circle*)
The great wheel of the mill;
And then the tall church steeple (*two hands clasped with index fingers up*)
The little church so still.

The bridge above the water (*clasp hands to represent a bridge*)
And when he stopped to rest
He saw among the bushes
A wee ground-sparrow's nest. (*make nest*)

And as he watched the birdies (dramatize each line)
Above the tree-tops fly,
He saw the clouds a-sailing
Across the sunny sky.

He saw the insects playing,
The flowers that summer brings,
He said, "I must hurry home
And tell about the many pretty things."

DRAMATIC REPRESENTATION

There is a strong drive toward social interaction among children. Dramatic representation meets the emotional needs for the children's desire for adventure and excitement. Often such activities serve as emotional releases for feelings which the children themselves do not understand. Through play the children review and assimilate information about their home and community; and in upper grades, the entire world. The three types are:

a. Dramatic play
b. Dramatization
c. Role playing or sociodrama

DRAMATIC PLAY

Purposes

1. Dramatic play provides a motivating factor for research, construction, and other experiences.
2. It provides an opportunity for the teacher to observe the behavior of the children.
3. Children gain information and learn to develop sequence and unity.
4. It reveals the new information gained by the children.
5. It leads into aesthetic expression in language, arts, music, and the like.
6. It promotes democratic living.
7. Children have fun while they are learning.
8. It offers a means of emotional release.

Procedures

The first time the children play, there should be only a few things to play with, and the children play only a few minutes. Following such a playtime, the teacher talks with them and helps them to see their own needs, such as more space, more playthings, or more information.

The teacher does no directing. The children identify themselves with their environment by reproducing activities they have experienced in the home, or those that they have heard about or seen. Dramatic play emerges quite naturally and is usually introduced by the children themselves.

Frequently the five- and six-year-olds will play at what is called "parallel" play. One end of the box may serve a child as an airplane, while the other end of the same box is a ship for another child. Older children make their play more formal, and they want something worthwhile about which to play. They usually continue their activity over a period of several weeks, while the small children use smaller play patterns.

The smaller children like to make sounds and movements of such things as animals, boats, or airplanes. They identify themselves with the fireman or the pilot and express themselves as the other person feels and thinks.

Dramatic play in the middle grades needs planning and research.

Evaluation

The evaluation period following dramatic play is very valuable. The children are brought together, and they make suggestions for improving their play and discuss problems and ask questions. Such questions as these may be asked:

What did you like about our play?
Did we clean up after the play?
Why is it important to come together in a group after cleaning up?
Why did you enjoy the play so much?
Did each person do his job well?
Did we talk like the people we were playing?
How did we share today?
What did you learn today?
What do we need to learn more about?

DRAMATIZATION

Dramatization is more formal than dramatic play and follows a definite pattern.

Purpose

1. Learning sequence
2. Interpreting characters
3. Developing sensitivity to emotional content
4. Creating new interests, problems, and needs
5. Contributing to democratic group activities
6. Stimulating language growth and development of concept
7. Learning and using new concepts

Procedures

Dramatization requires more memorization and is less creative. It takes more planning. The teacher or children may read a story or an experience. They plan the characters and what they will say; and sometimes they plan costumes and scenery. The dramatization is rehearsed until the children feel they have developed the production to their satisfaction. Radio plays, recorded programs, puppet shows, and television shows can be developed in this activity. Children find impromptu inventions satisfactory for their dramatization; but more formal dramatizations which are often used for entertainment for the public require more elaborate stage sets, costumes, and properties. The steps in the procedure are:

1. Selection of a story or situation which is appealing to the children.
2. Reading or telling the story and discussing the incident.
3. Planning the division into scenes or acts, the place, time, and sequence; then assignment of parts together with selection of a stage manager.
4. Conducting rehearsals.
5. Presenting the play.

Evaluation

After the performance the children gather in a group, and questions similar to the ones below may be asked:

Did the audience like the dramatization? Why?
Was the committee work carefully planned and carried through?
Did everyone use his imagination?
What behavior patterns were developed?
Was the committee work worthwhile?
What did the children learn?
How can the next production be made better?

ROLE PLAYING OR SOCIODRAMA

Sociodrama is a spontaneous play acted out under capable direction. The subject matter is a real-life situation common to all and is concerned with intergroup relationships.

Purpose

1. Helps the children identify the character to be depicted, to see themselves in different relationships, and widen their social understandings.
2. Helps the children see life around them with greater understanding.
3. Develops social sensitivity, and relieves tensions and emotions.
4. Develops spontaneous expression in the child.
5. Conveys information and facts.
6. Serves as group therapy.
7. Provides the teacher with an effective way of learning about the children's backgrounds, their personalities, and cultural levels.
8. Changes attitudes and develops democratic values.
9. Helps the group to resolve difficulties arising from interaction with different values.

Procedure

The teacher must exercise care in helping set up a sociodrama, in the selection of the situation and the characters. Each character is described with the problem and idea which the children will interpret and to which they add their own ideas. The play is unrehearsed and unprepared. The players will need a few moments to concentrate individually on their roles and the setting while the teacher prepares the audience by telling them to watch for certain action and suggests questions they should keep in mind. Problems too personal to be discussed in the first person may be looked at through the less direct process of playing out a situation.

Specific problems can be solved through the use of sociodrama. For example, the upper-grade children are going to have a dance and they do not know how to act, so they play out a school dance. Or the children are taking a bus trip and they want to know what to do. The roles can be played again and again to portray a different way of behaving under the circumstances. The roles can be reversed to see how the other person feels. The problem and the alternative ends are acted out. Participation must be entirely voluntary.

Sociodrama is very satisfactory for presenting problems at faculty meetings or parents' meetings. Teachers play the roles in this case.

Evaluation

There are four specific steps in evaluation:

a. The areas of conflict may be listed.
b. Labels may be given to actors. (This is optional.)
c. Solutions acted out should be discussed.
d. The play should be summarized and recommendations made.

The situations need to be clear and brief, and the description of the situation should not imply answers. Questions to ask are:

What were the good points about the way the situation was solved?

Was it better than a prepared play?

Did the students accept the informal role playing as "real" or as play acting with little meaning or involvement on their part?

What do you know about the situation that you didn't know before?

(Role playing is not suitable for grades below four.)

BLOCK PLAY

Purpose

The activities provide development of the children. It provides for free bodily expression, muscular coordination, manipulation, experimentation, and eye-hand coordination. Emotional and social development is encouraged through intelligently guided play. The children learn to work together and adjust their behavior to the group. They have a feeling of accomplishment and satisfaction. The use of blocks motivates learning and develops dramatic play expressions.

Materials

Large hollow blocks and solid floor blocks are used, together with small blocks of varying sizes. These are introduced later. Accessories include trees, people, signals, airplanes, trains, trucks, farm and wild animals, etc. Materials for painting and construction are also included. A small platform with casters makes a convenient way of moving materials. The blocks should be neatly piled in their bins or on the shelf when not in use.

Procedure

There should be sufficient work space for satisfactory block play, with at least 70 hollow blocks and 576 floor blocks. There should be ample time to work with the blocks and ample time allowed for putting them away. At the beginning stages of block play the teacher plans with the children. They decide the space in which to work, the safe way in which to take materials from the storage place, the signal which tells them the time to discontinue the work, the time signal for good housekeeping period, the way to share in a group, and a safe and orderly way to handle the blocks.

The children progress from working alone to group work. The block play may have been motivated by an experience, or a story told by the teacher. At first the children use the large blocks only. Accessories are introduced as the children ask for them and pictures are shown to clarify concepts. The working group usually consists of three or four children. Frequently the children participate in a parallel play at first. Blocks are frequently used in dramatic play experiences. Sequence usually can be developed from the block play.

Evaluation

Since the children frequently work in small groups, the teacher may be able to help them with on-the-spot evaluation. For older children the group evaluation is more satisfactory. Questions similar to those used in evaluating dramatic play are used, since dramatic play quite often does evolve in the block play.

PUPPETS

Purpose

The use of puppets makes an excellent lead-up activity for dramatic play or dramatization. It teaches the children to speak with self-confidence and to develop poise. It helps the shy child to overcome bashfulness before the group. The creating of puppets develops art appreciation and skills used in art work. Children gain information about the subject they are going to develop.

Procedure

The story or play is introduced by reading or telling. The teacher may show the children a puppet or pictures of some puppet plays. The children discuss how they can develop the story into a puppet play and what puppets they will need. The puppets may be made from paper bags, newspapers, cloth, papier-mâché, or wood. There are four types of puppets:

a. Marionettes—manipulated from strings on a control.
b. Hand puppets—held over the hand.
c. Stick puppets—drawn on paper and fastened to a stick.
d. Paper-bag puppets.

The children work in committees on the stage with the props, the puppets, and the script.

Evaluation

The children evaluate with regard to their growth as a whole. The activity will be evaluated with regard to its merits and how well it accomplished the purpose mentioned above. Did the class profit from the experience? Was there enthusiasm shown by the class? Did the children enjoy it?

CHORAL SPEAKING

Purposes

1. To develop the ability to participate successfully with the group, thus fostering social attitudes.
2. To increase the memory span and develop the ability to memorize.
3. To give self-conscious and reserved children an opportunity for expression.
4. To develop the ability to use good speech, enunciation, articulation, inflection, and tone of voice.
5. To increase the ability to interpret the printed page.
6. To provide an opportunity for rhythmic expressions.
7. To introduce poetry and its appreciation.
8. To develop readiness in reading through the use of choral speaking of nursery rhymes and simple poetry.
9. To encourage better oral reading.
10. To serve as relaxation for children when tired.
11. To improve breath control.
12. To expand the power of imagination.
13. To develop auditory acuity.
14. To develop greater grasp of verbal meanings.
15. To give the pupils an opportunity to interpret their own reactions to ideas, thoughts, and feelings as expressed in poetry.
16. To give the teacher the opportunity to observe the children's behavior.

Materials

The selections suitable for choral speaking must be adapted to the age and grade. The selection should have strong rhythm, beautiful language, stimulating ideas, repetition of phrases, and short sentences. Usually a selection having humor and gaiety is more suitable for the children.

Procedures

A poem that will be suitable for choral speaking is first read to the children, pictures are shown, and discussion held. The children should be encouraged to bring poems they think would be suitable for this type of reading. The choral reading of a poem should be the culminating, climaxing activity in its study. The voices are grouped as high and low voices. Each part of the selection is studied to discover its particular mood, then arranged for the group to speak. The pupils are encouraged to make suggestions. Vowels and verbs are stressed, but not nouns and the group avoids sing-song speaking, keeping their voices soft. The pupils need help in expressing different emotions by the voice alone. Tape recordings of different arrangements may be made to give the children an opportunity to select the one they think most suitable. One of the children should act as conductor.

A few of the arrangements are:

Refrains: The refrains are for the group to speak, while the stanzas are for the individual or a small group.

Dialogue or antiphona: A question is followed by an answer. The class is divided into two groups facing each other. One group states the question, the other gives the answer.

Sequential speech: This is sometimes called "line a child" speaking because each individual follows another in saying a small part.

Unison speech: Voices blend together, the words sound as one with perfect timing, and voices are controlled in tone and volume.

Choral drama: This type of material contains narration and impersonation for the children.

Evaluation

Choral speaking may be evaluated by the teacher in terms of the pupils' growth in self-control, participation with the group, appreciation, and improvement in speech skills. There should be a period for pupil evaluation at which time they discuss their growth, understandings, and appreciations.

PANTOMIME

Purposes

1. To develop self-expression.
2. To increase initiative and creativeness.
3. To release or eliminate tensions and self-consciousness.

Materials

No materials are needed, but a few small props may be available. The students should suggest or provide these, rather than having the teacher tell them what to use. If the teacher wishes to demonstrate so that the students will understand what is expected, it could be helpful.

Procedures

Children may work in groups of five or six. Each group plans an activity they will pantomime. It may be some activity in the home, on the farm, in school, or on the street. Stories and rhymes may be acted out, or the actions of animals may be pantomimed. Parts of the social studies lessons may be used. The students act out the movements but no words are spoken. The others in the class are to guess what the pantomimists are doing.

COLOR IDENTIFICATION

Everyday things and everyday happenings offer endless means of enlarging and enriching the child's color awareness. Many children enter first grade with a deep appreciation for color, but many children have not learned to see color and to feel its joy and beauty. It is important that children develop this awareness during their reading-readiness period. Also, there may be a few children who are color-blind. Through the use of the suggested games and exercises, the teacher will discover which children do not see all the colors.

1. Can You Find the Color?

Readiness

Each child is given a color card of red, blue, green, yellow, violet, brown, orange, black, and white. The teacher holds up a color and says,

> "Someone is wearing a dress this color. Can you find other things in the room that are this color?
> "What is the name of the color?
> "Will you please hold up your card if it is the same color?
> "Can you name some other things that are this color?"

2. I Am Thinking of a Color

Readiness

Each child has a color card. One child holds up a card and says, "I am thinking of something that is this color." The children take turns guessing the object, and the child who guesses correctly may be *it*.

3. Matching Colors

Readiness

Squares and circles of colored cloth and paper are cut and distributed. The children sort these into their colors; or one child may hold up one of his pieces and the other children find a color similar in their squares and circles.

4. Which One Is Gone?

Readiness

Two or three circles of different colors are held up before the class. The children name the colors, then they close their eyes and one circle is removed. They open their eyes and name the color that has been removed.

5. Colored Beads and Blocks

Readiness

The children use colored beads or blocks. If the beads are used, the children may be asked to follow directions similar to, "Use one red bead, use a blue bead, use two green beads," and so on. If blocks are used, small towers may be built according to directions given by the teacher.

6. Booklets and Charts

Readiness and grade one

The children may make small booklets, pasting on each page colored paper and objects of the same color cut from magazines. When the children are able to print, they write the name of the color. Suggestions for color booklets are: colored cars, vegetables, fruit, flowers, toys, and the like. Charts with the color and its name may be made for the bulletin board.

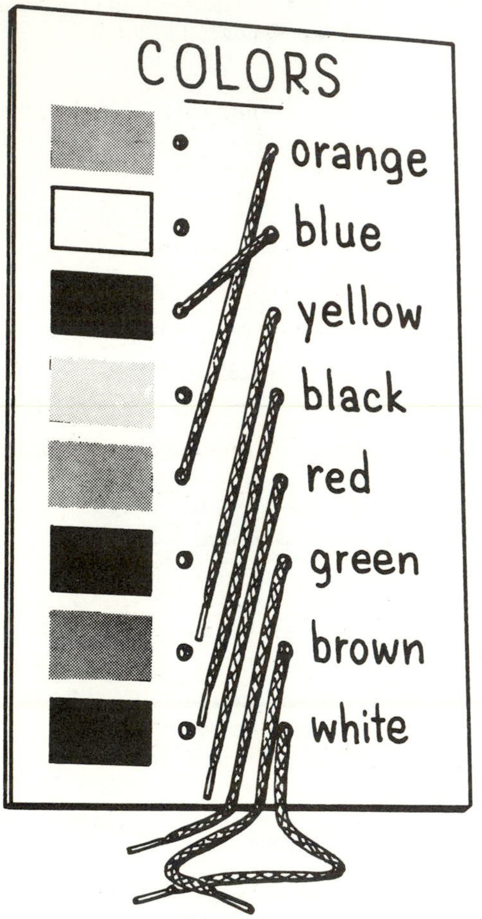

Figure 2.10 Color Chart

7. Lacing Games

Grade one

The names of the colors can be quickly learned by making cards with the color on one side and the name on the other. Shoelaces are cut in two, and half a shoelace is connected to each color. A hole is punched beside the color name. The child connects the color and its name with the shoelace (fig. 2.10).

8. What Does This Color Make You Think Of?

Grades four, five, and six

The pupils write the first word they think of as the color card is shown to them. This may be done orally, but the practice in writing is a good learning activity.

Example:

The orange color is shown to the class. The pupils might write sunset, orange juice, orange, crayon, and so on.

For red they might write anger, fever, danger, apple, and so on.

9. Using a Prism

Grades one, two, three, four, five, and six

The teacher may refer to a science book for suggestions for the many ways the prism may be utilized in working with color. It is a fascinating study for all ages.

10. Learning About Color

Grades one, two, three, four, five, and six

Use red, green, blue, yellow, white, orange, and black paper and cut out six-inch circles. Show the pupils a red and a yellow circle. Ask them what color can be made by mixing these two colors together. Query them about the red and blue, the yellow and blue, and white and black, in the same way. If a drill is available, cut parts of colored circles, stick a nail through the center and fasten to the bottom of the drill. By turning the handle of the drill, it is possible to mix the colors. Colored transparencies may also be used to demonstrate the mixture of colors.

11. Color Classification

Grades one and two

Several of these classification boxes can be assembled for learning colors. Use a shoe box for each classification box. Place the following items in each box: six or eight small boxes or box lids, colored buttons, screw-on tops of plastic bottles, marbles, plastic toys, strips of fabrics, and such. The child places objects of similar color into each small box.

12. Learning to Color With the Alphabet

Grades one, two, and three

Tell the children that adults sometimes paint by number or letters. These kits can be found in stores. They will be able to do this also.

Draw and duplicate pictures on regular sized paper. Divide areas and mark them with letters of the alaphabet which will be colored according to directions given.

These pictures may be correlated with the reading and social studies material and also with holidays. Begin with simple directions and then as the children become more proficient, increase their difficulty. The children should be encouraged to submit pictures that can be used in the class.

Numerals and exercises in comparison and contrast can be used similarly. For example, the directions can ask that the tallest flower be colored red, the largest blue, etc. An illustration follows.

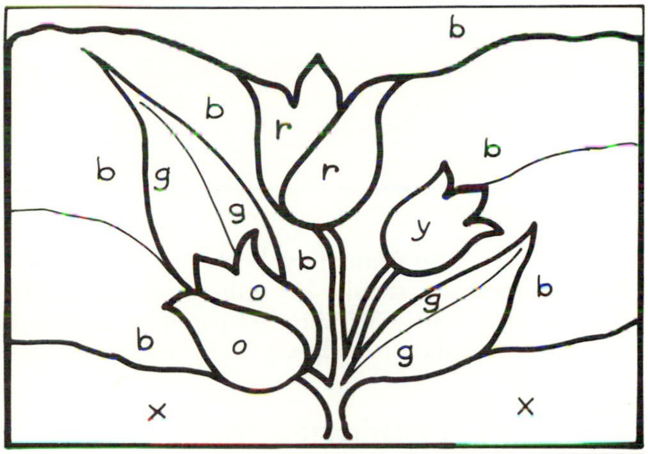

Color the areas marked **r** red.
Color the areas marked **o** orange.
Color the areas marked **y** yellow.
Color the areas marked **g** green.
Color the areas marked **b** blue.
Color the areas marked **x** brown.

Figure 2.11 Coloring by the Alphabet

13. A Jar of Jellybeans for Many Activities

There are many possibilities for the jar of jellybeans. The picture is duplicated and various words and number combinations are printed on the beans. This copy is duplicated for each child. A few suggestions are given below.

Long and short vowel sounds: Words with long and short vowel sounds have been printed on the beans. Ask the children to color all words with a long *a* sound green, all words with a short *a* sound yellow, etc.

Beginning and ending consonant sounds: Print words from reading assignment on the beans. Ask the children to color the ones beginning with the same sound as in *bird* red, etc.

Rhyming words

Parts of speech: Color all the verbs green, all the nouns blue, etc.

Number combinations: Color all the means with the sum of eight blue, etc.

Classification; Color all the beans with words that relate to the farm blue, etc.

The list of activities is endless and the teacher will find many varied uses for this activity.

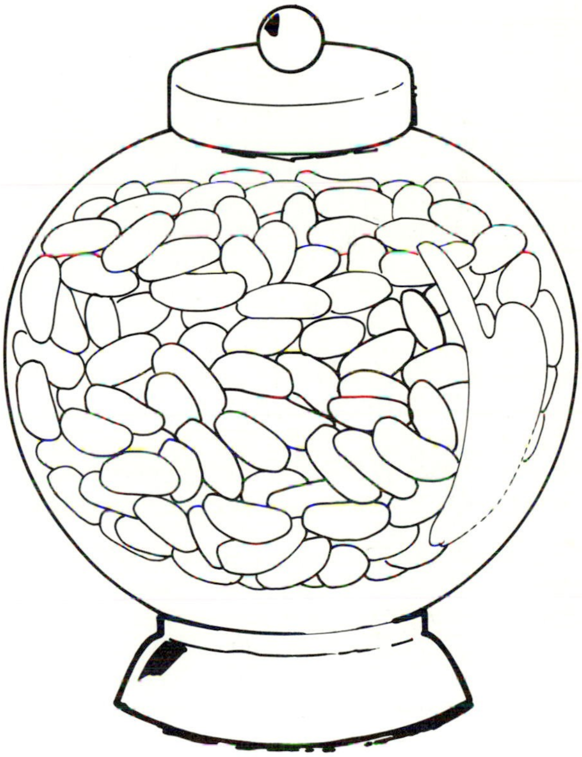

Figure 2.12 Jelly Beans

3 Cognitive Interpretation

Years ago, the Lamaistic priests of Tibet used a wonderful means of hailing their gods. They wrote their prayers on long strips of paper, which they wound around a cylinder. This cylinder revolved on an axle, and to pray, they spun the prayer wheel. The faster the wheel turned, the more prayers could be sent out to their gods. They must have expected their gods to read with great rapidity, and they must have expected them to interpret what they read, too. This type of prayer wheel is still found today in Tibetan Buddhist temples.

With the amount of printed material available today, it would be helpful if it were possible to read and interpret with the rapidity that the priests expected of their Tibetan gods. However, today, readers are able to read more rapidly and with greater understanding than they have ever done before. And they read with greater appreciation and more critically than in previous years.

Reading is a process of getting meaning from printed word symbols. Reading is more than a mechanical process, although the mechanical process of pronouncing words is necessary in beginning reading, especially, and in certain forms of communication.

Learning to read is a complicated process. There must be interaction between the reader and the printed symbols. Comprehension is the most important skill that must be developed in the reading process.

Too often teachers and parents deliberately or inadvertently compare the child with others in his peer group. Learning to read is an individual process and pupil differences must be a primary consideration in reading instruction. The teacher must be aware of the reasons for the child's inability to achieve and then help the child in overcoming the problems. Teachers and educators must be able to evaluate teaching materials and their impact on learning and reading instruction.

The principles of teaching reading successfully must evolve from the best knowledge available in the fields of psychology, educational psychology, curriculum planning, and child growth and development.

If a reader has a limited background in the material being read, it may be impossible to fully comprehend the information being purused. To overcome this, easier material on the subject should be made available. First hand experiences with the subject is very helpful. This is more easily achieved in lower grades. However, audio-visual assistance can be an added incentive in higher grades. Supplementary books magazines, pictures, and models should be utilized to enrich the child's environment. Children and parents usually appreciate being asked to help supply needed materials.

CONCENTRATION

Motivation and interest are two vitally important elements in developing and increasing the attention span. For the preschool and first grade short listening periods, finger plays, dramatic play, and other activities suitable for this level of learning are described in Chapters Two and Three. Suggestions for improving concentration will be discussed in this chapter.

In the lower grades the young child's attention span is very short and the children must learn or rather understand that quietness is most helpful in attaining that ability to attend to what is at hand. An atmosphere conducive to concentration is one of consideration for others and holding noise to a minimum, unless of course it is such an activity that all will participate in.

It is not always easy to concentrate when one is reading, and it takes time to develop the habit. It is not easy to put all else out of one's thoughts. It is not easy to focus one's attention on the printed page when a television set is on full-blast or the radio is going. Even worse a distraction is that of people conversing and laughing in a room where the child must study. If the child is expected to do homework, it should be arranged that he has a specific area, or at least a specific time to work.

It is difficult for many people to concentrate while they are reading or doing other work. They begin thinking about things they should do, what their friends are doing, or almost anything to use as an excuse to themselves for not attending to the business at hand. Concentration is developed through practice, supplemented by a great deal of self-discipline.

There are times when the teacher may believe that some of her students are not too bright because they do not achieve nor apply themselves to the task at hand. It is safe to say that many of these students judged dull may be brighter than some of the better achievers. The teacher might do well to look to herself and evaluate the motivation that is involved in the project.

There are other reasons for poor concentration. A child cannot achieve as successfully as he should if he is physically uncomfortable, malnourished, or mentally uncomfortable. Proper foods and self-well-being are very important to achievement. If one is hungry, the stomach muscles detract from the function of the eyes and the brain. Emotional disturbance will upset the entire well-being of the individual.

The environmental climate also plays a major part in the ability to concentrate. Poor ventilation, inadequate lighting, and inappropriate room temperatures all contribute to poor concentration.

Slow readers usually permit too many unnecessary ideas to pass through their minds while reading. If the material is too difficult and the reader does not understand the words in the text, it will naturally slow him down and therefore these unrelated thoughts come into his mind. If at all possible, reading materials at an easier level should be supplied, otherwise the teacher must see that the vocabulary is defined for the pupil.

A favorable environment and good motivation are important to any child's achievement. A strong motive strengthens the interest, and the individual attends to the task at hand more readily and with greater confidence. The teacher should recognize lack of concentration among the students, and then set about to remedy the situation. A class discussion can be helpful, but individual help must be given where it is needed. Good concentration is vital to good reading and achievement in all classwork.

DEVELOPMENT OF COGNITIVE SKILLS

Comprehension or reading for meaning is one of the first skills to be taught in the first grade. Comprehension is a complex activity which involves understanding, evaluating, organizing, and verifying. The child's comprehension depends upon his background of experience, his general intelligence, and his keenness of insight. His depth of comprehension is dependent upon his maturity.

Effective reading is an active process which involves thinking as one reads. Comprehension is more important than speed in reading. To read comprehensively, the student must read searchingly and critically.

Development of Skills

1. There must be an awareness of printed symbols and of the fact that they convey a meaning.
2. Reading is not a word-analyzing, sound, and memorizing process, but rather a thought-getting process.
3. Concepts are developed from experiences.
4. Visualizing in reading is important.
5. A background for the reading assignment must be established. The child should understand why he is reading. He should not read merely because he is told to do so.
6. Rather than say, "Read the next four lines," the teacher should say, "Let's read to find out ...."
7. The basic text is for the purpose of developing reading skills and not for oral reading around the class.
8. There is no law against not completing a story on the same day that it is started. If not completed, the children have something exciting to look forward to for the next day.
9. The teacher should not feel that she must hurry on to the next story.
10. For first grade the children should
    a. read for meaning at the very outset,
    b. dramatize stories,
    c. paint or draw parts of the story,
    d. have many learning activities, such as matching pictures, and later on words and pictures, finding right answers, telling how they think the story will end, etc.
11. Pictures and supplementary materials should be brought to the reading class. The children should learn about the period in which the story took place.
12. The child should emerge from his reading with a clear thought.
13. Simple outlining helps in comprehension. A simple form of outlining may be used in the third grade, beginning with the main idea of a paragraph and two or three supporting details.
14. New words are best introduced in context and reviewed promptly in varied context.
15. The children should be encouraged to conduct their own study of new words.
16. The introduction of too many words in a single lesson is to be avoided.
17. The knowledge the children already have on the subject needs to be recalled.
18. Use of the glossary, the table of contents, and the index will be of value.
19. Supplementary material pertaining to the story should be provided for the free-reading period.
20. For the slower learner, interesting but sufficiently challenging material can be found.
21. The children should learn to know guiding words:
    a. Contrast words: *but, however, nevertheless*
    b. Reference words: *former, the latter, the following*
    c. Number words: *fourth, fifth, sixth.*
22. Children should learn that the first paragraph of the story usually tells what it is about; the last paragraph summarizes the story.
23. In a paragraph, the first sentence is usually the key sentence.
24. There should be a purpose for reading and for rereading a selection.
25. The children should learn to use the *five w's: what, who, where, why,* and *when.*
26. Catch questions are to be avoided. Interrogative or imperative-type questions are useful but should not be combined in the same lesson because the children often become confused.
27. The questions should be at the learner's maturity level.
28. Repetition by the children of the exact words in the book is not to be encouraged.
29. Sequential questions are desirable, especially for guiding the first silent reading. One question should lead into another. Questions can be stimulating.
30. Children can learn to find proof for the correctness or incorrectness of a statement.
31. Comprehension should include phrase meaning, sentence meaning, and paragraph meaning.

Factors Affecting Comprehension

1. Instructional
   a. Failure to use related facts
   b. Inability to draw conclusions
   c. Inability to get meaning from context
   d. Inability to get the main idea
   e. Extremes in reading rate—too slow or too rapid
   f. Careless reading
   g. Lack of imagery
   h. Inadequate vocabulary
   i. Inability to concentrate
   j. Lack of retention
   k. Short memory span
   l. Lack of purpose for reading
2. Mental
   a. General intelligence
   b. Maturity
   c. Emotional stability
3. Environmental
   a. Meager home background and experiences
   b. Poor school attendance
4. Physical
   a. Ill health
   b. Poor vision or hearing

Ways of Checking Child's Comprehension

1. Matching pictures and sentences.
2. Writing answers to definite questions.
3. Finishing incomplete sentences.
4. Drawing illustrations of characters, actions, or scenes.
5. Collecting main points to be written on the blackboard and discussed.
6. Finding key words.
7. Dramatizing or dramatic play.
8. Discussing and reporting by pupils.
9. Proving or disproving a statement.
10. Classifying words which describe a given object, person, or time.
11. Selecting the part of the story liked best.
12. Discussing an important character in the story.
13. Making outlines.
14. Selecting the sentence which tells the story best.
15. Selecting the best title for the story or paragraph.
16. Telling in what way two characters were alike and in what way unalike.
17. Discriminating between crucial and incidental facts.
    a. The most important part of the story is................
    b. Some incidents I liked are......................................

SUGGESTIONS FOR ACTIVITIES IN DEVELOPING COMPREHENSION SKILLS

1. The Five W's

Grades two, three, four, five, and six

The children write *What, Who, When, Where, Why* to head columns at the top of their papers. They look through the story to find the answers.

This may be done as a class project, or the children may do it individually. This same idea may be used by having the children find all the words in the lesson that could be classified under these five headings.

2. Questions and Answers

Grades one, two, three, four, five, and six

Two sets of cards are used. One set has questions which pertain to the reading assignment, social studies, or science. The second set of cards gives the answers to the questions. Two or four children can play the game, or the teacher may use the question cards and have the child who has the right answer read it.
Example:

Set 1	*Set 2*
Who sells sugar?	The grocer sells sugar.
Who digs coal?	The postman carries mail.
Who sells postage stamps?	The miner digs coal.
Who carries mail?	The postmaster sells stamps.

—and so on

These packs of cards may be placed in envelopes or boxes and used over and over again. The number of questions to prepare will depend upon the number of children using the game at one time.

3. Matching Paragraphs and Titles

Grades two, three, four, five, and six

Paragraphs from old readers or science books may be pasted on 2½-by-5-inch cards. Titles that fit these paragraphs are typed on another set of cards with numbers for use in preparing a key. Children may work individually or in pairs, reading the paragraphs and deciding upon the best title for each paragraph. They may write their own paragraphs and titles.

4. Multiple-Choice Questions

Grades one, two, three, four, five, and six

The teacher duplicates this exercise. She uses sentences taken from the lesson and gives three or four choices for completing the sentence correctly.

Example:

Draw a line under the correct answer.

a. The man had a..
tame bear.
wild bear.
white bear

b. The bear could ....
march and sing.
dance and hop.
walk and jump,
etc.

5. Guessing Riddles

Grades one, two, and three

The teacher or the pupils make up riddles about animals or people in the story. One child reads the riddle, and the others guess the answer. The teacher may duplicate the riddles and the children write the answers. For first grade, the child may draw a picture of the object described.

Example:

I have a long neck.
I have a big bill.
I have webbed feet.
I am ....; and so on

6. Matching Sentences

Grades one, two, and three

The exercise using sentences or words from the reading lesson may be duplicated, written on the blackboard, or printed on strips or cards for individual activities.

Example:

A.	B.
a. We write	1. in the air.
b. Bread is baked	2. on a tree.
c. Birds fly	3. with a pencil.
d. Snow falls	4. in an oven; and so on

7. Sentence Completion

Grades one, two, three, four, five, and six

Sentences from other assignments may be used. All necessary words may be given for the lower grades, but older pupils should be able to complete the sentences from their recall of the materials read. The exercises are either duplicated or written on the blackboard.

Example:

Draw a line to the correct endings.

a. My dog ....sat on a tuffet.
b. Miss Muffet ....can bark.
c. Jack and Jill ....sat in a corner.
d. Little Jack Horner ....went up the hill; and so on.

8. True or False Statements

Grades one, two, three, four, five, and six

Some true and some false statements which refer to the reading assignment may be used. For lower grades, the children write *Yes* or *No* after the sentences. The material may be duplicated or written on the blackboard.

Example:

Write *Yes* after the sentences that are true and *No* after those that are not true.

a. Elephants are larger than tigers. ....
b. The little boy can run as fast as a horse. ....
c. The crow could talk as well as the boy. ....; and so on.

9. Watching for Key Words

Grades five and six

This exercise may be duplicated or printed on cards and kept in envelopes. The children may do these exercises during their independent activity period if the teacher prepares a sufficient number and provides a key so the children may check their answers.

Example: **Find the Key Words.**

Read the sentences and do what you are asked to do.

a. If squirrels are rodents, cross out the first verb in this sentence.
b. If June comes before March, write your name.
c. Write the first letter of the name of the largest city in the United States—and so on.

10. Words That Tell Time

Grades three and four

Sentences are prepared which contain reference to time, using words from the reading lesson. These may be duplicated or written on the blackboard.

Example: **Find the Words That Tell About Time**

Underline all the words that tell about time.

a. The week seemed to pass slowly.
b. In one year, the rosebush had grown a great deal.
c. Everyday I find something new and interesting.
d. I will be there in ten minutes.
e. He will come while you are here—and so on.

The children may be asked to go through their reading lesson and write all the words referring to time. Another activity which children enjoy is to take the newspaper and underline in red all the words referring to time and in blue all the words meaning numbers.

11. Sentence Completion with the Aid of the Readers

Grades two, three, and four

The teacher writes a part of the sentence on the blackboard. The children find the sentence in the reader and complete it.

Example:

a. Every morning the squirrel went out to ....
b. He saw tracks on the ....
c. Tomorrow I will set a ....

12. Making Comparisons

Grades three, four, five, and six

The children prepare a chart, showing the difference between two animals, people, or plants about which they have read. They may use reference books to complete the chart.

The teacher may give each child a duplicated outline or the outline may be written on the blackboard (fig. 3.1).

13. Answering Questions Through Recall

Grades three, four, five, and six

Questions are prepared that deal with topics covered in reading or other subjects. These may be duplicated or written on the blackboard.

Example: **How Well Do You Remember?**

Check the correct answers.

a. What is the lead in your pencil?
   graphite   clay   graphite and clay

The Porcupine and the Raccoon		
	Porcupine	*Raccoon*
1. Appearance		
2. Kind of home		
3. Food		
4. Means of protection		
5. Habits		
6. Young		
7. Size		
8. Hibernation		
9. Usefulness		
10. Where found		

Figure 3.1 Making Comparisons

b. How many meals should your dog have daily in July?
two three one

14. Finding the Paragraph

Grades three, four, five, and six

The exercise using the assignment in reading, science, or social studies may be written on the blackboard or duplicated.

Example:

Find the paragraph that begins with each sentence. Give the page and number of the paragraph. Read the paragraph and find one or two facts which support the sentence.

a. The women hurried into the cabin.
b. The Indians were watching from behind the trees.
c. There was little time left to warn the stranger; and so on.

15. Reading to Find Out

Grades one, two, three, four, five, and six

The children are asked to read a selection. After reading they are to answer the questions which the teacher has prepared and written on the blackboard or duplicated.

Example:

Read to find out

a. What color is the river?
b. How many boats were sailing down the river?
c. How many people were in the larger boat?—and so on.

16. Quiz Shows

Grades two, three, four, five, and six

The children prepare questions from their lessons and then conduct a quiz program similar to those seen on television. Strange incidents taken from the lessons may be used as models, and the students may then be required to discover other "believe it or not" situations or incidents.

17. Can You Answer?

Grades two, three, four, five, and six

A picture is pasted on a 6-by-9-inch card. This is followed by a short story or description. An envelope is pasted on the back of the card containing some words that tell about the picture and story and other words that do not belong. Without referring to the picture or story after it is once read, the child sorts the words that belong to the story. A key is provided so the child can check his work.

18. Comprehension

Grades two, three, four, five, and six

Sentences that will supplement work in science, social studies, and other assignments are printed on 9-by-12-inch cardboard pieces. Holes are punched after each subject and before each predicate in the second row. A shoestring or cord is fastened through each hole in the first row. The object of the game is to place the loose end of the string in the hole that represents the correct ending of the subject. This is an individual activity (fig. 3.2).

What Happens in Spring?	
1. The birds......................•	• get shorter.
2. The days......................•	• go up.
3. The seeds....................•	• make honey.
4. The nights....................•	• open.
5. The bees......................•	• build nests.
6. The weather................•	• are planted.
7. The cocoons..............•	• get longer.
8. The thermometers......•	• gets warmer.

Figure 3.2 Comprehension

19. Sentence Completion

Grades one and two

Across each of twenty 3-by-4-inch ovals, an irregular line is drawn lengthwise with the subject of a sentence above the line and the predicate on the lower half. These sentences contain words that the children encounter in their reading. These parts, together with the directions for using and the key, are stored in a labeled box. The child is to match the subject and predicate. After all parts have been matched, the child may read the sentences. Stories may be made from these sentences (fig. 3.3).

20. Matching Pictures and Sentences

Grade one

Pictures from magazines and workbooks are pasted on cards. A sentence for each picture is printed on a separate card and placed in an envelope or a box. Chil-

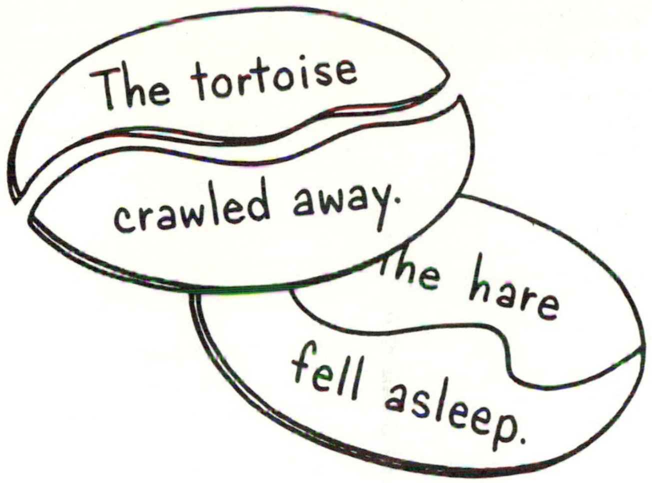

Figure 3.3 Sentence Completion

dren are to match pictures and sentences, then check with the key.

21. Matching Pictures and Paragraphs

Grades one and two

Pictures from magazines and workbooks are pasted on cards. A paragraph about each picture is printed on a separate card and placed in a box or envelope together with a key. The child matches pictures and paragraphs.

22. Matching Pictures and Paragraphs

Grades three, four, five, and six

The idea for grades one and two in the exercise above can be applied with pictures on science and social studies. Old books or stamp books are very useful for this.

23. Paragraph Meaning

Grades one, two, and three

Pictures that relate to the children's center of interest are pasted on each page of a booklet made by fastening 8-by-10-inch sheets of tagboard together with metal rings. A short paragraph about each picture is written on a 2-by-4-inch card, kept in an envelope on the back of the book. A pocket is under each picture or photo corners are placed there to hold the card the children choose as a match for the picture. A key gives the children an opportunity for self-checking.

24. Paragraph Meaning

Grades four, five, and six

Pictures about science, geography, or social studies can be obtained from travel folders, magazines, National Geographics, and post cards, and pasted in booklets similar to the ones described above. A paragraph about each picture is written on a 2-by-4-inch card and placed in an envelope at the back of the booklet. The children are to place the paragraphs in a pocket under the correct picture (see fig. 3.4).

Figure 3.4 Paragraph Meaning

25. Sentence Completion

Grades one and two

Folders are made with a picture on one side and sentences to be completed on the other. A picture may be pasted on the cover of the folder. Words that appear in the reading lesson are printed on small strips of paper to fit in the blanks in the sentences. Photo corners may be used to hold these word strips. The child is to place the words so that each sentence is completed. A small envelope at the back of the folder holds the key and the word strips (see fig. 3.5).

26. Finding Pairs

Grades three and four

Sentences containing pairs of words may be duplicated or written on the blackboard. The second word of each pair is omitted in the sentence and the child is to supply it.

Example: **What Word Is Missing?**

Write the word that is missing.

a. The table and .... were in the kitchen.
b. He wore a hat and ....
c. She sewed with a needle and ....
d. Mary washed the cup and ....
e. Bob likes bread and ....

27. Taking a Trip

Grades three, four, five, and six

The children make a list of cities they will pretend to visit, and prepare questions about each. Committees may be formed to report on each city. Countries may be used instead of cities. Travel agencies will usually cooperate in supplying materials.

28. Who Said It?

Grades one, two, three, four, five, and six

Quotations from the texts used may be duplicated or written on the blackboard.

Example: **Who Said It?**

a. "It must be the wind, no one would dare strike double knocks on our door." ....
b. "I'm sorry to hear that. How long may I stay?" ....
c. "Off and be hanged."..

29. Who?

Grades one, two, three, four, five, and six

Phrases from the reading lesson may be duplicated or written on the blackboard.

Directions:

Read the first phrase. Look in your reader to find the name of the animal described by the phrase. Write the name of the animal in the blank beside the phrase.

a. eating candy ....
b. always showing off ....
c. a very long neck ....
d. sleeping all winter .... etc.

30. Booklets for Developing Comprehension

Grades two, three, four, five, and six

The pupils should be encouraged to make scrapbooks or booklets about their hobbies and the topics they

Figure 3.5 Sentence Completion

are studying about in their classes. The books can be illustrated with their drawing or with pictures cut from magazines. The pupils should write captions under the pictures. They should refer to books, encyclopedias, and the like for information. Taking an imaginary trip can be a very interesting project. Pupils can write to the chambers of commerce in the various places that they plan to study and explain their project.

31. Understanding the Paragraph Organization

Grades five and six

Explain to the pupils that there is always a main idea in each paragraph. Duplicated paragraphs may be given to the pupils, who are to underline the topic sentence or the main idea.

32. Understanding Sentence Meaning

Grades four, five, and six

Write sentences on the blackboard, or duplicate the sentence for the pupils. Ask them to read the sentence and write *who, what, when, where,* or *why* after each sentence to show what the part of the sentence that is italicized tells.

Example:

a. The truck *went down the dusty street.* where
b. *Every day* the old man hurried down the street. ....
c. He ran as *fast as he could go.* ....
d. *Last summer* he went on a trip. ....
e. Jack made the boat *all by himself.* ....
f. They hurried indoors *when it started to rain.* ....
g. *The frost* killed many vines. ....
h. The knights *rode horses* when they invaded England. ....
i. Horses can be easily trained *because of their intelligence.* ....
j. *As the weather turns colder,* birds begin to fly south. ....

—and so on

33. Who, What, When, Where, or Why

Grades four, five, and six

Give the pupils phrases that may be taken from the reading assignment and ask them to write *who, what, when, where,* or *why* following each phrase.

Example:

1. on the table ....
2. a beautiful picture ....
3. playing ball ....
4. in order to talk ....
5. beside the car ....
6. at nine o'clock ....
7. because he's late ....
8. at the store ....
9. because it is broken ....
10. in the sky ....
11. a little boy ....
12. a happy child ....
13. in the morning ....
14. because of the heat ....
15. sometime later ....
16. finding some nuts ....
17. closed the door ....
18. next summer ....

MAIN IDEAS

A reader should know what he is looking for in his reading, and he should know how to read various materials in different ways. He should learn to think while he is reading.

The teacher should explain to the students that each paragraph consists of a group of sentences which deal with a specific topic. Each paragraph contains a topic sentence which may also be called the main idea or central thought.

A good reader is interested in the thought of the paragraph, which is usually expressed in a group of words. Students find it interesting to underline the main idea in paragraphs which may be taken from some of their own written work or newspapers may be used for this.

Since the good reader may have little difficulty in finding the main idea, it usually requires less time to develop this skill. However the teacher must be concerned with those students who have difficulty in recognizing the topic sentence.

1. Finding the Main Idea

Grade one

The children look at the picture in the reader and discuss what it is telling them.

2. Selecting a Picture to Illustrate the Main Idea

Grades one and two

Paragraphs are duplicated, and the children either find or draw pictures to illustrate them. The teacher may have pictures pasted on cards which the children can use for this activity. The child summarizes the paragraph he has read by choosing a suitable picture.

3. Finding the Main Idea and Supporting Details

Grades three, four, five, and six

Selections from books, magazines, editorials, and the like may be used. After the article has been read, the children decide on the main idea and the supporting details. If the material has been duplicated, each child may draw a red line under the main idea and blue lines under the supporting details.

4. Giving the Paragraph a Title

Grades two, three, four, five, and six

Children select a title for a duplicated paragraph either by multiple choice or by free selection.

5. Classifying the Main Ideas

Grades two and three

By using words found in the readers, exercises similar to the example below are duplicated. The children write *what* happened, *when* it happened, or *where* it happened.

Example:

a. on the floor ....
b. in the barn ....
c. ten minutes ago ....
d. because it rained ....
e. in the evening ....
f. because of the fire ....
g. much later ....
h. under the tree ....

6. Identifying the Central Idea

Grades four, five, and six

Simple paragraphs and questions similar to the ones given below may be used.

Example:

The doctor was in the best condition. He looked especially strong and young. The resemblance between him and his daughter Mary was very strong at times, and as they sat side by side, she leaning on his shoulder and he resting his arm on the back of her chair, it was very easy to trace the likeness. The central idea is:

a. The doctor's good health
b. Resemblance of the doctor and his daughter
c. Father-daughter relationship

7. Stating the Central Idea

Grades four, five, and six

A well-written paragraph usually has the central idea stated in a sentence called a topic sentence. This is generally the first sentence in the paragraph, and it may contain a key word. Paragraphs having the topic sentence containing a key word should be selected. The pupils are asked to underline the topic sentence and to encircle the key word.

8. Checking the Main Idea by Using a Picture

Grades one and two

A hosiery box with a picture and written directions pasted on the cover is suitable. Pictures from magazines or books are pasted on small cards about 2 × 3 inches. Eight or ten paragraphs, one about each picture, are written on 3½-by-8-inch cards, allowing space for the correct picture described at the bottom or on one side. Use eight or ten paragraphs and pictures. Each child may check his work from a key if the paragraphs are numbered and letters used for the pictures. The pupils match picture with paragraph.

9. Testing the Ability to Find the Main Idea

Grades four, five, and six

Paragraphs from the reading lesson are selected, and the directions are written on the chalkboard, together with the different main ideas used.

Directions:

Choose the main idea of each of these paragraphs from those given. Write only the answer you think is correct.

a. What is the main idea of paragraph 2, page 64?
b. What is the main idea of paragraph 3, page 65? —and so on.

RECOGNIZING THE SUPPORTING DETAILS

A good reader looks first for the main idea in a paragraph, and then for the supporting details. Each paragraph is a small unit of information. It gives information about one thing which is called the *main idea,* and in order to make this main idea more interesting, supporting details are included.

The reader should watch for words which may change the meaning of a sentence, such as *but, however,* and the like. These words usually make a great deal of difference in the meaning of the sentence and the paragraph. Sometimes, too, it is difficult to know what some pronouns are referring to. If the reader is uncertain as to the antecedent, the word to which a pronoun refers, he should reread the sentence or paragraph.

The reader should look for the main idea by asking himself *Who?* and *What?* These answers usually help in locating the main idea. Then he should look for the answers to *Where? When?* and *Why?* These will give the supporting details of the paragraph. Some details are more important than others, too, so the student should learn to find those that are of greater value to him in helping him understand the material he is reading. The information that is of greater importance to the understanding of the main idea is called a *major detail.* The minor details are not as important, but they add a little more thought to the subject.

Making a mental outline of what is being read is very helpful in remembering the important points in the material. The mind is very quick, and it is possible to develop this habit with little effort.

Sometimes written practice in filling in an outline can help in learning to find the important points in each paragraph. The reader should ask himself: Who or what is this about? Who is speaking? To whom? What is he saying? What is happening? Why did it happen? How did it happen? When did it happen?

ACHIEVING SKILL IN READING FOR DETAILS

Reading for details is one of the important skills in reading, and its development should begin in the first grade. Suggestions for developing this skill are given below. Paragraphs from the textbook may be duplicated or written on the chalkboard.

1. Finding Details in a Paragraph

Grades two, three, four, five, and six

About ten test items, such as true or false, multiple-choice, or completion are constructed for each paragraph. Once the child has read the selection, he is not to refer to it while answering the questions.

2. Recalling Details

Grades three, four, five, and six

Test items on a selection that is to be read in class may be duplicated or written on a chart. By noting the name of the book and the page number, these and the key may be filed and used again when another group is ready to read the book. Material from social studies or science lessons may be used.

Example:

In 1492, Columbus left Spain with three small ships. He wanted to find a new route to India. After many months at sea, land was sighted. Columbus called the strange people who lived on this land Indians because he thought he had reached India. The land he had found was America but the descendants of the people who lived here when he found this country are still called Indians.

Why do we call the people who lived in America when Columbus landed, Indians?

a. Which of the following facts are you to find?
........The year Columbus sailed from Spain.
........The number of months at sea.
........Why the natives are called Indians.

b. Which of the following facts are in the paragraph just read?
........The number of days Columbus was at sea.
........Columbus found a new route to India.
........Columbus thought he had landed on the shores of India.

c. Which of these questions are answered by facts in the paragraph?
........Where did Columbus land?
........Why is this country called America?
........Why did Columbus set sail from Spain?

3. Reading for Details

Grades two, three, and four

After the lesson has been read, questions on it are used as follow-up work. A key is provided. The material may be duplicated, written on the blackboard, or given orally.

Example:

a. Who said he was not well?
a dog a fox a pig

b. Who believed the pig?
a dog a goose a lamb

c. Who said, "Come into the house"?
Mary Jack Jill

4. Rereading for Detail

Grades three, four, five, and six

The children read the selection and then reread it to give the correct answers. Test items may be multiple-choice or completion.

Example:

a. What group of people is this story about?
Norsemen Indians Pilgrims

b. What was the name of the settlement?
Plymouth Plum Valley Jamestown

5. Locating Details in Sentences

Grades three, four, five, and six

Sentences, which have information about the subject being studied, are duplicated. The children read one sentence at a time and are asked to draw a line under the best answer to the question asked.

Example:

a. Many years ago there were no white men living in this country. There were only Indians.
Who lived in our country many years ago?
Pilgrims farmers red men

6. Locating Details

Grades two, three, four, five, and six

The children are asked to skim through the story in order to find the answers to questions given them. They are to write the page number, the paragraph, and the line where the answer was found.

Example:

a. Who liked the chocolate cake?
b. Who found the round stone?
c. Who made the dog bark?—and so on.

The children's answers will look like this:

a. page 43, para. 3, line 4
b. page 44, para. 6, line 1
c. page 46, para. 2, line 3—and so on.

7. Finding Details in Pictures

Grades one, two, and three

Each child is given a picture, which has been pasted on a sheet of cardboard, about 8 × 10 inches. A designated length of time is given to look at the picture, then without referring to it again, he answers questions similar to the ones given below. The questions may be duplicated or placed on a chart. When the child has used a picture, he may initial it so the teacher will not give it to him a second time.

Example: **What Did You See?**

a. Were there three boys in the picture?
b. What time of day was it?
c. What do you think happened?
d. What do you think is going to happen? etc.
For first grade, *yes* and *no* questions may be used.

8. Mapping Story Events

Grades one, two, three, four, five, and six

After reading the story, the children may, as a group or individually, make a map of some part of the story. They may indicate where certain events took place.

9. Understanding Details

Grades four, five, and six

Prepare sentences similar to the ones given below. These may be taken from students' textbook and pertain to the lessons. The student is to write *who, what, when, where, why,* or *how* to indicate what the italicized part of the sentence tells.

Example:

1. The truck went *down the dusty road.* where
2. *Every day* the old man hurried to the post office. ....
3. He ran *as fast as he could go.* ....
4. *Last summer* he went on a long trip. ....
5. Jack made the boat *all by himself.* ....
6. They hurried indoors *because it started to rain.* ....
7. *The frost* killed many vines. ....
8. *As the weather turns colder,* birds begin to fly South. ....
9. The knights *rode horses* when they invaded England. ....

10. Finding Words That Relate to When

Grades four, five, and six

Duplicate the paragraph below and have the students underline the words that relate to *When.*

The history of newspaper advertising has been traced back 5,000 years to ancient Greece. There at water fountains ads were posted regarding the sale of chariots, slaves, or household goods. In the seventeenth century, just after the great fire of London, the first printed ads appeared. Today our newspapers give many pages to ads, and even the many people who do not intend to buy enjoy reading them. A new form of advertising has appeared in the last several years which reminds one of the ancient ads of early Greece. Most supermarkets have poster boards on which anyone may place a card telling of some article he wishes to sell or buy. Rather than chariots and slaves, present-day ads are more likely to be for cars, washing machines, or pets.

CLASSIFICATION

The purpose of classification is to develop the idea that many words or ideas fall into general classification. The teacher may direct the pupils' thinking by talking about the classroom and what is found in it; then the discussion is directed to the home, and ultimately to other areas.

1. Classification of Pictures

Readiness activity

Pictures of fruit and vegetables, cut from magazines, readiness workbooks, and the like, pasted on 2-by-3-inch cards are to be placed in the lid and bottom of a box by the child. Using *fruit* and *vegetables* as an example of classification, a picture of some fruit and vegetable may be pasted on the lid of a tie box and the words *Fruit* and *Vegetables* are printed on the lid. Inside the lid of the box the picture of a vegetable is pasted, and in the bottom of the box, a fruit picture is pasted. "We belong here" may be printed under the pictures pasted in the top and the bottom. The child places the pictures in the proper place. A key may be provided so that the child can check his work. A few suggestions for classification of pictures follow:

School—Home	To live in—To wear
Farm—City	Grocery—Bakery
We run—We fly	People—Pets
Work—Play	To ride—To smell
Long—Short	To hear—To feel
Big—Little	To eat—To hear
Fast—Slow	Trees—Flowers
Toys—Pets	Wild flowers—Domesticated flowers
Clothes—Tools	Wild animals—Tame animals
Make—Grow	Summer—Winter
Vegetables—Fruit	Halloween—Thanksgiving
Night—Day	Kitchen—Bedroom
Time—Place	For baby—For me
Breakfast—Dinner	Animals—Birds
Fly—Swim	Live on land—Live in water
Wheels—Wings	Color—Things

2. Things That Belong Together

Grades one and two

Two-inch squares are marked off on a cardboard folder about 11 × 16 inches. One picture of each category, such as animals, fruit, flowers, toys, and transportation, is pasted in the first square of each line on the folder. Several pictures for each category are pasted on 1¾-inch squares of cardboard. The children place these pictures in the correct spaces on the folder. The folder and the pictures are kept in a box or in an envelope with a key for the children's use (fig. 3.6).

3. Words That Belong Together

Grades one, two and three

Spaces measuring 1¾ inches × 1¾ inches are marked off on 8¾-by-12-inch pieces of cardboard. Categories, such as color, toys, people, time, trees, fruit, food, numbers, action words, clothing, home, school, and animals, are printed in the top spaces of the cardboard. Words that belong to these categories are printed on 1-by-1½-

Figure 3.6 Things That Belong Together

inch strips, and the child is to place the names of the objects under the right category. The material may be stored in a labeled cardboard box or an envelope with the directions for using the game (fig. 3.7).

4. We Belong Here

Grades one and two

Two pictures, such as a store and a farm scene, are each pasted on an 8-by-10-inch sheet of cardboard and the sheets hinged together with tape. Under each picture there should be a pocket with the words "We belong here" on it (fig. 3.8).

For beginning readers, words from their reading books which pertain to each picture should be printed on 1-by-2-inch cardboard, one word to each strip. For reading readiness, pictures may be used instead of words. Complete sentences should be used as soon as possible. The children are to place the strips with the correct words or sentences in the pockets under each picture. There may be a third pocket with "We do not belong" in which words or sentences which do not fit may be placed. The material may be stored in a box or an envelope with a label and directions.

5. Classifying Ideas

Grades two, three, and four

Words that are found in the readers or other textbooks may be used in questions as suggested below. The material may be duplicated, written on the blackboard, or made into chart form.

What Would You Find?

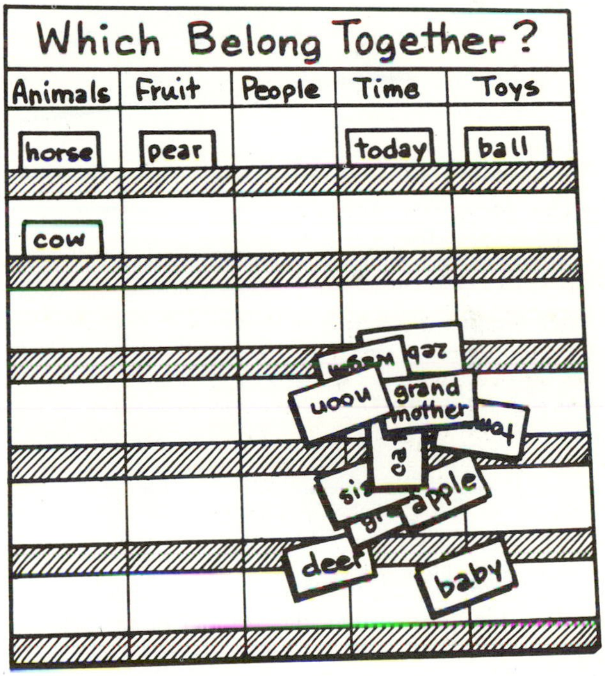

Figure 3.7 Words That Belong Together

Check the right answers

1. What can you see on a street? ....a truck ....a table ....a car
2. What is good to eat? ....a ball ....a cookie ....a pear
3. What has long ears? ....a calf ....a rabbit ....a dog
4. Where can you find a tulip? ....in a garden ....in school ....in a ball

—and so on

Figure 3.8 We Belong Here

6. What Are They?

Grades two, three, and four

This exercise is in a way similar to the one above.

What Are They?

Check the right answers

1. What is good to ride in? ....a boat ....a stove ....a car
2. What is too heavy to carry? ....a shoe ....a lion ....a goat
3. What is used on the farm? ....a hoe ....a circus ....a puppy

—and so on

7. Classification of Ideas

Grades one, two, three, and four

In the first and second grades, words appearing in the reader should be used. Categories, such as animals, action words, food, people, toys, and pets, may be used. In grades three and four, similar categories may be used, and words used in science and social studies may also be categorized. Words in the spelling lists may be included in the exercises. The material may be duplicated, written on the blackboard, or made into a chart.

Which Words Belong?

Check the names of animals in the words below:

country	breakfast	rabbit	trunk
tree	goat	fox	horse
elephant	hose	rubber	jungle

—and so on

8. Classification of Ideas

Grades one, two, three, and four

In this exercise the child has two directions to follow instead of one as in the preceding exercise.

Find the Right Words

Draw a *line* under the things you eat. Put an *x* over the things you play with.

apple	corn	cat	bread
ball	run	balloon	wagon
dog	cake	banana	chair

—and so on

For upper grades, the children may find rivers, mountains, states, inventors, scientists, etc.

9. Classifying Words

Grades two, three, and four

This exercise may be duplicated, written on the blackboard, or made into a chart, using words found in the readers, science books, and social studies texts.

Which Words Belong?

Cross out the words that do not belong in the lists:

Animals	*Plants*	*Fruit*	*Time*
cow	cactus	apple	yesterday
bell	lemon	potato	quick
sheep	sponge	peach	today
horse	tree	jelly	suddenly
butter			

—and so on

10. Classification

Grades two, three, four, five, and six

Categories suitable for the grade level of the children may deal with science, social studies, arithmetic, and so on. The exercise may be duplicated, written on the blackboard, or made into a chart.

Classification

Look at the first two words in each line, then write three other words that belong to the same class. You may use the word list in the back of your reader or other books.

1. bear .... donkey..
2. ears .... eyes..
3. dandelion .... rose..
4. eight .... eleven..
5. gloves .... hat..

—and so on

11. Classification

Grades two, three, four, five, and six

Classifications, suitable to the grade level, from science, social studies, arithmetic, and other categories may be used similarly to the exercises above.

Which Belong Together?

Choose the right answers.

1. A train goes with ....station ....snow ....railroad
2. A farm goes with ....tractor ....tickets ....fences
3. Snow goes with ....weather ....skating ....letters
4. Sandwiches go with ....country ....picnics ....sunshine

—and so on

12. Classification

Grades two, three, four, five, and six

Exercises suitable for the grade level may be prepared, using the words in readers and other textbooks. The material may be duplicated, written on the blackboard, or made into a chart.

What Will You Need?

Check the things you will need.

1. You are hungry ....milk ....napkin ....sandwich
2. You are writing a letter ....paper ....book ....pen
3. You are going to a circus ....tickets ....popcorn ....envelope

—and so on

13. Classification

Grades one, two, three, four, five, and six

The words found in the readers, science books, and social studies books may be used in exercises similar to the one shown in the next column.

Find the Right Words

Three of the words in each "set" go together. Find those words and draw a line under each one.

nickel dime	penny roof	branch hammer	bark leaves	hung pie	cake cookie
jump step	hop bite	sled skates	flour scooter	churn roof	chimney door
soft gentle	quiet harsh	great tiny	big large	roar whisper	scream cry

—and so on

14. Suggestions for Exercises Requiring Classification

Grades one, two, three, four, five, and six

Topics for classification are listed below. These may be developed according to grade level as in the foregoing examples. Some of the exercises may be placed in labeled boxes and others may be placed in envelopes.

Action Words
Animals, Domesticated and Wild
Activities
Birds
Countries
City and Country
Zoo and Farm Animals
Communication
Clothing
Colors
Cities and States
Dogs
Explorers
Farm Activities
Flags
Flowers
Food
Fruit
Fish
Homes
Houses
Inventions
Inventors
Now and Then
Insects
Mountains
Rivers
People
Playground
Products
Reptiles
School
Seasons
States
Time
Measure
Transportation
Weather
Fruit and Vegetables
We Run—We Fly
Home—School
Farm—Store
Things to Eat—Things to Wear
Things with Wheels—Things with Wings
Things That Float—Things That Soar
Shells

15. Classification of Word Forms

Grades five and six

List words used in the reading, science, mathematics, and other assignments. Ask the students to classify these words under nouns, adjectives, verbs, and so on. The students may refer to the dictionary when necessary.

Example:

Nouns *Adjectives* *Verbs*

Words to be classified:

ordinary	screw	ringing	magnetic
energy	magnet	touch	complete
unfasten	wire	stronger	change
compare	connect	circuit	
flow	electricity	strike	

16. Classifying Words

Grades five and six

Use the word lists in the index of the book. The students are to classify the verbs that refer to movement as climb, crawl, flee, quiver, and so on. Other categories can be:

Verbs that refer to sounds as groan, laugh, growl, hum, and so on.

Nouns that refer to time as day, minute, week, and so on.

Nouns that refer to money as quarter, greenback, buck, and so on.

Nouns that refer to food as fruit, energy, vegetables, and so on.

Adjectives that refer to speed as rapid, slow, speedy, swift, and so on.

17. Dramatizing and Pantomiming

Grades one, two, three, and four

The children select slips with the names of animals that live on the farm and those that live in the zoo. Write the words *FARM* and *ZOO* on the blackboard.

The pupil imitates the actions of the animal named on his slip. The class guesses the name of the animal the pupil is imitating. The pupil guessing the name of the animal may write the word on the blackboard, putting it in the right classification. Suggested names are bear, antelope, cat, cow, duck, dog, elephant, lion, hen, horse, turkey, and the like.

Other categories may be used.

18. Classification

Grades three, four, five, and six

The pupils look through the selection and write words that relate to a certain category. A few suggested classifications are color, animals, action, time, money, food, places, home, tools, happiness, occupations, and so on.

Example:

Climate

Words relating to climate may be temperature, hottest, summer, low, cool, ice, air, heat, cools, rays. The pupils may be asked to alphabetize these words for practice in this skill.

19. Booklets

Grades one, two, three, four, five and six

The children make booklets that are to be used for classification. Children in the lower grades may paste pictures of similar things in their books. The upper level can use words instead.

20. Grouping Words

Grades three, four, five, and six

Select words that are suited to the grade level.

Example:

Write three more words that belong to the groups below. Use the spaces following the words. Use a dictionary if necessary.

1. carrot .... beet
   ....
2. oak .... maple
   ....
3. ask .... inquire
   ....
4. said .... replied
   ....
5. bake .... cook
   ....
6. barge .... boat
   ....
7. kite .... jet
   ....
8. bright .... shiny
   ....
9. shoe .... moccasin
   ....
10. camel .... lion
    ....
11. cow .... dog
    ....
12. comma .... period
    ....
13. collect .... gather
    ....
14. creep .... slither
    ....
15. glance .... look
    ....
16. grimy .... untidy
    ....
17. hear .... smell
    ....
18. pinch .... nip
    ....
19. frighten .... terrify
    ....
20. tremble .... shake
    ....

21. What Are They?

Grades three, four, five, and six

Write the general classification on one side of the blackboard and the words to be classified on the other side. This activity may be duplicated if the teacher wishes.

General Heading

birds	grains
clothes	months
colors	noises
days	shapes
directions	sports
flowers	tools
fowls	trees
fruit	vegetables
furniture	

Words To Be Classified

apple	bed	cabbage	downward
axe	blue	circle	daisy
apron	bang	chair	desk
banana	baseball	coat	December
bluebird	beet	corn	dove
bluebell	bench	crawl	dog
bonnet	buzz	couch	drake

duck	hue	pink	Saturday
basketball	hawk	purple	Sunday
east	iris	quail	August
eagle	June	red	south
elk	January	rooster	triangle
elm	jacket	rice	Tuesday
Friday	kitten	rye	Thursday
fir	kingfisher	February	upward
fizz	lemon	March	tulip
fig	lark	robin	green
finch	May	April	west
file	Monday	May	wheat
gray	mouse	July	whisper
gander	moo	spade	football
gown	mittens	squash	tennis
hoe	November	squeak	soccer
hatchet	October	scarlet	lettuce
hat	oats	skating	potato
hoot	orange	swimming	tomato
howl	plow	spruce	whistle
hen	plum	sofa	Wednesday
horse	palm	square	
hammer	pine	crimson	

CONTEXT AND PICTURE CLUES

Children should learn to make use of picture and context clues at the very outset of reading. Too frequently the teacher overlooks the importance of the pictures that accompany the story. The suggestions that follow may prove helpful.

1. Picture Clues

Grade one

Children should be encouraged to study the pictures that accompany the reading materials because they give important clues to new words. The four levels of pictures of reading are:

a. Enumeration—name the objects
b. Description—what is happening
c. Interpretation—what is going to happen
d. Inference—why

Questions to ask the children:

a. What is happening?
b. What has happened?
c. What do you think will happen next?
d. Have you ever seen anything like this happen?
e. Why is this person doing this?
f. What does the picture tell you?

2. Context Clues

Grades one, two, three, four, five, and six

When a child sees a new word, one he does not recognize, he should be encouraged to read the entire sentence and then come back to the word. In the lower grades simple exercises help the child to develop the skill required to get the meaning of a word from context. Examination of the picture, too, may help him learn the new word. Introduce the new words in sentences that give the meaning of the words. The context clues may be of several types as:

a. *Definition* as in "The *reaper,* which cut the grain, etc."
b. *Synonym* as in "The next-door *neighbors,* etc."
c. *Comparison* as in "It is no longer hot, but *cold.*"
d. *Experience* as in "The mouse found some cheese to *nibble.*"

3. Visualizing the Word

Grades one, two, three, four, five, and six

By reading the sentences that have been duplicated or written on the blackboard, and by looking at the size of the blank, the children learn to recognize new words.

Example:

a. Please bring the xxxxxxxx so that I can cut the cloth.
b. Mary baked the cake in a xxx.
c. The xxxxxx of the trees moved in the breeze.

4. Noticing Clues

Grades two, three, four, five, and six

If words which will give the pupils difficulty are anticipated and used in sentences as shown below, they are easily learned.

Example:

The little girl was sitting on the porch. A little sparrow came hopping up the steps and eagerly picked up some bread crumbs. The little girl had dropped the .... that she had been eating.

5. Getting Word Meaning from Context

Grades four, five, and six

Sentences which contain words the children are finding difficult may be constructed to show meaning.

Example:

a. The brave man saved the others from *peril.*
Peril means ....
b. He hurried down the street with great *strides.*
Strides means ....

6. Judging Meaning by Context

Grades four, five, and six

Exercises, similar to the examples given below, should show two or more meanings for a word or words from the reading assignments.

Directions:

Read each sentence in the left-hand column and then find the definitions of the underlined words in the right-hand column. Write the number of the definition in the space provided for it.

Example:

a. He *rattled* on with the story. ....
b. He was *rattled* by the confusing tales told to him. ....
c. The dishes *rattled* in the sink. ....
d. The baby shook his *rattle.* ....

4. rapid succession of noises
3. confused, agitated
2. chattered continually
1. a toy

7. Meaning from Context

Grades three, four, five, and six

Sentences, similar to the examples below, using words and sentences from the reading lesson are duplicated or written on the blackboard.

Example 1.

Directions:

Read each sentence and then answer the questions about it.

a. The rabbits felt safe from the dreaded hawk as long as the faint light could be seen.
   Which word tells you that the light was dim?
   Which word tells you that hawk was feared?
b. The farmer whistled merrily as he rode down the shady lane.
   Which word tells you that the farmer was happy?
   Which word tells you that the sun was not shining on the lane?

Example 2.

Directions:

Fill in each blank in the following sentences, using words from your reader.

a. The farmer got out of his car when he had reached the ....
b. The chipmunk jumped .... to the next branch.

8. Using Context Clues

Grades two and three

Sentences, similar to the examples below, may be duplicated, using words from the lesson.

Directions:

Read each sentence to see if you can discover the word that belongs in the blank. Write the word in the blank by filling in the missing letters.

a. Take the d......y clothes out of the basket.
b. The dog d....g a deep hole.
c. The boy listened for the call of the o....l.
d. The Eskimos live in i......s.
e. The girl wore m...................s on her hands.
f. The man climbed to the top of the m.......................n.

9. Using Context

Grades one and two

Short paragraphs may be duplicated or written on the blackboard. Phrases are taken from these paragraphs and the children are to find the ending that completes each phrase. If the material is presented in duplicate form, the children may draw lines between the two parts of the sentence. If the sentences are to be copied from the blackboard, the sentence is to be written in its correct form.

Directions:

Jane and Bill went to the park. Jane took her doll. Bill took his boat. He sailed his boat on the water. They saw a squirrel. It ran up a tree.

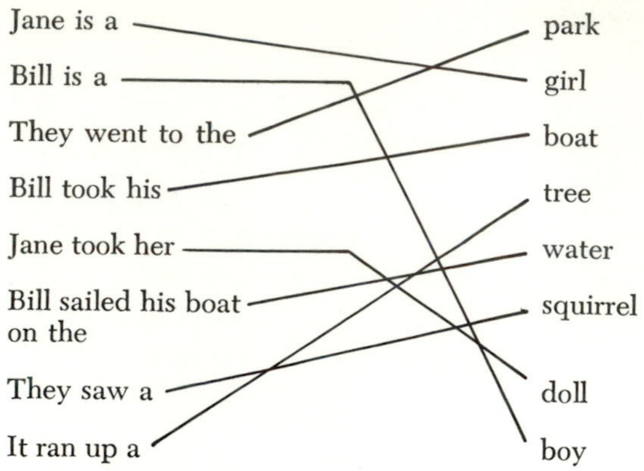

10. Recognizing Context Clues

Grades five and six

The teacher prepares exercises similar to the example given below. These may be developed from paraphrased information from reference books or magazine and newspaper stories.

Example:

Read the paragraphs below and then answer the questions that follow.

Today when you buy a ten-cent ice cream cone, and you give the clerk a quarter, you expect to receive a dime and a nickel in change. But what would you have done thousands of yars ago when there were no dimes, nickels, or pennies?

At one time there was no money at all. Men lived in caves and hunted and fished for their livelihood. All they needed in order to exist was shelter, food, and clothing. But even in these early times, people had different tastes and habits. Some men liked to hunt and fish; others liked to stay at home and make things. The man who hunted brought back meat and furs which the man at home needed for food and clothing. The man at home made spears, hatchets, arrows, and pottery which the hunter wanted. So the men traded with each other and the first barter began.

As time went on, more and more animals were killed, and more and more animal skins accumulated. Then people began to exchange furs for pottery, weapons, and food. They would agree upon the number of furs which would buy the things they needed. So furs became the first money because everyone needed them. They were easy to keep and carry, and they were readily exchanged for other things. People used many other things for barter, too, such as shells, dried fish, tobacco, and anything that was needed by someone else.

Later, when people began to farm the land, to raise grain, sheep and cattle, there was less hunting of wild animals, and wealth was estimated by the number of cows a man owned. Cows became money instead of furs.

Reread the entire sentence that contains the words listed below and from the context clue, determine the meaning of each word. Write the definition.

a. livelihood ....
b. barter ....
c. accumulated ....
d. readily ....
e. estimated ....

11. Enumeration

Grades one and two

Paste pictures on manila paper or cardboard so that they can be handled more easily. The questions can be printed on the back of the pictures for the second grade and the pupils can answer the questions on paper. For first grade, hold the picture so the children can see it. Ask them to tell how many things they see that are red, that can run, and so on.

12. Descriptions

Grades one, two, and three

Use pictures as described above. The questions may be printed on the back of the pictures for grades two and three. Ask questions pertaining to the picture.

Example:

What do you think will happen next?
What time of day is it?
In what part of the world was this picture taken?—and so on.

Other suggestions for using pictures are comparison of size, distance, weight, color, emotions.

13. Picture Clues

Grades one and two

Make folders with a picture at the top and questions on the bottom half of the paper. These may be used by the children for independent activities.

FOLLOWING DIRECTIONS

If children know how to follow directions carefully, their work will usually show the results of having developed this important skill. Whether the child follows directions given orally or from the printed page, he must learn to give attention to the details in the order of their sequence. In the readiness period the directions are given orally, then as he advances to the other grades, some directions are printed and become more and more complex. A few suggestions are given for training in the following of directions.

1. Readiness Exercises

a. String beads. "Take a red bead, now two blue beads," and so on.
b. Read a story and have the children draw a picture about it.
c. Color pictures according to oral direction.
d. Suggest activities which involve hopping, running, and the like.
e. Supply each child with a picture. The children follow directions as, "Make an *X* over the animal that barks," and so on.

2. First-Grade Exercises

The following directions may be written on the board, printed on a card, or duplicated:

1. There are __________ ducks in the picture.
2. A baby duck is called a ______________.
3. Ducks like to __________ in water.
4. The mother duck is taking them to their ____________.
5. Color the mother duck brown and the babies yellow.
6. You may color their beaks orange.
7. Color the water__________.

blue. . six. . swim. . nest. . duckling

Figure 3.9 Picture Clues

Example:

Make one ball. Make it big. Color it red.	Draw two cars. Make one car big. Make one car small. Color them blue.

3. Making Pictures

Grade one

Directions: Draw a picture for each group of words.

A green chair	A hen and five chicks	A big tree
Five stars	Two little wagons	A big and a little house

4. Following Directions

Grades one and two

Directions:
Put X's before the names of animals and circles around the things that grow in the garden.

bear	flowers	beans
pony	grass	cats
goose	carrot	horse
squirrel	hens	cabbage

5. Identifying the Word

Grade one

Directions:

Write the name of the animal that belongs in the blank.

"Moo," said the ....
"Quack," said the ....
"Meow," said the ....

6. Following Directions

Grades one and two

Exercises are duplicated, using words found in the reader.

Directions:

Put *lines* under the things you eat. Put X's over the play-things.

apple	wagon	ball
cat	fish	dog
bread	drum	airplane
corn	crayons	butter
pear	cookie	

7. Pantomiming

Grades two, three, four, five, and six

Each child draws a slip telling him what to do. The other children guess what each child pantomimes. Parts of a story may be used for the pantomiming.

8. Finding Information for Reports

Grades four, five, and six

Directions such as those shown in the example below are given, and each child gives a brief report on the topic he has chosen.

Example:

a. Look in the encyclopedia to find out about a titmouse. Give the volume and the page number.
b. Look for a story about a little toad. Where did you find it?

9. Following Directions in Map Reading

Grades four, five, and six

A map in the geography book may be used or one may be duplicated for the children. They are to answer questions similar to the following:

Example:

a. How are ocean currents shown on the map?
b. How many miles is Phoenix, Arizona from here?
c. Give the name of the longest river shown on the map.

10. Making Charts and Graphs by Following Directions

Grades four, five, and six

Explicit directions are given which will culminate in definite charts.

11. Following Printed Directions

Grades one, two, and three

The children follow instructions printed on cards. Occasionally, the entire group may do the same thing in unison.

Example:

a. Put your feet together.
b. Raise your left hand.
c. Put your left hand at your side.

12. Identifying the Sound

Grades one and two

The teacher writes a list of action words, such as jump, skip, run, walk, hop, sing, read, and laugh, on the board. A pupil is selected to go to a corner and blindfold himself. The teacher or a child points to one word on the board. Someone is selected to come to the front of the room and perform the action, emphasizing the sound of the word. The child takes his seat again. The blindfolded child uncovers his eyes, goes to the board, and points to the word expressing the action he heard performed. He then guesses who did it.

13. Playing Make-Believe

Grades two, three, and four

Each child selects a card, and when he is called upon, he acts out the directions written on his card. The other children guess what was on the card.

Example:

Make believe that you are a mailman. You have many letters to deliver and it is very warm. First you meet a little boy, then you meet a dog which barks furiously at you.

14. Following Directions

Grades two and three

A story is read or told to the class as the basis for the directions that follow it.

Example:

Today is Jane's birthday. She is seven years old. Her mother had a birthday party for her and invited three girls and three boys. Bob gave her a string of red beads and Mary gave her a box of paints. The children had ice cream and a cake with pink candles.

a. Get a piece of paper.
b. Write the number that tells how old Jane is.
c. Draw the pictures of all the children who came to the party.
d. Draw what Bob gave her.

15. Reading Directions

Grades two and three

Duplicated stories and directions similar to this example are given to each pupil.

(story)

Example:

a. Draw a blue circle around the word that tells what Helen found in the box.
b. Draw a red circle around the name of the noisiest thing in the room.
c. In sentence four, draw a green line under the name for an inland body of water.
d. In sentence six, draw a line under the word that tells what time of day it is.

16. Matching Pictures and Words

Grades one and two

Pictures are pasted in columns one and three, and words are printed in column two.

Directions:

Draw a line from each picture to the word that belongs to it.

Picture of a woman	food woman	Picture of a basket
Picture of pennies	town basket	Picture of a town
Picture of food	store pennies	Picture of a store
Picture of an animal	animal road	Picture of a road

17. Understanding Directions

Grades one and two

Pictures are provided and directions as shown below given to pupils.

Example:

a. Put an *X* under the woman.
b. Put a line under the apple.
c. Put a ring around the pennies.

18. Following Written Directions

Grades one and two

Duplicated directions are given as shown below:

Directions:

a. Write your name.
b. Draw a line.
c. Draw a house.
d. Next to the house, draw a tree.
e. Color the tree green.

19. Doing Magic

Grades four, five and six

Directions for doing simple magic tricks are given to the pupils.

Example:

Put a coin through a paper without tearing it.
Trace around the coin on the paper.
Cut a hole one-eighth of an inch smaller than the circle drawn.
Place the coin on the hole.
Take the tip of the coin and ease it through the hole.

20. Reading to Follow Directions

Grades three and four

Directions similar to those shown below are prepared using stories from the reading lesson or science books.

Example:

Many years ago, people believed that the world was full of wonder-working creatures. They believed that there were both good and bad spirits.

Directions:

a. Find the antonyms that describe spirits.
b. Find the places where spirits were found.
c. Find the paragraph that describes a fairy animal with a horn.

21. Following Directions

Grades three, four, five, and six

Slips are prepared as follows:

a. Read the title of the story.
b. Read the part that tells what Janey wished she could do.
c. Read the part that tells what Jack said to Janey.
d. Read the two pages about Jerry.

The children draw slips upon which directions have been written. After reading the directions and the assignment silently, they take turns reading orally to the group.

22. Hunting Game

Grades two, three, and four

The children are given slips of paper telling them to find something.

Example:

a. Find a stone that is bigger than an egg.
b. Find an insect.
c. Find a leaf from a tree, etc.

23. Following Directions for Making Things

Grades one, two, three, four, five, and six

Directions are given for making craft objects or for doing science experiments. These may be printed on charts or the chalkboard.

24. Following Directions for Playing Games

Grades one, two, three, four, five, and six

Directions for playing a new game are printed on a poster. The directions are read with the children and questions they may wish to ask are answered.

25. Learning Activities

Grades one and two

Folders from 9-by-12-inch pieces of cardboard are made by fastening the sheets together with tape. On one side of the folder simple directions are printed, and pockets are placed for holding the pictures of the objects to be used in the activity.

On the other side of the folder six houses, one green, one blue, one yellow, one red, one white, and one black, are pasted so that the bottom of each is loose. The houses may be made from colored oilcloth, felt, or other material so that they are easily manipulated (fig. 3.10). The children follow the directions given on the folder, such as:

Put the wagon under the blue house.
Put the ball under the yellow house.
Put the flag under the green house.
Put the money under the white house.
Put the airplane under the red house.
Put the chair under the black house.

Other objects may be used in place of the houses, such as cars, planes, and squares.

Figure 3.10 Learning Activities

4 Discriminative Reading

Fact or Opinion?
Drawing Conclusions
Predicting Outcomes
Making Inferences
Perceiving Relationships
Making Judgments
Problem Solving

Discriminative or critical reading is developmental in nature. If children are to become adept at critical reading, they must be guided toward this goal from the outset of their experiences with reading. There are many opportunities to sharpen critical powers through stories children read. Children should learn to interpret stories to determine whether places and characters are real or imaginary, they should learn to recognize moods of character, and to give explanation of why persons feel or speak as they do.

One of the important tasks of the school is helping children develop critical reading ability. Critical reading is not simply getting answers. It is analyzing and recognizing meaning and drawing inferences. This is the highest level and the most satisfying and rewarding form of reading that a student can achieve.

Critical reading is an important skill that the student must acquire if he is to become an efficient reader. To develop the skill is not difficult if the student learns what he is to look for.

The student must learn to examine and evaluate facts. Some people still think that anything that is in print is true. It is necessary to read between the lines and to draw upon past experiences and previous readings on the subject matter. Through the teacher's guidance, the pupil will learn to make inferences and draw conclusions from the reading materials.

Vocabulary is important. It usually is not the big word that makes the difference and gives meaning to the phrase or sentence, but rather words like *moreover, however,* and *nevertheless* that will change the entire meaning of a sentence. Words like *yet, otherwise, although, in spite of,* and so on will change the flow of thought. They are called *contrast words.*

Critical reading is especially important in the field of social studies and science. A good reader is interested not only with what is being said but why it is being said.

There is no short cut to critical reading. It is a continuing skill. A student learns through practice and by knowing what to look for.

FACT OR OPINION?

From the first grade on, children should learn to determine what is fact and what is opinion. The children should learn to listen critically and be aware of phrases such as, "I think," "It was said," "It is thought," "I believe," and so on.

When your author taught a first grade class, the children would whisper, "Make-believe," whenever a story was read or told that began with, "Once upon a time." This was a great game for them and as they began reading by themselves they always looked for fact or opinion.

Activities for developing skill in finding facts are suggested below.

1. Identifying Facts

Grades three, four, five, and six

Paragraphs from the reading text, social studies and science books should be used.

Example:

Long ago, people thought that a narrow stretch of land looked like a neck of some ancient animal and they called it an *isthmus. Isthmus* was the word for neck. This word now is used in many languages. Panama is called an isthmus because ....

2. Finding Evidence

Grades three, four, five, and six

Selections in the texts will provide material for this type of activity.

Example:

In the story we discover that:

a. Hubert forgot his former companion.
b. Hubert performed a brave deed.
c. The route was very difficult.

Evidence for *a* is ....
Evidence for *b* is ....
Evidence for *c* is ....

3. Answering True or False

Grades one, two, three, four, five, and six

Statements, some true and others improbable, should be given the children to check with those in the lesson to determine if they are true or false. For lower grades *yes* or *no* should be used instead of *true* or *false.*

4. Discriminating Between Fact or Fiction

Grades two, three, and four

The children are to tell which one of two stories presents true facts and which one describes events that are improbable. Paragraphs may be used in place of stories.

5. Selecting Passages that Support Fact

Grades three, four, five, and six

This may be done by having the two parts of each sentence used in different columns so the children can connect the corresponding parts with a line. These may also be written on cardboard strips and matched.

6. Using Multiple-Choice

Grades two, three, four, five, and six

Statements from the reading text are used with three choices for completing each.

Example:

As a child, Pete had many interests because

a. he lived near the seashore.
b. he had many interesting pets.
c. many strange visitors came to his home.

7. Classifying a Story

Grades one, two, and three

The children are to tell if the story really could happen or if it is make-believe. Children learn to recognize the fact that most make-believe stories begin with "Once upon a time."

8. Answering Yes or No

Grades one and two

Exercises similar to the example shown below are given, and the children answer *yes* or *no* on their papers.

Example:

The cat likes to

a. catch mice.
b. play with a ball.
c. play in the rain.
d. drink milk.

9. Locating Information

Grades three, four, five, and six

Questions are listed before the story is given, and the children locate the information needed to answer the questions as they read. The story is printed below the questions.

Example:

a. May the hunters kill the elk?
b. Where do the elk live?
c. Who are their enemies?

(Story)

10. Locating Details

Grades three and four

Questions are duplicated or written on the chalkboard.

Directions:

See how easily you can find the answer to these questions:

a. In what story did the animals help the little rabbit?
b. Who liked chocolate cake?—and so on.

The children answer the questions, giving the title, page, and paragraph, as:

Example:

a. Little Forest Friends, page 9, paragraph 1.—and so on.

11. Making Sentences True

Grades three, four, five, and six

Exercises similar to the example given below are used.

Directions:

Draw a line under the word below that makes the sentence true.

a. When it is dark, it is ....
   tight   light   night   winter
b. When it snows, we can ....
   skate   slide   sleep   picnic

12. Giving the Reason for Your Opinion

Grades four, five, and six

The children give the reason for their answers.

Example:

Do you think
a. that the mountain people had a hard life?
b. that Peggy was afraid to go away?

13. Comprehending and Locating Information

Grades four, five, and six

The material may be duplicated or written on the blackboard.

Directions:

The main idea for each paragraph listed under *A* may be found in column *B*. Match *A* and *B* columns.

A

a. page 342—paragraph 1
b. page 343—paragraph 2
c. page 345—paragraph 1
d. page 345—paragraph 3

B

1. It was Jefferson's duty to go to Washington.
2. Suffering causes revolution.
3. A committee was chosen to prepare the Declaration.
4. Jefferson worked without thought of himself.

14. Determining if a Statement Is True

Grades two, three, four, five, and six

Reread the lesson to see if these sentences are true.

Directions:

Write *yes* if they are true and *no* if they are not.

a. Rex wanted the tail. ....
b. Kitty could not run fast. ....
c. The children rode the pony. ....

15. Recognizing Fact or Opinion

Grades five and six

Duplicate sentences or write them on the blackboard. The students are to write *F* for fact and *O* for opinion.

........a. There are seven days in a week.
........b. It often rains on Wednesday.
........c. We think it will be cloudy tomorrow.
........d. The boys seemed to enjoy the game.
........e. The merchants sold silks and spices.
........f. The moon is thought to have volcanic formations on it.
........g. The old house in the woods is believed to be haunted.
........h. It is thought that over half of the students will attend the game.
........i. In the opinion of the judges, the first speaker appeared to be the best.
........j. The audience thought he made an excellent speech.
........k. The entire audience applauded.
........l. Having spent a month in Mexico, he felt that he knew a great deal about the country.
........m. Several students did not attend class.
........n. The climate in Louisiana is mild.
........o. Mary thinks her sister is pretty.
........p. The Romans invaded England.
........q. I like lettuce better than cabbage.
........r. Dr. Smith is the best doctor in the city.
........s. He was wrong about the decision.
........t. Jack knows he is right.
........u. Books on science are always popular.
........v. Mr. Adams believes that a student should read only the best literature.
........w. The purpose of the Hopi Snake Dance is to plead for plentiful rain and good crops.
........x. Sue began complaining of a headache.

16. Recognizing Fact and Opinion

Grades five and six

Duplicate paragraphs for the students. They are to determine if they are fact or opinion.

Examples:

1.

The largest of all fish, the whale shark, is completely harmless to man. This shark sometimes grows to the length of sixty feet and weighs 24,000 pounds. It eats only very small sea creatures and is a very mild animal. The whale is not a fish but a warm-blooded animal. It has lungs instead of gills and must breathe air. The whale can descend to great depths, possibly a mile below the surface, but it must come to the surface at intervals to breathe.

Is this fact or opinion? ....

2.

The human brain is probably the most wonderful thing in all the world. It is strong and sturdy, although it is a delicate mechanism. The thinking capacity of the brain has ten to twelve billion extremely tiny cells. The wisest man who ever lived came nowhere near using the full capacity of his mental ability. If a person does not use his thinking ability, he fails to make use of the full mentality that he has, and the more he uses it, the more alert he will remain.

Is this fact or opinion? ....

3.

Probably the most savage of the insect-eating plants is the Venus flytrap which grows only in North and South Carolina. A fly lights on the leaf and instantly, like jaws of a bear trap, the leaf folds together with its spines interlocking. There is no escape for the insect unless the trap opens again. The insect is digested by an acid secretion. Small stones and other indigestible objects are released after the insect has been digested.

Is this fact or opinion? ....

4.

September and October are the months when summer begins to wane. It is believed that the days will soon be cooler because the summer months were hot and dry. There are signs that the heavy hand of summer will soon be lifted because a cool spell usually follows a hot, dry summer. The Indians believed that if the animals' fur was heavier than usual, the winter would be extremely cold, and since many of the animals are getting heavy winter coats, we can look forward to a cold winter.

Is this fact or opinion? ....

17. Critical Analysis of the Information Read

Grades five and six

Prepare selections similar to the example below. These can be duplicated, or newspaper articles and editorials may be used.

Example:

The first raisin-type grapes were brought from Europe to California in 1861. Many were planted in the San Joaquin Valley, but it was twelve years before there was a raisin crop, and this was by accident.

In 1873, just before the September harvest, the San Joaquin Valley had an unusual hot spell. The heat wave came so unexpectedly and with such fierce heat that grapes dried on the vines before the growers could gather them. The growers feared their crops were a loss, since raisins were a little-known delicacy to Americans. But one grower was stubborn. He sent his dried grapes to a grocer friend in San Francisco.

The grocer was an idea man. He heard that a Peruvian ship was in San Francisco harbor, so he labeled the raisins "Peruvian Delicacies." They sold quickly. And so the San Joaquin raisin industry, now the largest in the world, was born.

More than 200,000 tons of raisins, over half the world's supply, are produced annually.

More than 5,000 growers supply the raisin grapes to some twenty packers.

The entire United States raisin crop is grown in California, and most of it within a 75-mile radius of Fresno. The city likes to call itself the "raisin capital of the world."

a. Is this fact or opinion? Why? ....

b. How were raisins introduced? ....

c. Is the author trying to influence you? Explain. ....

d. What past experience or knowledge can you apply to this? ....

e. Where would you look for further information on the raisin? ....

18. Fact or Opinion

For grades four, five, and six

Read the sentences careful and then determine whether they are fact or opinion. Write *F* for fact or *O* for opinion.

.... 1. There are seven days in a week.
.... 2. We think it well be cloudy tomorrow.
.... 3. The boys seemed to enjoy the game.
.... 4. The merchants sold silks and spices.
.... 5. It is believed that cats bring bad luck.
.... 6. The old house in the woods is believed to be haunted.
.... 7. In my opinion, the first speaker was the best.
.... 8. They thought he made an excellent speech.
.... 9. He felt that he knew a great deal about the subject.
........10. Several students did not attend class.
........11. The climate in Louisiana is mild.
........12. May thinks her sister is pretty.
........13. The Romans invaded England.
........14. I like lettuce better than cabbage.
........15. I think cabbage is hard to digest.
........16. Dr. Smith is the best doctor in town.
........17. People think Dr. Jones is the best dentist in the city.
........18. He was wrong about the decision.
........19. The purpose of the Hopi Snake dance is to plead for rain.
........20. Sue began complaining about a headache.

19. Paragraph Interpretation.

For grades five and six

Read the paragraphs below and determine whether they are fact or opinion.

1

The first horse was called Eohippus and lived fifty-five million years ago. It was a small animal no larger than a fox. It lived in the swampy woodlands of western North America and in Europe. It was called the *dawn horse.* The little animal had four toes on its front feet and three on the back feet. There were just a few stiff hairs instead of a mane, and its tail was more like a dog's. The prehistoric horse had no way of fighting its enemies, so it had to run very swiftly to get away.

Is this fact or opinion? ....

2

It was supposed that there was gold in the mountains. Rumors had come into town about the mines that had been lost, so the next few days were filled with excitement. Jim kept asking his father to let him go along up to the mountain to help him look for the gold. When his father finally consented to take him along, Jim thought he was the luckiest boy who ever walked the face of this earth.

Is this fact or opinion? ....

3

Probably the most vivid use of figurative phrases comes at the end of the poem, "Jesse James." It is stated that Jesse James will never die. Instead he lives on as a sunset overhead and a flash of lightening in a rainstorm. Jesse is described as being "ten foot tall" and a Hercules." The author believed that Jesse James rode a pinto horse and feared no enemy. When he robbed a stage, he divided the loot with needy people.

Is this fact or opinion? ....

4

Andrew Jackson was elected the President of the United States in 1828, and he was reelected in 1832. At the time that Jackson took office, there were only twenty-four stars in the flag, and the population of the country was 15,900,000. After seeing his friend, Martin Van Buren sworn in as President, Andrew Jackson went to the Hermitage to live for the remainder of his life.

Is this fact or opinion? ....

DRAWING CONCLUSIONS

In drawing conclusions, the known facts must be related to each other, the cause and effect relationships must be examined, and the reader must weigh the evidence. Conclusions should not include wishful thinking or personal preference; they must relate directly and impersonally to the problems.

Drawing conclusions may be a fairly simple matter when the facts are presented in logical order. But at times the author uses another form of organization which requires more careful thought on the part of the reader.

The student must learn to think while he reads. He must interpret, evaluate, make inferences, and then draw conclusions. He must learn to become aware of the time and the place while reading the selection. This is important, because as one knows, the types of things that took place fifty or even twenty-five years ago are in many respects quite different from what is occurring today. This is social change and progress. We cannot get away from it. A reader is not only aware of changes in the ways people live, but he must make use of his knowledge and awareness in making comparisons between things as they were, and as they are occurring at present. A good reader sifts out facts and knows why they may differ, one from another, in the drawing of inferences and the forming of conclusions.

Many articles and stories that are written today do not give one the ending or the conclusions written out in so many words. The author wants the reader to add his own store of knowledge to the information that is given him, and he also expects the reader to read between the lines and bring his own thinking into focus. By reading between the lines and using judgment, the reader learns to discover the conclusions or the reason for the resulting reactions.

Examples of exercises in developing skill in the drawing of conclusions are given below. These exercises may be duplicated, written on the chalkboard, or made into chart form. They should be modified according to the needs of the pupils.

1. Drawing Conclusions from Sentences

Grades two, three, four, five, and six

Sentences should be selected from the reading lesson.

Examples:

A. The old man went merrily down the street, whistling all the way.
The old man was happy because ....
....

B. "I am in a hurry to get home," the man said to his pig.
What did the man want the pig to do?
....

2. Drawing Conclusions from Paragraphs

Grades two, three, four, five, and six

Paragraphs are selected from the reading lesson and completion and multiple-choice test items prepared.

Example:

The Yellow River rises in Central Asia and flows silently toward the morning sun. Its course is soon interrupted by landslides. It switches northwest, curves south, and then east again. Finally the swishing, muddy stream crawls like

........a barber arrow ....a snake ....turtle.

3. Predicting Outcomes

Grades one, two, three, four, five, and six

After reading part of the lesson, children predict what is going to happen next. Older children may write the prediction on a sheet of paper and tell why they think this will happen.

4. Giving Reasons for Action

Grades one, two, three, four, five, and six

Paragraphs from the reading lesson may be used for this exercise, or the teacher may write the paragraphs. If the paragraphs are used from the reader, the first type of exercise may be developed.

Example:

A. Read paragraph 2, page 56.
Why did the lion roar so loudly?

B. The bear hurried down the shady path when he saw some bees flying overhead. They were heading straight for their home. "Mmmm! Some honey for my supper," said Mr. Bear.
Why did Mr. Bear think he would have honey for his supper?
........He smelled honey.
........He knew he could follow the bees home and find honey.
........He knew his wife would have some honey waiting for him.

5. Drawing Conclusions

Grades one, two, three, four, five, and six

Selections from the reader or science and social studies texts are used and questions prepared similar to the ones listed below.

a. What time of year is it?
b. Did this happen within recent times? Reason?
c. Where did this take place?
d. Do these people live the same as we do?
e. What would you like about doing these things? etc.

6. Giving Reasons

Grades one, two, three, four, five, and six

Multiple-choice items on the selection, reading similarly to those listed below, are prepared.

Example:

The logs were hard to load because
........the loggers had improper tools.
........the logs were too large.

7. Implying Meaning

Grades three, four, five, and six

Sentences from the reading assignment can be used for this exercise.

Directions:

Match the phrases in the first column with those of the second.

I	II
a. The owl thought	it was evening.
b. The wren thought	it was morning.
c. The dog thought	it would rain.
d. The boy was afraid	it would soon be dark.

—and so on

8. Drawing Conclusions

Grades three, four, and five

Sentences pertaining to the reading assignment, similar to the examples below, are prepared.

Example:

a. Four owls were flying around in the forest at midnight.
What? ....
When? ....
Where? ....
How many? ....

b. A long time ago Indians lived in tepees made of skin.
What? ....
When? ....
Where? ....
How many? ....

9. Solving Riddles

Grades two and three

Sentences similar to those below may be prepared, using words with which the children are familiar.

Example:

What is it?

a. Smoke comes out of it. ....
b. Bees make it. ....
c. We use it in cold weather. ....
d. We go there to swim. ....

10. Finding Conclusions

Grades one and two

Exercises similar to the examples below are prepared, using words from the reading lesson.

Example:

Write *yes* or *no* after each phrase.

a. A dog likes to:
run and jump ....
climb a tree ....
chase a kitten ....
fly a kite ....
b. The horse likes to:
eat green grass ....
drink milk ....
gallop and run ....
chase rabbits ....

11. Making Comparisons

Grades two and three

Questions similar to those given below are prepared, making use of information the children are learning in arithmetic, social studies, and science. The children write the answers.

Example:

a. Which is shorter, your thumb or your foot?
b. Which is thicker, a sandwich or a cracker?
c. Which is faster, a train or an airplane?

PREDICTING OUTCOMES

Explain to the student that the ability to predict outcomes is part of critical reading. To learn to do so, one must look for the reason for the action, find the implied meaning, and make comparisons; just as in drawing conclusions, the reader must remember previous information he has gained and compare it with what he is now reading. It is something like problem solving. However, sometimes he will come to material that is contradictory. He must learn to make comparisons and look at both sides. Also, knowing whether the material is fact or opinion will help in predicting the outcomes. There are two sides to every issue, and the reader must be able to see both sides of the issue and to evaluate them.

Children should learn to anticipate outcomes of stories and to predict the behavior or reaction of the characters. In introducing a story to the children, the teacher may ask them to tell what they think will happen and why. A few suggestions for developing a keener insight into predicting outcomes are given below.

1. What Is Going to Happen?

Grades two, three, four, five, and six

A story without the ending is duplicated. The ending may be duplicated on a separate sheet if the teacher wishes to have the ending in printed form. The children are to read the story and to write the conclusion they think should be given to the story. The children may give their predictions of the outcome orally if they wish. The reasons for their answers should be given. If the ending of the story is duplicated, the children may check their answers with the printed form.

2. Predicting the Outcome of the Story

Grades two, three, four, five, and six

After reading a part of the story, the predicted outcome of the story is discussed. The children tell why they think this character acted as he did and what they would have done in a similar situation and why.

3. Choosing the Right Ending

Grades two, three, four, five, and six

Short stories are pasted on cardboard sheets. The conclusions of these stories are put on another card. The children are to read the stories and the conclusions and then match the stories with the endings.

MAKING INFERENCES

To assist the pupils in developing the skill of making inferences, the teacher may use exercises similar to those detailed below. These should be modified according to the needs of the class.

1. Making Inferences about Materials Read

Grades two, three, four, five, and six

Short stories from the science and social studies materials may be used. The vocabulary should be chosen from the reader. The children are asked to make inferences as shown in the example below.

Example:

Mr. Brown brought home a package about six inches square. The package was carefully wrapped and tied. Mary picked it up and shook it. When Jack picked it up, he smelled it. Penny took it next and held it to her ear. Penny said, "I know what it is! It's a ...."

2. Using Riddles

The children may write riddles which they keep in a book. They ask the others to guess the answer.

3. Identifying a Description

Grades one and two

Each child selects a picture and then describes something he sees in the picture. This may be done orally, or the material may be written.

Example:

It can go. It cannot see. Billy played with it. It is a............ .

4. Making Inferences

Grades two and three

Directions:

Draw a line under all the groups of words that answer the question: Where do we see the birds?

in the tree	in a picture
in a nest	on a horse
on the ice	in the air

5. Making Inferences by Identifying an Action

Grades three and four

Directions:

Some of the groups of words tell things that are done by people and some things that are done by animals. Put *P* before the group of words that tell what people do. Put *A* before each group that tells what animals do.

........put on a dress
........paint with a brush
........bark at the moon
........sit in the sun
........flap their wings
........like to swim

Use various categories, like fruit and vegetables, inventors and explorers, and so on.

6. Making Comparisons

Grades two and three

Questions similar to examples given below can be used.

Example:

a. Which is faster, a horse or a train?
b. Which is thicker, a nickel or a dime?
c. Which is smaller, a cow or a cat?

7. Giving Reasons

Grades three, four, five, and six

The selection the children are reading is the basis for questions such as:

a. What two reasons are given for his actions?
b. What was the difference between John's and Henry's action?

8. Making Inferences

Grades four, five, and six

Duplicate sentences or write them on the blackboard. Write the words that describe the sentence above or below the sentences.

Example:

a. This animal looks like a horse but it has stripes. ....
b. This musical instrument is played with a bow. ....
c. This cry is long, loud, and mournful. ....
d. This animal carries its house with it wherever it goes. ....
e. This animal can change its coloring to match the background. ....
f. This is used to hold fish. ....
g. This means very small but in correct proportions. ....
h. This has whirling overhead blades which are used in propelling it. ....
i. This was once the shelter for some North American Indians. ....
j. This is a cigar-shaped balloon. ....
k. This is a two-wheeled cart, used in ancient times. ....
l. This is a group of persons who have the right to represent others. ....
m. This is a compulsory payment of a percentage of a person's income to help support the government. ....

zeppelin	cello	snail
delegation	taxation	howl
wigwam	helicopter	minimum
zebra	chariot	aquarium
chameleon	miniature	

PERCEIVING RELATIONSHIPS

The skill of perceiving relationships can be divided into time relationships, sequence, cause and effect, and seeing relationships. The exercises below are suggestions for activities which can be prepared to develop the awareness of relationships for children.

TIME RELATIONSHIPS

1. When Did It Happen?

Grades one, two, three, four, five, and six

When reading the assignment, the children find the sentences that tell when the story took place.

2. Time Words

Grades two, three, four, five, and six

The children look through newspapers, magazines, and so on, and underline the words that tell about time.

3. Perceiving Time

Grades three, four, five, and six

Phrases from the reading and social studies assignments are used. The children tell when the story or event happened and draw a line under the words that give the time.

Example:

a. The boy ate deer stew.
b. The jet bomber soared through the sky.
c. Jane brought candles into the parlor.
d. The boy slept on a bearskin in the cave.

—and so on

4. Clock Booklets

Grades one and two

Children may make booklets containing clock dials, showing when they do certain things, such as eat breakfast, go to school, and so on.

5. Time Relationships

Grades two, three, four, five, and six

The teacher writes sentences containing words about time. The children underline those words.

6. Making a Date Line

Grades three, four, five, and six

A line is drawn across the chalkboard or on a large sheet of paper. An inch is marked off for every 100 years. The children fill in events that they read about that have happened within each period. The children may illustrate the Time Line Chart by drawing the main events, clothing worn at that period, types of houses used, and so on.

7. Pictures Showing Time

Grades two, three, four, five, and six

Pictures of different periods are used. The children tell what period is depicted by looking at the picture and giving the main reason for making the time judgment.

SEQUENCE

1. Sequence of Events

Grades two, three, and four

A map showing streets, buildings, playgrounds and the like, is drawn and properly labeled. The children tell the things that Johnny will see from the time he leaves home until he arrives at school, or what Mrs. Jones will see when she goes to the grocery store. The children may tell what they see on the way to school or to the store. This activity trains pupils in the matter of safe routes to school and safety on the streets.

2. Paragraph Sequence

Grades two, three, four, five, and six

A story is cut into paragraphs. The paragraphs are pasted on cardboard and coded, so that the children may correct their work with a key. The children are to read the paragraphs and place them in proper sequence. This may be an individual, independent activity.

3. Sentence Sequence

Grades one, two, and three

Sentences are listed in incorrect sequence. The children number the sentences to show the sequence in which the events took place.

4. Sequence of Statements

Grades three, four, five, and six

Statements from the study assignments are used. These statements are placed in incorrect sequence. The children are to place them in proper sequence.

Example:

a. Put straw in the bottom of the barrel.
b. Put grease and lye into the kettle.
c. Pour water into the barrel.
d. Test the lye with an egg.
e. Stir the liquid while it boils.
f. Put ashes into the barrel.
g. Bore a hole in the barrel.
h. Save ashes and greases.
i. Let the soap cool.

5. Sequence of Events

Grades two, three, and four

A story pertaining to some of the children's experiences is written on the chalkboard or duplicated. The children make a list in the proper sequence of the things the child saw.

Example:

Mary went to the seashore. The first thing she saw was a little pink shell. She picked it up and put it in her pocket. As she walked along, she almost stepped on a clam shell, and so on.

Directions:

Write the things in the order that Mary saw them.

6. Order of Events

Grades three and four

Short paragraphs may be taken from the reading lesson. The children are to complete the sentences or answer the questions as shown in the example below.

Example:

When the poor woman returned with her basket of food, the children eagerly peeped into the basket. The woman quickly hurried to the cupboard, etc.

The first event was ....
The second event was ....etc.

or questions may be used as:

What happened first?
What happened next?
What happened last?

7. Finding the Sequence

Grades five and six

Prepare stories that have established sequences and ask the student questions pertaining to them.

Example:

In 1920, the New York Fair opened; Joe Brown had just finished painting the sign for his ice-cream parlor, and he felt that he had picked the right spot because the people who were on their way to the Fair, or on their way out, would pass by his little place.

More and more people stopped to buy ice-cream sandwiches, and Joe and his sister were kept very busy making sandwiches by spreading ice cream between waffles. There was no competition for them, and they felt very fortunate.

Then one day, they noticed some men putting up a building across the street. Then they saw a sign go up, "Ice-Cream Palace." Joe and Rose were afraid they were going to lose some of their business to the new place.

That same day, Joe brought Rose a small bunch of flowers. Rose wondered where she could put the flowers, and then her eyes fell on a waffle. Rose rolled the waffle into a cone and put a little water in it.

Rose didn't want to waste the other half of the waffle so she rolled it into a second cone and put some ice cream into it and ate it. Here was a new idea! And it would take less waffles to make their ice-cream sandwiches if they used just a half a waffle and rolled it into a cone!

They began calling their new idea "ice-cream cones" instead of ice-cream sandwiches. The cones were talked about by everyone at the New York Fair. The people liked them much better than sandwiches bcause the ice cream did not drip out of them.

The Ice-Cream Palace across the way began having fewer customers, and so the man who owned it stopped by to see Joe one afternoon. He said it was the ideas that count if you plan to succeed.

a. Underline the words that helped you find the proper order of events.
b. How long ago did this event take place? ....
....
c. What words are not used very often today? ....
....
d. How much do you think the ice-cream cones cost at that time? ....
e. What is the meaning of the word *competition*?.............
....
f. What is the opposite of *fortunate*? ....
....

CAUSE AND EFFECT

1. Cause and Effect

Grades three and four

Paragraphs from the stories read may be used. The children are to match the beginning and ending phrases.

Example:

Two cruel brothers wanted to get rid of the third one. They wanted to send him to free the princess because they thought the giants would kill him. A fairy came to Jack's rescue. He used a pearl necklace to climb out of the window. The necklace stretched to the ground. Jack took the princess for his bride.

Match these phrases:

The cruel brothers sent Jack away because
Jack saw through the castle wall because
Jack could walk down the wall because
The princess got to earth safely because

the shoes did not slip.
they hated him.
the necklace stretched.
he had magic glasses.

2. Implied Cause

Grades three and four

Paragraphs from the reading books may be used. Questions similar to the example can be developed.

Example:

Late one winter, Mr. Rabbit heard wild geese honking high overhead. He looked up and saw them flying to the north. He thought, "Spring is coming."

Why did Mr. Rabbit think that spring would come soon?

a. He heard some honking.
b. He saw some geese flying north.
c. He was lonely.

3. Matching for Cause and Effect

Grades three and four

Sentences are prepared from the reading assignment similar to the example given below.

Example:

a. Because of the action of the wind for many years.
b. Because of the stillness in the air. ....

—and so on

1. there was great danger.
2. the soil was bare.—and so on.

4. Cause and Effect

Grades two, three, and four

The story in readers or other books is used. Sentences similar to the example given below may be given to the children.

Example:

a. If Mary had gone to the marketplace, she would have heard ....
b. If Jane had not waited so long, she would have ....

—and so on

SEEING RELATIONS

1. Perceiving Relationships

Grade one

The children sort pictures and words that belong together, such as things we eat, things we wear, things that grow in the garden, and so on.

2. Seeing Relationships

Grades one and two

Pictures of community helpers or any objects that can be described in a sentence are used. The children match the picture and a sentence describing the picture.

Example:

He cuts our hair at his shop.
He brings mail to our houses.
He builds houses and stores.—and so on.

3. Ideas That Go Together

Grades three and four

Exercises similar to the example given below may be prepared for the children.

Example:

a. Chin is to head as knee is to—
   level body leg foot
b. Dim is to bright as smart is to—
   low big shiny dull

4. Perceiving Relationships

Grades four, five, and six

Prepare groups of words which have a relationship. The students are to write another word that is related to the other four words.

Example:

a. ache	injury	hurt	sting	....
b. land	ground	dirt	loam	....
c. gun	rifle	arrow	cannon	....
d. saw	hammer	plane	ruler	....
e. England	Denmark	Spain	Norway	....
f. strolled	leaped	skipped	walked	....
g. said	replied	answered	spoke	....

5. Finding Relationships

Grades five and six

The students are asked to read the paragraphs prepared by the teacher and then answer the questions regarding the relationship of two places or things.

Example:

The Dead Sea is the lowest area of land on this globe. Its shore is 1,290 feet below sea level. Death Valley in California, which is the lowest spot in the United States, is only 282 feet below sea level. There is little plant life in that area because the water is so salty. Death Valley has little vegetation due to the lack of rain and the intense heat. Borax deposits were discovered in the Valley in 1873. Borax mining began in the early 1880s. The Dead Sea contains large quantities of minerals, which include common salt and magnesium bromide.

a. What relationship do you see between the Dead Sea and Death Valley? ....
....
....
....

b. What differences do you see in the two places? ....
....
....
....

MAKING JUDGMENTS

Skill in making judgments should be developed through discussion of stories and through the use of exercises as shown below.

1. Choosing the Best Answer

Grades one and two

Directions:

Check the best answer. All the answers are possible.

a. Father works for us because
   ....he is big
   ....he loves us
   ....he has to work
b. The flowers make
   ....our yard pretty
   ....us work and work
   ....us pick them

2. Choosing the Right Answer

Grades one and two

Directions:

Which of these things can you eat?

bread	apples	coal	cars	cake
bears	oranges	cotton	money	candy

Such questions as the following may be used:

Which would you see in summer?
Where would you go to skate?
Which would you wear?
What is sticky?
What is silvery?
What is soft?

3. Making Judgments

Grades three and four

Parts of stories in readers, similar to the example below, may be used.

Example:

A miller was troubled with a rat eating his grain. He set a trap and used some cheese for bait. When he came back later, the miller heard some loud squeals and groans coming from the trap. In the trap was the old rat. The old rat started to beg, "Please open the trap, kind miller. I want to see whether the door swings in or out."

Was the old rat's reason real or pretended? Why?

4. Deciding What to Do

Grades three, four, five, and six

Directions:

What would you do?

You stayed in the sun too long and got a painful sunburn. Would you:

a. mention your trouble to everyone you met?
b. rub oil on your sunburn?
c. hold an umbrella over your head?

5. Analyzing Materials Read

Grades four, five, and six

Questions somewhat like examples given below can be used with selections from the textbooks.

Example:

a. How would you interpret the sentence on page 235, line 6?
b. Why did Mary act as she did? page 236, line 7.

6. Deciding Which to Do

Grades four, five, and six

Two courses of action are listed and the children are asked to tell which they would take and why.

Example:

Bobby was only a year old. He watched the children playing games in the room. Suddenly he began to cry. Would you talk to Bobby and try to find out why he was crying or would you rush to the telephone and call the doctor?

7. Giving Reasons

Grades three, four, five, and six

Sentences from the reading materials can be used.

Example:

The horses were shod with sharp shoes because:

a. their feet were tender.
b. they gripped the icy road.

8. Making Judgments

Grades two and three

Questions like the following may be asked on the reading assignment:

Example:

Our New Friends: pages 6 to 12

Do these lines tell about a boy or a pet? Write *boy* or *pet*.
a. page 6, line 2
b. page 9, line 4
c. page 11, line 5

9. Matching the Answers to Questions

Grades two, three, and four

The children match the answers with the questions.

Example:

The men put up a detour sign one morning before they began to repair the road.

1. Who put up the sign?	a. in the morning
2. When did they put it up?	b. on the road
3. What kind of a sign was it?	c. the workmen
4. Where did the men work?	d. a detour sign

10. Deciding on Reality

Grades three, four, five, and six

In phrases similar to those given below, the children are to place a line under everything that they can read about in storybooks but cannot see anywhere on earth. They may also make their own lists by scanning or rereading materials.

Example:

a. a merry-go-round in a park
b. a woman talking to herself
c. a rooster that can wake the sun
d. a pig making herself a pie
e. a pig rolling down the hill in a churn
f. two wagons tied together
g. a country mouse that can talk

11. Making Sentences True

Grades one, two, and three

Sentences similar to the example given below should be used.

Directions:

Draw a line under the word that makes the sentence true.

a. When it is dark, it is
   tight winter light night

12. Choosing the Best Answer

Grades one and two

Several sentences are printed on a folder and numbered. On slips of paper, which are in an envelope, are several answers for each sentence, with the number of the sentence written on each. The child places the slips with the right answers after each sentence and then chooses the best answer.

Example:

a. I will help mother because
   (a) I am six years old.
   (b) she works for me.
   (c) she says I must.
b. I will put away my toys
   (a) to keep the house neat.
   (b) to hide them
   (c) to keep them clean.

PROBLEM SOLVING

When a student reads something that involves problem solving, it will be necessary for him to read more slowly than when he reads for general information. Problem solving is a study-type learning, and at times it becomes necessary to go back and reread the entire paragraph or selection in order to be certain of all the steps.

Some individuals show a great deal of insight in problem solving. Insight is defined as a sudden illumination or awareness of the solution of the problem. One can see the solution without going through all the usual steps required in the solution of a problem.

The steps in problem solving are:

1. Defining or knowing what the problem is.
2. Drawing upon past experiences and knowledge to decide how to solve the problem. This is called the hypothesis.
3. Evaluating the hypothesis.
4. Solving the problem.
5. Verifying the problem—proving the accuracy of the solution.

There are many different kinds of problems. There are mathematical and scientific problems, and there may be problems that apply to the reader's own situation.

There are too many occasions when we waste much of our time by using the *trial and error* method instead of solving our problems the logical way. The reader should read the entire problem carefully and reread parts if necessary. Then he should define the problem and find the necessary information. With the information at hand, the reader should come to an unbiased conclusion.

Another way to solve the problem is to use inductive and deductive reasoning. Inductive reasoning begins with the known facts and goes to the unknown, moving from the part to the whole. In deductive reasoning we begin with general statements and go to specific facts. We move from the whole to the part.

We use inductive reasoning in our lives each day. We ask ourselves questions; our experiences help us find the answer. In the same manner, the reader must ask himself questions about the printed page, and he must evaluate the answers.

The reader should be aware of words such as *usually, nearly, few,* and *seldom.* What is the difference between *usually* and *some of the time*? *Very few* and *less than half*? *Nearly all* and *most*? These words can make a great difference in the reaching of conclusions or in solving the problem.

Children need training in learning to solve problems, whether in everyday life or in their arithmetic problems. Many children are able to do arithmetic computation but are unable to do successful work in arithmetic reasoning. If the child receives training in problem solving from his reading assignments, that training will carry through and can be applied to his other subjects. Only a few suggestions are given below for work in problem solving, but from these the teacher should be able to develop many other types of material according to the pupils' varied needs.

1. Arithmetic Problems

Grades one, two, three, four, five, and six

Stories in the arithmetic text may be utilized, or problems involving daily activities may be used.

2. What Would You Do?

Grades one, two, three, four, five, and six

Paragraphs from textbooks are used; stories in each of which there is a problem to be solved, may be written. The children are to tell how they would solve the problem and give the reasons for their decisions. They should discuss these with one another.

3. Jo-Jo and Josephine

Grades one and two

Each child is given a box of buttons or beans which he will use to illustrate the teacher's story. The teacher can make up various situations dealing with problem solving. The children should be encouraged to make up problems which the others help solve. An example of a story is given below.

Example:

Jo-Jo and Josephine were two little squirrels. They lived in a nut tree. One day Jo-Jo found two nuts and brought them back to the nest. (Children move out two buttons or beans.) Then Josephine went out and found two more nuts and brought them home. (Children move out two more buttons.) Do you know how many nuts they had now? Josephine was hungry and ate one nut. (Remove one button.) Then Jo-Jo found three more nuts, and so on.

The squirrels moved into an orange tree because they wanted orange juice for breakfast. There was a magic orange on the tree and they were warned to stay away from it. One day their little cousin Ronald, a very inquisitive little squirrel, came to visit them. They told little Ronald to stay away from the magic orange, but one day he went to take a look at this strange orange. Well, the orange sucked little Ronald right into it. If you want to know what happened to the inquisitive little squirrel, be sure to be in class tomorrow morning, and so on. Flannelboard figures may be made to accompany stories. This story can be continued throughout the year, using Halloween cats and jack-o-lanterns, turkeys, Christmas decorations, valentines, Easter eggs and rabbits, flowers, and the like.

4. Reading to Solve Problems

Grades five and six

Prepare problem-solving paragraphs as shown in the examples below.

Examples:

a. There are seven amoebas in a bowl. They multiply by dividing in two every minute. At the end of forty minutes the bowl is completely filled. How long did it take to get the bowl half-filled? (Answer: 39 minutes)

b. Bessie Johnson, age three, was given a bag of marbles by her uncle John. Not wanting marbles, she decided to give them to her friends. She gave one to Freddie, one to Lucy, one to Harriet, two to Henry, two to Robert, six to Peter, and dropped the others into the wastebasket. How many marbles did Uncle John give Bessie? (Answer: ?)

c. Divide a circle into as many segments as you can with four straight lines. (Answer: 10 segments)

d. Multiply the number of men in a tub by the number of days the pease porridge was in the pot. Subtract from that the number of blackbirds baked in a pie. Then add the number of wives of the man whom I met on the road to St. Ives. Add to that the number of the thieves Ali Baba met. What number did you get?

e. You remember the story about the hare and the tortoise. The tortoise moves at the speed of 1/100th of a mile an hour, while the hare runs at the speed of 45 miles an hour.
   (a) How long will it take the tortoise to run one mile?
   (b) How long will it take a hare to run one mile?

f. A court jester pleased his master, the king, so much that the king told the jester he would give him anything he wished as a reward. The jester said his wish was a simple one. Showing the king a chessboard, he asked the king if he would place a penny on the first square, double the amount on the second square, then double that amount on the third square, each time doubling the last amount until he had reached the sixty-fourth square. The king thought that this was indeed a modest request and granted the jester's wish. How much money did the king owe the jester?

g. *How quickly can a car be stopped?*
   If a car is on a level road and the surface is good, the driver is able to determine how quickly he can stop the car. To find out, take the speed of the car and divide it by 20. Add one and multiply the result by the speed of the car. The answer will give you the number of feet the car will travel before stopping.
   What distance in feet would a car going sixty miles an hour require before stopping?

5 Locational Skills

Locating Information
Reference Reading
Becoming Acquainted with the Book
Map Reading
Reading the Newspaper
Organization

There are many places the student can go to look for information which is to be found in untold numbers of magazines, newspapers, pamphlets, and books. Or he can, in some cases, go to the source itself and make first-hand observations.

Most obvious of all is the library, a storehouse of knowledge, and the student should be shown how to use it successfully. There is always a card catalog, which is the heart of the library. Every book in the library has three cards in this card catalog. One card gives the author and the title, another card lists the title first, and the third card, the subject card, names the general topic—what the book is about, and then gives the title and the author. So if the student does not know the title or the author, he can always refer to the subject card. Explain to the student that there are small numbers on the left side of the card, and if he wishes to look for the book on the shelves, or to check out the book, he should be sure to copy those numbers down. This will tell him and the librarian exactly where the book is on the shelves.

There are many, many books. The students might be interested to know that if they read eight hours a day, seven days a week and fifty-two weeks a year, it would take more than six hundred years of reading to read all the books that are in print. It has been estimated that our modern world turns out about four hundred and fifty thousand books and 60 million pieces of literature each year. Every forty minutes, it is said, enough new material is produced to fill a twenty-four-volume encyclopedia.

There are many kinds of books in the libraries. These include innumerable encyclopedia, almanacs, and other general guides. These are called reference books and are on virtually every subject you can name. Some books are biographies, others are factual, and still others are fictional.

If a student is assigned a special report, show him how to use the *Reader's Guide* or the *Education Index* in the Reference Room. Show him how to look under the topic assigned to him. He will find the names of articles referring to the subject. He selects some of the listed articles and writes down the name of the books or magazines with the volume number and the date. The librarian will get these for him. Some students have magazines at home that can be good sources of information. The newspapers carry information about the most recent current topics.

LOCATING INFORMATION

In order to learn to locate information effectively, children should develop the ability to:

a. Determine from the title of the book if it contains information they need.
b. Use the table of contents in locating information.
c. Use chapter and section headings.
d. Use the index and glossary.
e. Use the encyclopedia, atlas, and other reference material.
f. Learn to use the authors' names.
g. Use pictures and captions.
h. Use maps, graphs, and charts.

Suggestions are given below for developing skill in locating information. These may be modified according to the needs of the children.

1. Learning to Use the Index

Grades two, three, and four

Words from the reader's index are listed on the chalkboard. The children find each word in the index and write the number of the page on which information about each subject is found.

Example:

a. Sheep
b. Safety
c. Desert
d. Ivory
e. Outlines
f. South America
g. Lion cubs
h. Dogs
i. Markets

2. Locating Information for Answering Questions

Grades two, three, and four

Questions from the reading lesson, similar to those in the example below, are answered by the pupils, who give the paragraph and line number where the answer was found. These exercises may be duplicated and filed with the key for use with the next group that will read the book.

Example:

a. Page 94. What does Rusty want to do?
b. Page 95. What must Jerry do?

c. Page 95. What animals did Nancy feed?
Key: a. Paragraph 3, lines 7 and 8—He wanted to find a playmate.

3. Using the Table of Contents

Grades four, five, and six

Directions:

Use the table of contents to answer these questions.

Example:

a. How many stories are there about Holland?
b. Who wrote the story about the ocean liners?
c. What is the name of the story that tells about Gretchen?

4. Locating Information on Time, Place, and Cause

Grades four, five, and six

The children write *Time, Place,* and *Cause* as headings on their papers. They read through an assigned story and select the words that express time, place, and cause, listing them under the correct headings. The children may work in small committees to check their lists.

5. Finding Information in Reference Books

Grades four, five, and six

The children look in reference books for the answers to questions written on the board or given to them in duplicated form.

Example:

a. What are rocks?
b. How does water make rocks?
c. How does heat make rocks?

6. Locating Items in the Newspaper

Grades five and six

The index of features from the daily paper may be duplicated or a collection of such clippings used.

7. Using the Library

Grades four, five, and six

Discuss the use of the library with the children and then take them to find information for some definite assignment. Explain that the first time they go into a library they may not know exactly where to go to find what they are looking for, but if they will ask the librarian to show them or tell them where to find the card catalog, they will be able to find almost anything they want.

REFERENCE READING

Pupils should learn to use encyclopedia, dictionaries, atlases, books, and magazines in locating information as soon as the need arises. They should learn where to find information quickly by knowing what the encyclopedia will tell them, what the dictionary contains, and how to find reference material through the use of subject indexes to books. Below are listed a few suggestions designed to help them acquire the skill of reference reading.

1. Locating Information

Grades three, four, five, and six

Questions similar to those in the example below will be useful.

Example:

a. Where in the encyclopedia would you find information about a flying squirrel? Give the volume and page number.
b. Where would you find information about wild horses? Give the volume and page number.

2. Do You Know Why?

Grades four, five, and six

Questions similar to the example below should be prepared.

Example:

Where would you find the information?

a. If a candle flame is held too close to glass, carbon forms on the glass. What kind of chemical change has taken place? (Give the answer and reference.)

3. Library Story Titles

Grades three, four, five, and six

The children fill in the blanks, as they would for the exercise example below.

Example:

Find a title for each type of story listed below.

a. A science story ....
b. An adventure story ....
c. A dog story ....

4. Using the Encyclopedias

Grades three, four, five, and six

A picture of a set of encyclopedia is duplicated so as to show the volume number and letters on each book. The children are asked to tell in which volume they will find information about the following:

a. A kangaroo—Volume ....
b. A carnival—Volume ....

5. Using Reference Materials

Grades four, five, and six

What kind of information would you find in each of the following sources?

a. Magazines ....
b. Dictionaries ....
c. Newspapers ....
d. Atlases ....
e. Encyclopedia ....
f. Television ....
g. Radio ....
h. Globes ....
i. Weather maps ....
j. Textbooks ....

6. What Would You See?

Grades three, four, five, and six

A list of the different cities the children choose to visit on an imaginary trip is given them. They are to find information similar to that called for in the outline below.

a. Things to see
b. Things to do
c. Places to stay
d. Distance from home
e. Means of travel, cost, time, and so on
f. Foods to eat

7. Reference Reading

Grades three, four, five, and six

A paragraph from the text may be used, or the teacher may revise material from the reference books, using incomplete statements similar to the following examples.

a. The largest bee in the hive is the ....
b. The queen bee lays .... eggs.
c. The bee that does the least work is the ....

—and so on

BECOMING ACQUAINTED WITH THE BOOK

From the first day of school, the teacher can encourage children to become interested in books. The classroom collection of books should have a sufficient number of books that all the children can have one available. New books should be added from time to time and the children should be encouraged to discover them. Too many books in the lower grades may make it difficult for the child to make a choice. Both hardback and paperback belong in the collection. As soon as children begin reading fluently, they should become acquainted with the school and public libraries and they should be shown how to withdraw books.

Effective use of library resources is often one of the most undertaught skills. The library is a place where children get a great deal of information. It is the teacher's place to instruct the child in the make-up of the book.

The students should learn to look at the table of contents in the front of the book. This will tell them what the book is about. To find the exact pages where specific information can be found, they should use the index at the back of the book.

Pictures, maps, and illustrations are put in the book for a purpose, and they should not be overlooked.

Children in the first grade should learn to use their books correctly. At the very outset, they should learn to read page numbers and the titles of the stories. Later they should learn to use the table of contents. With a little training, children in the third grade will be able to make use of the index. Suggestions for exercises in becoming acquainted with a book are given below. These may be duplicated and given to each child, or the teacher may write the material on the blackboard or make a chart which can be used year after year.

1. Using the Table of Contents

Grades one, two, and three

The table of contents of the book the children are using can be the basis of questions similar to those given below. Each teacher may devise her own exercises.

Table of Contents

	Page
The Spotted Dog	3
The Robin's Nest	7
The First Bluebird	13
The Little Black Pig	18
The Red Automobile	22

—and so on

1. On what page will you find a story about a dog? ....
2. On what page will you find a story about a pig? ....
3. On what page will you find a story about a bird? ....
4. On what page will you find a story about a car? ...., and so on.

2. Becoming Acquainted with Your Book

Grades three, four, five, and six

The following questions may be duplicated, written on the blackboard, or made into chart form.

Becoming Acquainted with Your Book

1. The name of the new book is ....
2. The stories were selected by ....
3. The stories were written by ....
4. The artist who drew the picture was ....
5. The book is about ....
6. The book was published .... (*give date*) ....
7. The publishing company is ....

3. Finding a Story in the Book

Grades three, four, five, and six

The table of contents of the book being used in the class is used for answering questions similar to those in the examples given below.

Where Would You Look to Find Each Story?

Give the page number.

1. A story about a boat ....
2. A story about doing experiments ....
3. A story about the telephone ....
4. A story about air travel ....

4. Unit Titles

Grades three, four, five, and six

The table of contents of the book being used in the class will provide material for this activity.

Directions to students:

Use the table of contents and write the page number of each unit in this book.

1. Something about Indians ....
2. Something about homes ....
3. Something about travel ....

—and so on

5. Developing Location Skills

Grades four, five, and six

Exercises similar to that below may be duplicated for each pupil, written on the blackboard, or made into a permanent chart.

Locational Skills

The meaning of the words in Column I are found in Column II. Find the meaning and write the letter that matches each number.

I	II
1. Title	A. Alphabetical list of topics and page numbers.
2. Publication date	B. Name of person who wrote the book.
3. Index	C. An introduction at the beginning of the book.
4. Author	D. Name of the book.
5. Preface	E. When the book was printed.

6. The Index

Grades four, five, and six

Directions to students:

Open your geography book and look at the index at the back of the book. The words in the index are called *key words.* The page numbers following the key words tell you on what pages you can find information about this particular topic. These key words help you find the information quickly. Choose five key words from the index, find the page number for each, turn to the pages. Write the key word, the page number, and two things that you find about it on the pages shown in the index. Write your key words in alphabetical order.

7. Getting Acquainted with Your Reader

Grades four, five, and six

The following exercise may be duplicated for each child, written on the blackboard, or made as a permanent poster.

Getting Acquainted with Your Reader

1. Write the title of your new reader. ....
2. From this title, when would you expect that most of the stories took place? Check one answer.
   ....Long ago
   ....Within the last year
   ....Within the last twenty-five years
3. Write the title of the chapter which you think will fit each description below:
   Stories about famous inventions ....
   Stories about adventure ....
   Stories about transportation ....
   Stories about animals ....
   Imaginative stories ....

8. Using the Glossary

Grades four, five, and six

Words from the assignment in the class text may be used in questions to be answered by the use of the glossary. It is important that these words actually appear in the glossary.

Directions to the children:

Do you know the meaning of the italicized words?

Look in the glossary of your book and find the definitions.

1. Page 102........he had a *notion* to find out.
2. Page 106........he *trudged* down the lane

etc.

9. Table of Contents

Grades four, five, and six

The children use their books and turn to the table of contents. The teacher asks questions either orally or in written form. The children may answer orally or in writing.

Example:

1. Is there a story in this book about a beaver?
2. Who wrote the story?
3. Are there any poems in this book?
4. Are there any stories in this book about make-believe?

—and so on

10. Using the Textbook

Grades three, four, five, and six

Use the index of any of the textbooks the pupils use. Make a list of questions that will correspond with the index. Examples of questions are given below:

1. How many pages tell you something about birds?
2. What pages tell you about the food used by animals?
3. How many different kinds of animals are listed?
4. Where will you learn about the homes of hibernating animals?
5. On what pages will you find information about animal tracks?

11. Bookmaking

Grades one, two, three, four, five, and six

Making booklets on various subjects can be very informational to the pupil. These books may be on any topic or hobby the pupil is interested in. Loose-leaf notebooks are the most desirable form to use because pages can always be added when the child finds additional material. The first-grade pupil may want to make a picture book and use only the few words he knows. He may draw the pictures or they may be cut from magazines. In the other grades, the pupils will want to write about the subject. Pictures may be drawn, or cut from magazines. Reference reading should be encouraged.

12. Reference Reading

Grades three, four, five, and six

Explain to the students that when they are asked to find information for their social studies and science classes, they will want to know where to find the information quickly. List the following reference works on the blackboard and explain what they will find in each:

1. Encyclopedia
2. Atlases
3. Almanacs
4. Dictionaries
5. Maps
6. Readers or books containing selections about subjects.
7. Pictures, graphs, and charts
8. Brochures
9. Newspapers and magazines.

Older children should know how to use the card index in the library.

Write the questions below on the blackboard, or you may duplicate them if you wish.

Finding Information

Where would you look to find the following information? List several references for some.

1. The average rainfall in Arizona ....
2. The date of Benjamin Franklin's birth ....
3. The baseball scores for a recent game ....
4. Early explorers ....
5. The size of Australia ....
6. Animal life in Hawaii ....
7. Safety rules ....
8. The weather prediction for tomorrow ....

—and so on

MAP READING

Maps are of interest to most children, and they enjoy learning to read them. In the primary grades the children make their own maps on the floor or in the sand table. They frequently use blocks, and dramatic play about the home, community, airport, harbor, and the like, is involved. Older children like to make maps showing historic scenes, population, products, flowers, animals, trees, current events, stamps, industry, and so on. An opaque projector can be used for enlarging a small map and projecting it on paper fastened to the wall; then the children draw the projection on the paper.

Children in the upper grades should be able to locate places on globes and maps, recognize surface features and make use of lines of latitude and longitude. They should be able to answer such questions as:

a. What direction from us is ....?
b. How many miles away is ....?
c. How many miles from ....?
d. How does it compare with ....?

Even in the primary grades, if the children are reading a story about Jane, a map can be made of her community. Interesting questions could be asked such as: What route did she take going to school? How did she get to the store? For children in the third grade on up, maps should be used whenever possible.

Materials for Maps:

Floor, or sand table
Relief map of papier mâché, or salt and flour
Window shades
Oilcloth
Cloth
Poster paper
Flannel board
Masonite, plywood, or other compressed woods
Newsprint, wrapping paper
Construction paper
Cork

1. Studying the Globe

Grades four and five

Questions similar to those below can be used.

a. Which color stands for water on the globe?
b. What do the other colors stand for?
c. Is the greater part of the earth made up of land or water?
d. How much water surface is on the globe in comparison with land?
e. Which two continents form one large land mass?
f. What ocean is west of North America?
g. Are there more large cities north or south of the Equator?

2. Reading the Scale of Miles

Grade six

The children examine geographies, encyclopedia, and the like, to find as many different examples of map scales as they can in each book. They will discover that the scales differ from one map to another.

3. Making Map Collections

Grades two, three, four, five, and six

Pupils are encouraged to make map collections. They may keep them in folders or make booklets. They find keeping a scrapbook of maps cut from the daily newspapers a very interesting hobby.

4. Learning About Your Neighborhood

Grades two, three, and four

Draw a map of the neighborhood. This may be duplicated for each pupil, or it can be made on poster paper. Ask questions that pertain to the community.

Example:

a. If you start from the corner of Third Street and Highland Avenue and walk three blocks east, where would you be?
b. How many blocks would you walk to get from the drugstore to the library?
c. What building is located at the corner of Third Street and Highland Avenue?

—and so on

5. Map Games

Grades three, four, five, and six

Make a folder for the maps and questions about the country. The maps may be drawn by the children, or maps from travel bureaus and magazines can be used (fig. 5.1). A card containing directions is made for the game. The pupils write the answers on their own paper. A key is provided for the game.

Example: **How Far Is It?**

Directions:

Take out the big map and get a piece of paper and a pencil. Look at the scale showing miles per inch.

a. How many miles is it from Chihuahua to Mexico City? What direction is Chihuahua from Mexico City? From the United States?
b. How many miles is it from Taxco to Torreon? How would you go to Torreon from your home?
c. You are in Puebla and want to go to the seashore. How far would you have to travel?
d. What is the shortest distance between the Gulf of Tehuantepec and the Gulf of Campeche?

—and so on

READING THE NEWSPAPER

To read the newspaper effectively, the student must first know how it is organized. If an opaque projector is available, the Index of Features may be projected on the screen and the main topics or headings discussed. If the projector is not available, the Index of Features can be duplicated. Some papers are glad to furnish a copy of a previous day's paper for each student. Questions such as "Where would you find the weather report?" are asked.

In most newspaper writing, the main idea is stated in the first sentence of the paragraph. The pupils should be aware of the fact that the first page is the most important part of the paper. Ask them why the papers carry headlines.

Some people believe that if something is in print, it must be true. This fallacy should be pointed out to students. They should learn that the newspaper carries the opinions of its editor and writers. Students should know how to distinguish between fact and opinion.

A good activity for students from fourth grade on up, is to study the editorial page. Ask them to bring in editorials they wish to discuss or have discussed. The editorials reflect the editor's point of view, and the editorial page is where he sets down his thoughts about various topics. Whereas he has a right to his point of view, and to state matters as he sees them, he must depend upon people to buy his paper, so he will try not to offend his customers any more than a shopkeeper would purposefully annoy his customers. The students may wish to write a letter to the editor to express their views.

The class should learn to read more than one newspaper at times when there are vital issues to be con-

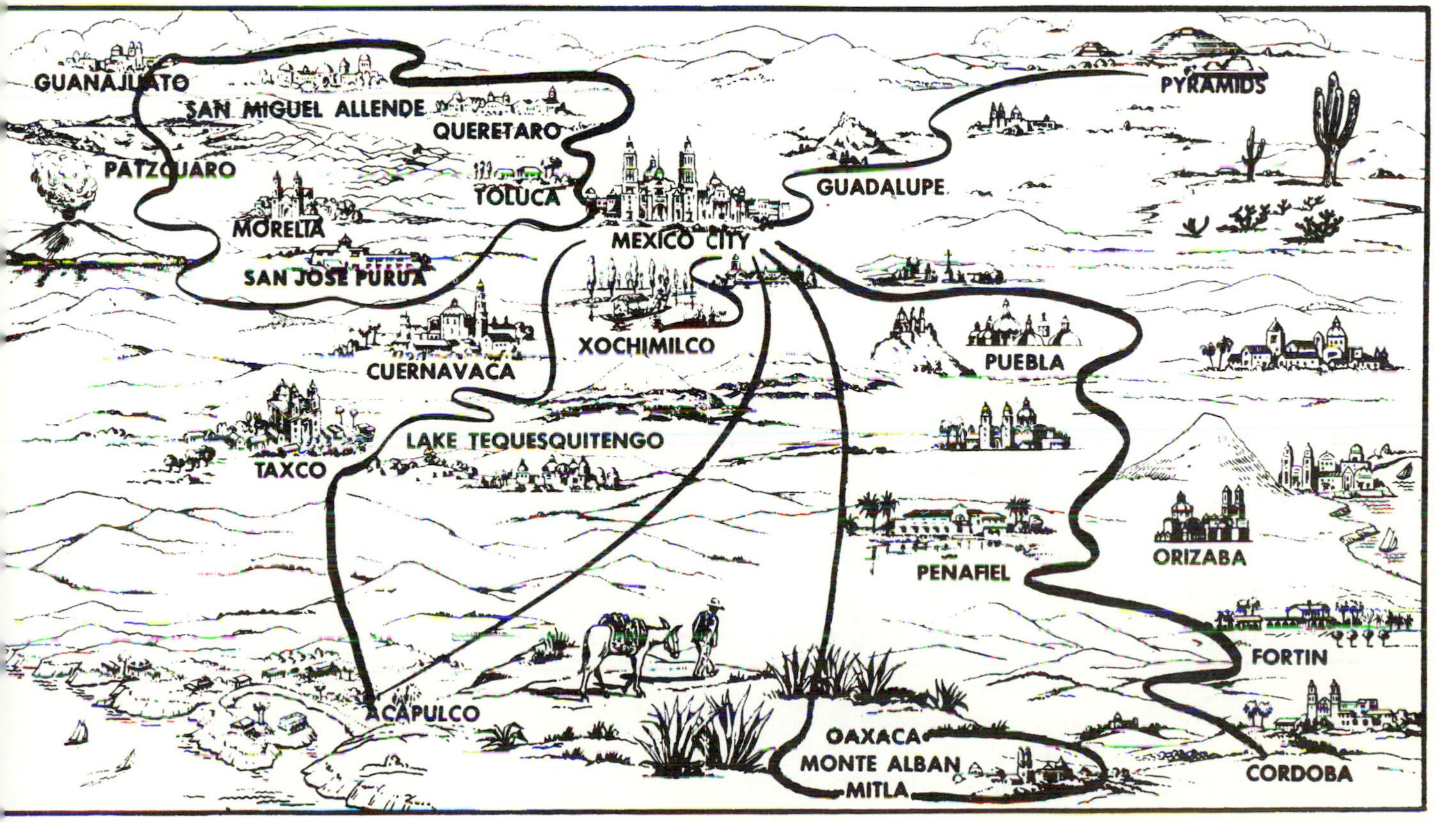

Figure 5.1 Map Game

sidered. They should learn to think for themselves and to make decisions about the facts as they are presented for both sides about any matter of importance.

The cartoons, charts, graphs, and maps should be examined and discussed. Students have found that making scrapbooks on maps, cartoons, and so on can be very interesting and worthwhile.

Even the comic strips may have some value. Some of the characters in these strips carry a worthwhile message, while others seem rather unimportant. The clues to the character of these comic strip people can make interesting class discussions.

The class may wish to have its own paper. Class members select their editor, reporters, and other members of the staff. Parents are generally pleased with such papers, and the activities of their children in preparing them.

Students should learn to increase their word power through the use of the newspaper. They may look for new or unusual words, and they may be given assignments in underlining certain words found in the paper. The use of colored pencils or pens will help the teacher check the work more easily. For example, the students might be asked to underline all action words with a green pencil and draw a circle around all figures of speech. These words can be kept in a notebook or file.

ORGANIZATION

If the pupils have not already learned about organizational patterns in paragraphs as a guide to finding the main idea, this skill should be presented before work is begun on learning the author's form of organization.

The author uses some form of organization to help the reader follow his pattern of thought. It will be an enjoyable surprise to the student when he discovers how easy it is to recognize the type of organization that is being employed by the writer.

The author may use the *chronological* pattern in organization. This is a time-sequence, and the author goes from one thing to another in the order that the events occurred. This is one of the most frequently used patterns of organization.

Sometimes the author describes everything just as it would meet the reader's eye. This form of organization is used in descriptive materials, whether scenery or some form of action is being described. This is called *spatial* organization and is used generally when writing about geography and physical subjects.

Enumeration is one of the simplest forms of organization. The reader goes from one thing to another, like beads on a string. The author tells the reader how many things he will discuss, and then proceeds to do so. If he says "The six most important things to remember are . . . ," you will know that there are six facts to remember.

The *problem-solving* organization can be found in mathematics, social studies, science, and other subjects, as well as in mystery stories. The reader is given a problem with the facts that have some bearing upon it. Sometimes the author includes possible solutions. The readers is to determine which solution to use. In other instances, the author will conclude the article with a solution and explain why he used it.

Another type of organization is that of *comparison* and *contrast.* In this type of organization, the reader is to evaluate the situation and make comparisons or contrasts. Frequently, the author makes an evaluation that lies somewhere between two ideas he has presented.

In *deductive* organization, progress is made from the known and the author gives a rule toward the application of it. First the reason is given and then its application is shown.

Inductive organization is just the opposite. The progress is made logically or mathematically from given instances toward a rule or conclusion.

The organization pattern can be identified by quickly skimming the material. The patterns may be identified by the use of specific words, such as *first, second,* which would indicate enumeration. Phrases such as *conversely, on the other hand,* will indicate comparison. Words like *and then, later,* point to the narrative or chronological organization.

Outlining can be helpful to the students in finding the main idea of the selection, as an aid in retention, and for use in future reference and study.

1. Outlining

Grade three

After reading the lesson, the teacher places an outline on the board, and the children fill in the blanks.

Example: **Indians**

I. Homes
  A. ....
  B. ....
  C. ....
II. Food
  A. ....
  B. ....
  C. ....
III. Dress
  A. ....
  B. ....
  C. ....

2. Making an Outline

Grades four, five, and six

After reading an article, the children fill in the main and subpoints. A hint may be given for the main heading.

Example:

I. .... (hint)
  A. ....
  B. ....
II. .... (hint)
  A. ....
  B. ....

3. Putting Words in Proper Place

Grades three and four

From a given list of objects pupils fill in the blanks in an outline.

Example:

grandmother	tulip	horse
horses	carrot	rose
monkey	children	uncle
captain	goat	bear
mice	radish	tree

I. Growing things
   A. ....
   B. ....
   C. ....
II. People
   A. ....
   B. ....
   C. ....
III. Animals
   A. ....
   B. ....
   C. ....

4. Organizing Information and Ideas

Grades three, four, five, and six

Stories from the reading book are used. The child writes the number of the paragraph of a story before the sentence expressing the main idea of that particular paragraph.

Example:

a. ....The horse wanted to go home.
b. ....The grass was wet.

5. Outlining the Reading Assignment

Grades four, five, and six

Directions:

Write a sentence in your own words, telling what the main thought of the first paragraph of the story is.

6. Outlining Several Paragraphs

Grades five and six

Directions:

Reread several paragraphs and write the reasons or proofs for the main thought. Be sure your reasons tell how or why. Use this outline.

I. .... Main thought
   A. .... Reason how or why
   B. .... Reason how or why
II. .... Main thought
   A. .... Why or how
   B. .... Why or how

7. Outlining Information

Grades four, five, and six

The major heading, as given below, is written on the board and then the outline is filled in.

Example:

A. The major causes of accidents involving children are:
   1. ....
   2. ....
   3. ....
   4. ....
   5. ....
   6. ....

8. Organizing Ideas

Grades four, five, and six

Headings are written on the board and lists of words given to the children to place under the proper headings. Social studies and science words lend themselves very well to this exercise. The children may also prepare their own lists by looking in their texts. A variety of headings may be used.

Headings:

ANIMALS PEOPLE THINGS WE USE

Words:

grandmother	horses	trunk	captain	monkey
kettle	wagon	chairs	carpet	mice

—and so on

9. Outlining

Grades four, five, and six

The children are to copy the headings of the outline. Under each heading they are to write the phrases that belong to it.

Example:

Henry's clothes *Henry's home*
The Bolder Land

Phrases:

tight waist and wide cuffs
long benches
head ornaments
mittens
red geraniums
cost millions of dollars
coal-burning fireplace
gold buttons for ornaments

10. Finding Information

Grades three, four, five, and six

The index of any textbook will furnish a list of topics to give to the pupils for this exercise. Within a time limit, they are to look in the index or table of contents and note the pages on which they would find these topics discussed. They may also list from the book one fact about each topic.

11. Selecting Titles

Grades three, four, five, and six

Under each paragraph of three or four sentences, several possible titles for the paragraphs are listed. The pupils are to choose the title which best gives the main idea of each paragraph.

6 Developing Word Power

Phonics
Dictionary Usage
Alphabetizing
Syllabication
Accents
Contractions
Compound Words
Synonyms and Antonyms
Latin and Greek Roots
Prefixes and Suffixes
Spelling as Related to Vocabulary Development
Word Lists

While it is agreed that comprehension is the most important phase of efficient reading, it must be realized that without an understanding of the individual words, there can be no comprehension. The individual's success in reading depends upon his understanding and interpretation of words. Merely pronouncing a word without knowing the meaning or the concept is of little value.

It is important for the student to develop an ever-increasing knowledge of words and the corollary knowledge of how they work. From the outset the teacher must instill an awareness of words within the student. Words represent facts, observations, principles, and feelings. We receive knowledge, experience, and thought of others through the medium of words, and the greater our knowledge of them, the better informed we are.

Word power can be developed through the presentation of a programmed word attack and by providing for the individual differences. The teacher must identify the pupil's strengths and weaknesses and schedule him for reinforcement activities. These games or activities that are presented are not just for fun, but for the reinforcement of learning.

To develop greater word power, the following procedures should be used:

1. Structural analysis, which includes the identification skills, the appearance of words, the distinctive parts as beginning and ending elements, Latin and Greek roots and stems, the common endings, suffixes and prefixes, compound words, syllabication, and phonetic elements.
2. Recognition skills, which include context clues and picture clues.
3. Phonetic analysis.
4. Dictionary usage.

Children should learn that they must not stop with the first clue, but should go on to the next and the next, until they can identify the word. Just looking up the meaning of the word in the dictionary is not enough. The student must see and use the word many times in order to make it his own. The size of the student's vocabulary will depend upon his experience background, the amount of reading he does, and his ability to attack new words.

Educators have attempted to establish the size of the vocabulary for each grade or age level, but because of differences in backgrounds and general abilities, there is no definitive agreement as to the number of words a student should know at any given level. It is estimated that by the time the student completes the sixth grade he should have a reading level of at least 15,000 words.

The following formula for estimating the approximate number of words in the student's reading vocabulary is fairly reliable and may be used. It should be applied on an individual basis, however, and is applicable from first grade through college.

The directions are as follows:

1. Use an abridged college edition dictionary.
2. Select 100 pages at random. The student views the word in the upper right-hand corner and defines it.
3. Record the number of words the student can define correctly.
4. Multiply the number of correctly defined words by the total number of pages of words in the dictionary.
5. Divide the results by 100.
6. Multiply this number by the average number of words on a page.
7. This will result in the approximate number of words in the student's reading vocabulary.

Example:

25 correctly defined words
× 1,500 – pages in dictionary
37,500 – divided by 100, equals 375.

375
× 40 (average number of words per dictionary page)
15,000 words—the approximate number of words in reading vocabulary.

One way of knowing if the material is too difficult for the student is to have him read orally a selection of 100 words in his reading book. If he misses more than five words in 100 running words, the material is too difficult for him. Unfamiliarity with the subject may prevent him from knowing the words, too. Of course, merely pronouncing the words without knowing or sensing the meaning doesn't help his comprehension. After reading the 100 words, ask a few questions about the selection to discover if he is comprehending what has been read.

There are two types of vocabulary: (1) the technical vocabulary, which is encountered in science and social study texts; and (2) the general vocabulary which is found in magazines, newspapers, and many books.

There are ten words that make up 25 percent of all the words used in all ordinary writing. They are:

a	be	in	the	we
and	I	of	to	you

The following fifty words make up nearly 50 percent of all running words used in all ordinary writing:

a	do	if	one	very
all	for	in	our	was
and	from	is	put	we
are	get	it	she	when
as	go	letter	so	will
at	good	me	that	with
be	had	my	the	would
been	have	not	this	you
but	he	of	time	your
can	I	on	to	yours

A brief outline for developing word recognition by grade level follows. There will be some deviation according to the needs of each child.

FIRST GRADE

1. Sight Vocabulary

a. Chart stories are used first. They should be properly motivated in order to bring out the children's own words in every case (choosing ones which coincide with those used in their first preprimers) so that the children may see their own words being put into printed symbols.

b. Use words in oral discussion; help children become secure in use of basic vocabulary by providing situations wherein the basic words may be used.

c. Label objects and pictures in the room.

d. Show the same word, or words, in many different contexts—such as different experience stories using same word.

e. Use clear enunciation and pronunciation of words when a story, phrase, or sentence is read.

2. Context Clues

a. Call children's attention to the form of a word—its general length, shape, size, and configuration without reference to individual letters. Indicate such by left-to-right motion.

b. Read a short sentence, a phrase, or a word to the children. Display the word or words. Show two pictures. Ask the children to choose the correct picture for the word or phrase.

c. Continue to encourage careful observation of any part of the environment; help children note likenesses and differences as they study leaves, seeds, insects, landscape, pictures.

d. Show children a word; tell them what it is; take the word away; ask them to close their eyes and "see" the word. Show two words; ask the children which one of the two is the one they saw before.

e. It is better to present at first as basic sight words those words which are quite unlike in appearance, and to save the words which are similar until the first words are thoroughly learned. For instance: be sure that a child can easily identify *same, saw, bed, funny* before he is introduced to *game, was, red,* and *sunny*.

3. Structural Analysis

a. Begin by asking the question, "What part of the word helps you remember it?"

b. Present a familiar word like *help*. Then show a new word form, as *helps*. Ask children to discover the difference between the two. Pronounce the two words for them so that they may hear the difference. Use the two forms in conversation. Help the children to do the same. Use pictures to illustrate.

4. Phonetic Analysis

a. Place before the children a list of words, all well known and easily recognized by them—words with the same initial consonant. Ask children to read the words silently. Call on one child to read the list aloud (*said, Sally, sand*). Ask children if they hear a sound that is the same in all the words. Point out that the first part of each word is the same. Ask children to think of another word that begins with the same sound.

b. Present a simple, two-line poem or jingle. Let the children enjoy it and learn it by rote. Ask them to observe the similarity of sound—the rhyme of the words.

c. Have fun creating, with the children, humorous jingles, riddles that rhyme, or verses with repetitious sounds.

SECOND GRADE

1. Sight Vocabulary

a. In preparation for reading a given story, new words should be presented in conversation with the same meaning associations with which they are used in the story. (Also as the same form of speech—verb, noun, adjective.) Show the new word on a card or on the board.

b. Present a new word in the midst of known, familiar words. (To be kept in mind when using experience charts for reading.)

c. Present a new meaning association for an old, familiar word as if the word were new (first discussion, oral use of the word); presentation of the written form, then in the story context after silent reading.

2. Context Clues

a. Help the children gather meaning from the sentence as context for a new word: Present a short sentence containing well-known words, except for one new word, such as "See Sally jump down" (down is a new word). Ask children to read the line silently. Ask them to raise their hands if they see an unfamiliar word. Talk about the picture: "Where was Sally? What did she do?" "Which way did she jump?" Ask children to read the sentence again, silently. Then call on a child to read it aloud.

b. Continue to use pictures and oral discussion as context.

3. Word Form Clues

a. Write a familiar word on the board (*funny*). Ask children to notice how the beginning of the word looks, the middle, the end.

b. Write another word beside the first (*funny, fell*). Lead the children to notice where the words are different. Point out that it is necessary to observe all parts of the word, not just the beginning.

c. Write the sentence on the board with one word missing and the blank space indicated. Offer two words as choice to complete the sentences, like "Look, Sally," said Father. "Look ...." (*in, up*)

Use pictures whenever possible to strengthen the meaning.

d. Place on the board, or on paper, two vertical lists of words. Use the same words in each column, but arrange them differently. Ask children to draw lines between the like words.

Example:

up	go
go	it
it	up
oh	oh

Use the same word, one capitalized, the other not, after such forms are made familiar through reading.

e. Make a list of familiar words, i.e. point to and ask children to pronounce *come*. Then ask children to find all the words in the column that are just like the first word and to underline them.

come
look
come
down
funny
come

4. Structural Analysis

a. Use the same procedure as suggested under 3, d, except that words to be matched will be the same but for the addition of *s* as an ending. Use words already familiar to the children:

see	helps
runs	sees
help	run
rides	ride

b. Use sentence completion with a choice of word forms.

Example:

Puff .... away. (run, runs)
Jane can .... fast. (run, runs)

c. Familiarize children with capitalized words, using same practice game as suggested under a. Use words already found and discussed in reading material.

5. Phonetic Analysis

a. Continue initial consonants. Place a letter on the board or paper, both lower and uppercase forms. Below this letter put a list of words already known to the children. Ask children to pronounce the words as they are indicated. Repeat this latter procedure while another child circles the words that begin with the letter indicated at the top of the column:

g G

good
Goodby
Baby
Get
Good

6. General

a. Always provide time for children to read the material silently that they are to read aloud. This applies throughout all reading levels.

b. Always provide opportunity and logical motivation for silent rereading of the passage read aloud, as, for example, 1. "Do you think Father was surprised? What makes you think so?" (Father said, "Oh my!") 2. "How many, altogether, had cookies?" (Sally said, "Cookies for Jane, and Dick, for Mother and Father.")

c. Always make reading a time for enjoyment and fun.

THIRD GRADE

1. Sight Vocabulary

a. Continue to help children acquire a larger sight vocabulary by associating words with meaningful situations, with pictures, and with objects.

b. A sight vocabulary of 250 words provides a good basis for the introduction of other methods of word attack, such as structural analysis and phonetic analysis.

c. Let each child keep an alphabetized file of his own basic sight words. Let him trace and write these words as he needs them for captions and stories.

2. Context Clues

a. Give children an opportunity to read (silently) a sentence in which one new word appears; a word which might be understood as a result of knowing the meaning of the rest of the sentence. Ask if any child thinks he knows the new word. If he does, ask him how he discovered its meaning. If he does not, ask him to read the sentence aloud, skipping the word not known. See if others in the group can tell what the new word could be.

b. Continue to use pictures as context clues.

3. Word Form Clues

a. Help children observe finer distinctions in word forms, as for example, *bump, jump; them, then; was, saw; quite, quiet.* Show children one of a pair of familiar words. Indicate by pointing left to right the contour of the first word. Have children say the word. Ask children to close their eyes and see the word. Go through the same procedure with the second word. Ask them to tell what the difference is, like "*Bump* goes up at first and down at the end. *Jump* goes down at first and down at the end, too." Do the same thing with the next pair, and so on.

4. Structural Analysis

a. Introduce variant forms of verbs (*paints, painted, painting*). Discuss an experience (such as painting trucks). Encourage description of the process and provide opportunity for the various uses of the verb *paint.* Repeat for the children some of the phrases used ("We painted our trucks today." "Dick is painting his truck green." "Mary paints very quickly.") Show the sentences lettered on tagboard or on the chalkboard. (Perhaps they are all included in an experience story.) Ask children to find the words, *paint, painted, painting.* Show individual word cards for those, or use words in text. Ask them to find the part of the word that is the same in all three forms. Ask them to show the parts that are different.

b. Find in a story a compound word composed of two words well known to the children, as *something.* Ask children to look for a part of the word which they already know, then another part. What do they make together? For emphasis another story on a chart could be used:

"This *thing* in my hand is a camera.
I will take *some* pictures with it.
I will take a picture of *something.*"

5. Phonetic Analysis

a. Introduce other initial consonants not yet used. Suggested order is: *s, t, d, m, b, j, p, g, l, v, w, n, h, c, x, z.* Suggested technique: "Say the word *look* to yourselves and think how it sounds at the beginning. Now say the words *laugh* and *light.* Do these words begin with the same sound as *look?* Yes, they all sound alike at the beginning, don't they? Now I am going to say some other words. Tell me the ones that begin with the same sound as *look, laugh,* and *light.*" Pronounce such words as *left, lemon, dentist; lesson, juice, lid; finger, lift, letter; letter, lip, saucer.* (Children could be asked to raise their hands if they hear a word that does not begin with the same sound.)

b. Continue to use matching games.

c. Use initial consonant substitution. Approach from children's familiarity with rhymes. Place two sentences on board or paper:
"The man is tall."
"Don't fall."
Ask the children to read sentences (known words, of course). Ask children to find two words that rhyme. Add another sentence: "The ball is blue." Ask children what is different about the three words. At another time review the sentences and words used; then add others: "It is in the hall." "The wall is high."

d. Provide children with opportunity to read a sentence containing all well-known words except one new word, *kitten.* Ask children if they think this new word reminds them (looks like) a word they already know. If they cannot remember, present a word card of kitten; then take it away. Ask children to think what sound the new word begins with (be sure to introduce only the new words whose initial consonant is already familiar to the children).

6. Combining Structural and Phonetic Analysis

a. Children may begin to have opportunity to combine structural and phonetic analysis by observing and comparing the similarities in words:

Extra mark above *fails.*
The baby *falls* down.
I see four *balls.*
There are two *halls* in our house.
The room has four *walls.*
The rain is *falling.*

Present such sentences as the above in which all the words are familiar. Ask children to find (a) the word that tells what baby does, (b) the word that tells what I see. Ask children what is alike about these two words. What is different? Ask about a third word "What are there in our house?" Find likeness and difference in the three words. Add the fourth and fifth in the same manner. Compound words may be compared in like manner:

"Will you *walk* with me?"
"No, we will *ride.*"
"I will sit on this *side.*"
"I can *talk* to you."
"We step on the *sidewalk.*"

FOURTH GRADE

1. Sight Vocabulary

a. Continue to increase the children's vocabulary through oral discussion, experiences of value, objects for observation.

b. Continue providing many different contexts for known words.

2. Context Clues

a. Continue to give opportunity to discover new words by means of general comprehension and interpretation. Shift emphasis from dependence on pictures alone to use of sentence and paragraph.

b. Provide a partial sentence to be completed by a choice of phrase:

A basket could have nuts in it.
could have water in it.
could have eggs in it.

3. Word Form Memory

a. Check pupil's ability to recall known word forms from memory.

b. Help children notice similarities and differences in words.

4. Structural Analysis

a. Introduce the process of recognizing verb forms.

b. Point out that *y* is changed to *i* when adding the endings.

5. Phonetic Analysis

a. Introduce visual-auditory perception of words.

b. Develop phonetic understandings.

DO'S AND DON'TS FOR THE TEACHER IN VOCABULARY DEVELOPMENT

1. Do not teach structural analysis until the child has a sight vocabulary of at least seventy-five words.
2. Establish the habit of using the context for recognition of words during the sight-recognition stage.
3. Give practice in auditory perception and pronunciation before presenting the visual form of the words.
4. Call attention to general configuration and visual clues while the child is learning his first sight vocabulary.
5. Word study should include only those words which are met in meaningful context.
6. Do not give isolated word drills.
7. The child should know at least fifty words before he begins phonetic analysis.
8. Teach one skill at a time and when it is needed.
9. Avoid rules.
10. The child must identify phonetic and structural elements before he can blend them to sound a word.
11. Structural analysis should precede phonetic analysis.
12. Never assume that a child knows more than he does.

There are many activities which can help the child learn new words and retain them. The activities that follow may be modified according to the pupil's needs and abilities.

Scrutiny of the total word form is one of the most important steps in attacking any new word, and the activities that are presented are for the purpose of providing added interest to the learning of new words, but not to the exclusion of developing the important work habits implicit in the noting of the phonetic, structural, and context clues in words.

There is a close relationship between the size of a pupil's vocabulary and his school achievement. Helping the child develop word power means that he will be able to work more effectively in all his studies.

1. Adding a Word

Grades one, two, three, four, five, and six

This exercise may be duplicated or written on the board.

Directions:

Write as many words as you can think of under each heading. Use the words from your reader and other books. You may use the dictionary if you wish.
Shoemaker Night Winter Skating
Cucumber

Words that might be listed under these headings are:

herdsman	skiing	morning	spring
grocer	lettuce	summer	fall
noon	cabbage	sledding	peas

2. Adding a Word to the Sentence

Grades one and two

Cards with small pictures of animals are presented. The first child picks a card and says, "I went to the circus and saw a ...." Name animal on card. The next child picks a card and says what the first child said and adds the name of the animal on his card. Later, words may be added to the pictures and finally only words may be used. This game may be used for "Going to the Grocer," "Going to the Farm," and the like. Use the appropriate pictures and words.

3. Add-to Game

Grades one, two, and three

In first grade the work may be oral; but for second and third grades phrases should be printed on slips. The first child draws a slip and reads the phrase; the next child repeats what the first child has read and adds another word; they continue taking turns until they can think of no other adjectives. Example: "The duck ran." The next child could say, "A yellow duck ran." The next child could say, "A little yellow duck ran." The next child could say, "A little yellow quacking duck," and so on.

4. Alphabet Blocks

Grade one

Commercial alphabet blocks may be used, but small wooden blocks can be substituted by placing masking tape on all six sides and printing a letter of the alphabet on each of the sides. At the beginning a child uses about three blocks. He tosses these on the table and tries to make a word from the letters that are up. Later, more blocks are added. A piece of felt on the desk top will help soften the sound. The children may take turns tossing the blocks, and score may be kept of the number of words each child can make.

5. Anagrams

Grades two, three, and four

Envelopes containing cardboard letters of the alphabet are distributed. A short story is written on the chalkboard together with questions. The children answer the questions by using their letters to make the words.

Example:

The old dog was sleeping soundly in front of the fireplace. He was dreaming about a rabbit that was leading him farther and farther into the woods. The rabbit crawled into a hollow log and the dog tried to follow him.

a. Where was the dog sleeping?
b. What did he dream about?
c. Where did the dream take place?

6. Anchors Aweigh!

Grades two and three

The children sit in a circle. The player who starts the game holds a small ball in his hand. He starts with, "Anchors Aweigh! The ship is filled with *Bananas*." He hands the ball to another child who must give another object beginning with the letter *B*. He in turn gives the ball to another child who names another object beginning with *B*. They continue until some child fails to name an object. The child who last had the ball begins the new game. Any letter of the alphabet may be used. A stopwatch may be used and scores may be kept.

7. Antonyms

Grades two, three, four, five, and six

The class is divided into teams of six members each. The teacher pronounces a word and uses it in a sentence. Each child on a team in turn gives a word of opposite meaning. A point is scored for each child who is able to give an anonym. Words used in the classwork should be used whenever possible.

8. Antonyms

Grades one, two, and three

Sentences are written on the board. The children read them and write a word meaning the opposite of the word that is *italicized*.

Example:

a. The soup is *hot*.
b. The hat is *old*.
c. The tree is *big*.
d. He always *sings*.

9. Around It Goes

Grades three and four

A twelve-inch circle has a hand or indicator of heavy cardboard fastened in the center with a brass fastener. Around the edge of the circle the endings, *ly*, *s*, *tion*, *y*, *ness*, *ing*, *ful*, *er*, *ed*, and *est* are printed. Each child is given six cards with words printed on them. The leader spins the indicator and if it should stop at *ly*, the children look to see what words they have that could be used with an *ly* ending. They write this word, together with the ending *ly*, on their papers. Words used in the reading lessons should be printed on the cards.

Example:

Look, little, play, imitate, quick, happy, and so on.

10. Authors with Endings

Grades two, three, and four

Four different endings on each root, as *grow, grown, growing, grows,* are each printed on a card. Twelve sets of roots are needed. The cards are shuffled and dealt, six cards to a player, with the remaining cards face down on the table. The object of the game is to get four cards with the same root. The players take turns asking another for a card (he must have one of the four in his hand). The child must relinquish all the cards with the root word that he has been asked for. After the child has asked another child for a word, he draws a card from the pile. When he has four cards with the same root word, he lays them on the table. Words that may be used are: *rain, thank, wait, throw, polite, wish.*

11. Ball Game

Grade one

The children stand behind their chairs. Each child has a word card which he puts on his chair. One child bounces the ball to another child who catches it and says his word. If he says the word correctly, he picks up his word and another word is placed in front of the first word. At the end of the game, the child with the most cards wins.

12. Balloon Game

Grades one and two

A clown picture is drawn on the board or on paper. An equal number of balloons with a word printed on each are drawn on each side. A set of colored circles represents the balloons. There should be the same number of circles as balloons. On each circle a word which corresponds to a word on one of the balloons is printed. In playing the game, the circles are shuffled and divided equally between the two players. The children take turns reading the words on their circles. When a word is read correctly, the circle is placed over the balloon with the same word. They may be fastened on with plastic tape. Each player tries to cover balloons on his side of the clown first, but if a player gets a word not contained in the balloons on his side, he must put it on the other side. The player wins when his balloons are covered.

13. Baseball

Grades one, two, and three

Eighteen cards, each with a word printed on it, are shuffled and divided between the two teams of nine players each. A scoreboard is made to record the number of runs, and a baseball diamond is drawn on paper or the board. A child reads the first card. If he reads it correctly, he makes a home run and it is recorded on the scoreboard. If he fails on the first try but succeeds on the second, his card goes to third base. If he has two unsuccessful attempts, second base is reached; three unsuccessful attempts places the card on first base. If he has to make four tries, he is out and the card is set aside. If a player is on a base and the next player makes a home run, it forces the player off base. If a player advances to a base already occupied, it automatically advances the player on the base to the next one. Three outs and the other team is up to bat. Markers may be used for the men at the bases.

14. Book Games

Grades one, two, three, four, five, and six

Words that the children will need help with are printed on cards, three copies of each word. Fifteen or twenty sets of cards are shuffled, and each player is given six cards. The remainder of the cards are placed face down on the table. Three cards with the same word make a book. The first child asks another child, "Do you have ....?" He cannot ask for a word unless he has one in his hand. The child asked must give up all the cards with that word. The first child then draws a card, and the play goes to the second one. The children lays their *books* on the table before them.

15. Building

Grades one and two

A house with an incomplete roof is drawn. Cards are made to represent the shingles. A word is written on each shingle. The child reads the word and puts it on the house. If the picture of the house is tacked onto a bulletin board, the shingles may be stuck on with pins or thumbtacks. If this is not possible, small pieces of Scotch tape may be used. The house may be outlined for bricks in a similar way.

16. Buying a Toy

Grades one and two

Animals and toys are cut out of construction paper. On the backs of these objects are written words with which the children have difficulty. The objects are placed on the chalk ledge or tacked to the bulletin board. The children take turns going to buy a toy. They must read the word on the back of the picture to get it.

17. Call Game

Grades one and two

Words, phrases, or sentences are written on the chalkboard and numbered 1, 2, 3, 4, and so on. The children draw numbers from a box, and each reads the word or phrase that corresponds to the number drawn.

18. Card Game

Grades one and two

Three pictures of each of the following are drawn on cards: apple, flower, bird, house, tree, ball, wagon, cat, dog, and duck; and a different word is printed on each card. The cards are shuffled and given to each player. The remainder of the cards are placed face down on the table. The object of the game is to get a book of three similar pictures and to be able to read the words printed on the cards as well. The first child asks another if he has a flower. If he has, he must give it to the child who requested it. The child receiving the card must pronounce the word or he will be unable to keep it. He then draws one card from the pile. The next child then asks for a picture he wants.

19. Card Reading

Grades one and two

Words are printed on 2-by-3-inch cards which are placed face down on the table. The children take turns drawing cards. When a player takes a card he reads the word printed on it. If he reads it correctly, he keeps the card in front of him. If he cannot read it, he returns the card, face down, to the bottom of the center pack. The child with the most cards wins.

20. Catch

Grade one

Words are printed on the chalkboard or on a chart. The teacher throws a ball to a child who pronounces the first word in the list. If the child can read the word, he throws the ball back to the teacher. If he cannot read it, he passes the ball to the next child, who says the word if he can.

21. Choosing Words that Mean the Same

Grades three, four, five, and six

The exercise is duplicated or written on the chalkboard. Words from the reading assignment may be used.

Directions:

Read the sentence. Write a word on the line that means the same as the *italicized* word. The words to be used may be written on the board if the teacher wishes.

a. The woman prepared a *delicious* meal. ....
b. He *decided* he would leave. ....
c. He lived in a *cottage*. ....

22. Circle Game

Grades one and two

The children sit in a small circle on the floor. The word cards are placed face down in the center. The first child picks up a card and reads it. He keeps the card if he reads it correctly. If he cannot, he puts it back on the bottom of the pack. The next child draws a card and reads it.

23. Change the Letter and the Word

Grades two, three, and four

The exercise is duplicated or written on the chalkboard. Words are taken from the reading assignments or other lessons.

Directions:

Change one letter of the *italicized* word to make a new word.

a. Change one letter in *house*, and make an animal to ride.
b. Change one letter in *can*, and make a person.
c. Add a letter to *got*, and make an animal with horns.

24. Checkers

Grades one, two, three, four, five, and six

The easiest procedure is to duplicate thirty or forty outlines for checkerboards. However, masking tape on regular checkerboards works very well. In the squares where the checkers are to be placed and moved, print each word right side up and upside down so both players can read it. The children play checkers in the usual way, but they must be able to read the word in the square or they cannot move into it. Science and social studies words may be learned this way (see fig. 6.1).

25. Choose the Word

Grades one, two, three, and four

Words are to be chosen from the list to answer the riddles.

Example:

Riddles	*List*
a. What is the opposite of down?	evening
b. When does the sun set?	wife
c. Who helps the farmer?	up

26. Completion

Grades one, two, three, four, five, and six

A list of words and several incomplete sentences that are numbered are written on the chalkboard.

Directions:

Number your paper to match the sentences on the board. After each number write the word that will complete the sentence correctly.

a. The little brown child could not ....
b. Tom and Jack were good ....

27. Conductor

Grade one

One child is the conductor of the reading train. He stands behind a seated child. The teacher shows them a word card. The child who says the word first wins. If the conductor says the word first, he moves behind the next child in the circle. If the seated child says it first, he changes places and becomes the conductor.

28. Configuration

Grade one

The children may be given wooden blocks. The teacher shows the children a word card and they put together the number of blocks required to make the word. A three-letter word would require three blocks. After they

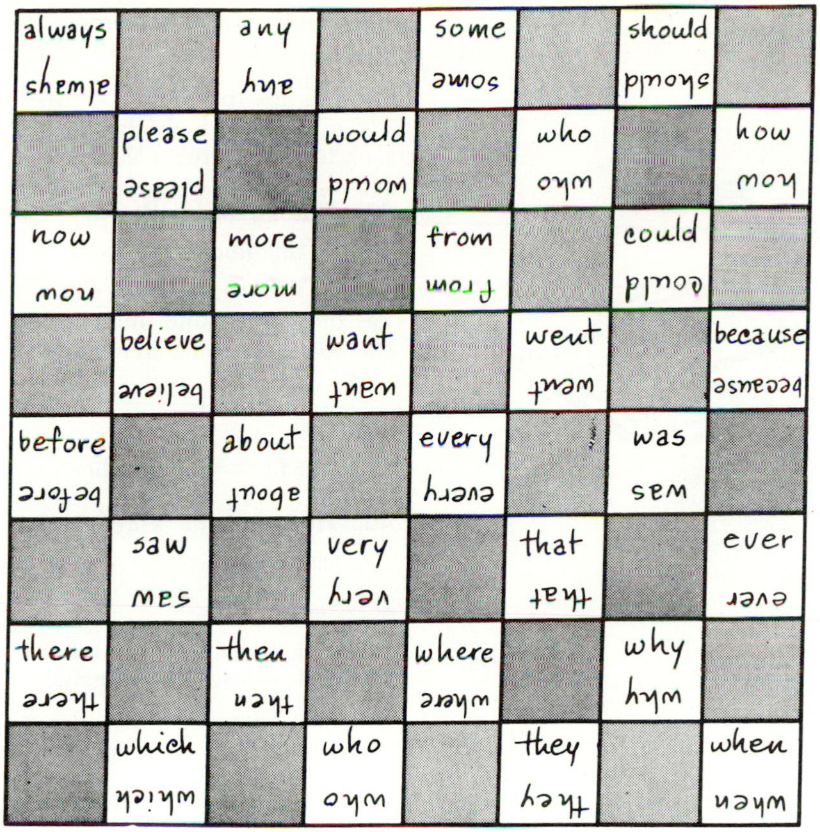

Figure 6.1 Checkers

are able to do this they may match the words to blocks as shown below.

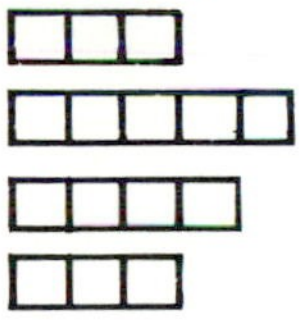

why

who

where

what, —and so on

29. Contractions

Grades two and three

Cards with contractions and the words for which they stand may be printed. The children may match the two or they may play a card game, asking for the words to make a book. They may also be asked to write the words for these contractions:

aren't	can't	doesn't	haven't	hasn't
he'd	he's	he'll	couldn't	wouldn't
shouldn't	didn't	don't	hadn't	I'm
I'd	I'll	I've	it's	isn't
let's	she'll	she'd	there's	they'll
they're	they'd	they've	that's	weren't
we'll	we'd	we've	wasn't	we're
you're	you'd	you've	you'll	hadn't
won't	what's			

30. Description

Grades two, three, four, and five

Words from the reading lesson similar to the example given below, are duplicated or written on the board.

Directions:

Draw a line under the word that best describes the first word.

a. butter....black....yellow....brown....cake
b. ice...........melt......warm....cold........tall

31. Detective

Grades two, three, and four

Directions:

Look through your reading lesson and see how many compound words you can find. Write these on a piece of paper.

32. Diacritical Markings

Grades four, five, and six

Each pupil writes a code message, using the respelling of the words in the dictionary or the glossary. The children exchange messages and decode them.

Example:

The jentl wind barli bloo.

33. Dominoes

Grades one and two

A set of word cards is made up to look like dominoes. The set should contain about twenty-four different phrases or words, four copies of each phrase. Two phrases or words are on each card. A few of these should be doubles. The game is played just like dominoes (fig. 6.2).

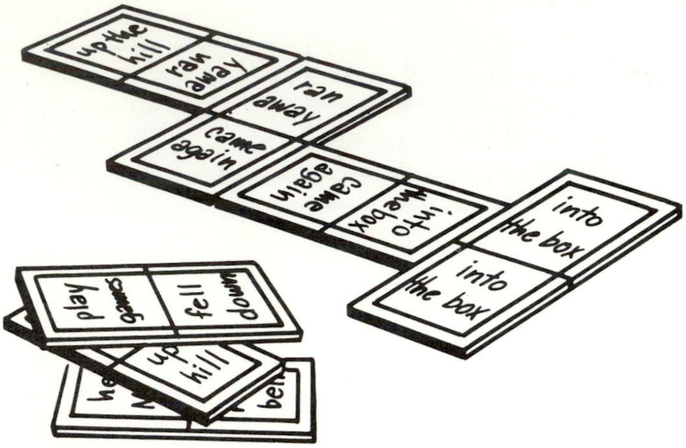

Figure 6.2 Dominoes

34. Do This

Grades one and two

Print action verbs on cards, such as *clap, crawl, shiver, smile, throw, wave,* and so on. The leader draws a card and indicates which child is to pantomime the action.

35. Emotive and Informative Words

Grades five and six

The children are to write *E* in front of each sentence that contains emotive language. They underline the word that creates emotions. They write *I* in front of those sentences that contain information only.

Example:

a. The delicate fragrance drifted through the air.
b. Mary was elected class president.
c. The child cried violently.

36. Duck Shooting

Grades one and two

A row of ducks is drawn on the board and a word written under each duck. The child is given a rubber dart. If he shoots the duck, he must read the word under it.

37. Fairy Door

Grades one, two, and three

Each child thinks of a word and tells it to the teacher who writes it on the chalkboard. One child has a "fairy wand" and touches a word, asking another child to read the word. If he can, he may go through the Fairy Door. The game may be played by giving the opposite of the word or by using the word in a sentence. This is a good game to play just before recess or at dismissal time, because then the children can go through the door.

38. Find a Picture Game

Grade one

Pictures are placed about the room. The pupils are given words which illustrate the pictures, and they look for the pictures that match their cards.

39. Finding Short Words

Grades one and two

Words that contain the letters of a shorter word that has the same sound units are duplicated or written on the board. The children are to find the shorter word in each.

Example:

band fit cup thin call

40. Finding Little Words

Grades one and two

Directions:

If you can find a little word in the big word, write it beside the letter with which it begins.

call bee jumping any doing yesterday
a........b......j..................a........d............y................

41. Finding Two Words in a Large Word

Grades two and three

The children find the two words in the compound words *farmyard, upon, everywhere, sometime, everyone, somebody.* The words may be written singly on cards, as *sun, yard, stairs, shine, up, farm, snow, some, shoes,* and *time,* and the children put the two words together to form the compound word.

42. Find the Word

Grades three, four, five, and six

Directions:

Look at the first word and then find its meaning in the second column. Put the letter of the word beside its meaning.

a. frisky	........not happy
b. discontented	........a green field
c. meadow	........very lively

43. First-Chair Game

Grades one and two

One chair is designated as the first chair. A child may stay in this chair only until he misses a word. Then he goes to the end chair and the other children move up a chair. Any other child who misses a word goes to the end chair, and the others move up to fill his place.

44. Fishing

Grades one and two

Words from the lesson are printed on cards. These may be cut in fish shapes if the teacher wishes. A paper clip is attached to each card or fish. A fishing line is made with a string, pole, and magnet. The child fishes for a word, pronounces it, and keeps the card. If he cannot give the word, he studies it until his turn comes again; then he puts it into the pond and fishes again.

45. Football Game

Grades one, two, and three

A football field is made of cardboard. Words are printed on cards. The ball is placed on the fifty-yard line. The first player reads the word on the first card. If he reads the word correctly, he moves the ball ten yards toward the goal; but if he misses, the ball goes back ten yards. When a child crosses the opposite goal line, his score is six. If he reads the next word correctly, he adds the one extra point to his score.

46. Football Game in Oral Reading

Grades one, two, and three

A football field is drawn on a 26-by-20-inch paper, including goalposts, and a paper football three inches long. This game is played by four pupils with two on each side. The rules are as follows:

a. Five lines read without an error is the first down.
b. Each player may have one chance to recover the fumble (correct error) before losing the ball.
c. A team may keep the ball as long as its members are able to make first downs.
d. When one team loses the ball the other team must take over from its position on the field.
e. The ball must be read over the goal line for a touchdown.
f. A touchdown counts six points.
g. One sentence must be read correctly for an additional point.
h. A team may be penalized five yards for unnecessary talking.

47. Following Directions

Grades one and two

Directions:

Read each sentence and show the meaning of each italicized word.

a. Put the red ball *on* your desk.
b. Put the blue ball *in* your desk.
c. Put the red ball *by* your hand.

48. Freight Train

Grades one and two

Outlines of train and freight cars are made for each child. An envelope or pocket is on the back of each car and the engine. The teacher shows a word printed on a card. If the child knows the word, he places it in one of the cars. The player whose cars are filled first wins.

49. Gaps

Grades one, two, and three

A list of words that have one or two middle letters missing is duplicated. The player who completes the largest number of words in a given time wins.

Example:

l........g (long), b........l (ball), g........t (got)

50. Get Away

Grades one and two

Words from the reading lesson are on cards. One child holds the cards in front of the class, showing one card at a time. He designates which child is to pronounce the word. If that child can say the word, he takes the card.

51. Giant

Grade one

The teacher holds up a word card. If a child knows it, he stands up; for the second word correctly read, he gets to stand on his chair; and if he gets a third, he raises his arms, becoming a giant. He may sit down because holding up both arms might prove too tiring. He may become a giant a second or even a third time.

52. Going on a Trip

Grades one, two, and three

Word cards are prepared from words in the reading lesson. These may be placed inside a box which is to represent a trunk or luggage. The first child takes a card and says, "I am going on a trip and I will take .... (word on card)." He places the word card on the board ledge. The next child draws a card and says, "I am going on a trip and I will take .... (word on card) and ....(word previously drawn)." The others take their turn.

53. Guessing Game

Grades two, three, four, and five

Each child folds a sheet of paper into four sections. In each section he draws a picture to represent the words he is thinking of. He puts the first letter of the word in each section. The other children guess the words. For example, the child draws a picture of a dinosaur and has a *p* written in the corner. The word would be prehistoric.

54. Guessing Game

Grade one

Directions:

When I say a word, think of as many words as you can that go with this word.

Example:

Milkman—The children could name bottles, milk truck, cream, eggs, etc.

55. Guessing Game

Grades one and two

Words are printed on a chart or written on the board. A child selects a word and says, "Guess which word I am thinking of." The children take turns guessing. The one who guesses correctly is *it*.

56. Guiding Words

Grades four, five, and six

Children look through their reading lesson for guiding words. Pages from newspapers and magazines may be used. The children underline one type with green, another with blue, and another with red.

a. Contrast words as *but, however, nevertheless,* and the like.
b. Reference words as *former,* the *latter,* and so on.
c. Number words as *fourth, second,* and so on.

57. Hide and Seek

Grades one and two

Three columns of words are written on the board. One child covers his eyes while another child points to a word. The first child opens his eyes and takes three guesses as to which word has been indicated. If he cannot guess, he is told which column it is in and he has another guess. If he guesses correctly, he may indicate the next word to be guessed.

58. Hide and Seek Game

Grades one, two, and three

Cards with words are hidden about the room, and the children hunt for them. The pupils receive a point for each card they find and can read correctly.

59. Homonyms

Grades four, five, and six

The children fill the blanks with the homonym that completes the sentence.

Example:

need........knead
a. Mary will .... a pencil.
b. Mother will .... the bread.

60. Hopscotch

Grades one and two

Draw a hopscotch pattern on a sheet of wrapping paper. Place a word card in each space. The child hops through the spaces, saying the words as he hops into the spaces.

61. Hunting Game

Grades one, two, three, and four

Words from the science books may be used very successfully for this. Each child draws a slip that lists things to find for the next day. If the game is to be played indoors, it may include such items as:

a. Find a piece of paper that is smaller than your hand.
b. Find a pencil as long as your thumb.

For outdoor activities, the directions could be:

a. Find a stone that is bigger than a chicken egg.
b. Find a twig that is more than two inches long.

62. If I Had a Zoo

Grades one and two

Each child selects a picture of an animal. He matches the picture with the name of the animal. He then gives one fact about the animal, as "The elephant has a long trunk."

63. I Have a Secret

Grades one, two, and three

The children are seated in front of the blackboard. The leader starts the game by writing a word that is about the secret. The other children have three guesses; if they cannot guess, the leader writes another word. This continues until someone guesses the secret. The child who guesses the secret becomes the leader.

64. I Know It

Grades one, two, and three

Two to four children can play the game. A different word is printed on each of fifty 2-by-3-inch cards. The cards are shuffled and placed in the center of the table, face down. The children take turns drawing a card and reading it. If he can read it correctly, he places it in front of him. If he does not know the word, the card is placed to the right of the center pile. The next player can say, "I know it." If he reads the word correctly, he takes the card and puts it in front of him, he also draws a card from the pile. The game continues until all fifty cards have been drawn.

65. Illustrated Words

Grades three, four, five, and six

The teacher makes charts for word lists. These charts are illustrated by the children. One chart might consist of words that mean *pretty,* such as *comely, gorgeous, beautiful;* another chart could have words used in place of *said,* as *replied, answered, requested.*

66. Indians

Grades one and two

A picture of a house, tepees, and trees is drawn. A word is printed on each tree. A path is drawn between the trees. The child moves a marker along the path and says the words on the trees as he passes them. If he succeeds in returning safely home again, his name is written on the house. If he does not know a word, he is captured by the Indians and his name is written on a tepee.

67. Ladder Game

Grades one and two

Word cards are arranged in packs of ten. A pack is given to each child and he is asked to make a ladder with them. The first card goes into the bottom slot of the chart holder. Each succeeding card goes into the next higher slot. The child may use only the words he knows. He tries to climb to the top of the ladder.

68. Learning Word Meanings

Grades two, three, and four

The children read the sentences and then write the letters to complete the words in the blanks.

a. It is the opposite of down. u....
b. We keep it in the garage. c........
c. It is something we live in. h...............

69. Letter Chains

Grades one and two

The children make words with paper chains, using letters of the alphabet which have been printed on strips of paper. This device is very good for reversals as *was* and *saw*, and the like. Entire sentences may be made this way. Two blank links are left between each word.

70. Magic Beanstalk

Grades one and two

After telling the story of Jack and the Beanstalk, a beanstalk is drawn on the chalkboard. Leaves are cut from green paper and words are printed on the leaves. These leaves are fastened to the stalk with Scotch tape. The player climbs the beanstalk by reading the leaves in the correct order. As he reads the leaf, he removes it from the stalk. Beans may be planted in a jar, and the children will enjoy seeing them sprout.

71. Mailbox Game

Grades one and two

This activity provides motivation for children who have difficulty with their words. A shoe box marked "DEAD LETTER OFFICE" is used. A 6-by-9-inch mailbox is drawn on green paper. A slit is made for the letters. On the back is pasted a small paper bag which will hold the cards. The children drop all the words they know in the mailbox. Those they do not know go into the Dead Letter Office. The children may make their individual mailboxes and drop their *letters* in these.

72. Malapropisms

Grades five and six

Sentences, using the incorrect form of a word, are prepared. The child reads the sentence orally and corrects the sentence. Example: The man's *preposition* (proposition) was not pleasing to me.

73. Matching Words

Grades one, two, three, and four

Words needed in the reading lesson are used.

Example:

After each word in the first column, write the number of the word in the second column that best describes it.

I	II
a. sharp	1. night
b. dark	2. elephant
c. huge	3. knife

74. Matching Words with Pictures

Grade one

Pictures are used to illustrate the words. These may be placed in boxes in groups of twenty, and labeled. The child matches the pictures and words. A key is provided so that he can check his work.

75. Minister's Cat

Grades three, four, five, and six

The teacher may begin by saying, "The minister's cat is an *acrobatic* cat." The next child says, "The minister's cat is an *anxious* cat." After about six words have been given using *a*, the children go on to the next letter of the alphabet, as "The minister's cat is a *bewildered* cat," and so on.

76. Mr. Webster Says

Grades four, five, and six

Three judges are appointed and the remainder of the class is divided into two teams. The leader of the first team gives a word. The first team must know the meaning of the word. The second team defines the word and gives an acceptable sentence. Words may be selected from the glossary of the textbook.

77. Multiple Choice

Grades one, two, three, four, five, and six

Sentences, using words from the reader, are prepared. The sentence is completed by selecting the best word from three or four listed words.

Example:

a. The little puppy fell into a big ....
well hole river sink
b. The little rabbit is ....
brave timid clumsy large

78. Nine Pins

Grades one, two, and three

Nine 3-inch squares are marked off on a sheet of paper and placed on the floor. Words are printed on cards which are to be placed on the squares. An empty milk carton is placed on each card on the floor. Children take turns rolling a small ball toward the milk cartons. They are to say each word that has been uncovered by the rolling ball. A point is scored for each word that is pronounced. The words are changed as needed.

79. Nouns and Adjectives

Grades four, five, and six

A chart containing twenty-five nouns such as *mountains, clouds, airplane* is prepared; and strips containing descriptive phrases such as, the fleecy white ...., snow-capped ...., are made. The phrases are distributed to the children who match them with the nouns.

80. Opposites

Grades one, two, three, four, five, and six

The children read the sentences which have been duplicated or written on the chalkboard. They are to write a word that means the opposite of the italicized word.

Example:

a. She wore a *bright* dress. ....
b. It was *cool* last night. ....

81. Pantomime

Grades one, two, three, four, five, and six

In the lower grades, the children may select cards with directions printed on them. They are to act out the word or sentence. The other children are to guess what the action is. Older children may act out occupations as artist, teacher, lawyer, and so on. They may also pantomime words such as *horrified, delighted, amused,* and the like. They may select the words from the reading assignments, or words may be printed on cards which the children select.

82. Part of What?

Grades two and three

Words found in the readers are used. This exercise may be duplicated, written on the chalkboard, or printed on 9-by-12-inch cards. If the cards are used, shoelaces may be used for lacing the matching words together.

Example:

Write the number of the object in the second column that the one in the first column matches.

branch..	1. donkey
pillow..	2. tree
tail..	3. bed

83. Parts of Speech

Grades four, five, and six

Ads in magazines may be used. The children are to underline the adjectives in red, the adverbs in green, and so on.

84. Pick a Slip

Grades one and two

Words or phrases are printed on strips of paper. The number 1, 2, 3 is printed in the upper right-hand corner of each slip. Two or more children may play the game. The children take turns picking a slip and reading it. They receive the score written on the slip.

85. Picking Apples

Grades one and two

A large tree is drawn on the chalkboard and words are printed on the apples. The children are to take turns picking the apples from the tree. A flannel board apple tree may be made, and the children may make small paper baskets to hold the fruit. Oranges, nuts, plums, cherries, bananas, and other tree fruits may be picked in the same way.

86. Playing Opposites

Grades two and three

Cards with words and their opposites are printed. The children on the first team are given one set of cards and those on the other team the opposites. A child in the first group stands and reads his card. The child in the second group, who has the opposite word, stands up, reads his card, and joins his partner.

87. Playing Partners

Grade one

Cards, using the characters in a story, as *Betty said, Tom said,* are printed. On other cardboard strips, are printed what the characters said in the reading lesson. The children find their partners.

88. Polly Parrot

Grades two and three

The first child says, "Polly Parrot wants a *cracker*." The next child adds an adjective beginning with *c* to the phrase, the next child repeats what has been said and adds another adjective, beginning with the same letter. Each adjective scores a point except the last adjective, which scores five points. Words beginning with the different letters of the alphabet are used.

89. Post Office

Grades one and two

The chartholder is filled with word cards. Each word represents a letter in the post office. The children come, one at a time, and ask, "Do you have a letter for (give word)?" When all the words have been removed from the chartholder, the children mail their new letters by putting them into the chartholder.

90. Princess and the Pirate

Grades one and two

Cards with a word on one side and a number on the other are prepared. A child is selected to be the princess and another to be the pirate. They stand on one side of the room and the other children stand in a line on the other side of the room. The princess indicates a child, and the pirate shows a card. The indicated child says the word and takes as many steps toward the princess as the reverse side of card indicates. The child coming to the princess first wins.

91. Rebus

Grade one

The children may make their names by rolling plasticine into long coils and forming the letters. The teacher may cover cardboard with plastic or waxed paper. The children make words from the rolled clay and lay them on the cardboard. (A picture may be clipped on the side of the cardboard for words which the child cannot spell.) Children in first grade enjoy this activity very much.

92. Rewriting Stories

Grades four, five, and six

The children are given a simple story which they are to rewrite, using words entirely different from those used in the story, but which have the same meaning. They may use their dictionaries.

Example:

A mouse wished he had a bushy tail like a squirrel. A grey hen, feeling sorry for him, gave him some feathers. The mouse glued the feathers on his bare tail and went away happy. He sat in a tree and curled his tail over his back. A man with a gun came along. He cried out, "One more squirrel skin and my wife will have enough for her coat."

The story rewritten:

A rodent desired that he possess an overgrown hindmost similar to a spermophiles. A darkish fowl, reflecting sympathy over the animal, decreed to him a quantity of plumage. The rat adhered the fringe of hair upon his naked appendage and scurried off felicitously. The mammal perched in a sycamore and spiraled the rear end of his body beyond the part of himself which is opposite to the front. A Homo sapiens in company of a revolver ambled progressively forward. The male shrieked forth, "A single phalanger epidermis addition and my spouse is capable of obtaining a sufficient amount of pelt to be designated to a garment worn out-of-doors over one's usual clothing."

93. Send-Away

Grades one and two

A word is written on the board while the children watch. The word is erased as soon as it is written. "What word did I send away?" This may be varied by having a great many sight words written on the board. A child may erase any word he knows.

94. Scrambles

Grades four, five, and six

Words from science or social studies may be used. The children unscramble the words.

Example:

State Capitals

a. BALYAN .... b. RCCOODN ....
b. NUTSIA .... c. SILVENHAL ....

95. Simon Says "Thumbs Up"

Grades one and two

The teacher has a pack of word cards and a pack of picture cards to correspond with them. In playing the game, she holds up a picture card and places a word card underneath it, exposing the two for just a moment. If the word is the name of the picture, the children hold their thumbs up; if not, they put their thumbs down.

96. Similarities and Opposites

Grades two, three, four, five, and six

A list of words, similar to the example below, is made. If the words mean the same, the children write *S*; if they mean the opposite, they write *O*. This is a good way to learn the meaning of the new words in the reading lesson.

Example:

a. strong ....weak
b. huge ....immense
c. delicate ....frail

97. Sound Words

Grades two, three, four, five, and six

Words from the reading lesson are used, and the exercise is duplicated or written on the chalkboard.

Example:

Match the word and the phrase

a. rumble ....distant thunder
b. patter ....falling rain
c. tinkle ....ringing of a tiny bell

98. Speed Race

Grades one and two

A racetrack is drawn on a sheet of paper. The track is marked off in squares. In each square a word that the children need help with is printed. Each child has a toy car. He follows the racetrack and pronounces the words as he pushes his car along. He is timed to see how quickly he can go around the track.

99. Spinning Wheel Game

Grades one and two

A large circle is cut from cardboard. A pointer is fastened to the center of the wheel with a paper fastener. Words are printed around the edge of the wheel. The child spins the pointer and says the word on which the pointer stops. The children take turns spinning the pointer and saying the word. If a child does not know the word, the one who says it first is credited with it.

100. Steeple Chase

Grades one and two

Phrases are printed on cards that have been folded so they will stand. These are placed on a table. The children move small figures of a horse and rider over these hurdles as they pronounce them.

101. Stoop Game

Grades one, two, and three

Words from the reading lesson are printed on cards. The cards are shown one at a time and in turn to each child. If the child does not know the word, he must stoop. If he is quick enough to read another card before the next child is able to say it, he may rise and that child must stoop. The children who do not have to stoop win the game.

102. Stop and Go

Grades one and two

Words or phrases from the reading lesson are printed on cards. STOP is printed on eight cards. These STOP cards are placed at intervals among the other cards. The first child says the words in the pack and continues until he comes to a STOP. He then counts the words he knew and marks down his score. After shuffling the cards he has just read, he places them at the bottom of the deck. The next child starts to pronounce the words until he comes to STOP or until he does not know a word.

103. Structural Analysis

Grades two and three

Words may be written on the chalkboard or may be duplicated. The children put the words in the right groupings, as *call, called, calling, calls.*

Example:

want	calls	wants
calling	wanting	wished
wanted	jumped	wish
called	wishing	jumping
wishes	jumps	call

Suffixes such as *ful, able,* and the like, may be included.

104. Surprise Box

Grades one and two

A package is wrapped attractively. Some small object, such as a peanut, or a stick of gum, is placed in the package. It is put on the reading table with a sign, "What am I?" Clues are printed on strips of paper. The children take turns reading the clues and guessing. The child who guesses correctly may have the package. The children may take turns working in committees and preparing the surprise box and clues.

105. Synonyms

Grades three, four, five, and six

Exercises similar to the example below, using words found in the reading lesson, are prepared. The children write the synonym.

A	*B*	*C*
a. Reply to a question	nasrew	(answer)
b. Alter	gechan	(change)

106. Synonyms and Antonyms

Grades three, four, five, and six

Exercises similar to the example below are prepared. Words from the reading lesson are used.

	Synonym	*Antonym*
a. courage	....	....
b. strong	....	....

107. Take Away

Grades one ad two

Word cards are placed on the chalk ledge or in a chartholder. The children may take all the cards they can pronounce correctly.

108. Target

Grades one and two

A target is made by cutting circles of different colored paper and of varying sizes. When completed it should look like a target for archery. A child is given a pack of words which he is to study. If he can pronounce each word correctly and in a given time, he scores a bull's-eye. If it takes him sixty seconds to say the words, his name is tacked in the circle next to the center ring, and so on.

109. Tick-Tack-Toe

Grades one, two, and three

This game can be used for reviewing words, number combinations, phonics, and the like. The teacher puts the words or phonics elements in the tick-tack-toe. The children play the game by making *x* and *o* in the spaces. These exercises may be duplicated for the children. In phonics, the initial blend or ending may be used and the children give a word beginning or ending like it.

110. Train Game

Grades one and two

The children are divided into two groups, each group representing a train. The words are shown to the children in turn. Any child who does not know the card shown to him is given the card. The train is not ready to go if any child on the train has a card.

111. Treasure Hunt

Grades one and two

Small objects and pictures are collected. Word cards are printed which correspond to these. The cards are arranged on the chalkboard ledge or in a chartholder. The objects and pictures are placed in a box. The child closes his eyes and draws an object or picture. He places it with the corresponding word on the chalkboard ledge.

112. Two Things to Watch

Grades one and two

Words are placed in a chartholder. A number is written on the board. The child indicated is to draw that number of cards. He receives a point for each card he is able to read correctly.

113. Using New Words

Grades two and three

"The Straw Ox," pp. 103-8, from *I Know a Story,* by Huber.

Name ....
Date ....
Score ....

Directions: Please write the correct words in the blanks.

1. The old man sat down to sharpen his .... (page 103)
2. The old man wanted the bear's fur for a .... (page 103)
3. The old man let the bear .... (page 103)
4. The bear said he would get a .... (page 103)
5. The wolf said he would get some .... (page 104)
6. The fox said he would get some .... (page 105)
7. The dog said he would get a .... (page 106)
8. The bear was there with the .... (page 107)
9. The dog was there with the .... (page 107)
10. Now the old man and the old woman have all they want to .... (page 108)

coat	cow	go	knife
goat	eat	ducks	hens

114. Using New Words

Grades four, five, and six

Children should be encouraged to use "grown-up" words that they hear on television or elsewhere. They may keep a notebook for this purpose. They may write the definitions for the words. A few words that are heard frequently are: *invisible, enthusiastic, antique, investigate, insufficient.*

115. Using Other Words for "Said"

Grades three, four, five, and six

The children rewrite sentences and substitute other words for *said.* They may substitute such words as *whispered, repeated, replied,* and the like.

116. Word Building

Grades two, three, four, five, and six

Exercises similar to the one below are duplicated, and the children try to spell as many words as possible, going from one square to another. They may move up, down, across, and diagonally.

Directions:

By moving from one square to the other, up and down, sidewise, or crosswise, see how many things you can find that you would be able to buy in a grocery store.

E	N	G	F	L	N	B	R	S	E	H	A
U	G	I	S	O	P	E	A	N	E	C	R
T	L	M	H	U	B	Y	T	D	M	D	R
S	E	K	O	R	I	U	T	A	S	P	A
A	T	G	N	A	S	N	J	E	P	L	E

117. Word Consciousness

Grades three, four, five, and six

The children keep individual notebooks for words that they find. The children place them under such categories as:

Aviation words:	jet, helicopter, propulsion
Beautiful words:	geranium, vermilion
Childish words:	naughty, kitty
Dignified words:	gentleman, revere
Emotional words:	sympathy, pity
Geographical words:	oasis, peninsula
Historical words:	colonial, knight
Humorous words:	hilarious, comical
Plain words:	man, run
Undignified words:	junk, bawl
Action words:	run, jump
Quaint words:	thou, demure

118. Word Meaning

Grades two, three, four, five, and six

This exercise is modified according to the grade and ability of the children. Words from the reading lesson are used. This work may be duplicated or written on the blackboard.

Example:

a. Atmosphere means ....
page ...., paragraph ...., line ....
b. Improbable means ....
page ...., paragraph ...., line ....

119. Word Recognition

Grades one and two

Pictures of objects from a readiness book, magazines, and so on, are used. Cut cardboard 8½ × 15 inches. (The size is optional.) A second strip 1½ inches wide but the same length as the larger piece is cut. This is fastened to the larger piece with masking tape, hinging it so it folds over the first sheet. Divisions about 1½ inches wide are made, as shown in the illustration below. Pictures are pasted to the far left. On the flap that folds over, the name of the picture is printed on the underside so the child can use it as a check on his work. Strips about 1½ × 3 inches are cut and on these are written the same words that are printed on the underside of the flap. A small pocket is placed on the outer side of the flap to hold these word strips. The child places the words on the open spaces beside each picture. He checks his work by opening the flap after he has completed his work (fig. 6.3).

120. Word Fan-Tan

Grades two and three

Fifteen sets of cards, four cards for each category (set), are printed. The categories could include *farm* words *like barn, dairy, pasture, tractor; kitchen* words *like dishwasher, sink, oven, knife.*

One card of each category is placed in one pile, and the leader is given the remaining cards. Each child draws a card. The leader shows his cards, one at a

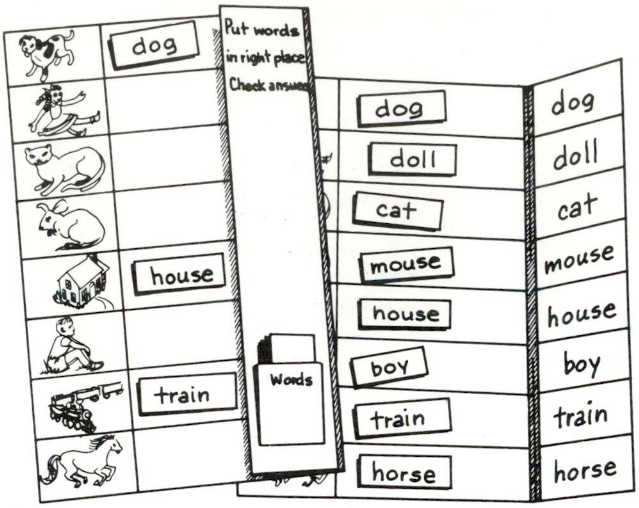

Figure 6.3 Word Recognition

time. The child whose card belongs to the same category as the one shown by the leader calls "Fan-Tan" and claims the card. Unclaimed cards go back into the pack and are shown a second time. A child has a "book" when he has the set of four cards. He places these on the table and draws another card to start another book. The child with the most cards wins.

121. Words for Stories

Grades three, four, five, and six

Word lists are printed on the board. The children are to tell what type of story the word would be found in.

Example:

magic .... dude ....
brave .... pasture ....
dwarf .... bullet ....
lasso .... rescue ....

122. Word Hunt

Grades three, four, five, and six

The teacher writes one or two new words on the chalkboard and then uses them in a sentence. The next day each child reports *when, where,* and *how* he heard or saw each new word used. The child may hear the words several times and should report on each use of it.

Example:

alternate

123. Words Ending in Silent "e"

Grades one and two

The teacher shows the children that words ending in silent *e* drop the *e* when adding *ing*. She may tell them that she will put the *e* to bed and the *ing* family moves in.

Example:

change....by adding *ing*....change to changing
bite..........by adding *ing*....bite to biting

124. Word Categories

Grades four, five, and six

Outlines similar to the following below are prepared. These may be duplicated or drawn by the children themselves. Any four- or five-letter word may be used across the top. The children fill in the blanks.

Example:

Put the words in the right category.

	B	*A*	*L*	*D*
Cities	Boston	Austin	Los Angeles	Denver
Automobiles				
Rivers				
Trees				

125. Which Is It?

Grades three, four, five, and six

Material similar to the example below may be duplicated.

Example:

Each word has two different meanings. After each word, write the phrase numbers that mean the same as the word.

a. pen ....1. where pigs are kept
b. pound ....2. something to make a cake
c. light ....3. something to write with
4. to hit something hard
5. not hard
6. a measure

126. Wordo

Grades one, two, three, four, five, and six

This may be played by two children or the entire group. Words may be duplicated on paper or cut apart and pasted on cardboard sheets that have been marked off in 1-by-½-inch rectangles. There may be spaces for twenty-five up to forty-eight words. The words should not be placed in the same position on each cardboard sheet. If the teacher wishes, she can print the words directly on the cardboard; but it is much simpler to use the duplicated words. Phrases may also be used. The players play this just like bingo. One child reads the words or phrases and the other players cover up the phrases or words with buttons or pieces of cardboard. The child who has a straight row covered says "Wordo." He then reads back the covered words. This activity may also be used for social studies, science, and so on. The children may be asked to find "a river in Asia," "a mountain in Europe," and the like.

127. Word Squares

Grades three, four, five, and six

The children may draw their own squares by following directions and using their rulers, or the teacher may prepare the material in duplicated form. Words needed in the reading lesson or in other assignments are used.

Example:

Fill in the squares.

a	b	c	d	e
b				
c				
d				
e				

a. Natives of Scotland
b. Chocolate drink
c. Sea
d. Browned bread
e. He comes at Christmas

a	b	c	d	e
b				
c				
d				
e				

a. Part of a flower
b. Rub out
c. A city in Florida
d. Tree whose leaves quiver.
e. Not standing straight

128. Word Puzzle

Grades two, three, and four

The children read the first sentence and then find the right answer in the words listed above it. They are to write it in the puzzle on the first line.

Example:

low .... arm .... cap .... dust .... band .... end .... catch .... stamp .... fall .... beat

c........... A boy wears it on his head.
l .... It is not high.
a........... Your hand is on one end of it.
e........... It is the last part.
b........... People dance when it plays music.

129. Where Will You Find It?

Directions:

There are words in the story that have meanings opposite to those of words listed here. Find the page and line. Write the word that means the opposite of each word. Read the sentence to prove that your answer is correct.

Word	*Opposite*	*Page*	*Line*
a. go before	....	....	....
b. known	....	....	....
c. friend	....	....	....

130. Word Hunt

Grades one and two

Directions:

How many times can you find *did* in your story? Use the words that the children find difficult. Stories may be duplicated and the children may draw a green line under one word, a blue circle around another, and so on.

131. Word Clues

Grades one and two

Pictorial word cards, 3 × 5 inches in size, are printed. These may be prepared in several ways.

a. Print the word on one side of the card and paste a picture of the word on the other side.
b. Print on one side of the card, "A bear is brown." On the other side of the card paste a picture of a bear with the word *bear* printed under it. Also paste a piece of brown paper on this side and print *brown* under it.
c. Paste a picture of a bear on one side and print "I am brown. I like to climb. I like honey."

132. What Is the Hidden Word?

Grades one and two

Sentences are printed on cardboard strips. One word is covered with a small card that is fastened to the strip with a paper clip. The children are asked to read the sentence and tell what they think the hidden word is.

Example:

The little bird will sing. Cover *will.*

133. Vocabulary Development

Grades one, two, three, and four

Sentences similar to the exercise below are duplicated. The material may be taken from the reading lesson, social studies, or science.

Example:

Read each sentence and the words directly below it. Draw a ring around the right words.

a. We saw these animals at the zoo.
   fox raccoon raincoat halibut
b. These are bodies of water.
   sea canals candles landscapes

134. Vocabulary Study

Grades one and two

Objects are cut from colored paper, using the color designated. These are pasted on 4-by-6-inch cards. Under the object is printed the color and the name of the object as "brown bear." All the cards are cut in half. These pieces are placed in a hose box that has been labeled, or an envelope may be used. Examples of cards are: red hen, yellow butterfly, red apple, green leaf, orange box, blue house, black car, pink flower, grey bird, etc.

135. Vocabulary Meaning

Grades four, five, and six

Words from the reading lesson similar to the example given below are prepared.

Example:

Give the meaning of the italicized words. Find them in the story.

a. *nimble* hoofs .... page 326

....

b. *previous* autumn .... page 327

....

c. beyond *pursuit* .... page 328

....

136. Vocabulary Exercise

Grades three, four, five, and six

Example:

Select the words from the given page which mean the same as the words below.

a. page 213.............................left
b. page 224.............................peak
c. page 219.............................thief

Select the word from the given page which means the opposite of the word listed below.

a. page 220.............................rough
b. page 212.............................forward
c. page 213.............................calm

137. Variation of Wordo

Grades three, four, five, and six

Cardboard sheets as for Wordo (see #126) are prepared, using homonyms, antonyms, or synonyms.

138. Word Wheel

Grades one and two

A circle eighteen inches in diameter is cut from cardboard. Holes are punched an inch in from the edge. These should be two inches apart. These are threaded with a string by going in and out of the holes. The string is tied tightly. These will be used for holding cards. Holes are punched about four inches out from the center. These will also be threaded with string to correspond to the outer threading. Cards containing words will be slipped under these strings. The children match pictures with these words and slip the pictures, which have been pasted on cards, under the outside string (fig. 6.4). Some teachers like to use clip clothespins to hold the pictures in place.

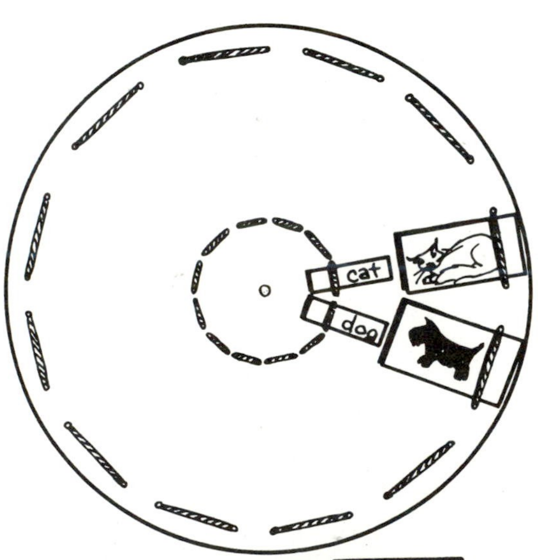

Figure 6.4 Word Wheel

139. What Do These Words Make You Think Of?

Grades two, three, four, five, and six

The words may be written on the chalkboard or on a chart. The children are asked to write about a picture which is put on the chart or the chalkboard, and words are given as clues.

Example:

A picture of two puppies is shown. What do these words make you think of?

bright	furry	sleepy	paws
friendly	friends	meal	nose
tired	wiggly	white	hair

140. Word Files

Grades one, two, three, four, five, and six

The children should be encouraged to keep word files. They should learn to alphabetize the words. In the first grade, the children may paste a picture on the back of each card to help them remember. These files may be used in many ways. The child might have the words he needs help with at the front of the file and those he knows at the back. As he learns the word, he places it back into the known-words section. The children may refer to their files for writing stories, and the like. The files can be made from boxes which may be covered with wallpaper.

141. Word Folders

Grades one, two, and three

A folder may be made for each child. There is a pocket at the bottom of each side of the folder. The children place words they will need for their reading lesson in the pocket "Words to Learn." As they master the word, they place it in the pocket "Words I Know." They review their words before the reading period (fig. 6.5).

Figure 6.5 Word Folders

142. Words We Know

Grades one and two

Two sheets of 8-by-10-inch cardboard, hinged with tape, are used to make a folder. Squares and spaces are marked off as shown below. A picture is pasted in each square. Words are printed on small strips to correspond to the picture. These strips are kept in an envelope on the back of the folder. The children are to place the words in proper sequence in the space provided for them to correspond to the pictures (see fig. 6.6). A key is provided so that the children may check their work.

143. Words to Know

Grades one and two

This activity is similar to the preceding one, only the words are printed in the column on the left-hand side, and the child places the picture cards in the squares in proper order (see fig. 6.7).

144. Matching Game

Grades one, two, and three

Forty-two pieces of construction paper are cut to card-size, 4 × 6 inches. A half inch on each piece is turned up and stapled or pasted to form a pocket at the bottom of the card. A picture is pasted on each card. A short paragraph about each picture is typed on a sheet of paper and pasted on a 3-by-3-inch square of paper. The object of the game is to match the paragraphs and the pictures (see fig. 6.8). A key should be provided for self-checking.

Directions:

Divide the picture cards among the players. These are laid face up in front of the players. The paragraph cards are placed face down in the center of the table. The children take turns drawing the paragraph cards. If the card that is drawn matches one of the picture cards he has, he places it in the pocket of that card. If it does not match, he lays it face up beside the paragraph cards. He must read his card before he can match it. The next player may select the card that has been discarded if it matches one of his cards. If it does not, he draws from the pile. Three completed sets make a book. Continue until all the cards are matched.

A child may play the game by himself, too.

Suggested paragraph:

There are six of us.
One is the mother.
We hang on Mother's tail.
We hang by our tails when we sleep.

The cards are placed in a labeled box with directions.

145. Matching

Grades one and two

Pictures from magazines and readiness books are used. An arrow is drawn from each object to the margin. The names of these objects are printed on strips of paper. The child is to place each word beside the right arrow (see fig. 6.9). These slips may be attached with paper clips. The slips may be kept for further use in an envelope pasted on the back of the picture.

146. Matching Words and Pictures

Grades one and two

A folder is made from two 8-by-10-inch pieces of cardboard which have been taped together. A picture is pasted on one side, which has each object numbered. On the opposite side may be written directions such as,

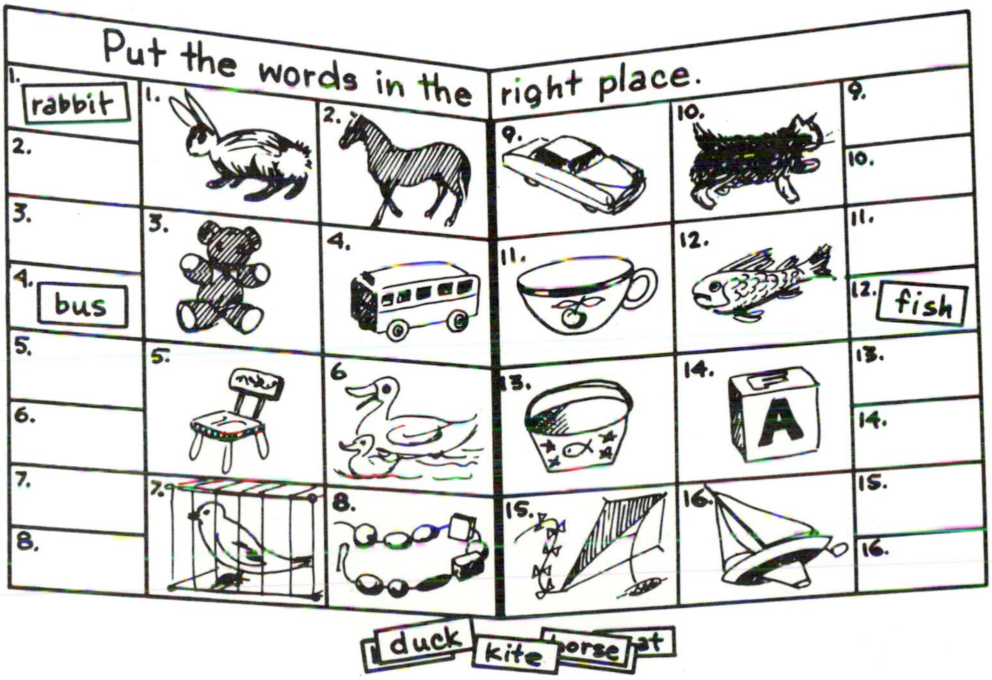

Figure 6.6 Words We Know

Figure 6.7 Words to Know

Figure 6.8 Matching Game

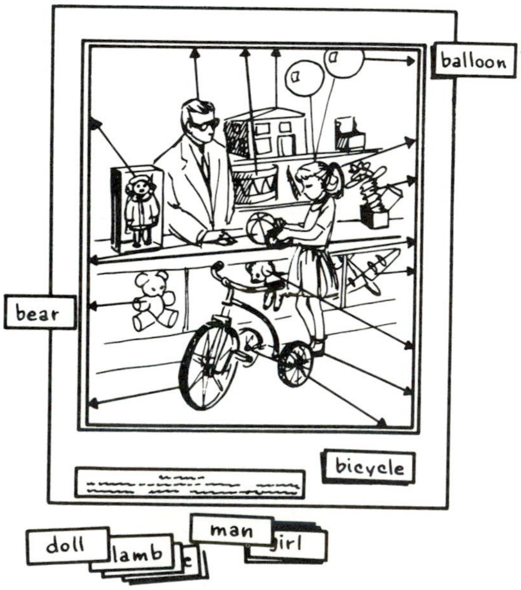

Figure 6.9 Matching

"Look at the picture. Match the numbers with the names of things." The names of the objects are printed on this side of the folder and numbers are printed on small squares of cardboard. The children place the number in the correct place. This activity may be correlated with social studies by using pictures of the home, the family, the farm, and so on (fig. 6.10).

147. What Shall We Wear?

Grades one and two

Folders as described in the preceding activities may be prepared. Pictures of the four seasons are shown. Pictures of various types of clothing are pasted on small cards which the children will place in the pockets under the seasons. For second-grade children, the printed

Figure 6.10 Matching Words and Pictures

names of clothing, as well as the pictures, may be used (fig. 6.11).

148. Ways We Travel

Grades one, two, three, and four

Folders similar to those already described may be prepared. The children are to match the words or paragraphs describing the modes of travel with the pictures, as shown in figure 6.12.

149. Find the Answer

Grades one, two, and three

Folders similar to those described previously may be made. Each child may have a folder, but the pictures are arranged differently on each folder. The children are to take the sentence strips out of the envelopes at the back of the folder and lay them face up alongside the folder. Sentence clues are printed on the master card which is to be used by the teacher or group leader. As the clues are read from the master card, each child looks for the sentence that will describe what has been read, and he then places the sentence over the picture it represents. The child who completes two rows first says, "I have it!" and reads his sentences. As he does so the children find these sentences and put them in similar sequence beside their folders. Another way this game may be played is to have two players. The card swith the sentences are placed face down. The children take turns in picking up a sentence, reading it, and placing it on the right picture.

Example of master card:

a. Find the sentence that tells what the bee says.
b. Find the sentence that tells about the animal with a long trunk.
c. Find the sentence that tells what the duck says.

Figure 6.11 What Shall We Wear?

Figure 6.12 Ways We Travel

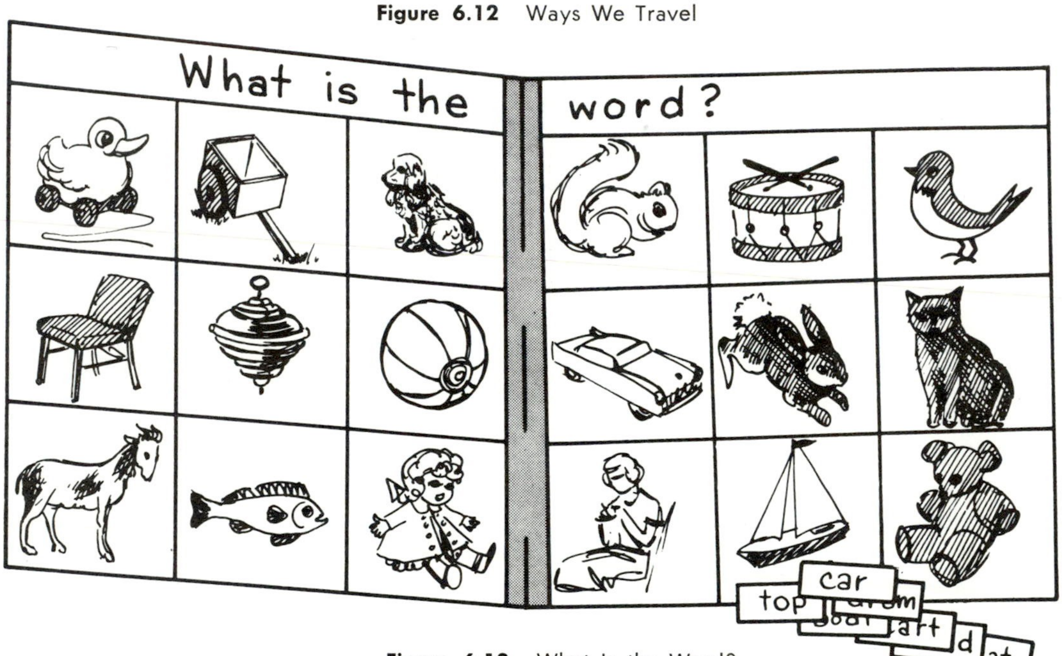

Figure 6.13 What Is the Word?

150. Five Senses

Grades one, two, three, four, five, and six

For the first grade only picture cards are used, but the children in the other grades may combine words and pictures. Pictures of things to smell, hear, feel, taste, and see are collected and pasted on small cards. Slips that stand are made and "Things we see," "Things we hear," "Things we feel," "Things we smell," and "Things we taste" are printed on them. A picture may be pasted beside each phrase for the first grade. In the other grades the children are to place the pictures and words beside the correct label. The children may help find the pictures and the words and actually prepare the game (fig. 6.14).

Figure 6.14 Five Senses

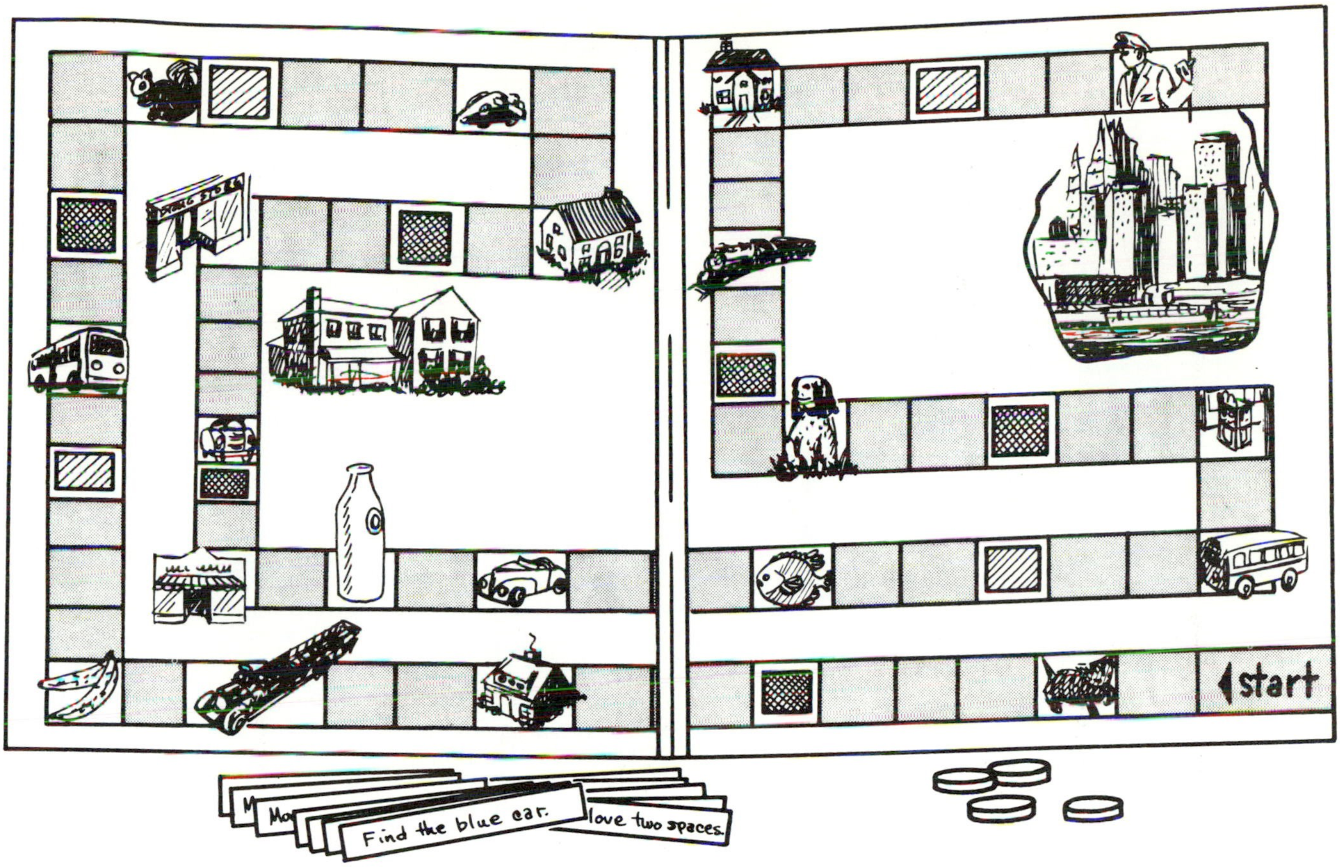

Figure 6.15 Word Travel Game

151. Word Travel Game

Grades one, two, three, and four

A game board is made similar to the example shown in figure 6.15. Any type of route may be made. In the third and fourth grades social studies and science may be used as the theme. The cards giving the directions may contain phrases or clues taken from the lesson. The players move their markers between the heavy lines from the starting point to *home* according to the directions they read from the cards. Directions are printed on the cards, which are shuffled and placed face down on the table. The children take turns drawing the cards. They read the directions before they may move. The rules may be changed according to the needs of the group.

Suggested rules are:

a. If two players land on the same space, the first must move back five spaces.
b. Green is the safety zone. The player need not move back if he is on one.
c. If the directions tell the player to go a space over ten points back, he need only go back ten spaces.

Suggested sentences are:

a. You are lost. Ask the traffic officer to help you.
b. Help the fireman put the hose onto the fireplug.
c. Go to the house with the red roof that stands on the corner.
d. Move four spaces.
e. Move back two spaces.
f. Go directly to ....

This game may be utilized in the learning of geography, history, and history dates.

Example:

Place dates in the square, such as 1492. The child draws a slip "Move to the date Columbus came to America," and the like.

Synonyms, antonyms, homonyms, roots, prefixes, and so on, may be used.

152. Lacing Activities

Grade one

Cards with pictures on one side and short sentences or paragraphs on the other may be prepared. The children lace the matching items with shoelaces or plastic cord (see fig. 6.16).

153. Learning to Remember

Grades one, two, three, four, five, and six

Cards with a picture at the top and a flap at the lower half of the page may be prepared. On the top of the flap may be printed the directions such as:

How well do you remember?

Look carefully at the picture. Then turn the flap up and follow the directions.

Figure 6.16 Lacing Activities

When the flap is folded back, it should cover the picture. Directions such as these are printed on the inside of the flap:

Please Do Not Look Back at the Picture

Answer *yes* or *no* to the questions. ....

a. A boy was cleaning an eraser out of a window.
b. A little girl fell off the teeter-totter.
c. The teacher was not on the playground.

About ten questions with the key may be given. For the lower grades, the exercises should be quite simple and only pictures with few details should be used (see fig. 6.17).

154. Stump the Experts

Grades four, five, and six

For differentiated reading groups, the children are divided into three sections. The lowest group may be the judges. The second group may find words for the first group to define. They may make up questions which the first group will answer. The children who make up the questions should tell the other groups where the questions will come from so that they may study for the panel.

155. Preprimer Bingo

Preprimer level

The bingo reading activity has been developed from the reading vocabulary taught to the children. It is

Figure 6.17 Learning to Remember

introduced immediately after the completion of the first preprimer and continued throughout the primary grades. It is used for reading as well as phonics, number work, and color recognition.

Three different sets of bingo reading cards are made from each preprimer and each unit in the primer and the other graded reading books.

The aim of the game is to have the child calling *Bingo* reread the words correctly to win the game or a point. A child who is unable to reread the word correctly does not win the game. The teacher notices the words and makes a notation next to the child's name for additional help.

Proper directions must be given the children as to how bingo is won. At first bingo is won horizontally only, then vertically only, then both are combined at a later period. Then the crisscross bingo is introduced after all understand the different ways of winning bingo.

To win bingo, a child must say the "Bingo Comes" word. For example, the child says, "I have Bingo Comes. My bingo is under the letter *C* or the letter the *bingo* is under." He then reads his words by reading the letter, as "under *C*, Spot, under *O*, jump," and so on. A child reading all words correctly wins a point or a game. A child winning five points or games is appointed captain of his group. Each group consists of five children. The child remains the captain until another child wins five points.

This game is played as a vocabulary check and seat group work. It is also excellent for rainy-day sessions (see fig. 6.15).

—by Stella Marie Nadeau

c	o	m	e	s
Tim	and	oh	look	see
down	Puff	up	Sally	Jump
funny	Dick		come	Jane
Run	Go	Tim	run	funny
Sally	Look	go	Spot	and

c	o	m	e	s
and	up	go	Jump	Dick
Tim	Sally	Jane	Run	Spot
oh	run		come	Tim
look	and	Puff	Jane	come
see	funny	and	Sally	oh

w	o	r	k	s
sees	my	red	big	play
me	want	two	mother	one
yellow	for		I	little
is	father	it	can	to
said	make	something	the	blue

c	o	m	e	s
see	oh	look	and	Tim
up	Sally	down	funny	See
come	And		Dick	Run
Jane	Down	run	Jump	Puff
jump	Look	Spot	Up	Go

Figure 6.18 Preprimer Bingo

PHONICS

While phonics can be a wonderful aid in learning to read, there must be one word of caution; not all words follow the rules. However, the wise teacher and the alert pupil will recognize this, and the knowledge of phonics then can be a great assistance in learning to read well and independently.

By *phonics* we mean the study of sounds as related to reading, and by *phonetics* we mean the science of speech sounds. Every basic reading series in the schools today devotes time to phonics. This process is usually referred to as *word analysis*. Phonics can help the child sound out a word, but it does not necessarily mean that it will give him the meaning of the word.

I. DEFINITIONS

1. Phonetics—Science of speech sounds
2. Phonics—Study of sounds as related to reading and enunciation.
3. Phonetic word—a word in which every letter represents a particular sound, like *run, sit, did.*
4. Phonograms—Word families like *run, fun, sun, gun*
5. Blend—Two or three letters whose sounds are both pronounced, like *bl, gr, st.*
6. Initial blend—The blend that begins the word.
7. Final blend—The blend that is at the end of the word.
8. Digraph—Two consonants or vowels that represent a single speech sound, as *ph, oa, ea.*
9. Diphthong—The slurring of two letters, as *oi, oy, ou* and *ow*. Some consonants also give the slurring effect.
10. Initial consonant—Single first consonant of the word, as *c* in *cat.*
11. Final consonant—Single consonant at the end of word, as *t* in *cat.*
12. Medial sound—Vowel or consonant sound in the middle of the words.

II. AIMS

1. Phonics provide the child with a tool that will help him attack unfamiliar words encountered in reading, but it will not give him the meaning of the word unless he can get that from context of the sentence.
2. Phonics can teach the child to associate the visual symbols with sounds known to him in oral-aural forms.
3. Phonics are a means to an end but not an end in themselves.
4. A wise teacher cannot depend upon phonics alone to unlock all new words that occur in a child's reading program.
5. Phonetic instruction should be a part of effective word analysis.

III. TEACHING PROCEDURES

1. The children should be shown how to use several methods of attack in word analysis. These are:
   a. Looking at the beginning of the word to see if it begins the same as some word already known.
   b. Looking at the ending of the word to see if it ends like a word already known.
   c. Looking at the ending of the word to see if it has a rhyming end similar to an already-known element.
   d. Looking at the word to see if a base word is recognizable, as *look* in looking.
2. No one method of attack is suitable for every word.
3. There are about forty-three separate and distinct phonic sound units in the general American speech. Certain symbols represent more than one sound.
4. Children should receive phonic training only when needed. A quick-learning child may not need much help in phonics.
5. During the reading class, if a child does not know a word, tell him quickly and later show him how to analyze it.
6. In all phonetic work, it is important to use words which have meaning, rather than using nonsense syllables.
7. Call the letters by their alphabetical names, not the sound. "This is *a* and it sounds like ...."
8. Some children learn to read without phonics, but it is advisable to give the children a working knowledge of them to use.
9. *Never drill* for the sake of drill alone.
10. Phonics cannot be done in chorus.
11. Five minutes a day for phonics should be sufficient.
12. Avoid distorting the sounds. Never add *uh* after the consonants, as *puh-an* for pan.
13. Phonics can produce natural articulation and assist enunciation and pronunciation if taught correctly.
14. Strive for intrinsic motivation.

In the first grade, the teacher begins her phonic training with ear training. It is only after the child becomes aware of the way words begin and end, and after he has a sight vocabulary of about 175 words, that she begins visual work in phonics. The children themselves notice that words begin or end the same, and it is at that time that the teacher introduces the printed words in phonics.

Initial Sounds

CONSONANTS		BLENDS		
b	n	bl	pr	spr
c	p	br	qu	squ
d	r	ch	sc	st
f	s	cl	sch	str
g	t	cr	scr	sw
h	v	dr	sh	th
j	w	fl	sk	thr
k	x	fr	sl	tr
l	z	gl	sm	tw
m		gr	sn	wh
		kn	sp	wr
		pl	spl	

Ending Sounds

ab	ape	ed	ift	oam	or	ub
ace	ar	ee	ig	oan	ord	ube
ack	are	eed	ight	oap	ore	uck
act	ark	eek	ike	oar	ork	uct
ad	arm	eel	ile	oat	orm	ud
ade	arn	eem	ilk	ob	orn	ude
ag	arp	een	ill	obe	ort	ug
age	art	eep	ilt	ock	ose	uke
aid	ash	eer	im	od	oss	ule
ail	ask	eet	imp	ode	ost	ulk
ain	ast	eg	in	oe	ot	ull
air	at	ell	ind	og	ote	um
ait	atch	em	ine	oil	other	umb
ake	ate	en	ing	oin	ound	ume
ald	aul	end	ink	oke	ouse	ump
ale	aw	ent	ip	old	out	un
alf	awl	ep	ipe	ole	ow	unch
alk	awn	er	ir	olk	owl	und
all	ay	es	ire	oll	own	une
am	each	est	irk	om	ox	ung
ame	ead	et	irt	omb	oy	unt
amp	eaf	ew	ise	ome	ood	up
an	eak	ib	ish	omp	ook	ur
ance	eal	ice	ist	on	ool	urn
and	eam	ick	it	ond	oom	us
ane	ean	id	itch	one	oon	use
ang	eap	ide	ite	ong	oop	uss
ank	ear	ie	oad	onk	oor	ust
ant	eat	ife	oak	op	oose	ut
ap	eb	iff	oal	ope	oot	ute

Figure 6.19 Sounds

IV. SUGGESTIONS FOR READINESS

1. Listening to Records

Play records that include rhythms, stories, poems, and songs. Encourage the child to retell parts of the story, to listen for certain parts, to tell what he has heard, and to keep time to the music. He may clap, bounce a ball, or skip to the music.

2. Listening to Sounds

Make a 2-by-3-foot screen by cutting the sides from a large cardboard box. The purpose of this screen is to hide what you are doing so the child will listen for the sounds and can guess what he has heard. The screen may be placed on a table or on the floor between you. A few suggestions for sounds are given, but you will find many other interesting sounds that you can use.

a. Show a piece of paper toweling and a piece of heavy typing paper. Tell the child that you will crush one of the sheets and he is to guess which one it is. Use other types of paper or materials in the same way.
b. Use a pencil and a fork. Show them to the child. He is to guess which one you are using when you tap on the table or the floor. Use other objects in the same way.
c. Use a fork or other object and tap a rhythmic pattern on the table or floor. It should be very, very simple at first, just two or three taps. Let the child repeat the pattern. Then let him tap and have you repeat what he tapped. He is to listen to see if you have it right.
d. Show the child a piece of wood and a tin can. Then tap on either one, and he is to tell you which one you tapped. Use other objects.
e. Use soft-toned bells. Let him guess which of the two bells you have rung. You may wish to have him tell you if it is a high or low tone. If there is a piano in the school, many games can be played by listening to high or low tones, or telling if tones are the same.
f. Show the child buttons or pennies which you will drop on a hard surface. He is to tell you if you have dropped one, two, or many. Then, give the child some buttons or pennies. He is to drop the same number that you have dropped.
g. Show a button or a penny. Drop one and the child is to tell you which one you dropped. Use other objects in the same way.
h. Use kitchen equipment such as an egg beater, or a can opener.
i. Tear paper, cloth, and like objects.
j. Bounce a ball and have the child imitate the rhythm.
k. Tap on an empty, half-full and full glass.
l. Echo game: Call out in any intonation you choose. The child is to repeat it. Then let him make intonations and have him listen to see if you or another child can imitate each.
m. Nursery rhymes: Familiarize the child with nursery rhymes. Ask him to listen while you say a part of the rhyme; then he is to add the word you omitted.
n. Picures: Cut pictures from magazines and mount them on cardboard. The child looks at the picture for a minute and then says as many words as he can that begin the same as the picture. Example: The child has a picture of a cat. He might say, for example, *call, come, cab, car, cabbage.*

3. I Am Thinking of a Word

Any words may be used but a few suggestions are given below. Make up any story you wish. Be sure the child knows what the word *rhyme* means. Develop word concepts and do not accept nonsense syllables.

a. I am thinking of a word that rhymes with *bake*. It is something good to eat. Can you think of some other words that rhyme with *bake?*
b. I am thinking of a word that rhymes with *mouse*. We live in it. Ask for other words for each word that follows.
c. I am thinking of a word that rhymes with *spool*. Jerry goes there.
d. I am thinking of a word that rhymes with *bag*. It is red, white, and blue.
e. I am thinking of a word that rhymes with *mile*. It is something you do when you are pleased.
f. I am thinking of a word that rhymes with *hand*. You can play in it.
g. I am thinking of a word that rhymes with *moon*. You eat with it.
h. I am thinking of a word that rhymes with *pick*. It is small and says, "Peep, peep."
i. I am thinking of a word that rhymes with *feed*. You can plant it.
j. I am thinking of a word that rhymes with *goat*. You can wear it.
k. I am thinking of a word that rhymes with *block*. It tells time.
l. I am thinking of a word that rhymes with *how*. It gives milk.
m. I am thinking of a word that rhymes with *throw*. It says "Caw-caw."
n. I am thinking of a word that rhymes with *rain*. It says "Toot-toot."
o. I am thinking of a word that rhymes with *those*. It is beautiful and has a sweet smell.

Other words to use are listed below. You will be able to make up your own clues for these.

treat-sweet	dish-fish	play-clay	can-ran
game-came	red-bed	bean-green	hole-roll
hook-book	gate-skate	cat-hat	toad-road
log-dog	wear-bear	boot-toot	tall-ball
nest-best	tie-pie	town-clown	hop-stop
floor-door	tail-pail	pig-big	same-came
right-night	light-kite	duck-truck	chair-hair
three-tree	grass-glass	pen-hen	—and so on.
bell-tell	spin-win	blue-glue	

4. Initial Sounds

Make up stories about animals and familiar objects using the initial sound. For example: Mary had a little gray *kitten*. The little kitten liked milk, and it liked to play with Mary. Can you think of a word that begins like *kitten?* Clues may be given. Ask for other words. If the child does not have a concept of the meaning of the word, help him get the right concept. Below are listed initial sounds, with suggested words.

b-baby, c-cat, d-dog, f-fairy, g-goat, h-hat, j-jam, k-kitten, l-lamb, m-mouse, n-nut, p-pear, r-rabbit, s-sugar, t-turtle, w-wagon, v-vase.

The initial blends may also be used. They are listed below.

ch-chair, br-brown, bl-black, cr-crib, cl-clown, dr-drum, fl-flag, fr-frog, pl-plant, sl-sled, sh-shower, sc-school, tr-train.

5. Packing My Bag

Explain the game to the children. You will name as many things as you can that begin with the same sound as the place you are pretending to visit. Use places that are familiar to the children, such as towns and cities, that he knows. Every time the player gives a correct word, he may take a button for his pile. The one who gets the most buttons wins. Start the game by saying, "I am going to California. I will take a cat." The child will say, "I am going to California. I will take a car," and so on.

6. Surprise Box

Place in a box small objects such as miniature toys, button, ruler, pencil, shell, marble, bead, spool, scissors. The child reaches into the box and pulls out an object. He names the object and then gives another word that begins with the same sound. Continue until all the objects are out. Change the objects in the box from time to time.

7. Mum Game

"We call this *Mum Game* because no one talks. I will whisper the name of something I can see right now. Watch my lips carefully and see if you can guess what I said." Let the child then whisper a word and have you guess.

V. SUGGESTIONS FOR FIRST GRADE

The materials and games suggested for the readiness period should be used if a child has not had this step in training previously.

It is urged that the parents keep in touch with the teacher at all times so that they will know what skills the child has developed in school. Most teachers appreciate having the parents help in the home provided that they follow the correct procedures.

The child must have a sight vocabulary of at least fifty words before he is able to work with the printed symbols in phonics. Usually the child notices that some words begin the same, and the teacher takes this opportunity to introduce him to the printed aspect of phonics. However if, after enough time has elapsed, the child still is unaware of the similarity, the teacher proceeds anyway. The child may have said "*mother* and *my* are alike." The teacher then puts the letter *m* on the blackboard. She asks the group to listen while she says the words. She asks, "Did you notice anything about these words?" The children will say, "Yes, they begin alike." The teacher then has them look at the words. "Do you see anything that looks the same in all these words?" The children will reply, "Yes, they all have the same beginning letter." The teacher then asks the children to think of other words that begin with this letter. She prints the words on the blackboard, and the children discuss them. She asks, "Did you notice anything that is the same about these words?" "Pronounce the words." "Now look in your book and see how many other words you can find that begin like these words."

In the first grade, present the single consonants first, and the double consonants only as needed. The short vowel sounds only are presented.

Games and Activities

1. Finding Initial Consonants

Stories containing many words that have the initial consonant that is being learned are duplicated and given to the children. The children should be able to read the story and then they are to circle all the words that begin with a designated consonant. Later endings may be used in the same way. After the children have mastered these two steps, they are asked to underline the designated initial consonant with a green pencil and the ending with a red pencil.

2. Rhyming Words

The children are to look at pairs of words and to put a line under the part that is the same.

Example:

house	swing	cake	tree	fun	game
mouse	thing	make	bee	gun	same

3. Rhyming Words

The children are to draw a red circle around the pairs of words that rhyme and a blue circle around those that do not rhyme.

Example:

take	far	make	fish	gone	will
make	farm	take	dish	done	wall

4. Picture Sorting

Small pictures are pasted on 3-by-3-inch squares of cardboard. The children are asked to sort the pictures according to initial consonants, and then according to rhymes. After they can do this, printed words that rhyme are included.

5. Finding Partners

Cards with initial blends and others with word endings are distributed among the children. The children are to find their partners and say, "We made .... with our cards." Sometimes more than one initial consonant will fit the ending. The teacher asks if there is anyone else who can help Mary make a word.

6. Throwing the Ball

A child throws a ball and says a word. The child catching the ball says another word that rhymes with it. Initial blends may also be used in a similar way.

7. Five Words

The teacher says, "Listen while I say five words . . . black, blue, place, blur, blot." Place the words, which have been printed on slips, in a wall-pocket chart. The children remove the word that does not begin the same. Endings may be used in the same manner. The children may play this game in groups of two or three.

8. Words that Rhyme

Four rhyming words are written in a column. The children are asked to write the words that have been written in columns of fours on the chalkboard. They are to write other rhyming words for each group. They may select the words, or the teacher may give the words they are to use.

9. Beanbag

Squares are marked off on a piece of wrapping paper. Each square has an initial consonant printed on it. The child is to throw his beanbag into a square and give as many words as he can that begin the same. He may be awarded a point for each word. A time limit should be set for giving words. Rhyming words may be used in a similar manner.

10. Chart and Blackboard Stories

Short stories are written on the blackboard or on a chart, using the initial consonant that is being learned as follows:

Example:

Mary s........... on the chair. She s........... a little s........... and so on.

The children read the story and put in the correct words.

11. Dart Game

A target is made from cardboard and initial consonants are printed in the squares or circles. The child throws a rubber dart and gives a word that begins with the consonant that he hits. Endings may also be used.

12. Bird, Beast, or Fish

Each child is given a letter of the alphabet. In turn the children give the name of a bird, beast, or fish whose beginning sound is the one they have been given. A child may ask another child to give the classification of bird, beast, or fish.

13. Making Words

Balls or squares are made as shown in figure 6.20. The ending is written on the balls, and a strip of paper containing the initial consonants is pulled through the opening as shown in the illustration.

14. Pictorial Rhyming Words for Phonics Games

tack....sack....track....black	pig....fig
rake....cake	crib....bib
car....star	ring....swing....king
ball....shawl	chick....brick....stick

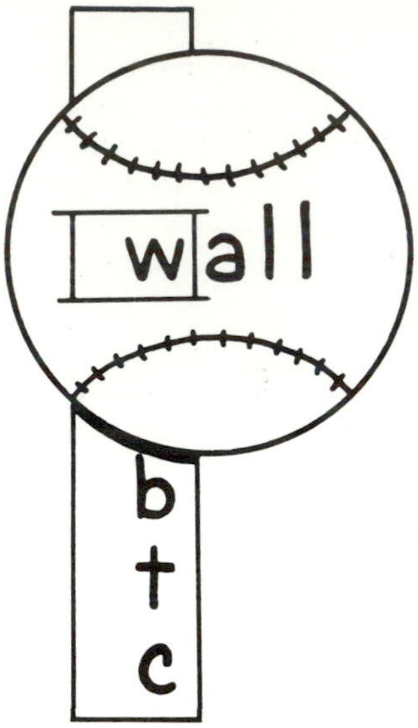

Figure 6.20 Making Words

cart....heart
hand....sand....band
pan....fan....can....man
stamp....lamp
cat....hat....bat....mat....rat
pail....tail....whale....snail
plane....train....cane....rain
skate....plate....gate
tray....clay....play
flag....bag
lamb....clam
saw....claw....paw
spade....braid
glass....grass
leaf—chief (Indian)
bead....seed
key....tree....pea....bee....three
beef....feet....seat....wheat
egg....leg....peg
nest....vest
bean....green
bed..sled..red..head..bread
pear....bear....chair....hair
wheel....seal
shell....bell....well
hen....pen....ten
mice....rice....slice
hill....pill....frill
ship....clip
chicks....six....sticks
tie....pie....fly
tire....fire
kittens....mittens
fish....dish
school....spool
mouse....house
socks....box....fox
book....hook
cow....plow....bough
rose....nose....hose....toes
door....floor....core (apple)
shoe....blue
clown....brown....town
owl....towel
coat....boat....goat
clock....block....sock
dog....frog....log
fork....cork
moon....spoon
cone....bone
crow....snow
toad....road
coal....pole
suit....boot
bug....rug
drum....plum
sun....gun....bun

VI. SUGGESTIONS FOR SECOND AND THIRD GRADE

A. Ear Training

Some children may need some auditory training, and the suggestions given previously may be used.

B. Visual Training

The children should be given a review of the materials covered in the first grade. After they have a good understanding of these phonetic elements, they may continue with the suggestions given below.

1. Long and Short Vowel Sounds

The word *dim* is written on the chalkboard and the children are asked to pronounce the word. An *e* is added to *dim* and the children are asked to pronounce the new word. This procedure is repeated with several other words and the children are asked to tell what they have noticed about these words. They will see that when an *e* has been added, the *i* has a long sound. The same procedure is followed for the remaining vowels. After the children have learned that a vowel followed by a consonant and a final *e* makes the first vowels long, the word *met* is written on the chalkboard. The words *meet* and *meat* are written, and the children are asked to pronounce these. Other words with double vowels are written. The children will be able to explain that when two vowels are together, the first is long and the second is silent. They may wish to remember the rhyme, "When two vowels go walking, the first one does the talking." The children are told that a single vowel is short in two-, three-, or four-letter words, when the vowels comes at the beginning or in the middle of the word, as *rang, pig, end.* Exercises are prepared in which the children are to cross out all the words with a long *i* sound, and they are to underline all the words with a short *i* sound.

Example: mice sit nine think tie white, and so on.
The other vowels are used in a similar manner.

Games and Activities

1. Change the Vowel to Make a New Word

Grades one and two

Words are duplicated or written on the chalkboard. Words that can be altered by changing the vowel are used.

Example:

Change the vowel and make a new word.

want	came	wish	fan	some	at
(went)	(come)	(wash)	(fun)	(same)	(it)

2. Add Another Vowel to Make a New Word

Grades two and three

The words may be duplicated or written on the chalkboard. Words that can be changed by adding another vowel are used.

Example:

Add another vowel and make a new word.

mad	led	dim	hat	at	din
(made)	(lead)	(dime)	(hate)	(ate)	(dine)

3. Quiz Bee

Grades four and five

A chart showing suffixes and prefixes is made and discussed with the children. Words whose meaning can be changed by adding prefixes and suffixes are written on slips of paper. Each child draws a designated number of slips and makes as many words as possible, using prefixes and suffixes.

Example:

trust—distrust, trusting, untrustworthy, trusted, and so on.

4. Find Us by Sounds

Grades one, two, three, and four

A folder is made similar to the illustration below. About fifty 2-by-3-inch cards, with directions for the moves, are printed. Two to four children may play the game; the object is to move the buttons between the heavy lines or path as directed by the cards, giving the moves to be made. The game may utilize initial blends, by having pictures of objects that begin with these sounds; or rhyming words may be used (fig. 6.18).

Directions:

a. Place the cards with the directions for the moves on the table, face down.
b. Children take turns drawing a card, reading the directions, and moving as indicated on the end.
c. The child must give the rhyming word of each picture he passes; if his directions designate to pass any of them or if the blends are used, he must give a word beginning like the picture he passes.
d. When the directions designate a picture he has already passed, he only moves back five spaces.
e. If two players should stop in the same space, the first one to occupy the space goes back ten spaces.

Directions for Pictures With Rhyming Words

a. Move one space ....make ten cards
b. Move two spaces ....make ten cards
c. Move back one space ....make four cards
d. Move to something that rhymes with *tie.*
e. Move to something that rhymes with *now.*
f. I rhyme with *Indian chief.*
g. Find a picture that rhymes with *duck.*
h. Move to something that rhymes with *fun.*
i. Move to something that rhymes with *goat.*
j. This rhymes with *chair.*
k. This rhymes with *dog.*
l. Move one space in front of something that rhymes with *coat.* It sails.
m. Move to something that rhymes with *make*—and so on.

Directions for Pictures Using Initial Consonants and Consonant Blends

a. Move to something that begins like *d*uck.
b. Move to something that begins like *bl*ue—and so on. (See figure 6.21.)

5. Pinwheel for Saying the wh Words

Grades one and two

The children make paper pinwheels as shown in figure 6.22. These pinwheels may be fastened to a pencil or a small stick. The child turns the wheel by saying words

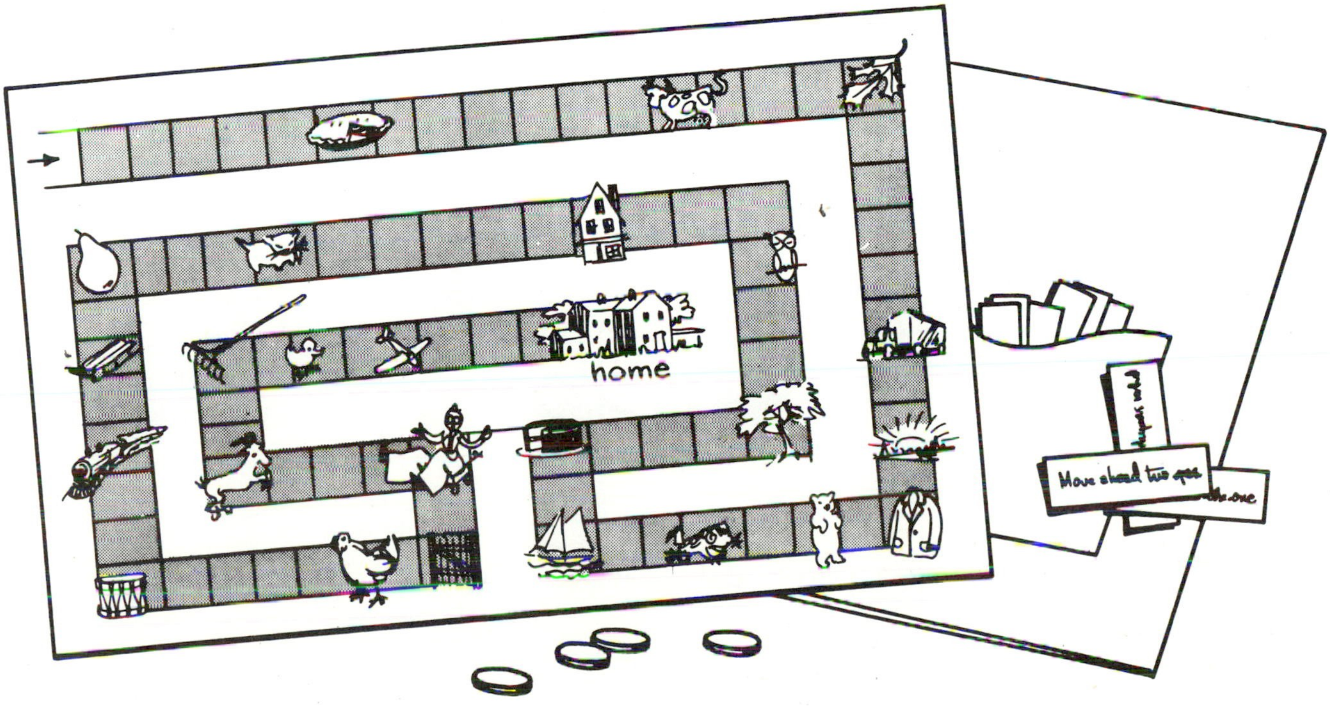

Figure 6.21 Find Us By Sound

which begin with *wh*. If he does not pronounce them correctly, the wheel will not turn.

Words beginning with *wh*:

when	whole	white	while	whistle	whisper
whale	where	whom	wheat	whirl	whose
what	who	why	which	whir	

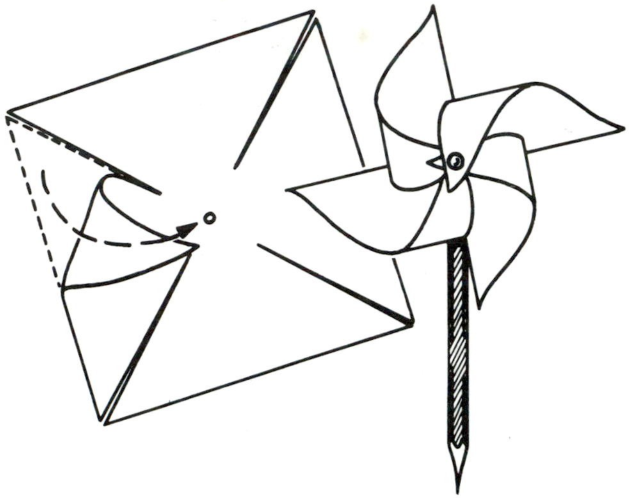

Figure 6.22 Pinwheel for Words

6. Words that Rhyme

Grades one, two, and three

Accordion folders with a train inside are made as shown in figure 6.23. Cards with word endings are made and placed in an envelope at the back of the folder. The children place these cards with the endings in the pockets under the train. They then look in their readers for words that end the same, or they may write any words they can recall that rhyme with the endings in the pockets. The children print the words and place them in the proper place in the opening on top of the engine and the cars. The children may take turns reading the words. A number value may be given to each car, and the children add up their scores at the end of a designated length of time.

7. Carnival Game

Grades one, two, and three

Folders similar to the illustration (fig. 6.24) may be made. This activity may be used for initial blends or for rhyming words and is played very much like the preceding game. For learning the initial blend, an initial blend is placed on each pocket. The children are to find words that begin with the same blend and write them on slips of paper. These slips are placed in the correct pockets. The teacher may duplicate words which the children can cut into strips and place in the right pocket.

—By Betty Rucker

8. Initial, Medial, or Final Sounds

This game can be played in the latter half of the first grade, and in the second and third grades. In all three grades only sounds that the children know are used. A list of eight words is given for each sound, but it is suggested that the teacher look at the word list in her reader and utilize those words also.

Directions: "Listen while I pronounce a word. I will ask you to listen for a certain sound and you are to think where the sound is in the word. Is it at the beginning, in the middle, or at the end? Will you listen for the *t* sound in this word *top*? Was the *t* at the end, the middle, or the beginning? Yes, it was at the beginning. Now place a marker at the beginning of the first line. (You may wish to illustrate these positions on the chalkboard.) Now listen again for the *t* sound and tell me where you hear it, *cat*. Now place

Figure 6.23 Words That Rhyme

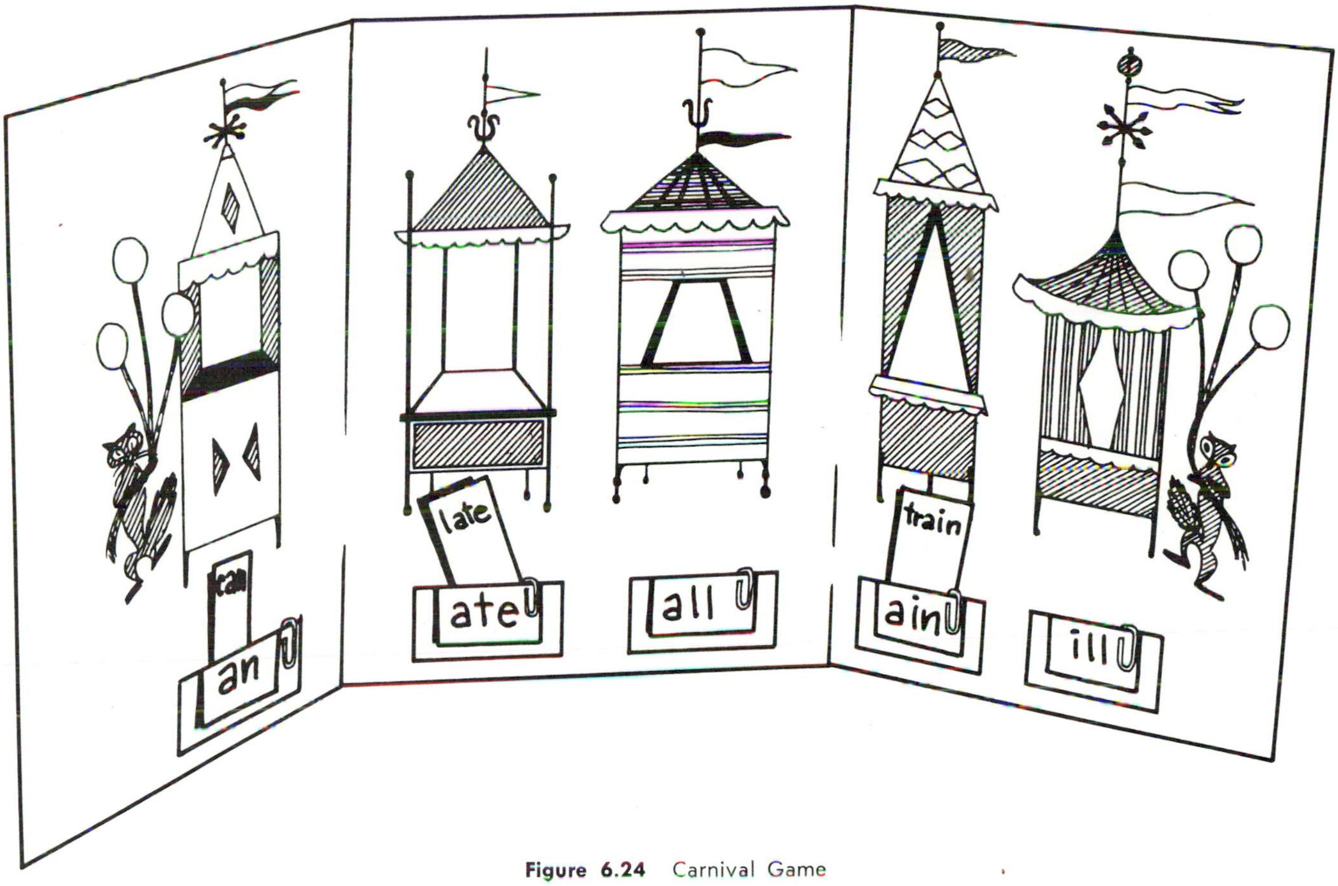

Figure 6.24 Carnival Game

your marker in the right place on the second line. Where did you place your marker, Jane? Now listen again—*kitten*. Put your marker in the right place on the third line. Where did you put your marker this time? Sometimes you will hear the sound twice.

"We are ready to play our game now. You have your card and your markers ready. Listen carefully while I say the word and then place the marker in the right place."

Initial, Medial, or Final Sound?

I.	II.
1.	1. ....
2.	2. ....
3.	3. ....
4.	4. ....
5.	5. ....
6.	6. ....
7.	7. ....
8.	8. ....

III.	IV.
1.	1. ....
2.	2. ....
3.	3. ....
4.	4. ....
5.	5. ....
6.	6. ....
7.	7. ....
8.	8. ....

After all the words have been pronounced, one child reads back the placement of the markers while all the children check their work. The children should contribute words for the game, too.

List of Words

t	*d*	*f*	*b*
1. winter	1. down	1. find	1. nimble
2. tumble	2. send	2. ruffle	2. bend
3. little	3. second	3. fluff	3. rob
4. went	4. fiddle	4. friend	4. Bobby
5. town	5. inside	5. stuff	5. pebble
6. kitten	6. double	6. muffle	6. crib
7. sit	7. under	7. filling	7. bread
8. tip	8. found	8. flew	8. able

p	*g*	*l*	*m*
1. pepper	1. pig	1. little	1. mouse
2. peep	2. get	2. while	2. mumble
3. jump	3. goose	3. light	3. drum
4. supper	4. giggle	4. lilies	4. mine
5. pump	5. dog	5. squeal	5. stumble
6. pluck	6. begin	6. leaf	6. clump
7. clipper	7. good	7. million	7. mama
8. crumple	8. beggar	8. lull	8. loom

n	*r*	*w*	*v*
1. dinner	1. rest	1. wonder	1. violet
2. win	2. river	2. wish	2. velvet
3. single	3. ever	3. slower	3. vase
4. never	4. mirror	4. will	4. salve

5. nine	5. remember	5. willow	5. vain
6. need	6. murmur	6. rewind	6. even
7. enter	7. runner	7. reward	7. woven
8. common	8. careful	8. winter	8. vowels

s	*sh*	*Long e*	*Long a*
1. send	1. shuffle	1. feet	1. tray
2. toss	2. wish	2. tree	2. ate
3. seven	3. shut	3. even	3. station
4. lesson	4. shovel	4. teepee	4. train
5. sings	5. fishes	5. eaten	5. able
6. season	6. crush	6. teeter	6. repay
7. seen	7. cushion	7. screen	7. complain
8. apples	8. shoes	8. evening	8. staying

Short a	*Short e*	*Long i*	*Short i*
1. apple	1. set	1. white	1. into
2. rat	2. ever	2. nine	2. kitchen
3. rat-a-tat-tat	3. ended	3. pie	3. sitting
4. another	4. went	4. bicycle	4. little
5. platter	5. elephant	5. idea	5. inside
6. flatter	6. seven	6. ice	6. riddle
7. afternoon	7. ten	7. inside	7. tip
8. added	8. egg	8. timing	8. until

Long o	*Short o*	*Long u*	*Short u*
1. over	1. top	1. cube	1. until
2. toe	2. come	2. due	2. sun
3. stolen	3. block	3. cucumber	3. under
4. open	4. October	4. unite	4. tumble
5. coal	5. bonbon	5. use	5. button
6. oatmeal	6. stop	6. rule	6. cutting
7. coconut	7. tiptop	7. useless	7. supper
8. cone	8. cock-a-doodle-doo	8. flute	8. crumble

ow and *ou sounds*	*th*
1. outside	1. mother
2. cow	2. then
3. town	3. with
4. our	4. another
5. powwow	5. thought
6. spout	6. farther
7. clown	7. they
8. hound	8. brother

9. Word-Building Game

Each holder may be placed in an envelope and should include the following 1½-by-4-inch cards:

1....a	1....j	3....t
1....b	1....k	1....u
1....c	3....l	1....v
1....d	1....m	1....w
3....e	2....n	1....x
1....f	2....o	1....y
1....g	2....p	1....z
1....h	2....r	
1....i	3....s	

There should also be ten blank cards included in each envelope in case other letters are needed.

The Game:

Each child in the group has an envelope.

1. The teacher says, "I am thinking of a word that begins like *have*. You wear this on your head." The children have the letter cards spread on their tables or desks. They select the letters they need and put them into the folders. They hold the folders up for the teacher to see (fig. 6.25).

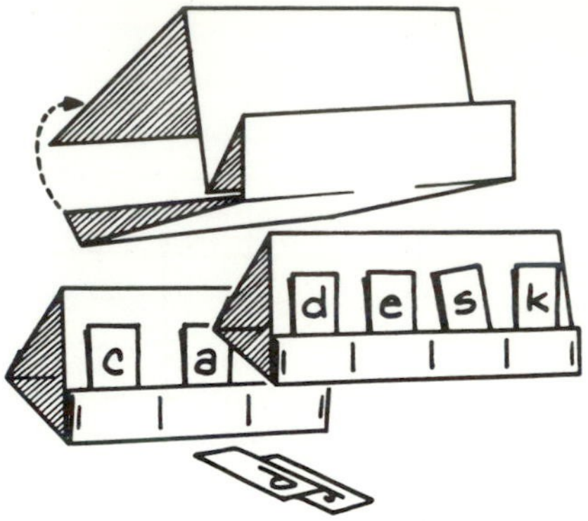

Figure 6.25 Word-Building Game

2. To learn the long sound of the vowels, the teacher shows the children the word *dim*. The children place the letters in their folders, leaving the space at the right empty. "Now what letter could we put in this space that would make the *i* have a long sound?" "What word do you have?" The children learn that when two vowels are together, the first one says its name and the second one says nothing, or if there is a consonant between two vowels, this also holds true. This activity is also good for spelling.

10. Long and Short Vowel Sounds

"Listen while I pronounce some words. I will tell you what vowel sound to listen for. Listen to see whether it has a *long* or a *short* vowel sound. Then place a marker on *Long* or *Short* on your card. When I have pronounced all twenty words, I will ask someone to read back the placement of the markers so that you can check your answers. I will tell you what vowel to watch for."

(The teacher should use words found in the reading lessons as well as in the materials used in other subjects for additional exercises.)

A	*A*	*E*	*E*
1. cat	1. clap	1. need	1. seed
2. came	2. game	2. bed	2. tell
3. matter	3. rattle	3. tender	3. red
4. make	4. claim	4. sentence	4. bend
5. tame	5. clapping	5. leaf	5. creep
6. rapping	6. wrap	6. weave	6. sleeve
7. strap	7. and	7. wet	7. met
8. apple	8. trample	8. dream	8. cream
9. sample	9. take	9. screen	9. green
10. tail	10. sail	10. bean	10. please
11. manner	11. table	11. sent	11. sent
12. chatter	12. clatter	12. heat	12. meddle
13. shape	13. cape	13. whether	13. fence
14. master	14. last	14. settle	14. kettle
15. appetite	15. map	15. steep	15. treat
16. name	16. claim	16. wheel	16. kneel
17. hand	17. land	17. never	17. enter
18. train	18. bait	18. fell	18. well
19. banner	19. saddle	19. feel	19. steal
20. wait	20. plane	20. bead	20. lead

I	*I*	*O*	*O*
1. bit	1. fit	1. ton	1. stone
2. bite	2. right	2. tone	2. known

3. kite	3. dime	3. coal	3. goat
4. white	4. mitten	4. cone	4. lone
5. riddle	5. wide	5. over	5. stove
6. slide	6. slim	6. bonfire	6. oak
7. trim	7. trip	7. toe	7. doe
8. kitten	8. thistle	8. hope	8. rope
9. ship	9. strip	9. hopping	9. stopping
10. spin	10. thimble	10. shop	10. chopping
11. whistle	11. fifty	11. roast	11. toast
12. thing	12. list	12. lock	12. clock
13. sixty	13. rise	13. float	13. bowl
14. size	14. twin	14. soap	14. October
15. fiddle	15. dish	15. note	15. wrote
16. sitting	16. twist	16. nose	16. goes
17. twist	17. knitting	17. knot	17. hot
18. shine	18. dinner	18. pod	18. shod
19. mist	19. middle	19. lot	19. trot
20. fish	20. inner	20. flow	20. row

U		*U*	
1. blue	11. shut	1. glue	11. gruel
2. nut	12. cud	2. but	12. bud
3. bun	13. bug	3. fun	13. rug
4. tune	14. flute	4. ruin	14. cruel
5. use	15. runt	5. useful	15. stunt
6. until	16. bump	6. under	16. dump
7. run	17. hunt	7. sun	17. shutter
8. cute	18. clutter	8. mule	18. custard
9. dues	19. cup	9. rude	19. puppy
10. crude	20. funny	10. hut	20. bunny

11. Phonics Bingo

Grades one and two

A. *Initial Sounds:* Two sheets of 8-by-10-inch cardboard are joined with tape to make a folder. Two-inch squares are marked off. In each square a picture is pasted that begins with the initial sounds you are working with. A folder is prepared for each child, but the pictures are placed in different sequence. The teacher says a word and the children cover the picture of the object that begins like the word the teacher has pronounced. Later, a printed word may be used to show the children and they are to cover the picture of the object that begins like the printed word shown to them. After the children can do this satisfactorily, the markers for covering the picture may have the initial sounds printed on them, and the children place these over the correct pictures. When a child has filled a line, he indicates with some word agreed upon, such as *Bingo* or *Phonics,* and he reads back the sounds he has covered. This may be alternated by placing the initial sound in the squares and showing the pictures (fig. 6.26).

B. *Rhyming Sounds:* This is used like the preceding game, except that the rhyming sounds or the endings are used instead of the initial sounds.

C. *Long- and Short-Vowel Sounds:* This game is used in the second and third grade. Use pictures of objects whose names contain long- and short-vowel sounds. The teacher pronounces a word and the children cover a picture of an object whose name contains that vowel sound. The game is played as described above.

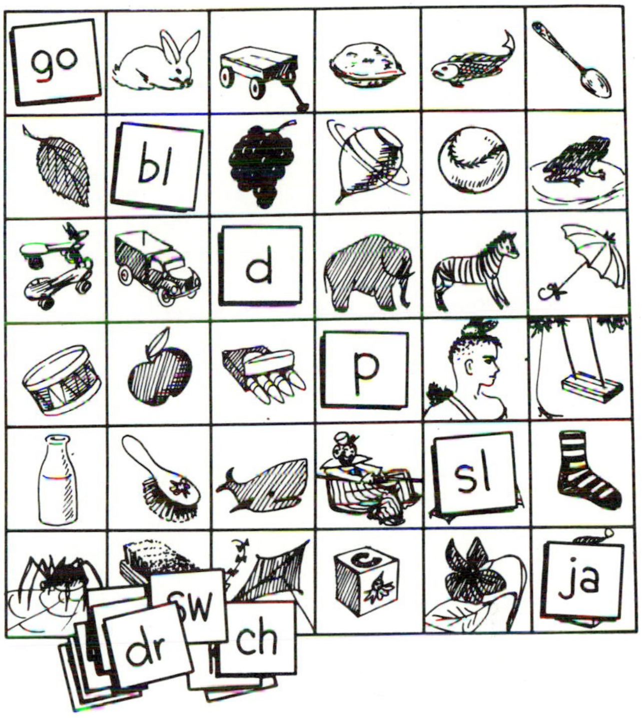

Figure 6.26 Phonics Bingo

12. The Long and Short Sound of Vowels

Grades one and two

Prepare sheets similar to figure 6.27. The other four vowels may be used in the same way. This activity may be prepared on a 12-by-12-inch cardboard and the children use colored squares of paper to place over the pictures.

Color green all the squares that have pictures of things that have the sound of *a* as in *man.*

Color yellow all the squares that have pictures of things that have the sound of *a* as in *make.*

13. Recognizing Digraphs

Grades one and two

Make work sheets similar to the one shown as figure 6.28 and put pictures of words beginning with the digraphs. If the teacher wishes, the activity can be put on a 12-by-12-inch cardboard, with twenty-five squares marked off. Use colored pieces of paper and have the pupils place the colored paper on the correct picture. Ending digraphs can be used in the same manner.

Color red all the squares with pictures of things that begin with *sh.*

Color blue all the squares with pictures of things that begin with *ch.*

Color green all the squares with pictures of things that begin with *wh.*

Color yellow all the squares with pictures of things that begin with *th.*

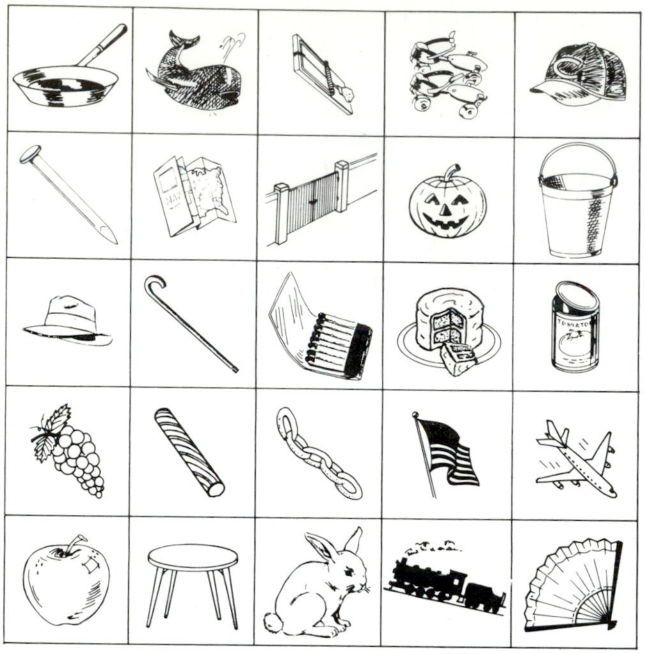

Figure 6.27 Long and Short Sound of Vowels

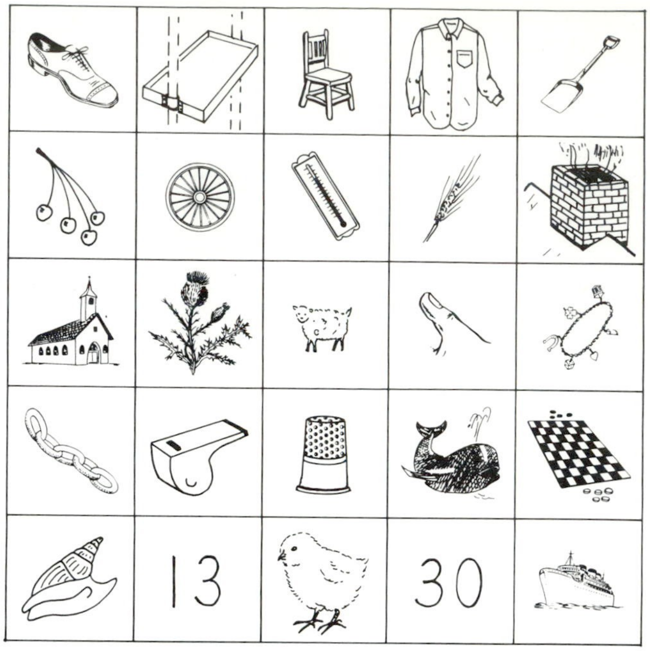

Figure 6.28 Recognizing Digraphs

14. Finding Vowels

Grades one, two, three, four, and five

Ask the children to find the number of vowels in the first paragraph of their reading text. Have them count the vowels in as many paragraphs as time permits. Long or short vowels may be counted, or digraphs can be assigned. The children may also write sentences and count the vowels as indicated here:

Mary had a little lamb. _7_ vowels

15. Silent Letters

Grades three and four

Use old books that have been discarded, or write short paragraphs or sentences for the children to use.

Write the rules on the blackboard or on the work sheet. Ask the children to circle the words that contain letter combinations where the rules apply and write the number of the *rule* over it.

Example:

1. When two vowels are together, the first is usually long and the second is silent.
2. When a vowel is before the letters *gh*, the vowel is usually long.

The flight of the seagull . . .

16. Same Sounds

Grades three, four, and five

The teacher prepares lists of words whch may be either duplicated or written on the blackboard. The children write *yes* or *no* after each group.

Example:

Do these words have the same vowel sound?

1. rose . . . clothes . . . shows . . . toes . . . rows. . . *yes*
2. roll . . . to . . . doll . . . pole . . . crow. . . *no*

—and so on

17. Rhyming Dominoes

Grades one, two, three, four, five, and six

With a paper cutter, cut cardboard to 1½ × 3 inches. Draw a line through the center of each piece to make two 1½-inch squares. For primary grades, paste or draw pictures on each square. Use words for upper grades. Each child draws six cards; the remainder are placed in the center of the table, face down. The game is played like the standard game of dominoes. A suggested list of dominoes is given for first grade.

Example:

cat—ball	tub—hat	rose—five	rope—star
shawl—pan	bat—bill	four—shoe	car—stool
fan—sand	hill—bone	two—man	spool—sun
hand—bear	cone—corn	pan—map	gun—tag
pear—sock	horn—house	trap—pen	bag—three
block—boat	mouse—clip	ten—rain	tree—thread
goat—clock	ship—cut	train—rake	bed—top
lock—ring	hut—dog	cake—road	fox—zoo
king—lamp	log—duck	toad—pie	box—pig
stamp—cent	truck—frog	tie—rug	twig—two
tent—bell	draw—hoe	bug—tail	whale—wheel
shell—beet	saw—dish	pail—skunk	seal—six
wheat—bug	fish—eight	trunk—duck	sticks—spoon
rug—crib	gate—five	truck—cot	moon—pin
bib—cub	hive—hose	pot—soap	

18. Guessing Game

Grades one and two

This activity may be oral or written. Questions similar to the ones below are used. The work may be duplicated, written on the chalkboard, or given orally.

1. What is in the zoo that begins with the letter *c*? It has the sound of *k*. (give sound of *k*)
2. What is in the kitchen that begins with the letter *p*? (give *p* sound)
3. What is in the circus that begins with the letter *l*? (give *l* sound)

—and so on.

19. Phonograms

Grades two and three

Write endings on the chalkboard. The teacher pronounces the word and the children write the number of the ending on their papers.

Example:

1. ....ank
2. ....ack
3. ....ink
4. ....ench, and so on.

The teacher says the word *track*. The children write *2* on their papers.

The teacher says *bench,* and the children write *4* on their papers.

20. Finding Words

Grades one, two, three, four, and five

The teacher lists words used in the reading lesson. She says:

a. I see a word that has a long *a sound*. Write it.
b. I see two words that begin with the same sound as table does. Write it.—and so on.

21. Which Words Begin Alike?

Grade one

Folders similar to that in figure 6.29 are prepared. The children match the words that begin alike. Words that rhyme may also be used. After the children have a sufficient number of sight words, they may match the word with the picture.

22. Matching Rhyming Words

Grade one

Folders as shown in figure 6.30 are prepared. In order to help the children locate the pictures with rhyming words, one folder may have pictures mounted on red, the next on blue, and the third on green. Small pictures that rhyme will be mounted on a corresponding color and pasted on small cards. These are placed in the pocket provided for that purpose.

23. Find the Words that Rhyme

Grades one and two

This activity is helpful in teaching word endings.

Example:

Look in your reader to find the words that rhyme with the following words. Give the page and line number.

a. Mary ....page .... line ....
b. hide ....page .... line ....
c. look ....page .... line ....

24. Find Words in Pictures

Grades one and two

Pictures from magazines, workbooks, and so on, are used. The children are to find as many words as they can that begin with *p*, or whatever consonant is decided upon.

25. How Many Words Can You Write?

Grades one and two

A small picture is pasted on a sheet of paper. The children are to write as many words as they can that begin like the name of the picture. Rhyming words and endings may be used in the same way.

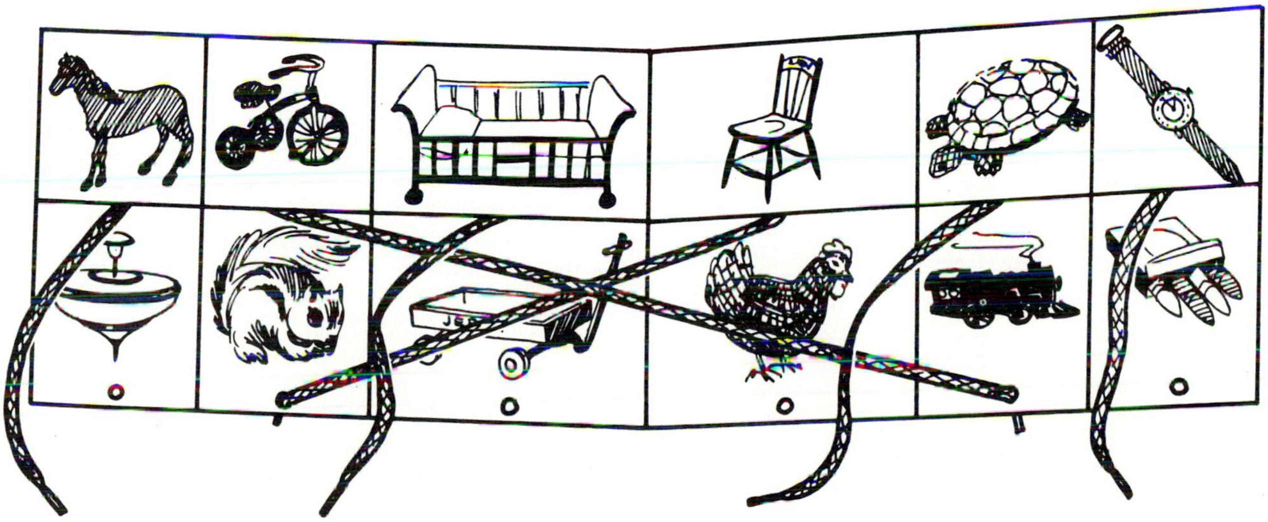

Figure 6.29 Which Words Begin Alike?

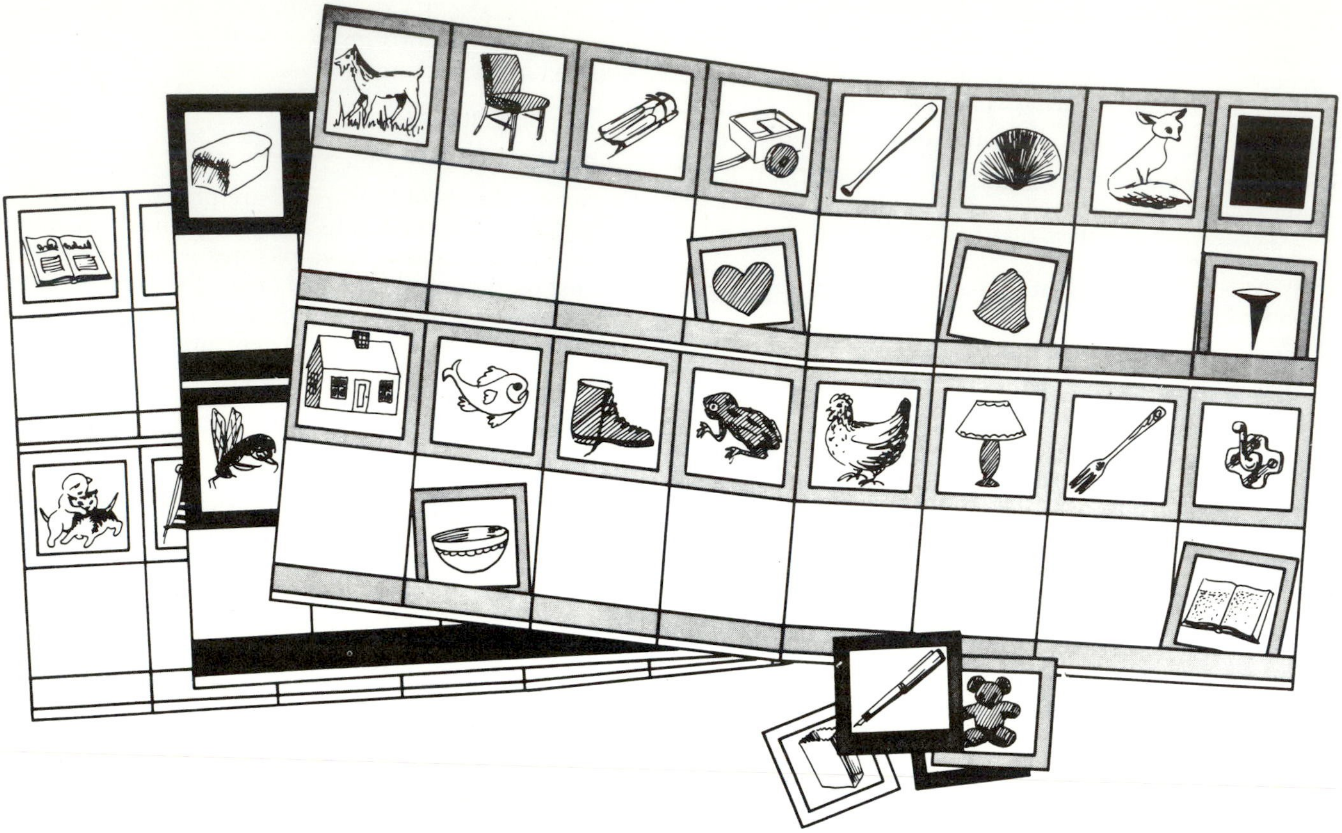

Figure 6.30 Matching Rhyming Words

SEQUENCE FOR PHONETIC TRAINING

A. Auditory

1. Listening to sounds around us, stories, rhythms, music.
2. Listening to words that begin alike.
3. Listening to words that have the same ending sound.
4. Listening to words that rhyme.

B. Visual

1. Matching pictures of objects whose names have the same initial sounds or blends.
2. Matching pictures of objects whose names have the same rhymes or final consonants.
3. Matching a picture of an object with a printed word for initial sounds and blends.
4. Matching a picture of an object with a printed word having the same ending or rhyme.
5. Matching a word with a letter for initial and final blends.
6. Matching rhyming words.
7. Recognizing short vowel sounds.
8. Recognizing diphthongs.
9. Recognizing digraphs.
10. Recognizing long- and short-vowel sounds.
11. Becoming aware of phonic irregularities.

PHONETIC IRREGULARITIES

There are only two letters in the alphabet that remain constant at all times. They are *m* and *v*. The vowels have a greater variance in sound than the consonants. Thus, you can see that phonics can help with spelling and in the pronounciation of words, children need to know that there are some irregularities. The list of irregularities is for the teacher's use and may be referred to as needed. If you will examine the pronunciation charts in various dictionaries, you will see that their markings differ. The schwa has come into use more frequently now. It is an unstressed midcentral vowel that is the usual sound of the first and last vowels of the English word *America*. The symbol ə is usually used to designate the schwa.

Many times the child can sound out a word and then get the meaning from the context clues. Every word has some phonetic element in it. The teaching of reading has paid relatively little attention to the phonic consistency of the English language. Authorities estimate that approximately 85 per cent of the words contain phonetically consistent elements. It should also be added that the pronunciation in dictionaries vary and the school should decide upon *one* dictionary.

The data obtained from the tabulation of the vocabulary found in twelve basic series of readers used in grades one through six indicated that there were 10,955 different words used. The chart that follows lists these phonetic elements. Variants were not included in this study.

Element	Applies No. words %	Does not Apply	r*
ai....long a sound	133– 98%	3– 2%	74
ar....as in car	194–100	0	
ar....as in care	98– 99	1– 1	
ar....as or...ar is preceded by w or qu	27–100	0	
ar....as er........used as a suffix	345–100	0	
age....as ij........used as a suffix	87– 96	4– 4	
au....as in caught	108– 97	4– 3	
aw....sound of aw when *a* precedes k, l, w	73– 99½	1– ½	
ay....long a when ay conclude word or syllable	49– 98	1– 2	
ea....long a	179– 85	32–15	8
ee....long e	145– 98	3– 2	41
ei....applicable rules	35– 93	2– 7	6
ew....long o when letters conclude word	49– 98	1– 2	
ey....no applicable rule			
i....long when followed by gh, ght, gn, ld, mb, nd+	40– 97	1– 3	
ie....no applicable rules			
oa....long o	48– 96	2– 4	11
oi....and oy....as in boy	47– 94	3– 6	14
o....long at end of two syllable words	46– 99	1– 1	
ou....no applicable rules........(nine sounds)			
ow....long o when end of two syllable word	36– 97	1– 3	
ui....as in ruin	37– 80	9–20	
igh....long i, gh silent	29–100	0	
y....long i when last and only vowel in word	16–100	0	
y....short i when preceded by consanant, ends word	786–100	0	
Only vowel at end of 2, 3, or 4 letter word is long	30– 89	4–11	
Vowel has short sound when between consonants #	3,236– 98+	78– 1=	
First vowel long in VCV pattern....(final e)	878– 98	11– 2	

* r following vowel, changes vowel sound
\+ concludes word
\# ild, ind, old not included

Element	Applies No. words %	Does not Apply	r
ch....has three sounds ch, k, sh			
c....as in cat when followed by a, o, u, l, or r	737–100%	0 %	
c....as in cent when followed by e, i, or y*	143– 98	3– 2	
ge....as in gem....beginning word or syllable	110– 90	12–10	
ge....as in edge....ends word or syllable	265–100	0	
gi....as in ginger	82– 82	19–18	
kn....k silent	64–100	0	
wr....w silent	62–100	0	
le....in syllabication, preceding consonant included**	420–100	0	
or....as in for	476– 99	20– 1	–w precade
oo....no applicable rule			11

* words containing ious, ial, etc. belong to another rule
** ck is a digraph, rule: never break digraph but divide after it

There is a 96.9 percent application of the phonetic elements as related to the pronunciation of words. Through the use of context clues and structural analysis, a child should be able to pronounce almost all words he encounters.

Our Vowels Have Many Sounds*

a
fate (ā)
fatality (ā̍)
care (â)
car (ä)
add (ă)
account (*ă*)
fall (aw)
ask (ȧ)
sofa (*ȧ*)
war (or)
many (ĕ)

ace
face (ā)
surface (ĭ)

age
age (ā)
village (ĭ)
garage (ä)

ai
plain (ā)
plaid (ă)
said (ĕ)
aisle (ī)
captain (i)
air (â)

ar
car (ä)
care (â)
coward (er)
war (or)

au
gauge (ā)
laugh (ă)
aunt (ȧ)
caught (ô)

aw
paw (ô)
away (*ȧ*)

ay
say (ä)
says (ĕ)
aye (ī)
Monday (ĭ)

e
eve (ē)
end (ĕ)
here (ĭ)
her (er)
event (e)
silent (*ĕ*)
feet (ēē)

ea
great (ā)
meat (ē)
bear (ĕ)
clear (ĭ)
beau (ō)
earn (er)
heart (är)

ee
meet (ēē)
matinee (ā)
coffee (ĭ)
been (ĕ)

ei
eight (ā)
receive (ē)
their (ĕ)
height (ī)
foreign (ĭ)

eo
leopard (ĕ)
people (ē)
Leo (ē-ō)

er
cherry (ĕ)
here (ĭ)
certain (er)
sergeant (ä)

eu
feud (ū)
Freudian (oi)
Europe (ū̍)

ew
dew (ū)
sew (ō)

ey
obey (ā)
eye (ī)
eyre (ar)
key (ē)
money (ĭ)

i
pique (ē)
in (ĭ)
ice (ī)
girl (er)

ia
fiance (*a*)
carriage (ĭ)
giant (ī-ŭ)

ie
soldier (yer)
field (ē)
tie (ī)
view (ū)
fierce (ĭ)
friend (ĕ)

o
note (ō)
obey (ō̍)
lord (or)
odd (ŏ)
toward (ŭ)
soft (ō̍)
connect (*ŏ*)
blood (ŭ)
food (oo)
out (ou)
core (or)
women (ĭ)
coin (oi)

oa
soar (or)
goat (ō)
broad (ô)

oe
toe (ō)
canoe (ū)
does (ŭ)
phoebe (ē)

oi
coin (oi)
choir (ī)
porpoise (ŭ)

oo
blood (ŭ)
good (oo)
food (o͞o)
poor (oor)
brooch (ō)
door (or)

or
sore (or)
morrow (ŏ)
word (er)

ou
cough (aw)
tough (ŭ)
though (ō)
could (oo)
out (ou)
group (o͞o)
pour (oŏr)
four (or)
journey (er)

ow
crow (ō)
cow (ou)

oy
boy (oi)

u
cube (ū)
unite (ū̍)
furl (er)
up (ŭ)
circus (*ŭ*)
busy (ĭ)
buy (ī)
quart (kwor)

ua
quart (kwor)
January (ū̍-ĕ)
piquant (*ă*)

ue
due (ū)
guest (ĕ)
bouquet (ā)
plague (silent)

ui
build (ĭ)
suit (ū)
genuine (ū-ĭ)
guide (ī)

ur
bury (ĕ)
fur (er)
sure (oŏr)
mature (ū)

y
sky (ī)
party (ĭ)
myrtle (er)
they (ā)
year (y) consonant
play (ā)
boy (oi)

* Phonics Book, Published by I-MED, Los Angeles, California 90025

Consonant Sounds*

c
cat (k)
cent (s)
ocean (sh)

ch
chick (ch)
chorus (k)
chiffon (sh)
sandwich (j)
yacht (silent)

d
hauled (d)
jumped (t)
waited (ed)
soldier (j)
handkerchief (silent)

f
five (f)
of (v)

g
gone (g)
giraffe (j)
garage (zh)
high (silent)

gh
ghost (g)
laugh (f)
sight (silent)

gn
gnat (n)
dignity (g-n)

h
have (h)
humble (silent)

j
judge (j)
hallelujah (y)

k
kite (k)
know (silent)

l
leaf (l)
talk (silent)

m
make (m)

n
not (n)
solemn (silent)

p
pan (p)
photo (f)
glimpse (silent)

ph
phone (f)
Stephen (v)

qu
queen (kw)
unique (k)
liquor (ker)

r
red (r)
murmur (rolled)

s
see (s)
days (z)
sure (sh)
vision (zh)

t
top (t)
listen (silent)
the (th)

th
teeth (breath)
they (voice)

ti
question (ch)
nation (sh)
prettily (t-i)

v
vine (v)

w
wind (w)
wh (digraph wh)
sew (silent)

wh
who (h)
whale (wh)

x
box (ks)
exist (gz)
xylophone (z)

y
year (consonant)
play (silent)
sky (ī-vowel)
ready (ĭ-vowel)
boy (oi)

z
buzz (z)
seizure (zh)

Key to Pronunciation of Vowels*

ā....as in ale
â....as in care
ä....as in car
ă....as in add
ȧ....as in ask
ȧ....as in sofa
ē....as in eve
ê....as in deer
ē̇....as in event
ĕ....as in end
ẽ....as in her
ī....as in ice
ĭ....as in sit
ĩ....as in bird
ō....as in old
ô....as in orb
ŏ....as in not
ȯ....as in soft
oi....as in boil
o͞o....as in food
o͝o....as in foot
ou....as in out
ow....as in cow
ōw̸....as in crow
oy....as in boy
ū....as in cube
û....as in urn
ŭ....as in up

*Phonics Book, Published by I-MED, Los Angeles, California 90025

There Are Many Ways to Spell the Phonemes

Long a
ai....plain
ay....play
ae....Mae
aye....aye
quet....bouquet
ee....matinee
ey....they
ei....veil
eigh....weigh
ea....great
a-e....cake
au....gauge
ce....fiance
ague....plague
que....pique
ao....gaol

Short a
a....an
ai....plaid
a-w....have
au....laugh
al....half

âr
ar....care
aer....aeruak
air....hair
ayer....prayer
ear....bear
eir....their
ere....there
eyr....eyre

är
ar....car
ear....heart
er....sergeant
oir....memoir

aw
aw....draw
au....cause
augh....caught
al....alk, ball
ou....ought
ah....Utah
o....offer, cost
ong....song
oa....broad
one....gone

Long e
ee....heel
ea....meal
e-e....these
ie....believe
ei....receive
ine....sardine
-e....me
ique....pique
ae....Aesop
ay....quay
ey....key
e+base word....equal
qui....mosquito
eo....people
oe....phoebe

Short e
e....get
ie....friend
ei....their
ere....there
err....cherry
ea....bear
ai....said
a....many
ess....guess
says....says
eo....leopard
u....bury
ae....aesthetic
ee....been

ẽr
er....her
ir....fir
ur....burn
our....journey
or....word
ar....dollar
yr....myrtle
ure....treasure
ear....earth
err....err

Long i
i-e....like
ie....tie
ight....sight
igh....sigh
ind....kind
ild....child
ei....height
y....fly
oir....choir
ye....rye
up....buy
eye....eye
aye....aye
coy....coyote
ia....giant

Short i
i....bit
o....women
ai....fountain
ee....breeches
ie....fierce
ui....build
y....nymph
ey....money
ed....added
ee....coffee
age....village
eo....pigeon
ay....Monday
re....pretty
ace....surface
ia....carriage
ea....guinea
e....England
ate....senate
u....minute
eer....deer
ere....here
ei....foreign
est....smallest
ear....clear
ive....give
usy....busy

Long o
oa....goat
old....cold
ew....sew
o....so
oe....toe
oh....oh
olk....folk
eo....yeoman
o-e....note
au....hautboy
ow....show
oll....roll
ou....dough
oth....both
owe....owe
omb....comb
oem....poem
eau....beau
oo....brooch
ou....soul

Short o
oll....doll
o....top
atch....watch
a....want
or....morrow
ou....bought

ôr
or....for
ore....core
oor....door
ar....war
ou....course
oa....coarse

ou
ou....mouse
ough....bough
ouw....cow

ȯ
o....off
ou....cough

Long u
u....cupid
u-e....tune
oo....goose
ou....through
oe....shoe
ou....through
o....do
ue....due
ew....dew
eu....feud
ie....view
to....toward
ui....suit
wo....two
eau....beauty
ieu....adieu
eue....queue
ove....move
ture....mature

Short u
u....sunk
oe....does
ou....tough
oi....porpoise
o-e....come
io....cushion
on....lemon
o....won
oo....blood
wo....twopence

u̇
u....full
oo....wool
ol....wolf
o....woman

Silent Letters in Words

b....The b is silent when preceded by m, as in lamb, climb
b....The b is silent when followed by t, as in debt, doubt
c....The c is silent in some words, as in scene, muscle, indict
d....The d is silent in some words, as in Wednesday, adjust
d....The d is silent after g, as in edge, badger, fudge
g....The g is silent before n, as in gnaw, design, sign
gh....The gh is often silent when preceded by a vowel, as in might
gh....The h is silent when the word begins with gh, as ghost
h....The h is sometimes silent when it is the first letter of a word, as in hour, humble
h....The h is silent when preceded by r, as in rhubarb, rhythm
k....The k is silent when it is followed by n, as in know, knit
l....The l is silent in some words, as in calf, talk, palm
n....The n is silent when it is preceded by m, as in solemn, autumn
p....The p is silent when it is followed by s, as in glimpse, psalm
p....The p is silent in some words, as in cupboard, receipt
p....The p is silent when it is followed by n, as in pneumonia
s....The s is silent in some words, as in isle, aisle
t....The t is silent in some words, as in listen, often
w....The w is silent when it is followed by r, as in wrong, wrap
w....The w is silent when wh is followed by o, as in who, whole
w....The w may be silent in some combinations of sw, as in sword, answer

Word List for Silent Letters

So that the teacher will not need to look for words to use in developing exercises in silent letters in words, this list is made available.

Silent b in words

bomb	dumb
climb	lamb
comb	limb
crumb	numb
debt	plumber
doubt	thumb

Rules:
1. In most words with only one syllable, the *b* is silent when it follows the letter *m*.
2. The *b* is silent when it is followed by the letter *t*.

Silent d in words

badge	hedge
badger	ledge
bridge	lodge
budge	pledge
edge	ridge
fledgling	sledge
fudge	sludge
gadget	trudge
grudge	wedge

Rules:
1. The *d* is usually silent when followed by the letter *g*.
2. The *d* is silent in some words, as in *handsome, Wednesday.*

The letters gh in words

bought	might
bright	neighbors
dough	ought
eight	right
fight	straight
freight	taught
frighten	though
ghastly	thought
ghost	tight
height	weigh
high	wrought
light	

Rules:
1. The letters *gh* are usually silent when they follow a vowel.
2. When *gh* is preceded by a single vowel *i*, it is silent and the *i* is usually long.
3. If *gh* comes at the beginning of a word, the *h* is silent, and the *g* is pronounced.

The letters gn

align	gnat
foreign	gnaw
gnarl	gnome
gnash	gnu

Rule:
1. When *g* is followed by the letter *n*, it is silent.

The letter h

heir	rhesus
heirloom	rheumatism
honest	rhinestone
honor	rhinoceros
hour	Rhode Island
hourly	rhyme
rhapsody	rhythm

Rules:
1. The *h* is sometimes silent when it is the first letter in a word.
2. When the *h* is preceded by the letter *r*, it is silent.

The letters kn

knack	knight
knap	knit
knapsack	knob
knave	knock
knead	knoll
knee	knot
kneel	know
knelt	knowledge
knew	known
knickers	knuckle
knick-knack	knurl
knife	

Rule:
1. When the letters *kn* are together in a word, the *k* is silent, and the *n* is voiced.

The letter l

balk	mild
balm	palm
balmy	psalm
calf	salmon
calm	salve
calves	should
chalk	stalk
child	talk
could	walk
folks	wild
half	would
halves	yolk

Rules:

1. The letter *l* is usually silent when it is followed by *f, k, m,* or *v.*
2. The *l* is silent when it follows *ou* and is not the letter in the word.
3. The *l* is usually not silent when it is preceded by *i.* The *i* has a long sound.

The letter n

autumn	hymn
column	solemn
condemn	synonym
homonym	

Rule:

1. The *n* is silent when it is preceded by *m.*

The letter p

cupboard	pseudonym
glimpse	pshaw
pneumonia	psychology
psalm	receipt

Rules:

1. The *p* is silent when it is followed by *s* and they are not the last two letters in the word.
2. The *p* is silent when it is followed by *n* and is at the beginning of the word.
3. The *p* is sometimes silent in some other words.

The letter t

batch	match
blotch	nestle
bustle	often
butcher	patch
castle	pitcher
catch	rustle
christen	scratch
Christmas	snatch
gristle	soften
hasten	stretch
hatch	switch
hachet	thatch
hitch	thistle
hustle	twitch
itch	watch
jostle	whistle
latch	wrestle
listen	

Rules:

1. If *t* is not the last letter in a word and it is followed by *l* or *ch,* the t is silent.
2. When *t* is preceded by *s* or *f,* it is usually silent.
3. In *tle,* the *t* is silent when preceded by *s.* The *l* is the last syllable sound.

The letter w

wrangle	wrist
wrap	write
wrath	writhe
wreath	wrong
wreck	wrote
wreckage	wrought
wren	wrung
wrench	who
wrestle	whoever
wretched	whole
wriggle	whom
wring	whoop
wrinkle	whose

Rules:

1. When the letters *wr* are together, the *w,* is silent and the *r* is voiced.
2. The *w* may be silent in some combinations of *sw,* as in *sword, answer.*
3. When *wh* is followed by *o,* the *w* is usually silent.

The f sound in ph and gh

alphabet	orphan
aphid	paragraph
autograph	Phillip
camphor	phlox
cipher	phone
cough	phonograph
dolphin	photograph
draught	phrase
elephant	physical
enough	rough
geography	sphere
gopher	telephone
laugh	telegraph
nephew	tough

Rules:

1. The letters *ph* in a word are usually pronounced as *f.*
2. The letters *gh* sometimes have the sound of *f.*

THINGS TO REMEMBER

1. Teaching phonetics by elaborate isolated drills cannot be justified; neither can taking the entire reading period be considered good practice.
2. Phonetics that are badly taught can be more harmful than none at all.
3. Overemphasis on phonetic elements can produce word-callers.
4. Phonics can help enunciation.
5. Just pronouncing the word correctly does not mean that the child knows the meaning of the word.
6. Give individual attention to the child's needs.
7. Phonetic rules are not taught.
8. Children should not respond in chorus or in group pronunciations. You have no way of knowing if the individual child is saying the words correctly in this type of activity.
9. Avoid distortions of sounds. Give true sound values.
10. Never ask the child to break up words into independent sounds.
11. Only eighty-five percent of all our words are phonetic, but no English word is wholly unphonetic.
12. Phonics can be an aid or a hindrance to spelling, depending on how they are presented.

DICTIONARY USAGE

There are many good primary dictionaries available, some costing as little as a dollar. (Children should be encouraged to make their own dictionaries also. The procedure will be described under the heading Alphabetizing that follows this section.) Children in the third grade ordinarily begin using a junior edition dictionary.

The dictionary exercises help the child locate words quickly and accurately, to learn word meanings, pronounce words correctly, and are an aid to correct spelling. Children can make a classroom chart similar to the following:

The Uses of the Dictionary

1. It gives the meaning of words.
2. It gives correct spelling.
3. It gives correct pronunciation.
4. It helps with abbreviations.
5. It shows changes in word forms.
6. It gives pictures of some words.
7. It has special lists of words.

There are three major classes of basic dictionary skills. The pupil must first learn to locate the word. Then he must be able to pronounce it, and finally he must be able to get the meaning of the word. The children must be able to apply their knowledge of alphabetical sequence and general alphabetical position. They must be shown how to use the guide words in locating the word quickly.

Several suggestions for exercises in learning to alphabetize in order to use the dictionary effectively follow.

1. Which Letters Come First?

Grades two and three

The exercises may be duplicated, written on the blackboard, or presented in chart form.

Example A.

a. What letter comes after *g*?
b. What letter comes after *c*?
c. What letter comes before *n*?

Example B.

Fill in the missing letters.
a b .... d e .... h .... k l .... etc.

2. Learning to Alphabetize

Grades two, three, and four

Each child opens his dictionary at random. He selects a new word, reads the definition, and uses it in a sentence. The teacher or another child writes the word on the blackboard. After all the children have had a turn at finding a word, the children arrange the words in alphabetical order.

3. Alphabetization

Grades two, three, and four

Exercises similar to the example given below may be constructed, using words found in the reading lesson.

Directions:

Put these words in the correct alphabetical order. Put a check in front of the word when you have used it.

like	rope	now
dare	enter	point
over	where	gone
make	under	here
bend	fun	jump
apple	come	kick
inside	quick	some
zero	time	yellow
visit	xylophone	

a	b	c ....
d	e	f ....
g	h	i ....
j	k	l ....
m	n	o ....
p	q	r ....
s	t	u ....
v	w	x ....
y	z	

4. Alphabetizing Words

Grades three and four

Children alphabetize words according to the first and second letters in the word as: *am, and, apple, ate.* After they can do this, they alphabetize words according to their sequence.

5. Using Guide Words

Grades three and four

Exercises similar to the example given below may be developed.

Directions:

Would each of the following words come before or after the page having the guide word *Edison*? Write *before* or *after* in each blank.

everyday	exhibit	ear ....
ebony	economy	effort ....

—and so on

6. Dictionary Fun

Grades four, five, and six

With the help of the dictionary, the children find the correct title or proverb given by the teacher.

Example:

a. Vertebrates that flit and have similar plumage congregate.
(Birds of a feather flock together.)

b. Refrain from enumerating your domestic fowl prior to the arrival of the entire brood.
(Don't count your chickens before they are hatched.)

Each child should be encouraged to rewrite titles and proverbs and have the other children guess them.

7. Guide Words Game

Grades three and four

Two guide words, such as *combat* and *council* are written on the blackboard. A time limit is given and pupils list as many words as they can think of that would appear between these two guide words. Each correct word scores a point. Incorrect words subtract from the score. Pupils can divide into two groups to compete against each other.

8. Relay Race

Grades three and four

Several words are placed on the chalkboard by the teacher. The pupils in each row or at each table constitute a team. Each pupil has a dictionary which lies closed on his desk. The first pupil in each row is given a sheet of paper and, when the signal is given, he selects the word nearest the beginning of the alphabet, consults his dictionary, and records the spelling, syllabication, part of speech (or whatever is decided upon) and then passes the paper on to the next pupil, who takes the next word in alphabetical order and records the required information. The game continues until all the pupils have finished or a stop signal has been given. The papers are corrected, and one point for each error is subtracted from the possible score.

9. Synonyms and Antonyms

Grades four, five, and six

Words from the lessons are selected and written on the blackboard.

Example A.

List three synonyms for each of the following words:
a. greedy ....
b. cordial ....
c. wisely ....

Example B.

List three antonyms for each of the following words:
a. unkind ....
b. simplicity ....
c. fretful ....

Example C.

List an antonym and a synonym for each of the following words:

	antonym	synonym
a. dry	....	....
b. bright	....	....
c. crisp	....	....

10. Correct Spelling

Grades three, four, five, and six

Words are written on the chalkboard, some of them incorrectly spelled. The students are to write all the words correctly. They may refer to their dictionaries for verification.

11. History Game

Grades four, five, and six

The teacher places on the blackboard a list of names, such as:

Buddha Cartier Jamestown Amundsen

The children refer to their dictionaries to find the suggested information and tabulate it as follows:

Example:

Name	Date	Information
Cartier	1491-1557	French explorer, etc.

12. Bird, Beast, or Fish

Grades two, three, four, five, and six

The pupil writes the name of a bird, beast, or fish, in each space. For fifth and sixth grades, both categories should be used. At the lower level the first category is given. The pupils should tell only if it is bird, beast, or fish.

Lower level:

A is for *ape* (*beast*)
B is for *bluebird* (*bird*)
C is for *catfish* (*fish*)

—and so on

13. Letter Additions

Grades three, four, five, and six

Write letters which are parts of words on the chalkboard. The pupils are to complete the words. Use words from the spelling list.

Example:

........gl........ (ugly)
........wf........ .... (awful)
........and........ (handy)

14. Hanging Dictionary

Grades one, two, and three

Materials needed are: (1) wire coat hangers, (2) shelf paper, wrapping paper, newsprint, or tagboard; and (3) a rack made from a reading-chart frame or a pole or dowel suspended from a frame. The paper is folded in half and hung over the hanger. The pupils add new words in the correct sequence. Miniature hanging dictionaries for individual use can be made from paper clips, 3-by-5-inch cards, and shoe boxes (fig. 6.31).

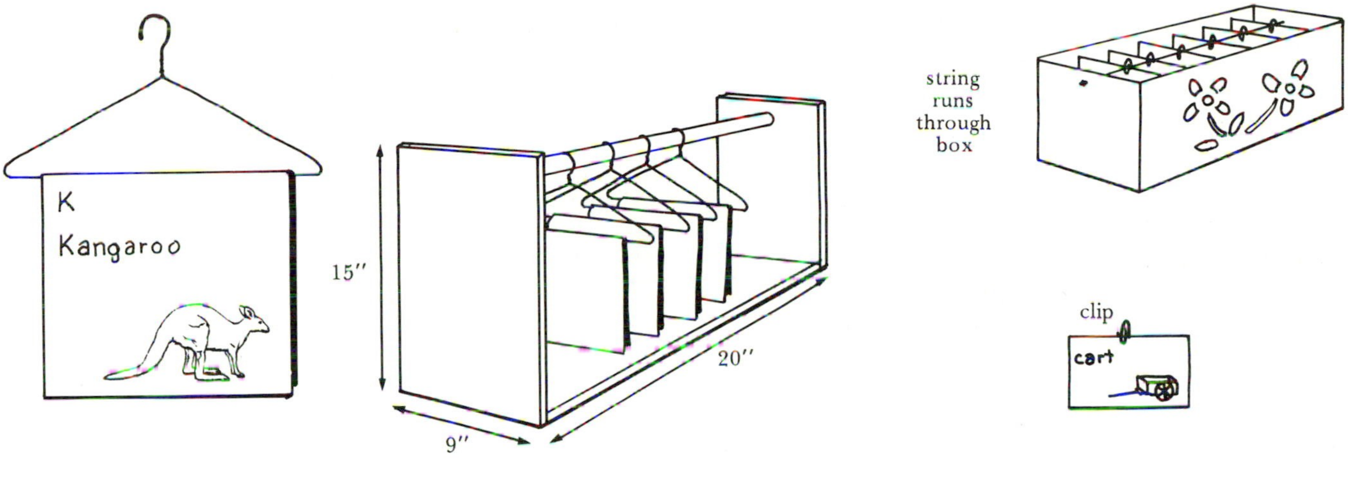

Miniature Hanging Dictionary

Shoe Box Decorated

Figure 6.31 Hanging Dictionary

15. Dictionaries

Grades one, two, three, and four

To teach the pupils to look for the guide words on each page in the dictionary, explain that the word in the upper left-hand corner of the page is the first word on that page and the word in the upper right-hand corner is the last word on that page. They are to prepare their dictionaries in the same way. They may use notebooks, or make the dictionary from shelf paper. The dictionaries may be illustrated (see fig. 6.32).

16. Building Game

Grades two and three

Each letter of the alphabet is printed on three 2-by-3-inch cards—a total of seventy-eight cards.

The cards are shuffled and six are dealt to each player. (This is a game for four to six players.) The remainder of the cards are placed face down on the table. The children take turns drawing a card and playing. If a child has four letters running in sequence (a-b-c-d, m-n-o-p), he may lay the cards down before

Figure 6.32 Dictionaries

him and draw other cards as he finishes his play with six cards in his hand. If a child draws a card and cannot play, he discards one. A child may build on another's sequence when the cards are laid on the table, but he keeps the cards he has played in front of him. The child who has the most cards at the end of the game wins.

This game may be modified by using words beginning with the letters of the alphabet, with the children alphabetizing the words.

17. Alphabet Game

Grades two and three

When the leader, standing before the group, names a letter of the alphabet, the children indicate whether it is a vowel or a consonant by raising the right hand for a vowel or the left hand for a consonant. Any prearranged sign may be used to indicate the letters. The leader, using only one minute, may try to confuse the group by raising the wrong hand at times. The leader or another child keeps score of the rights and wrongs by count. When the time is up, another leader is chosen.

18. Alphabetizing Names

Grade three

With a capital *A* written on the board, the pupils whose last names begin with *A* are asked to write their last names on the board under the letter. Then the question of which name should be written first is discussed—for example, *Adams* should be written before *Alexander,* and so on. The activity continues through the letters of the alphabet. Names in stories or in social studies may be used.

19. Alphabetizing

Grades two, three, four, and five

Each child is given a column clipped from a newspaper or magazine. He is to circle the first *a* that he finds in the print. He continues on to the first *b* that follows the *a* and circles it. The letters are circled in alphabetical sequence. For older pupils, they may be asked to circle the words that begin with the letters in alphabetical sequence.

20. Supply the Missing Letters

Grades three, four, five, and six

Words used in the current assignments may be used for this activity, or words from previous spelling lessons may be used. Ask the pupils to supply the missing letters. If necessary, they may refer to the dictionary.

Example:

ap-le	col-r	
ban-na	dre-m	—and so on

21. Finding a Word in the Dictionary

Grades three, four, five, and six

The pupils are to number the words to show the order in which they would appear in a dictionary. Use words suitable for the grade level.

......carrot	......diamond	......tumble	......nonsense
......elevator	......witch	......queer	......insect
......frog	......dozen	......vegetable	......jungle
......dictionary	......mouse	......quack	......manner
......blink	......glue	......yawn	......nowhere
......song	......giant	......special	......outside
......scold	......every	......cage	......remember
......answer	......end	......patch	......struck
......gather	......lamb	......knock	......tremble
......drank	......lost	......inside	......shelter
......harm	......hunt	......pearl	......wicked

22. Dictionary Practice

Grades four, five, and six

Use words that are being used in current assignments. The students are to find the words in the dictionary, look for other information about the kind of word it is and then write the meaning on the line following the word.

Word	*Meaning*
repair	....
clutter	....
extremely	....
vanished	....

23. Using the Dictionary

Grades four, five, and six

Duplicate paragraphs from the reading or social study books which will pertain to the subjects being studied. An example is given below.

Example:

One of the most valuable and interesting achievements of science was the laying of the Atlantic Cable—a telegraph stretching from Ireland to Newfoundland, upon the bed of the Atlantic Ocean. After failing in the attempt in 1857, 1858, and 1865, it was at last accomplished, in 1866, by means of the Great Eastern, the largest steam vessel constructed up to that time. The Atlantic Cable is about two thousand six hundred miles long, and its strength is sufficient to bear a strain of nearly twenty-eight tons. The success of this enterprise was largely due to the intelligence and untiring energy of Cyrus W. Field.

a. Find the word *achievement* in the dictionary.
The long vowel sound in the word is ....
The word has .... syllables.
It means ....
The suffix of the word is ....
and means ....

b. Find the word *enterprise* in the dictionary.
(noun, verb, etc.)
The word is a ....
The meaning of the word is ....
The word comes from the Latin *inter,* meaning ....
...., and *prendere,*
meaning ....
The word has .... meanings given.

24. Something About the Dictionary

Every student from the first grade on should get the dictionary habit. There are three kinds of dictionary skills. First the student must know how to locate the word, then he must be able to pronounce it, and finally he must be able to get its meaning.

As you look at a page in the dictionary, you see two words at the top of each page. These are called *guide words*. The word on the left-hand side of the page tells you the first word on that page, and the word on the right-hand side tells you the last word on that page. In looking up words, the students will find they can do so much more quicky if they use the guide words.

The uses of the dictionary are:

1. To give the correct meaning of words.
2. To give the correct spelling of words.
3. To give the correct pronunciation.
4. To give abbreviations of words.
5. To show changes in word forms, like *gain, gained, gaining, gains*.
6. To show the kind of word it is, as *verb, noun, adjective,* and so on.

Dictionaries have many other uses, too. There is a great deal of information in the big, or *unabridged*, dictionary.

Sometimes more than one meaning for a word may be given. If you will look in the unabridged dictionary, you will find that there are, for example, several pages devoted to the definitions for the word *run*.

A Chinese scholar, Pa-Out-She, made the first dictionary about 1,100 B.C. Others wrote dictionaries, too. Look on the cover of your dictionary. You will probably see the name of Noah Webster on it. He is the man who wrote the first dictionary in this country.

Benjamin Franklin had been in France for seven years and when he returned, he was shocked at the words that were being used. He said some of the words people were using were highly improper, like *progress, nice,* and *raise*. He felt that someone must write a book to guide people in the use of proper words.

Benjamin Franklin knew a young man by the name of Noah Webster who had written a spelling book called the *Blue-Back Speller*. Franklin thought that this would be just the man to write such a book, so he went to Noah Webster with his plan.

It took Mr. Webster, who accepted the idea, a number of years to collect all the words that were being used, and it took him twenty years to put the words in alphabetical order and to give the meaning and pronunciation of each word. This dictionary contained about 12,000 different words. Today there are over 600,000 different words in the unabridged dictionary!

ALPHABETIZING

There is no particular need for a child to be able to name all the letters of the alphabet or to give them in sequence at the prereading level. Children become aware of letters because of initials on clothing and handkerchiefs, and the letters in their names. Picture dictionaries are useful in the primary grades and their main purpose is to instill an interest in and develop an understanding of the dictionary. Suggested learning activities for alphabetizing and learning the letters of the alphabet follow.

1. Picture Dictionary

Grades one and two

When the children know about fifty sight words and are beginning to show an awareness of letters, they may begin to make their own picture dictionaries. These booklets may be made of newsprint or construction paper, with a separate page for each letter of the alphabet. These pages are sewn or stapled together. The children design a suitable cover and either print or cut out each letter of the alphabet. They may draw their pictures, or pictures from magazines are alphabetized and pasted under the correct letter. In the latter part of the first grade, the children may print the name of the object next to the picture (fig. 6.33). In the second grade the children are able to write a short sentence about each picture.

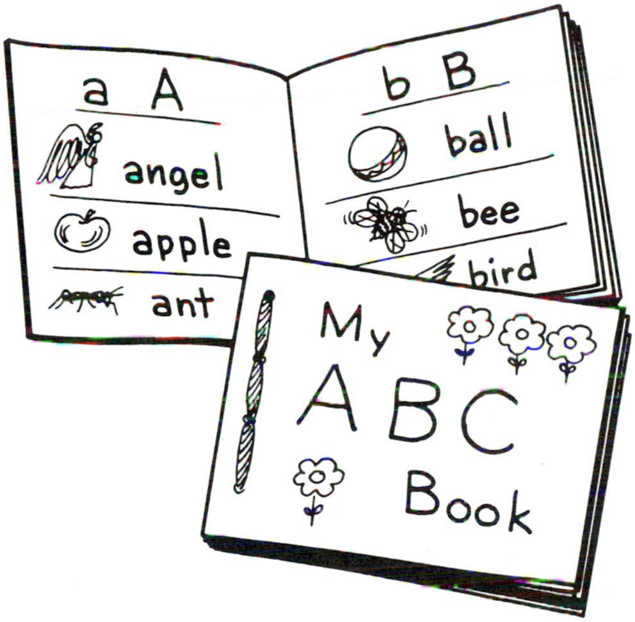

Figure 6.33 Picture Dictionary

2. Alphabet Posters

Grades one and two

Pictures to represent each letter of the alphabet, such as an apple for *A*, a bird for *B*, and so on can be pasted on 9-by-12-inch cardboard or tagboard with both the capital and the lowercase letter under the picture. The name of the object may also be printed on the card, if the teacher wishes. These cards may be set on the chalkboard ledge or put on the bulletin board in sequence by the children.

3. Alphabet Cards

Grades one and two

Pictures of objects representing each letter of the alphabet are pasted on 4-by-6-inch cards. A half-inch strip is pasted at the bottom of each card to make a pocket. This pocket is used for placing the letters of the alphabet under the appropriate pictures. Alphabet cards using both the capitals and the lowercase letters should be 1½ inches square. After the letters and the pictures have been matched, the child uses a self-checking key and then puts the letters in proper sequence. These cards, directions, and keys may be stored for future use in a cardboard box or an envelope with the name of the activity inscribed on the outside.

4. Flannelboard Letters

Grades one and two

The capitals and lowercase letters of the alphabet may be cut from flannel board or cardboard. If paper is used, cloth or sandpaper should be pasted on the back so the letters will stick to the flannel board. The children place the letters in proper sequence.

5. Learning Alphabet Sequence

Grades one and two

Using a box, such as hosiery comes in, twenty-six squares are marked off on the bottom and the lid of the box. On squares or circles of cardboard, slightly smaller than the squares in the box, the letters of the alphabet are printed. The child places the letters in proper sequence in the squares. Some teachers number the squares in the box. Provide a key for this project. The name of the activity is printed on the box and directions and a key for the project are enclosed in it.

6. Alphabet Sequence

Grades one, two, and three

Two 6-by-10-inch pieces of cardboard are hinged together with tape, and on the inside of this folder 2-inch squares are drawn, with a pocket for each square made by pasting a ½-inch strip of cardboard at the bottom of each square. These squares are numbered one through twenty-six on the pocket. On each of twenty-six 1¾-inch squares, a picture is pasted or drawn to represent each letter of the alphabet, as an airplane for *A*, a balloon for *B*, and so on. Fifty-two 1-by-1½-inch pieces of cardboard with the capital letters and the lowercase letters are provided in a box or an envelope.

The first step for the children is to place the pictures representing the letters of the alphabet in pockets, in proper sequence. They then use the small cards with the letters of the alphabet and place them in the pockets with the pictures (see fig. 6.34). Later, they may use the letters of the alphabet alone. They key for this activity and the directions are stored in a box or a Manila envelope that is labeled.

7. Alphabet Puzzle

Grades one, two, and three

The letters of the alphabet are printed in proper sequence on a 15-by-15-inch piece of cardboard and cut apart with scissors. The child is to place the puzzle pieces together. For a more elaborate puzzle, the letters may be painted on plywood and cut apart with a jigsaw. The puzzle with directions may be stored in a box that is labeled.

Figure 6.34 Alphabet Sequence

8. Building Game

Grades two and three

Each letter of the alphabet is individually printed on a 2-by-3-inch card, and three sets of these—for a total of seventy-eight cards—are made up.

The cards are shuffled and six are dealt to each player. The remainder of the cards are placed face down on the table. The children take turns drawing a card and playing. If a child has four letters running in sequence (a-b-c-d, m-n-o-p), he may lay the cards down before him and draw other cards as he finishes his play with six cards in his hand. If a child draws a card and cannot play, he discards one. A child may build on another's sequence when the cards are laid on the table, but he keeps the cards he has played in front of him. The child who has the most cards at the end of the game wins.

This game may be modified by having the children alphabetize the words used, in sequence, by their beginning letters.

9. Accordion Alphabet Book

Grade one

Children enjoy making small accordion books by folding paper for the pages. Tagboard or construction paper is cut into the longest strips possible. These strips may be four or five inches in width. The children measure off four- or five-inch squares on the strips and fold the paper to make the accordion. The strips are spliced with tape. After the accordion book has been completed with twenty-six pages, the children may either draw the pictures for the alphabet book or paste in those they have cut from magazines. They print the proper letters on each page of the book (see fig. 6.35). If it is not feasible for each child to make a book, the teacher can make a larger book, which may be placed on the reading table or on the window ledge.

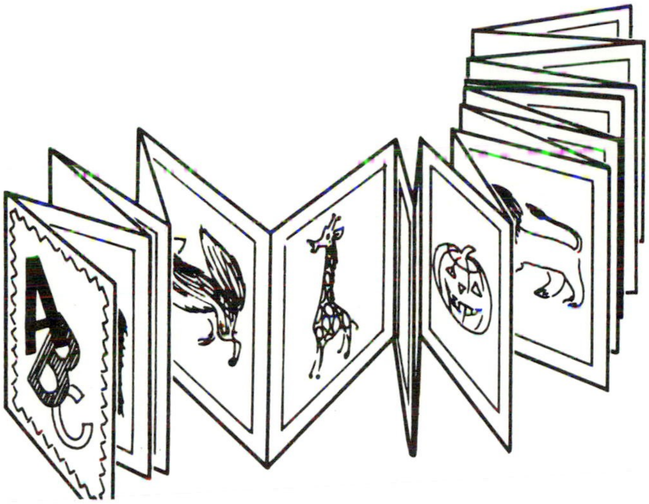

Figure 6.35 Accordion Alphabet Book

10. Alphabet Game

Grades two and three

When the leader, standing before the group, names a letter of the alphabet, the children indicate whether it is a vowel or a consonant by raising the right hand for a vowel or the left hand for a consonant. Any prearranged sign may be used to indicate the letters. The leader, using only one minute, may try to confuse the group by raising the wrong hand at times. The leader or another child keeps score. When the time is up, another leader is chosen.

11. Alphabet Pictures

Grade one

The letters of the alphabet are arranged in such a way that, as the child joins the letters in correct sequence, he draws a picture or design. Simple outline pictures can be made easily with a letter of the alphabet beside each dot. The children may enjoy making the dots, lettering them, and having their classmates make the pictures. The children guess what the picture will be before they begin joining the letters.

12. Alphabetizing Names

Grade three

With a capital *A* written on the board, the pupils whose last names begin with *A* are asked to write their last names on the board under the letter. Then the question of which name should be written first is discussed —*Adams* should be written before *Alexander.* The activity continues through the letters of the alphabet. Names in stories or in social studies may be used.

13. Alphabet Hopscotch

Grades one, two, and three

The hopscotch figure is made on a sheet of wrapping paper with the letters of the alphabet printed in the squares. The child says the name of the letter as he hops into the square, and keeps on hopping in correct sequence. If the child misses, he writes his name in that square and waits for another turn.

14. Computer Alphabetizing

Grades one, two, and three

Cut cards to represent IBM cards. Paste pictures of objects named A through Z on the cards. Draw a horizontal line one inch from the top of each card. With a paper punch, punch the first card about half an inch from the left, using the horizonal line for a guide. The card that comes next in alphabetical order is punched in the same place as the first card and a second hole is then punched about a quarter of an inch to the right of the first hole. The third card would have three holes, and so on. As you proceed making the cards, use a second and third row of holes.

The child can check his work as he works with the words. In the second grade, both the picture and the word is used. In the third grade, words only need be used, if the teacher wishes. In this case, the teacher may use several words beginning with the same letter, as table, take, there.

15. Subject Alphabetizing

Grades one, two, three, and four

Use the same procedure as for #14, but use pictures relating to birds, flowers, animals, farm, science, mathematics, and similar types of objects. If the category is birds, the following words would be appropriate: bill, bird, buebird, bobolink, claws, eggs, feathers, nest, etc. In the third and fourth grades, the pupils can select the words that will be used.

The pupils are to put the words in alphabetical order.

16. Footsteps

For grades one, two, and three

Cut footprints from wrapping paper or cardboard. The children can trace around their feet and cut them out. Print the letter of the alphabet on the footprints. The footprints are laid on the floor and the child begins with *A* and then steps to the next letter. He says the name of the letter as he steps on it. Score may be kept with the child receiving a point for each correct step. Both upper- and lowercase letters should be used. This exercise is helpful in developing coordination as well as teaching the letters of the alphabet.

17. Alphabetizing

Grades two, three, four, and five

Each child is given a column cut from the newspaper or magazine. He is to circle the first *a* that he finds in the print. He continues on to the first *b* that follows the *a* and circles it. The letters are circled in alphabetical sequence. For older pupils, they may be asked to circle the words that begin with the letters in alphabetical sequence.

SYLLABICATION

Developing the ability to divide words into syllables can be useful to the student in pronunciation, recognizing new words, and in learning to spell.

A syllable is a unit of speech and it forms either a complete word or a part of a word. There are a few principles involved in syllabication and when the student is aware of them, it will make him more proficient in reading and spelling.

1. Each syllable must have a vowel. To find the number of syllables in the word, the children should count the vowels. Double vowels with a single sound are counted as one and the silent *e* at the end of a word does not count unless it is preceded by the letter *l*.
2. A word is divided between two consonants unless the letters are the digraphs *ch, ck, ph, sh, th,* and *wh,* as in *but/ter* and *leath/er.*
3. When the single vowel in a syllable is preceded by a consonant and is followed by a consonant, the vowel is usually short, as in *can.*
4. You can usually tell how many syllables are in a word by placing the thumb and forefinger on the throat and saying the word. You can feel the movement of your throat as you say the word, and by counting the number of movements you know how many syllables are in the word.
5. If the last syllable of the word ends in the letters *le,* the consonant preceding the *le* is part of the last syllable, unless the letters are *ck* or *ch.* In that case, the *le* makes up the last syllable. The final *e* is silent and the *l* is the final sound, as in *pick/le* and *la/dle.*
6. When a single vowel is followed by a single consonant, the single vowel makes up the first syllable, as in *a/bide.*
7. When the letters *ed* are added to a word, the letters may sound as *ed, d,* or *t.* When the letters have a *d,* or *t* sound, they are not separated from the word as a syllable. If the letters have the *ed* sound, they make up a separate syllable. The suffix *ed* is a syllable only when it follows the sound of *d* or *t,* as in *wait/ed.*
8. When the first vowel in a word is followed by a single consonant and the vowel has a short sound, the consonant is included in the first syllable, as in *cab/in.*
9. If the first vowel in a word has a long sound, the consonant is included in the next syllable as in *clo/ver.*
10. Two vowels that make a single sound are counted as one vowel and are not divided, as in *toad.* When two vowels are together and have two distinct sounds, they are divided, as in *fu/el.*
11. If a suffix is added to the base word ending in two consonants, the division comes between the base word and the suffix and not between the double consonants, as in *hold/ing.*
12. If a prefix is added to a base word that begins with two consonants, the division comes between the prefix and the base word, as in *re/store.*

SUGGESTIONS FOR DEVELOPING SYLLABICATION SKILLS

The words given in the following activities are merely suggestions. Using words from the daily class assignments would serve as reinforcements.

1. Vowels and Syllables

Grades three, four, five, and six

The children fill in the number of vowels seen and heard and the number of syllables in each word in a given list.

Pronounce the words below, mark the vowels, and then write the number of vowels you see, the number of vowels you hear, and the number of syllables in the word.

2. Finding the Number of Syllables After Adding ed

Grades two, three, and four

Directions:

If *ed* is added to each word, write the number of syllables in the word.

Word	*One syllable*	*Two syllables*
jump	jumped	
wait	....	
end	....	

3. Words with Double Consonants

Grades two and three

Directions:

Divide the words into syllables.
digging dirty question often

4. Words with Short Vowel Sounds

Grades two and three

Directions:

Break these words up into syllables.
robin hotel wider cider tulip

5. Baseball

Grades two and three

The teacher writes about thirty words on the board. The children choose teams. A baseball diamond is drawn on the board. A child on the first team acts as "pitcher" and points to a word; he asks someone on the second team to tell the number of syllables in the word. If he answers correctly, he may mark the first base. When there are three outs, a child on the second team becomes the pitcher.

6. Long and Short Vowel Sounds

Grades three, four, five, and six

When the first vowel in a word has a short sound, the consonant that follows it is usually a part of the first syllable.

Example: cab/in

If the first vowel in a word has a long sound, the consonant that follows it is usually a part of the next syllable. If there are two vowels together and they have a long sound, the rule also applies.

Example: gro/cer

Pronounce each word below. Listen to the first vowel sound and then divide the word into syllables.

1. bacon	8. melon	15. present
2. basin	9. miser	16. profit
3. beacon	10. meter	17. raisin
4. major	11. panel	18. second
5. manage	12. petal	19. season
6. memory	13. peanut	20. notice
7. motion	14. pity	

7. Adding ed to Words

Grades three, four, five, and six

The letters *ed* may have one of three sounds when added to words. When they have the *d* or *t* sound, they are not a separate syllable but if the letters have the sound of *ed,* they are counted as a syllable.

Examples:

walked	(*t*)
pulled	(*d*)
started	(*ed*)

Pronounce the words below. Divide the words into syllables.

Write *t, d,* or *ed* after each word to show the sound of the letters *ed.*

1. batted	....	11. enjoyed	....
2. borrowed	....	12. knitted	....
3. camped	....	13. lighted	....
4. charted	....	14. marched	....
5. doubted	....	15. pouted	....
6. frightened	....	16. pounced	....
7. feared	....	17. stared	....
8. galloped	....	18. talked	....
9. halted	....	19. wished	....
10. jumped	....	20. filled	....

8. Pictures from Magazines

Grades one and two

Explain to the children that a syllable is a single unit or part of a word. Ask how many syllables in *cat, kitten, sometime,* and the like.

Have children cut pictures from magazines and mount them. Show the picture of a dog and ask how many units or syllables they can hear when they say the name of the picture. Show pictures and ask the children to tell how many syllables they can hear in each word. If the pictures are numbered, the children can work independently, giving the number of syllables for each picture word.

9. First Vowel Followed by a Single Consonant

Grades three, four, and five

If the first vowel is followed by a single consonant, the single vowel usually makes a syllable and the consonant that follows begins the second syllable.

Say these words and notice how many vowel sounds you hear. Divide the words into syllables and write the number of vowel sounds you heard.

able	emerge
abide	evict
afraid	evolve
again	icycle
agent	idea
ahead	idle
alarm	obey
alone	ocean
amend	odor
amount	open
aside	opinion
away	orient
elaborate	oval
elect	over
electric	unite

10. Long and Short Vowel Sounds

Grades three and four

If the first vowel in the word is followed by a single consonant and the vowel has a short sound, the consonant usually is part of the first syllable, as in *lem/on.* If the two vowels have a short vowel sound, the rule also applies as in *feath/er.*

If the first vowel in a word is followed by a single consonant and the vowel has a long sound, the consonant usually is a part of the second syllable, as in *de/cide.* If there are two vowels together have a long sound, the rule also applies, as in *trea/son.*

Say these words and divide them into syllables. Mark the vowels long or short.

baby	demand
bacon	depot
baton	docile
benefit	donate
body	dragon
cabin	feature
camel	feeble
camera	Friday
caterpillar	frisky
catalogue	habit
clever	lemon
clober	measure
comic	minus
copy	minute
cubic	reason
deacon	season
decide	weasel
delay	treasure

11. Words With Double Vowels

Grades three, four, and five

When two vowels are together and they have a single sound, they are usually considered one syllable. When the two vowels are not united in sound, the division is between the two vowels.

Say these words and divide them into syllables.

beach
bound
client
crown
cruel
deal
dial
diary
diet
duet
fuel
geography
giant
gradual
idea
influence
lion
loaded
manual
mean
meekly
piano
poet
quiet
really
reason
ruin
science
suitable
traitor
trial
trio
triumph
unusual
variety

12. Words With Syllables Ending in le

Grades three, four, and five

If the last syllable of a word ends in the letters *le,* the consonant preceding the *le* is part of the last syllable, unless the letters are *ck* or *ch.* In that case, the *le* will make up the last syllable. The final *e* is silent, and the *l* is the final sound.

Say these words and divide them into syllables. Mark the vowel sounds to show whether they are long or short.

able
battle
bottle
bubble
buckle
bustle
candle
cattle
circle
cripple
double
eagle
fable
gentle
handle
kettle
ladle
marble
muddle
nibble
paddle
people
pickle
puzzle
rattle
riddle
rustle
single
sparkle
sprinkle
tickle
trickle
trouble
whistle
wrestle

13. Words with Double Consonants

Grades three and four

When the only vowel in a syllable has a consonant in front of it and it is followed by a consonant, the vowel usually is short, and the syllable is called a *closed syllable.*

The syllable division is made between two consonants when there are two or more syllables in the word. The digraphs, *ch, ck, ph, sh, th,* and *wh* are *not* divided between the two consonants.

Say the words and divide them, write the number of syllables in the word after the word.

blossom
bobbin
bottom
button
camp
cannot
chipmunk
digging
dinner
funnel
gallon
goldfish
heather
lantern
listen
master
much
oppose
picket
pistol
pocket
princess
puppet
ragged
remnant
ribbon
ripple
section
thimble
tunnel
whether

14. Words with Double Consonants

Grades three, four, and five

If the vowel in a word is followed by two consonants, the word is divided between the two consonants, unless the consonants have a single sound as *th, sh, ck, ch, wh,* and *ph.* Whenever three or more consonants appear between the two vowels, learn to look for consonant blends or digraphs.

These are never divided, as in *em/pha/sis and en/thu/si/asm.* Say these words and divide them into syllables.

almost
apostrophe
arrow
basket
blanket
bracket
butter
cabbage
carrot
chatter
cotton
elephant
fragment
fundamental
grumble
hangar
hermit
hindrance
jungle
mention
method
mirth
mission
mongrel
monkey
normal
nothing
nowhere
number
pasture
pigment
plentiful
plunge
practise
progress
ransack
sense
sentiment
servant
smolder
sparrow
splendid
sympathy
telephone
thatch
thunder
within
wringer

15. Adding ed to Words

Grades two, three, four, and five

When the letters *ed* are added to a word, the letters sound as *ed, d,* or *t.* The *ed* is not a separate syllable when it has the *d* or *t* sound, but when it has the *ed* sound it is a separate syllable. The suffix *ed* is a syllable only when it follows the sound of *d* or *t.*

Say these words, divide them into syllables. Write *d, t,* or *ed* after each word to show the sound of the letters *ed.*

banded	mended
blocked	minded
called	mixed
carried	noticed
doubled	opened
doubted	pulled
ended	painted
fastened	pointed
fitted	rained
fixed	rested
glued	sounded
granted	started
happened	stretched
helped	tended
hinted	tired
jumped	walked
knotted	wanted
laughed	wasted
lifted	wished

16. Adding ed and ing to Words

Grades three and four

There are a few principles to remember when adding a suffix to a word. They are:

1. In *b, d, l, m, n, p,* and *t,* all seven of these letters are regularly dobled when the suffixes begin with a vowel as *able, ed,* or *ing* are added to the base word. They are not doubled, however, when the preceding vowel is a dipthong, as *schooling.*
2. When the last vowel in the word has a short sound and there is a single consonant at the end of the word, double the consonant and add *ed* or *ing,* as in *knot, knotted, knotting.*
3. When the vowel has a short sound and is followed by a double consonant, just add *ed* or *ing,* as in *fill, filled, filling.*
4. When a word ends in *w,* add *ed* or *ing,* as in *sew, sewed, sewing.*
5. Words with a single final consonant and two preceding vowels, just have *ed* and *ing* added, as *seed, seeded, seeding.*
6. When the vowel has a long sound and the word ends in *e,* drop the final *e* and add *ed* or *ing,* as *rake, raked, raking.*
7. When *y* is the last letter of the word and it is preceded by a vowel, just add *ed* or *ing,* as *toy, toyed, toying.*
8. When the final *y* is preceded by a consonant, add *ing.* When *ed* is added, change the *y* to *i* and add the *ed,* as *try, tried, trying.*

Add *ed* and *ing* to these words. Be sure to follow the above rules.

bake	cry	fool	mat	play	seat	trip
bat	draw	fry	mend	plow	sew	try
book	dry	heal	mew	pray	skate	wait
bray	fade	hint	need	pry	spoil	watch
call	fan	hope	pat	rest	start	wipe
comb	feel	knot	peel	sail	step	
cool	fill	leak	pet	saw	tap	
crow	fix	look	pity	seal	trail	

17. Adding s and es to Words

Grades three and four

Adding plurals to words can be made easy by remembering a few rules.

1. Add *es* to words ending in *s, ss, sh, ch,* and *x,* as in *bus, buses; mass, masses; dish, dishes; match, matches.*
2. When the word ends in *y* and the *y* is preceded by a consonant, change the *y* to *i* and add *es,* as *try, tries.*
3. When the final *y* is preceded by a vowel, add *s,* as in *day, days.*
4. Add only *s* to all other words.

Write the words below and add *s* or *es* to them.

bank	latch
bench	loss
box	march
bunch	match
bus	miss
carry	nest
catch	peach
crash	press
cry	purses
dash	rooster
desk	saw
dress	school
dry	spare
fence	spray
flash	tax
fox	toss
frame	track
free	use
freeze	watch
fry	write
inch	

18. Dividing Words Into Syllables

Grades three, four, five, and six

Complete these sentences.

1. You can tell how many syllables are in a word by pronouncing the word and................................the vowel sounds.
2. When the only vowel in the word has a consonant in front of it and one following it, the vowel sound is usually ....
3. When two consonant are together, you divide the word between the consonants unless they are the letters ...., ..., ..., or .... Thse letters are called digraphs.
4. When two vowels are together and have a single sound, they are considered as .... vowel.
5. When two vowels are together and they have two sounds, the syllable division is made by dividing ....
6. When the letters *le* are at the end of the word, the consonant preceding them is usually considered a part of the ....
7. If the letters *ch* or *ck* precede the *le,* they are considered a part of ....syllable.

8. When the first vowel in a word is short or pronounced as a schwa and it is followed by a single consonant, that vowel is considered as the first .... of the word.
9. When the letters *ed* are added to the end of a word, the *ed* will have the sound of ...., ..., or .... The letters are considered a separate syllable when they have the sound of ....
10. When the first vowel in a word has a long sound, the following consonant is included in the .... syllable.
11. If the first vowel in a word has a short sound, the following consonant is included in the .... syllable.

Divide these words into syllables and write 1, 2, 3, 4, 5, 6, 7, 8, 9, 10, or 11 after the word to show which rule you used. You may need to use more than one rule for the word.

acorn	hastened
appoint	hastle
camera	honored
candle	hurry
carry	lemon
counted	listened
cradle	meddle
cramped	mission
doubted	nestled
drowned	pickle
duel	picture
empty	presently
feather	weather
finished	wrestle
gentle	zebra
gracious	

19. Word Division at the End of a Line

Grades three, four, five, and six

You will need to remember some special rules for dividing words at the end of a line of your writing. Some syllabication rules may not apply.

1. If a word has only one syllable it cannot be divided. If you do not have enough space for it at the end of the line, start it on the next line below.
2. Surnames should never be divided. Titles and initials should not be separated from the surname.
3. Hyphenated words are divided at the hyphen only.
4. A single letter syllable at the beginning of a word should not be separated from the remainder of the word, as in *able*.
5. A single letter syllable at the end of a word is not to be separated from the word. If there isn't enough room at the end of the line, start to write the word on the next line below. Example: *windy*.
6. Never separate a two-letter syllable at the beginning of a word, as in *explore*.
7. A two letter syllable at the end of a word is never separated from the rest of the word, as in *hospitality*.
8. A single letter vowel syllable within a word is written with the preceding syllable, as *memo-rize*.
9. When the final syllable does not have a pronounced vowel, it is not separated from the rest of the word, as in comfort*able*.
10. Don't hesitate to use the dictionary.

ACCENTS

By accents we mean emphasis put on one part of a word more than another. When a word has more than one syllable, one of the syllables is spoken with more emphasis than the other. The accent mark (′) is placed to the right of the syllable that is to be stressed. Some words have two accented syllables with one of the accent marks heavier than the other, which indicates that one syllable is given a little more force than the other one. The vowel sound is stressed in the accented syllables.

There are some visual clues that will help the student determine the accented syllable in two-syllable root words. These words may either be with or without an ending or a suffix.

1. If the final syllable is a consonant followed by *y*, and the *y* has the sound of short *i*, the accent is usually on the first syllable, as in *ba′ by, sun′ ny*.
2. When the first syllable of the word is *de, be, re,* or *ex,* the accent is usually on the last syllable as *ex hale′, re turn′*.
3. When the last syllable of a word ends in *le,* that syllable usually is not accented as in *bot′ tle, ta′ ble*. When the final syllable ends in *le* and is preceded by a consonant, the first syllable of the word is accented as in *mid′ dle, set′ tle*.
4. If a word ends with a suffix, the root word is usually accented as in *bright′ er, a maze′ment*.
5. If the root word has more than one syllable, and there is a single consonant before the ending of the last syllable of the root word, the last syllable of the root word is usually unaccented as in *mod′ el ing*.
6. The first syllable of a word is accented when the letters *ck* follow a single vowel as in *pock′ et, chick′ en*.
7. When two vowels are together in a two-syllable root word, the final syllable is accented as in *ex plain′, re deem′*.
8. When the two-syllable root word ends with a vowel, followed by a consonant and a final *e*, the final syllable is accented as in *pro vide′, be have′*.
9. The first syllable of a word is accented when double consonants follow a single vowel as in *but′ ter, mat′ ter*.
10. Words that have four or more syllables often have two accents. One accented syllable is spoken with more force than the other and its accent mark is heavier.
11. A syllable with the soft or reduced vowel sound, or *schwa*, is not accented.

1. Using Accents

Grades four, five, and six

Words used in the reading, spelling, or science lessons may be used. These are written on the blackboard or duplicated for the pupils. Ask the students to divide the words into syllables and mark the accented syllable. They may check their work by using the dictionary, or the work may be checked as a class project. For the teacher's convenience, a list of words that utilize the visual clues listed at the left are given.

abandon	divide	kitchen	salute
active	doughnut	lantern	sardines
admirable	double	lesson	scenery
adjustment	dreadful	locomotive	scientist
alone	electricity	library	somewhere
appetite	elsewhere	location	superintendent
apron	engineer	marine	sprinkle
arena	entertain	manufacturing	suppose
arithmetic	explain	messenger	talkative
artist	everyone	microbe	taxi
ashes	flapjack	minutes	thermometer
badger	final	moment	torpedo
behave	furious	noble	trapeze
between	follow	never	twenty
bicycle	forget	nonsense	telegram
birthday	gather	nowhere	tropical
blackboard	goodby	obtained	tonight
because	government	orchestra	umbrella
battle	grasshopper	only	underneath
carefully	handiwork	oatmeal	unforgettable
carrot	happy	pancake	vacant
cement	hello	patient	various
complete	hopefully	peppermint	variety
complain	handkerchief	provide	vanish
companion	important	program	weapon
cyclone	improvement	possible	weather
comfortable	intention	postpone	welcome
circle	invite	rabbit	wonderful
delight	influence	rainbow	wrestle
decide	jiggle	repeat	whistle
degree	jingle	remember	worthless
demand	July	reply	worrying
development	jungle	ribbon	yellow
determine	knapsack	ruler	yesterday
digestion	jack-o-lantern	robin	yearly
direction	kangaroo	restlessness	zebra
delighted	kingdom	several	zigzag

Select only the words suitable for your grade level.

2. Accents May Determine the Meaning of Words

Grades five and six

The accent of words can determine their meaning. Here are a few troublesome words.

compress	conduct
close	address
present	perfume
permit	insert

August (august)

blessed	buffet
produce	commune
desert	envelope (envelop)
excise	expose
forearm	incense
invalid	learned
lighter	inlay
inquiry	menu
object	ordeal

CONTRACTIONS

A contraction is a shortening of a word or phrase. Explain this to the pupils by first putting examples on the blackboard, and then by having the pupils supply other contractions. Usually a good time to present contractions is when they first appear in the reading lesson. At that time, ask the children why the word is contracted and what words it represents. A list of the various contractions is given for the teacher's convenience.

LIST OF CONTRACTIONS

will

I will – I'll
you will – you'll
he will – he'll
she will – she'll
it will – it'll
we will – we'll
they will – they'll
what will – what'll
when will – when'll
how will – how'll
where will – where'll

am—is—are

I am – I'm
you are – you're
he is – he's
she is – she's
it is – it's
we are – we're
they are – they're
who is – who's
where is – where's
when is – when's
how is – how's
what is – what's

not

cannot – can't
will not – won't
shall not – shan't
could not – couldn't
should not – shouldn't
would not – wouldn't
must not – mustn't
have not – haven't
has not – hasn't
had not – hadn't
is not – isn't
are not – aren't
was not – wasn't
were not – weren't
do not – don't
does not – doesn't
did not – didn't

have—has—had

I have – I've
I had – I'd
you have – you've
you had – you'd
he has – he's
he had – he'd
she has – she's
she had – she'd
they have – they've
they had – they'd
it has – it's
it had – it'd

would

I would – I'd
you would – you'd
he would – he'd
she would – she'd
it would – it'd
they would – they'd
we would – we'd

others

of the clock – o'clock
let us – let's
over – o'er
ever – e'er
never – ne'er
it was – 'twas

COMPOUND WORDS

1. Word Match-up

Grades three, four, five, and six

Select words from the compound word list that are suited to the grade level. This activity may be written or oral. The teacher may write the first word of the compound word on the chalkboard, or the work may be duplicated. The students are to match the ending part of the word with the first part supplied by the teacher. If the teacher wishes to make this an oral activity, she or one of the students gives the first part of the word, and then a student supplies the ending orally.

The correct compound words are:

alter–	night–	alter ego	night hawk
blue–	nest–	bluebird	nest egg
Dutch	wheel–	Dutch oven	wheelbarrow
ice–	bean–	ice cream	bean bag

Note: There may be more than one answer, as in *blue*. The response could be *bluejay, bluebell, blueberry,* and so on.

2. How Many Words Can You Find Beginning with Cross?

Grades three, four, five, and six

Ask the students to list all the compound words beginning with *cross*. After they have named as many as they can, they may refer to the dictionary.

Example:

crossbones	cross section	cross out
cross-country	cross ventilation	crossover
cross-examine	crosswalk	crosspatch
cross off	crossword	crossroads

Other words that can be used are *over, under, foot, mid, back,* and *out.*

3. Did You Ever See?

Grades three, four, five, and six

Ask the student to use compound words to make nonsensical questions. These may be written or given orally.

Example:

Did you ever see a star fish?

—a horse fly?	—a cloud burst?	—a dragon fly?
—a cow slip?	—a bed spring?	—a fly paper ?
—a fire fly?	—a peanut stand?	—a nut hatch?
—a bag pipe?	—a door step?	—a tongue tied?
—a bell hop?	—a cat fish?	—a wind fall?
—a bed spread?	—a tail spin?	—a tooth pick?
—a home run?	—a ginger snap?	—a back stroke?
—a hat box?	—a table spoon?	—a saw dust?
—a mouse trap?	—a bill fold?	—an egg plant?

SYNONYMS AND ANTONYMS

Explain to the pupils that words which have the same meaning are called *synonyms*. Ask them to give a word that means the same as *big*. An antonym is a word that means the opposite of a given word. Ask them to give a word that means the opposite of *big*. Practice with synonyms and antonyms will help them develop greater word power.

1. Matching Words

Grades three, four, five, and six

Select synonyms that are used in the reading text and make 2-by-4-inch cards. Print or write a word and its synonym on each card. Various card games can be played with these cards, such as giving each pupil six cards and putting the remainder on the table face down. He lays down his pairs and draws a card. If he cannot lay down a pair, he discards one of his cards after he has drawn his card. The one who disposes of his cards first wins.

Antonyms may be used in the same way.

2. Synonyms and Antonyms

Grades three, four, five, and six

Select words that are found in the reading text. Duplicate the list and have the pupils circle the synonyms and mark an X on the antonyms.

Example:

able . . . capable . . . unable . . . special
active . . . working . . . passive . . . idle
above . . . beneath . . . over . . . behind
break . . . smash . . . mend . . . drop
brave . . . bold . . . fearless . . . fearful

3. Synonyms and Antonyms

Grades three, four, five, and six

Write sentences and omit the one word to be used as an antonym and a synonym. The child writes in both words and distinguishes whether it is a synonym or antonym by writing *s* or *a* after the word.

Example:

They found a (an) .... object in the road.
The house was very ....—and so on.

4. Synonyms and Antonyms

Grades three, four, five, and six

Prepare a list of words and place them on the chalkboard or duplicate them. The pupils are asked to fill the spaces.

Example:

Word	*Antonym*	*Synonym*
cold	....	....
deep	....	....
sour	....	....
under	....	....
back	....	....

5. Accordion Synonyms

Grades three, four, and five

Fold paper as in making paper fans. Write the word on every other section. The pupils write in a synonym on the side that faces the word.

The pupil folds his accordion and states his synonym. The class compares the synonyms (see fig. 6.36).

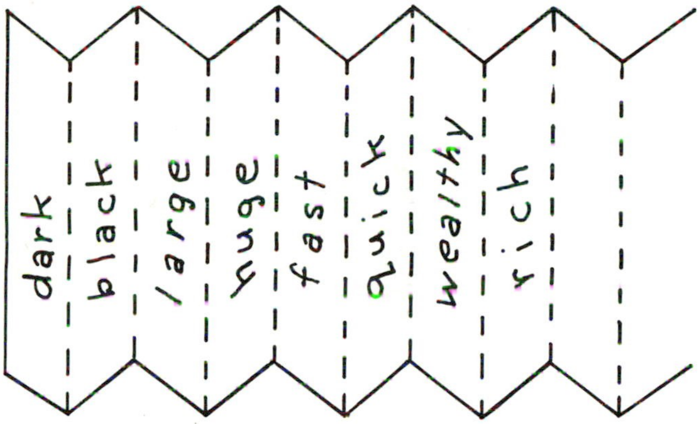

Figure 6.36 Accordion Synonyms

(This can be used for antonyms, too.)

6. Develop Your Word Power

Grades four, five, and six

Prepare exercises similar to the example below.

1. Write a synonym and antonym for each of these words.

	Synonym	*Antonym*
discovered	....	....
unhappy	....	....
tough	....	....

2. Add the prefix *un* to each of the words below and give the meaning of the new word.

able	....	....
noticed	....	....
used	....	....
covered	....	....
washed	....	....

3. The prefix *un* means ....
4. Add the prefix *un* to four other words and give their meanings.

....
....
....
....

7. Write the Synonyms and Antonyms for These Words

Grades four, five, and six

Duplicate or write on the chalkboard.

	Synonym	*Antonym*
1. swift	....	....
2. excited	....	....
3. difficult	....	....
4. sharp	....	....
5. borrow	....	....
6. broad	....	....
7. blunt	....	....
8. busy	....	....
9. polite	....	....
10. careful	....	....
11. correct	....	....
12. tidy	....	....
13. near	....	....
14. ordinary	....	....
15. end	....	....
16. coarse	....	....
17. different	....	....
18. below	....	....
19. subtract	....	....

8. Synonyms and Antonyms

Grades four, five, and six

Look at the words below and write S on the line if the words are synonyms and write A if they are antonyms. Use your dictionary if you need to.

1. huge .... large
2. alike .... different
3. blend .... mix
4. blunt .... sharp
5. broad .... narrow
6. bright .... brilliant
7. busy .... active
8. tidy .... neat
9. untidy .... spotless
10. careful .... careless
11. single .... one
12. quiet .... noisy
13. polite .... impolite
14. center .... middle
15. rapid .... speedy
16. clear .... cloudy
17. gather .... scatter
18. cheery .... gloomy
19. choose .... select
20. close .... open
21. coarse .... rough
22. clumsy .... awkward
23. crooked .... straight
24. come .... depart
25. common .... ordinary
26. commence .... finish
27. faithful .... loyal
28. follow .... pursue
29. strength .... weakness
30. lively .... frisky
31. gallant .... rude
32. greedy .... selfish
33. handsome .... homely
34. heavy .... light
35. heal .... cure
36. horrible .... dreadful
37. imitation .... genuine
38. humble .... proud
39. impure .... dirty
40. inquire .... reply
41. laugh .... weep
42. leave .... remain
43. misery .... pain
44. cunning .... clever
45. nothing ..... something
46. deeds .... acts
47. sensitive .... insensitive
48. meager .... plentiful
49. grasp .... hold
50. regret .... sorry
51. extend .... reach
52. occupation .... job
53. previous .... earlier
54. vigorous .... strong

9. Synonyms

Grades three, four, five, and six

Exercises similar to the example below, using words found in the reading lesson, are prepared. The children write the synonym.

A	*B*	*C*
a. Reply to a question	nasrew	(answer)
b. Alter	gechan	(change)

10. Synonyms and Antonyms

Grades three, four, five, and six

Exercises similar to the example below are prepared. Words from the reading lesson are used.

	Synonym	*Antonym*
a. courage	....	....
b. strong	....	....

11. Similarities and Opposites

Grades two, three, four, five, and six

A list of words, similar to the example below, is made. If the words mean the same, the children write S; if they mean opposite, they write O. This is a good way to learn the meaning of the new words in the reading lesson.

Example:

a. strong ....weak
b. huge ....immense
c. delicate ....frail

12. Synonyms and Antonyms

Grades four, five, and six

Words from the lessons are selected and written on the chalkboard.

Example A:

List three synonyms for each of the following words:
a. greedy ....
b. cordial ....
c. wisely ....

Example B:

List three antonyms for each of the following words:
a. unkind ....
b. simplicity ....
c. fretful ....

Example C:

List an antonym and a synonym for each of the following words:

	Antonym	*Synonym*
a. dry	....	....
b. bright	....	....
c. crisp	....	....

LATIN AND GREEK ROOTS

The youngsters in the sixth grade enjoy looking for roots and stems in words. It may interest them to know that of the 600,000 words in the English dictionary, 360,000 are derived from the Latin and Greek. A list of the most-used roots and stems is given. The teacher may check off the roots in the list as they are presented to the children. They should be presented only as the words are found in the reading materials being presented. The children should be encouraged to look for words containing these roots and stems.

Latin Roots

Root	*Meaning*	*Qualifying word*
aer	sharp	acid
annus	year	annual
aqua	water	aquarium
audio	hear	auditorium
bell	war	belligerent
bene	well	benediction
ced	move	secede
cent	hundred	century
cognos	know	recognize
col	care for	colonize
cor	heart	cordial
corpus	body	corporate
credo	belief	credence
crescere	grow	increase
cult	care for	agriculture
cur	run	current
cura	heal	curative
dic	say	dictation
doe	teach	doctrine
dominus	rule, lord	dominate
duc, ducto	lead	conduct
duras	hard	durable
exter	out	external
facilis	easy	facilitate
facio	make	manufacture
fides	faith	confident
fero	carry	ferry
fin	end	final
homo	man	homicide
ignis	fire	ignite
later	side	lateral
liber	free	liberate
liter	letters	literature
locus	place	locate
lucio, lux	light	translucent
magn	great	magnitude
mal	bad	malignant
man	hand	manufacture
mitto	send	remit
mob	move	mobile
multus	much	multiply
nomen	name	nominate
ocul	eye	oculist
omnis	all	omnipotent
pac	peace	Pacific
par	equal	compare
pater	father	paternity
pes, pedis	foot	pedestrian
popul	people	population
port	carry	portfolio
potio	strong	potent
primus	first	primary
scribo	write	subscribe
sect	cut	bisect
sed, sess	sit	session
solus	lone	solitary
spee	see	spectacle
super	above	superintendent
tempus	time	temporary
terr	land	territory
totus	whole	total
ut	use	utility
vag	wander	vagrant
venire	come	ventilate
ver	truth	verify
verbum	word	verbal
verto	turn	convert
via	way	viaduct
vid, visum	see	visible
viv, vit	live	vivacious
voca	call	vocal
vol	roll	revolve

Greek Roots

Root	Meaning	Qualifying Word
aer	air	airplane
arche	old, beginning	archbishop
auto	self	automatic
bi	two	bicycle
bio	life	biology
chrom	color	chromatic
chron	time	chronological
crat	rule	democratic
cycl	circle	tricycle
dem	people	democracy
derm	skin	epidermis
dyn	power	dynamo
geo	earth	geography
graph	write	phonograph
hydr	water	hydraulic
hyper	over	hyperactive
mania	madness for	pyromania
metro	measure	metronoscope
micro	small	microscope
mono	one	monotone
octo	eight	octopus
pan	all	panchromatic
path	feeling, disease	pathetic
phil	love	philosophy
phobos	fear	toxiphobia
phon	sound	telephone
polis	city	metropolis
poly	many	polysyllable
scop	view	telescope
syn, sym	together	symphony
tele	far	telegraph
tri	three	tripod

1. Recognizing the Latin or Greek Root

Grades four, five, and six

Write ten Latin or Greek roots on the board. Discuss their meanings, then ask the pupils to consult their dictionaries and find for each root five words in which that root is contained. Discuss the words and their meanings.

Example:

Root	*Meaning*	*Words*	*Meaning*
bene	well	benefit	promotes welfare
		benediction	to say it well, blessing
		benefactor	....
		beneficial	....
		benign	....

PREFIXES AND SUFFIXES

PREFIXES

The prefix is a syllable at the beginning of a word. Prefixes generally alter the aspect of the idea. (For example, *kindness* means a state of being kind.) *Unkind* means not kind. One-fourth, or 5,000 of the 20,000 words listed in Thorndike's Word List have prefixes, and a mere fifteen prefixes account for eighty-two percent of that group.

These fifteen prefixes are:

ab....from	*dis*....part	*pre*....before
ad....to	*en*....in	*pro*....in front of
be....by	*ex*....out	*re*....back
com....with	*in*....into	*sub*....under
de....from	*in*....not	*un*....not

Below are listed some of the most-used prefixes, together with their meanings and qualifying words.

Prefix	*Meaning*	*Qualifying Word*
ab	away from	absent
ad	to	adhere
ambi, amphi	both	amphibian
ante	before	anteroom
anti	against	antibody
auto	self	autobiography
be	by	beside
bi	two	bicycle
circum	around	circumference
com, con, co	together	combine
contra, counter	against	contraband
de	from, down	depart
dis	not, away	disagree
en	in	enroll
ex	out	export
hemi	half	hemisphere
hyper	above	hyperactive
hypo	under	hypodermic
in, im	into, not	impossible
inter	between	interstate
il, ir	not	illegal
mis	wrong	misinform
multi	many	multitude
non	not	nonskid
op	against	oppose
out	over, surpass	outshine
para	beside	paragraph
per	through	pertain
poly	many	polysyllable
post	after	postoperative
pre	before	preschool
pro	in front of, before	program
re	back	remit
semi	half	semicircle
sub	under	submarine
super	above	superintendent
syn, sym	together	sympathy
trans	across	transatlantic
ultra	above	ultramodern
un	not	unknown
with	against	withhold

A suggested study plan for words is given below:

Example: disablement

Stem: ....Meaning: ....
Prefix: ....Meaning: ....
Suffix: ....Meaning: ....

1. Recognizing Form and Meaning of Prefixes

Grades four, five, and six

Place the prefix *un* at the beginning of the words and give their meaning.

............settled ....
............important ....
............kind ....
............interesting ....
............healthy ....
............able ....

Use other prefixes in a similar way.

2. Becoming Acquainted with Prefixes

Grades four, five, and six

Decide on the meaning of each of the words by looking at the prefix.

............prepaid ....
............misspelled ....
............semicircle ....
............interstate ....
............transcontinental ....
............anti-slavery ....

3. Cross Out the Word

Grades four, five, and six

Choose the word that will complete the meaning of each sentence. Cross out the word that does not belong.
Mary (tied, untied) the package to see what was inside.
It is (necessary, unnecessary) to watch the traffic signals.

4. Knowing Prefixes

Grades five and six

Prepare exercises similar to those given below:

a. Write the prefix *mis* before each word and define the word.

............place ....
............understand ....
............direct ....
............conduct ....
............spell ....
............carry ....
............fit ....
............deed ....

b. Write the prefix *ante* before each word and define the word.

............bellum ....
............room ....
............diluvian ....
............chamber ....
............cedent ....
............orbital ....
............Victorian ....
............cede ....

c. Write the prefix *pre* before each word and define the word.

............fix ....
............historic ....
............view ....
............cook ....
............school ....
............dict ....
............determine ....
............paid ....

d. Write the prefix *im* or *in* before each word and define the word.

............patient ....
............possible ....
............perfect ....
............capable ....
............direct ....
............practical ....
............polite ....
............pure ....

5. Is It a Prefix?

Grades five and six

Checks the words that contain prefixes.

........impossible	........rejoin
........disorderly	........forearm
........incorrect	........uncle
........vite	........unafraid
........union	........disaster
........unexpected	........disobey
........understand	........improve
........incapable	........impure
........remodel	........imperfect
........inactive	........reappear
........dishpan	........foreground
........distrust	........incomplete

—and so on

6. Prefixes

Grades four, five, and six

Prepare the paper as shown below. Duplicate one for each pupil. They are to write as many words as they can that begin with the prefix in the box. They may consult a dictionary if necessary. After the work is completed, discuss and define the words.

1. ab	2. ad
3. an	4. de
5. dis	6. ex
7. im	8. in
9. mis	10. per
11. re	12. sub

13. syn, sym	14. trans
15. ultra	16. un

SUFFIXES

A suffix is a syllable at the end of a word and usually changes the original word to a different class or kind. Some of the most used suffixes are listed below:

able............capable of being
age............act or state of
al............relation to
ate (noun)............one who
ate (verb)............to make
ble, ible............capable of being
cy............state of
den, dom............state or condition
er............little, maker of
est............comparison
ful............capable of being
ian............relating to
ise, ize............to make
ish............state of being
ism............act of
ist, ite............one who
ity, ty............state of being
ly............like, in manner
less............without
ment............state or quality
ness............state of being
ship............relationship
some............state of being
ster............one who
tion............state or condition
tude............state or condition
ure............act or process
ward............direction of

1. Adding Endings to Words

Grades two and three

Directions:

Write *er* and *est* after these words. Then use them in sentences. Children should fill in blanks and then make use of the words in their written work.

old

....

....

long

....

....

short

....

....

2. Changing Words with Suffixes

Grades three and four

Directions:

Add the proper suffix to each word followed by a space to make the sentence correct.
The........art........was painting a picture.
The man appreciated his kind ....

3. Adding a Suffix

Grades three and four

Directions:

Write the suffix *ly* after each word and tell what it means.
exact....... quiet....... careful......., and the like.
Other suffixes may be used in the same way.

4. Recognizing Suffixes

Grades five and six

Write the meaning of the words below. Circle the suffix and underline the baseword.

1. painful ....
2. wonderful ....
3. wooden ....
4. quickest ....
5. farmer ....
6. smoother ....
7. unsuitable ....
8. disagreeable ....
9. kingdom ....
10. freedom ....
11. powerless ....
12. ruler ....
13. kindness ....
14. settlement ....
15. meaningless ....
16. homesickness ....
17. actor ....
18. miner ....
19. unkindly ....
20. weakly ....
21. improvement ....
22. thoughtfully ....
23. lonely ....
24. dreadful ....
25. enjoyment ....
26. movement ....
27. manly ....
28. unforgivable ....
29. ungrateful ....
30. slowest ....
31. slowly ....
32. silken ....

5. Using Suffixes and Prefixes

Grades five and six

Add prefixes and suffixes to the basewords. Make as many words as possible by using the basewords given below.

Using Prefixes and Suffixes

1. *kind*

2. *honest*

3. *believe*

4. *place*

5. *fit*

6. *carry*

7. *pay*

8. *like*

9. *comfort*

10. *pleasant*

11. *prove*

12. *complete*

6. Learning New Words

Grades five and six

Give the students lists of words and ask them to give the meaning by using their knowledge of prefixes, suffixes, and roots.

antechamber ....
antisocial ....
amphibian plane ....
bicycle ....
automatic ....
abnormal ....
beside ....
century ....
circumnavigate ....
companion ....
depart ....
decimal ....
discourage ....
enable ....
excursion ....
hexagon ....
hypersensitive ....
hypodermic ....
inability ....
intake ....
interstate ....
irregular ....
illegal ....
misrepresent ....
monoplane ....
multitude ....
nonessential ....
octagon ....
octopus ....
pentagon ....
centipede ....
polysyllable ....
collection ....
perfectly ....
hydroplane ....
quadrangle ....
prologue ....
preseason ....
retake ....
semicircle ....
submarine ....
supercharged ....
transmission ....
tricycle ....
unable ....
bisect ....
settlement ....
autograph ....
interstellar ....
predict ....
exponent ....
inconvenience ....
semicivilized ....
subscribe ....
wooden ....
misleading ....
lonesomeness ....
kingdom ....
hemisphere ....
exterior ....
by-product ....
receptacle ....

SPELLING AS RELATED TO VOCABULARY DEVELOPMENT

Although spelling a word orally is not used as a means of word recognition, yet being able to spell words can be an asset to the pupil in word recognition. The following activities can be used to make spelling more meaningful and enjoyable.

1. Using the Morse Code

Grades three, four, five, and six

The students learn the Morse code. The teacher may place words in code on the blackboard, and the students can decode them. The students can also write their words in code.

The Morse Code:

A • —	J • — — —	S • • •
B — • • •	K — • —	T —
C — • — •	L • — • •	U • • —
D — • •	M — —	V • • • —
E •	N — •	W • — —
F • • — •	O — — —	X — • • —
G — — •	P • — — •	Y — • — —
H • • • •	Q — — • —	Z — — • •
I • •	R • — •	

2. Speed Spelling

Grades two, three, four, five, and six

The pupils write the letters of the alphabet, one letter on each line. Opposite each letter they are to write as many three-letter words as they can that begin with that letter of the alphabet. Go to four-letter words, and for older students, five- and six-letter words may be used. Time the class.

Example:

A . . . ate, are, ant, ago
B . . . bug, big, bag, but, bin, and so on.

3. Visualizing Words

Grades three, four, five, and six

Write two letters on the blackboard and ask the pupils to find a word in the spelling list that contains those two letters.

4. Listening for Sounds

Grades three, four, five, and six

One pupil spells the word orally and asks another one to pronounce it. The child may continue spelling until he finds someone who cannot recognize the word. He then selects another child to spell the words.

5. Exploring

Grades three, four, five, and six

Give the definition of a word and ask the children to find the antonym and the synonym for it. This may be done orally or it can be used for a written activity.

6. Association

Grades three, four, five, and six

The children are asked to write the word that belongs to make up a combination. The words may be given orally or written on the chalkboard.

Example:

chair —	bread —
pen —	cup —

The children would write

table	butter
ink	saucer

7. Uncode Synonyms and Antonyms

Grades three, four, five, and six

Given words may be duplicated or written on the board. The children write the antonyms and synonyms in Morse code.

Word	*Synonym*	*Antonym*
cold		
fast		
small		

8. Finding Words

Grades three, four, five, and six

The teacher writes words on the board and writes questions to be answered by the pupils. This exercise may be duplicated if desired. For lower grades use ten words, but use about twenty words for upper levels.

Example:

1. Which word has an *f* sound that is spelled with a *gh*? ....
2. Which word has an *f* sound that is spelled another way? ....
3. Which word is the plural of *loaf*? ....
4. Which word rhymes with *way* even though the ending is not spelled the same? ....

Words: sleigh, enough, often, loaves, prophet, and so on.

9. Making New Words

Grades four, five, and six

The pupils are asked to add another word to the beginning or the end of the words given to them to make new words.

Example:

1. Add *end* to these words to make new words. Then write new words on line.
   anger........... ear........... less........... port...........
2. Add *rot* to car........... par........... ten........... ate...........
3. Add *so* to lo........... lid........... on........... me...........
4. Add *ten* to has........... ant........... fat........... pin.........
5. Add *ice* to not........... off........... just........... box.........
6. Add *rate* to mode........ pi........ lace........ able........
7. Add *get* to for........ mid........tar........ bud........
8. Add *duct* to pro........ con........ via........ in........

Students define the words. Encourage them to make up their own sets of words.

10. Fifteen Letter Puzzle

Grades two, three, four, five, and six

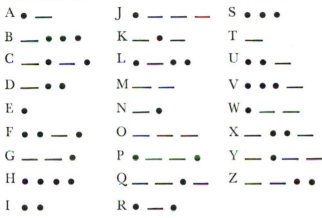

Use the letters *a b c d e f g h i j k l m n o* and make as many three-letter words as possible. Use a letter only once in each word. For older students four-letter words may be made.

Example:

act
aft
age
and,—and so on

11. Make as Many Words as You Can

Grades three, four, five, and six

Ask the pupils to write their names and then use the from the word *independence.* Use a letter only once in each word but it need not be in the same sequence as it is in the original word.

Among the other words that can be used are *stationery, photographer, understood, afterward, appearance, masquerade.*

12. Using Your Name to Make Words

Grades three, four, five, and six

Ask the pupils to write their names and then use the letters in making as many words as they can. A letter is used only once in each word. The pupils can display their results.

13. Hidden Words

Grades three, four, five, and six

Ask the pupils to find as many hidden words as they can in each word. The work may be placed on the blackboard, duplicated, or given orally. Segments of words, as well as entire words, may be used.

Example:

abed (*bead*)	burst (*rust*)
aster (*star*)	beast (*east*)
awful (*flaw, law*)	beneath (*then*)
aside (*aid*)	battle (*tale*)

The pupils can make up their own lists and try to stump the class.

14. Wordo

Grades three, four, five, and six

Make markers from cardboard, or use buttons, corn, or beans. Mark off squares on a piece of paper—one for each child. Write the words into the squares and as the child or the teacher pronounces the word, the children place the marker on the word. The arrangement of the words should differ on each sheet of paper. The child who gets the first row complete or filled calls "Wordo." Children can make up these sheets for classroom use.

15. Missing Word

Grades two, three, four, five, and six

Write the spelling words on the chalkboard. The children look at the words, then put their heads on their arms at tables or desks. The teacher or a child erases a word. The pupil is then called on to spell the missing word.

16. Touch

Grades two, three, and four

The children are in a circle and hold their hands behind their backs. Place an object in one child's hand. If he recognizes the object he spells the name. If he can't spell it, he passes it on to the next child.

17. Beheading Words

Grades three, four, five, and six

Write the directions on the chalkboard and ask the children to find the correct words. This activity may also be used as paper work.

Example:

Behead a garden tool and get a poor dwelling. (hovel)
Behead a group of animals and get a safety device. (lock)

The pupils can make up their own directions.

18. Hidden Pairs

Grades three, four, five, and six

Have the students find words in the dictionary that have something in common in a shorter word hidden in each pair of words.

Example: trimming wedge

1. dogma—catch	6. stilt—clean
2. carnival—cable	7. charm—legend
3. bold—sworn	8. addle—summary
4. respond—slake	9. chatter—capable
5. humble—missing	10. potato—company

19. Mixed-up Letters

Grades four, five, and six

The scrambled letters spell musical instruments when arranged in the correct order. The pupils are to spell the words correctly. They may make up exercises using other classifications such as fruit, vegetables, states, and so on.

1. glube	9. recont	17. anipo
2. rubematoni	10. oilivn	18. fetul
3. lovia	11. jobna	19. sonaobs
4. murd	12. raph	20. puremtt
5. noleypoxh	13. eboo	21. nearlict
6. coilcop	14. tuab	22. noterbom
7. labycm	15. lecol	23. nicotrance
8. uratig	16. groan	24. donnlaim

20. Twister Words

Grades two, three, four, five, and six

The pupils, using the same letters in each word make different words of them. Pupils can make their own twister words by using the dictionary.

Example: march—charm

Partial list of words.

act	amble	blister	cheater
acme	aster	bruise	cape
arch	ate	cheap	dear
arm	ample	clasp	drop
are	battle	clean	
acre	fowl	crate	

21. Word Wheels

Grades four, five, and six

The "spoke" words begin with the letter in the center of the wheel. The pupils, going clockwise, fill in the outside ring. The beginning of the word starts out with the last letter of the preceding word (fig. 6.37).

The pupils can make a wheel for each letter of the alphabet.

Example:

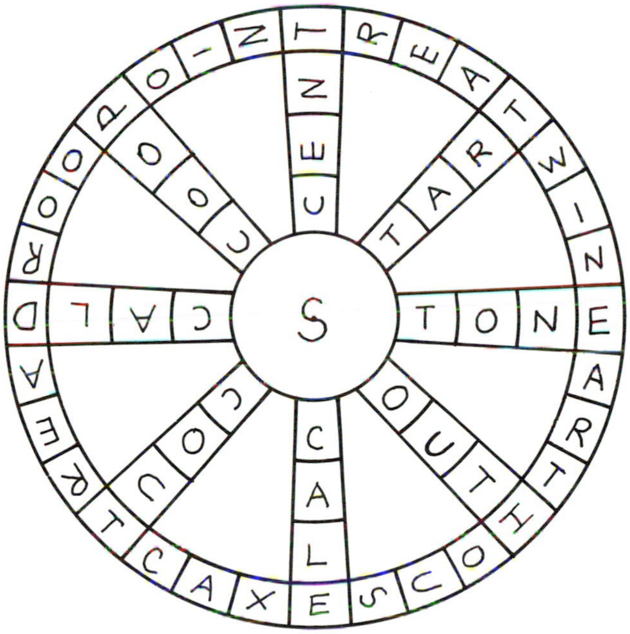

Figure 6.37 Word Wheel

22. Interesting Words

Grades four, five, and six

Ask the pupils to find origins of words.

Example:

1. *Disaster* comes from the Latin *dis* and *astre* (star). It means: if the stars are not right you have disaster.
2. *Volcano* is derived from the name *Vulcan*, the Roman god, who was the lame son of the Roman god Jupiter. Vulcan had his workshop under Mount Aetna.

23. Recent or Dated Words

Grades four, five, and six

Write the words on the chalkboard or duplicate them. The pupils write *R* for recent and *O* for outdated after the words.

Example:

doughboy	phonograph
orbit	surrey
tin Lizzie	square
transistorized	vamoose
	—and so on

Ask the pupils to make lists to be presented to the class. Their parents will enjoy helping them with their lists. *Overused* words can also be listed.

24. Word Letters

Grades three, four, five, and six

Present the words either on the chalkboard or on paper. The pupils are to write the word represented by the letters: I, T, J, PP, L, Q, C, U, G, O, MT, CD, IC, DK, IV, XS, LC, KT, FE, ME, K, AB, PT, LX, EZ, BD, NV, NME, XYC, PK, TP, SA, B, B4, 4, 2, 8, Y, 4T, 8T, R, YY,

Can you read? YY U R, YY UB, I C U R YY 4 me. O I C U R. I C U R YY. I C U 8 2, and so on.

Ask the pupils to find other letters.

25. How Many Ways Can You Use These Words?

Grades three, four, five, and six

Each of these words has more than one meaning. Give lists to pupils and have them use the words in sentences (each word to be used in two sentences to show different meanings) either orally or in written form. Ask the pupils to make lists of other words having more than one meaning.

Partial list:

arm	brood	fall	mind	shed
back	brush	felt	mine	show
ball	cane	fire	miss	sink
bank	call	firm	nail	spring
bark	card	fish	note	strain
bat	check	flat	peck	team
bay	chest	hand	pen	tip
bear	chief	hold	pick	tire
beat	chop	hose	point	top
bill	club	jam	post	train
bit	coast	jerk	present	well
block	comb	land	ring	will
blow	down	leaves	roll	work
board	drop	long	rose	
bow	duck	march	run	
box	eyes	may	saw	
break	fair	might	seal	

26. Silent Letters

Grades three, four, five, and six

Present the rules for silent letters when these letters appear in the spelling lists and in the reading assignment.

These letters are silent:

1. *b* is silent when followed by *t* as in *debt, doubt.*
2. *b* is silent when preceded by *m* as in *lamb, climb.*
3. *c* is silent when used in some words, like *scene, muscle.*
4. *d* is silent in some words, like *handsome, Wednesday.*
5. *gh* is usually silent when preceded by a vowel, like *might, caught.*
6. *g* is silent when it is followed by *n,* as in *gnaw, gnat.*
7. *h* is silent when it is preceded by *g,* like *ghost, ghastly.*
8. *h* is silent in some words, like *honor, hour.*
9. *k* is silent when followed by *n* as in *know, knee.*
10. *l* is silent in some words like *talk, should.*
11. *n* is silent when preceded by *m* as in *solemn.*

12. *p* is silent when followed by *s* like *glimpse, psalm.*
13. *p* is silent in some words, like *cupboard, receipt.*
14. *p* is silent when followed by *n* as in *pneumonia.*
15. *t* is silent in some words, like *listen, often.*
16. *w* is silent when followed by *r* as in *wrong, wrap.*
17. When *wh* is followed by *o*, the *w* is usually silent, like *whole, who, whose.*

27. Is it "os" or "oes" in the Plural?

Grades four, five, and six

List some words that end in *o*. Ask the pupils to form the plurals with the aid of the dictionary. Ask them to formulate a rule to follow about adding an *e* before the *s*.

Words ending in *o*

alto	buffalo	domino	junco
armadillo	cargo	dynamo	kimono
auto	cello	echo	lasso
banjo	cockatoo	Eskimo	lotto
bolero	credo	halo	mango
bolo	cuckoo	hero	memento
broncho	dingo	hobo	memo
motto	potato	solo	veto
mulatto	radio	tomato	zero
piano	ratio	tornado	zoo
piccolo	silo	torpedo	

28. Classification and Word Recognition

Grades one, two, and three

Use words found in the textbook to develop this activity. Vary the directions according to needs. Classifications may be names of plants, flowers, fruit, animals, verbs, nouns, and the like.

Color the squares red if they contain names of toys.

Color the squares green if they contain names of animals.

Color the squares blue if they contain names of food.

See example below.

29. Unscramble These Capitals

For Grades four, five, and six

Duplicate these scrambled capitals. Ask the pupils to write the word correctly and give the state.

cake	monkey	mule	sheep	hamster	cow	bread
cat	apple	jumping rope	top	blocks	grapes	horse
rabbit	toy train	rice	car	noodles	doll	zebra
pig	teddy bear	puzzle	milk	toy plane	hula hoop	deer
goose	jack-in-box	lettuce	jacks	hamburger	ball	wolf
lion	beans	marbles	wagon	toy boat	peas	bear
potatoes	frog	tiger	goat	fox	elephant	oatmeal

		Name	*State*
1.	Roved	....	....
2.	Lattana	....	....
3.	Sibco	....	....
4.	Feast An	....	....
5.	Doccorn	....	....
6.	Connill	....	....
7.	Skojnac	....	....
8.	Gommetryon	....	....
9.	Nixehop	....	....
10.	Vender	....	....
11.	Haltsaseale	....	....
12.	Lunohulo	....	....
13.	Heneceny	....	....
14.	Sonidam	....	....
15.	Pailomy	....	....
16.	Larckshonet	....	....
17.	Nutsia	....	....
18.	Vainshell	....	....
19.	Repire	....	....
20.	Naujeu	....	....
21.	Litter Lock	....	....
22.	Meanscroat	....	....
23.	Darthorf	....	....
24.	Sipoinlandia	....	....
25.	Prinsigeldf	....	....
26.	Men Soides	....	....
27.	Poetak	....	....
28.	Krafftorn	....	....
29.	Grant Oboue	....	....
30.	Nottern	....	....
31.	Sagautu	....	....
32.	Tobons	....	....
33.	Noccis Arty	....	....
34.	Hondcrim	....	....
35.	Leprominte	....	....
36.	Last Lacy Tike	....	....
37.	Baylan	....	....
38.	Hiraleg	....	....
39.	Bricksam	....	....
40.	Coumbial	....	....
41.	Bumsucol	....	....
42.	Cedrovepin	....	....
43.	Imohacoy Talk	....	....
44.	Meals	....	....
45.	Rashrugrib	....	....
46.	Snaponali	....	....
47.	Slingan	....	....
48.	Nofffericy Jest	....	....
49.	Up Last	....	....
50.	Nehela	....	....

30. Find the Fifty States

Grades four, five, and six

Duplicate the puzzle for each pupil and have them enclose each state with a pencil marking. They may be read forward, backward, upward, downward, or

G	E	N	I	A	M	R	A	M	A	B	A	L	A	N	O	Z	I	R	A	K	Y	Z	T
E	N	A	R	O	F	I	M	Y	L	T	E	N	N	E	S	S	E	E	R	R	S	R	U
R	E	I	V	F	Y	D	O	B	A	O	F	I	X	I	Y	X	O	H	I	O	M	H	Z
I	W	N	M	L	B	A	H	I	S	L	L	R	V	K	M	W	C	N	U	Y	X	O	A
H	J	A	Y	O	V	H	A	B	K	C	F	V	C	O	A	O	D	T	A	W	I	D	I
S	E	V	Z	R	Y	O	L	X	A	S	X	U	N	S	N	I	O	M	T	E	I	E	N
P	R	L	N	I	E	W	K	V	A	X	T	T	H	N	A	X	J	U	O	N	S	I	R
M	S	Y	P	D	R	L	O	S	V	N	A	I	E	N	X	N	U	V	S	T	C	S	O
A	E	S	S	A	U	G	N	T	E	N	N	C	A	D	G	E	O	R	G	I	A	L	F
H	Y	N	E	B	R	A	S	K	A	G	T	O	V	I	R	G	I	N	I	A	S	A	I
W	I	N	A	O	K	A	D	T	T	I	N	J	F	V	J	D	A	I	D	O	O	N	L
E	V	E	C	T	H	O	X	O	C	O	O	R	E	G	O	N	W	L	E	C	U	D	A
N	Q	P	T	J	O	B	N	U	P	W	M	Y	J	X	G	I	V	L	L	I	T	X	C
M	I	N	N	E	S	O	T	A	G	A	R	F	O	Z	S	K	S	I	A	X	H	M	N
R	C	K	X	F	X	H	C	D	Q	U	E	D	R	C	Z	Y	K	N	W	E	D	I	A
I	I	A	W	A	H	N	O	P	X	W	V	E	O	T	V	X	B	O	A	M	A	S	G
K	L	O	M	A	R	Y	L	A	N	D	P	N	B	E	K	H	S	I	R	W	K	S	I
H	J	E	E	X	J	S	O	B	O	C	S	F	Y	X	F	M	O	S	E	E	O	I	H
S	O	U	T	H	C	A	R	O	L	I	N	A	D	A	V	E	N	X	X	N	T	S	C
K	D	C	X	A	S	P	A	U	N	L	X	L	M	S	A	R	K	A	N	S	A	S	I
R	X	H	C	T	F	I	D	S	T	T	E	S	U	H	C	A	S	S	A	M	O	I	M
Q	L	K	E	U	O	B	O	A	I	N	I	G	R	I	V	T	S	E	W	X	Z	P	D
L	O	U	I	S	I	A	N	A	T	O	K	A	D	H	T	R	O	N	B	X	Q	P	G
A	N	I	L	O	R	A	C	H	T	R	O	N	W	X	M	I	S	S	O	U	R	I	C

diagonally to find the fifty states. This puzzle may also be drawn on a 15-by-15-inch piece of cardboard and covered with transparent plastic. The pupil then uses crayons to mark the states. After he has completed the project, it may be erased with Kleenex and used again.

WORD LISTS

These lists are prepared for the teacher's convenience. They are not complete and students should be encouraged to add to them. The lists may be used in many ways, such as classification, research, organization, mapmaking, date lines, spelling, phonics, science, and so on. Using barred paper, the teacher or the students can make puzzles similar to the one shown below.

Example: Find the Vegetables

You may read forward, backward, upward, downward, or diagonally to find as many vegetables as you can.

A	K	O	H	L	R	A	B	I	R	D	T	E	E	B
H	S	E	V	I	H	C	R	A	C	U	U	B	Y	E
A	E	P	E	A	S	A	O	K	R	A	D	C	O	A
R	U	T	A	B	A	G	A	N	Y	R	S	K	K	N
O	N	U	O	R	B	E	I	O	D	R	A	R	E	S
M	A	T	S	O	A	P	A	W	L	E	E	E	O	R
A	N	R	O	C	O	G	R	U	E	L	A	P	I	T
I	D	B	D	C	U	C	U	M	B	E	R	P	S	D
N	O	I	N	O	F	H	E	S	J	C	R	E	O	S
E	G	G	P	L	A	N	T	N	M	O	T	P	H	U
G	A	R	L	I	C	I	R	A	D	I	S	H	S	V
A	C	E	G	R	E	W	O	L	F	I	L	A	U	C
A	R	T	I	C	H	O	K	E	N	W	V	W	N	E
K	L	L	E	T	T	U	C	E	P	X	Y	E	L	N
C	A	B	B	A	G	E	P	K	A	L	E	O	S	T

1. A List of Flowers

Ask the students to make flower scrap books, pressed flowers, collect seeds, make maps on origin of flowers, and the like. The list can be used for classification of wild flowers, garden flowers, annuals, perennials, red, blue, and so on. The pupils can also learn how the plants reseed themselves.

adder's tongue
alyssum
anemone
arbutus, trailing
arrowheads
aster
bachelor's button
begonia
bellflower
black-eyed Susan
bleeding heart
bluebell
bluebonnet
bluets
bouncing Bet
butter-and-eggs
buttercup
California poppy
casam
camelia
candytuft
canna
carnation
chrysanthemum
clover
columbine
coneflower
cornflower
cosmos
cowslip
crocus
daffodil
dahlia
daisy
dandelion
day lily
dog violet
dogwood
evening primrose
forget-me-not
foxglove
fuchsia
galardia
gentian
geranium
gilia
goldenrod
hepatica
honeysuckle
hyacinth
iris
jonquil
jumping johnnie
lady's slipper
larkspur
lilac
lily
lily of the valley
lobelia
lotus
lupine
magnolia
mallow
marguerite
marigold
mariposa lily
May apple
Mayflower
milkweed
morning glory
mullein
narcissus
nasturtium
oleander
orchid
paintbrush, Indian
pansy
pasqueflower
penstemon
peony
petunia
phlox
pinks
poinsettia
poppy
portulaca
Queen Anne's lace
rhododendron
rose
sego lily
shooting star
Solomon's seal (false)
sunflower
sweet peas
sweet William
thistle
toadflax
trillium
tulip
vervain
vetch
viola
violet
wisteria
wood sorrel
yarrow
zinnia

2. A List of Vegetables

artichoke
asparagus
avocado (*fruit*)
bean
beet
broccoli
cabbage
carrot
cauliflower
celery
chives
corn
cowpeas
cucumber
eggplant
endive
gherkin
kale
kohlrabi
leek
lentils
lettuce
mushroom
onion
parsley
parsnip
pepper
potato
radish
romaine
rutabaga
squash
spinach
tomato (*fruit*)
turnip
yam

3. A List of Musical Instruments

autoharp
bagpipes
balalaika
banjo
bass horn
bassoon
bass viol
bazooka
bugle
cello
clarinet
concertina
cornet
symbal
dulcimer
drum
fife
flute
French horn
guitar
harmonica
harp
kettledrum
lute
lyre
mandolin
melodeon
oboe
organ
piano
piccolo
pipes
saxophone
spinet
tambourine
trombone
trumpet
tuba
ukelele
viola
violin
xylophone

4. Modes of Transportation

Suggestions: The various means of transportation may be classified according to whether transport is by water, air, or land; or they can be classified by datelines. The children should use reference books for identifying those they do not know. Transportation books and posters may be made.

airplane
automobile
balloon
barouche
barrow
bateaux
berlin
betjack
bicycle
biplane
bireme
boat
brig
brigantine
britzka
broughham
buckboard
buffalo
buggy
bull-boat
burro
bus
cab
cable car caboose
cabriolet
caique
calash
caleche
camel
canoe
car
caravel
carriage
carryall
cart
catamaran
catboat
chaise
chariot
clipper
coach
coble
Conestoga
coracle
corvette
coupe
curricle
cutter
dahabieh
dhow
dinghy
dirigible
dogcart
dogs
donkey
dory
drag
dray
droshky
dugout
elephant
elevator
escalator
felucca
ferry
fiacre
flatboat
freighter
frigate
galleon
galley
gondola
goofah
gunboat
hackney coach
hansom
helicopter
horse
horsecar
houseboat
hydrofoil
hydroplane
jaunting car
junk
kayak
ketch
landau
launch
lifeboat
liner
llama
locomotive
logs
motorboat
motorcycle
mule
omnibus
oxen
parachute
phaeton
prairie schooner
pram
proa
punt
racer
racing shell
raft
reindeer
rickshaw
rockaway
rowboat
sailboat
sampan
schooner
scooter
scow
sedan
shallop
ship
skate
skiff
sled
sledge
sleigh
sloop
sociable
stagecoach
steamer
sternwheeler
streetcar
stretcher
submarine
sulky
surrey
tallyho
tanker
taxi
trailer
train
tramway
trap
travois
tricycle
truck
tugboat
van
velocipede
victoria
wagon
whaleboat
wheelbarrow
wherries
yacht
yak
yawl
zeppelin

5. A List of Birds

Suggestions: The birds may be classified as, for example: land, water, wild, domestic, song, migrating, and so on. Students may make bird books and write stories and descriptions, and a bird-watching trip can be planned.

albatross
auk
avocet
bird of paradise
bittern
blackbird
bluebird
bluejay
bobolink
bobwhite
bowerbird
bunting
bushtit
canary
canvasback
cardinal
cassowary
catbird
chickadee
chimney swift
cockatiel
cockatoo
condor
coot
cormorant
crane
creeper, brown
crow
cuckoo
darter
dove
duck
eagle
eagle, bald
egret
emu
English sparrow
erne
falcon
finch
flamingo
flicker
flycatcher
gnatcatcher
goldfinch
goose
goshawk
grackle
grebe
grosbeak
grouse
guinea
gull
hawk
heron
house sparrow
hummingbird
ibis
junco
killdeer
kingbird
finglet
kite
lapwing
lark
lark, horned
linnet
loggerhead shrike
loon
macaw
magpie
mallard
martin
meadowlark
merganser duck
mockingbird
nighthawk
nightingale
nuthatch
oriole
osprey
ostrich
ovenbird
owl
owl, barn
owl, horned
owl, screech
parakeet
parrot
partridge
peacock
pelican
pewee
pheasant
phoebe
pigeon
pintail
pipit
plover
puffin
quail
rail
raven
redstart
reedbird
robin
rook
sandpiper
sapsucker
shrike
skylark
snipe
sparrow
spoonbill
starling
stork
swallow
swan
swift
tanager
teal
tern
thrasher
thrush
titmouse
toucan
towee
turkey
umbrella bird
vireo
vulture
warbler
waxwing
whippoorwill
willet
woodcock
wood duck
woodpecker
woodpecker, redheaded
wood pewee
wren
yellowlegs

6. A List of Trees

alder
ash
aspen
balsam
basswood
beech
birch
box elder
buckeye
butternut
catalpa
cedar
chestnut
cottonwood
cypress
dogwood
elm
fir
gum
hackberry
hawthorn
hemlock
hickory
holly
horse chestnut
Joshua tree
juniper
larch
laurel
linden
locust
magnolia
maple
mountain ash
mulberry
oak
olive
palm
pecan
pine
poplar
pussy willow
redbud
redwood
sasafras
sequoia
spruce
sugar maple
sumac
sycamore
tamarack
tulip tree
tupelo
walnut
willow

7. A List of Fruit

apple
apricot
avocado
banana
blackberry
blueberry
cantaloupe
casaba melon
cherry

chokecherry
crabapple
cranberry
currant
date
dewberry
elderberry
fig
gooseberry
grapefruit
grape
guava
hackberry
haw
hawthorn
honeydew melon
huckleberry
kumquat
lemon
lime
loganberry
mango
melon
mulberry
nectarine
olive
orange
papaya
peach
pear
persimmon
pineapple
plum
pumpkin
quince
raspberry
strawberry
tangelo
tangerine
tomato
watermelon

Nuts

acorn
almond
beechnut
Brazil nut
butternut
chestnut
filbert
hazelnut
hickory
pinyon
walnut

8. A List of Homes

Suggestions: This list may be used for classification, associating with who lives in each home, where the home is, matching occupant and home, and so on.

apartment
adobe hut
anthill
aquarium
ark
attic
bank (mud)
barge
barn
barracks
bowl (fish)
brook
billet
blockhouse
box
briar patch
cabin
cage
camper
castle
cave
chalet
circus
condominium
coop
cote
cottage
court
cradle
crib
dairy
den
farm
flat
fold (sheep)
forest
fort
garden
garret
grass
hedge
hogan
hole
hovel
hutch
igloo
lean-to
lighthouse
lodge
loft
log
longhouse
manor
manse
mansion
meadow
mobile home
monastery
nest
palace
park
pasture
pen
plantation
pool
puddle
pueblo
ranch
river
rock
sampan
shack
shanty
shed
shell
slough
sod house
sty
swamp
tepee
tent
thatched house
trailer
tree
villa
warren
web
wigwam
zoo

9. Picture Words

These words that can be illustrated are listed for the teacher's convenience in making up games and activities. It is suggested that the teacher and the pupils keep a file of pictures cut from magazines, catalogs, old books, and original drawings. Alphabetizing can be part of the activity.

acorn
ant
apple
apron
arm
arrow
axe
baby
bacon
bag
ball
balloon
banana
band
bank
barn
barrel
basket
basketball
bat (ball)
bat (mammal)
beads
beans
bear
beaver
bed
bee
beet
beetle
bell
belt
bench
berry
bib
bicycle
bird
blackbird
blackboard
blanket
block
blocks
blouse
bluejay
board
boat
bone
book
boots
bottle
bow (hair)
bow (arrow)
bowl
box
boy
bracelet
bread
bricks
bridge
bridle
broom
brownie
brush
bucket
buckle
bug
bus
buttercup
butterfly
button
cactus
cage
cake
calendar
calf
camel
camera
can
candle
candy
cane
cap
cape
car
carrot
cart
carton
castle
cat
celery
cent
chain
chair
chalk
charms
checkers
cheese
cherries
chick
children
chimney
chipmunk
church
churn
circus
city
clock
cloud
clown
coat
collar
colt
comb
cone
cook
cookie
corn
corncob
cot
cottage
cow
cowboy
crab
cracker
crayon
crib
cricket
crown
cry
cub
cucumber
cup
curtain
cushion
cut
daisy
dandelion
dart
door
deer
dentist
desk
dime
dinosaur
dish
doctor
dog
doll
dollar
dolphin
dominoes
donkey
dots
doughnut
dove
dragon
draw
drawer
dress
drink
drum
duck
dustpan
egg
eight
elbow
elephant
eleven
envelope
eraser
fairy
fall
fan
farm
farmer
father
feather
feet
fence
fern
file
finger
fire
fireman
fish
fist
five
flag
flame
flower
flowerpot
fly
foot
football
fork
fountain
four
fox
frame
fringe
frog
fruit
game
garden
gate
geese
geranium
giant
giraffe
girl
glass
glider
globe
glove
goat
goggles
goldfish
goose
grapefruit
grapes
grass
grasshopper
guitar
gum
gun
ham
hamburger
hammer
hammock
hand
handkerchief
handle
harp
hat
hatchet
hawk
heart
hay
haystack
heel
helicopter
helmet
hen
hill
hippopotamus
hoe
hook
hoop
horn
horse
hose
hound
house
hummingbird
igloo
Indian
ink
inkwell
jack (car)
jacket
jack-in-the-box
jack-o'-lantern
jacks
jam
jeans
jeep
jelly
jet
jewelry
jonquil
jug
jump
kangaroo
kettle
key
king
kite
kitten
knee
knife
knob
koala
label
lace
ladder
ladle
ladybug
lamb
lamp
lantern
leaf
leash
leg
lemon
letter
lettuce
lid
lightning
lily
lion
lips

lizard
lobster
lock
locket
log
magazine
mailbox
mailman
man
map
marbles
marshmallow
mask
mat
match
matches
men
melon
mice
milk
milkman
mill
mirror
mitt
mitten
money
monkey
moon
moose
mop
mother
motorcycle
mountain
mouse
mower
muff
mug
mule
nail
napkin
needle
nest
net
newspaper
nickel
nine
nose
notebook
numbers
nurse
nut
oar
octopus
olive
one
onion
orange
ostrich
oven
owl
oyster
package
page
pail
paints
pan
pancake

parachute
parakeet
parcel
paste
paw
peach
pear
pearls
peas
pen
pencil
penguin
piano
pickle
picture
pie
pig
pigeon
pillow
pin
pipe
plane
plant
plate
play
plow
plum
pole
poodle
pony
popcorn
poppy
post
postman
pot
potato
pump
pumpkin
puppet
puppy
purse
puzzle
quail
quarter
queen
quilt
rabbit
radio
radish
rain
rainbow
raincoat
rake
rat
rattle
read
records
refrigerator
rhinoceros
ribbon
ride
ring
river
road
robin
rock
rocker

rocket
roller skate
roof
rooster
rope
rose
ruler
run
saddle
sailor
sand
sandals
sandwich
saw
scarf
school
scissors
screw
seal
seven
shade
shadow
sheep
sheet
shelf
shell
ship
shirt
shoe
shovel
sink
sit
six
skate
skirt
skunk
sled
sleep
slide
slipper
smoke
snake
snow
snowman
soap
socks
soda
soldier
spade
spider
spire
sponge
spool
spoon
spur
square
squirrel
stalk
stamp
stand
star
stocking
stool
store
stork
stove
strawberries

string
submarine
sun
sunflower
sweater
swim
table
tack
tag
tail
tap (water)
teacher
tepee
teeter
teeth
telephone
television
ten
tent
thimble
thirteen
thirty
thistle
thread
three
thumb
tie
tiger
tire
toad
toast
toaster
toe
tomato
tool
top
towel
track
tractor
train
trap
tray
tree
tricycle
trout
truck
trunk
tub
tube
tulip
turkey
turtle
twelve
twig
two
umbrella
urn
valentine
vase
vegetable
vest
vine
violet
violin
waffle
wagon
wall

walrus
washing machine
watch
watercan
waterfall
water lily
watermelon

web
well
whale
wheat
wheel
wheelbarrow
whip
whistle

wigwam
window
window shade
wing
wishbone
witch
wolf
worm

yard
yardstick
yarn
xylophone
zebra
zeppelin
zipper
zoo

10. A Partial List of Compound Words

This list is prepared for the teacher so that she will be able to develop activities relating to them. If the teacher will help the pupils develop an awareness of these compound words, it will help them in the recognition of many words that are new to them.

afternoon
afterwards
airplane
airport
airship
airways
alleyway
another
anteater
anthill
anybody
anything
anytime
anywhere
apple pie
applesauce
apple tree
archway
armchair
backbone
background
backwoods
bagpipes
ball game
bandstand
barbershop
bareback
barefoot
baseball
basketball
bathroom
battleship
because
bedroom
bedspread
beehive
before
behind
beside
billfold
bird-dog
birdhouse
birthday
birthmark
birthplace
blackberry
blackbird
blackboard
blackout
bloodhound
bluebell

blueberry
bluebird
bluegrass
bluejay
bobcat
bobsled
bodyguard
bookcase
bookend
bookkeeper
bookmark
bookshelf
bookshop
bothersome
bottleneck
boxcar
breakdown
breakfast
breathtaking
broadcast
broadside
broomstick
buckskin
buckshot
bulldog
bullfrog
buttercup
butterfly
buttermilk
buttonhole
byway
campfire
candlelight
candlestick
candytuft
cannonball
cannot
cardboard
carport
castoff
catbird
catfish
catnip
cattail
checkerboard
chestnut
classmate
classroom
clockwork
clothesbasket
clothespin

clothesline
cloudburst
clubhouse
clubroom
coathanger
coattail
cobweb
collarbone
corkscrew
cornbread
corncob
corncrib
cornfield
cornhusk
cornstalk
cottonseed
cottontail
cottonwood
cowbell
cowboy
cowhand
cowhide
cowpuncher
cowslip
crabapple
crackerjack
crosscut
crosspatch
crossroads
crosswalk
crowbar
cuff links
cupboard
cup cake
curbstone
cut glass
cut-off
dairyman
dashboard
daydream
daylight
daytime
deerskin
dewdrop
dimestore
dining room
dinnerbell
doghouse
dollhouse
doughnut
downcast

downhearted
dragonfly
drainboard
drainpipe
drawbridge
dressmaker
driftwood
driveway
drugstore
drumstick
dumbbell
dustpan
earache
eardrum
earmark
earphone
earring
earthenware
earthquake
earthworm
eggplant
elsewhere
evergreen
everlasting
evermore
everybody
everyone
everything
everywhere
expressman
eyebrow
eyelid
eyesight
eyesore
eyestrain
fallout
fantail
farewell
farmhouse
farmyard
fencepost
ferryboat
fingernail
firecracker
firefly
firelight
fireman
fireplace
fireproof
fireside
firewood

first class
fisherman
fishhook
flagman
flagpole
flagstaff
flashlight
floodlight
flowerpot
flycatcher
fly paper
foghorn
football
footman
foot races
footsteps
footstool
footwear
forearm
forecast
foregone
forehead
foreman
foremost
foresight
forever
forget-me-not
foxglove
foxtail
freeway
frostbite
furthermore
gentleman
gingerbread
gingersnap
glowworm
godmother
goldenrod
goldfish
goldrush
glassblower
gooseberry
grandchild
grandfather
grandmother
grandstand
grapefruit
grapejuice
grapevine
grasshopper
greenback
griddlecake
grindstone
groundhog
groundwork
guesswork
hailstone
hailstorm
halfway
hallway
handbook
handcart
handcuff
handkerchief
handbag
handlebar
handmade
handout
handrail
handwriting
hangnail
hardhearted
hardware
hardwood
hatbox
hatrack
hayloft
haymow
haystack
headlight
hearsay
heavyweight
hereafter
herself
highlight
highway
high school
hillside
hilltop
himself
hitchhike
hobnail
homemade
homesick
homespun
homestead
homework
horseback
horsefly
horsepower
horseradish
horseshoe
houseboat
household
housekeeper
housemaid
housetop
housewares
housework
humbug
hummingbird
iceberg
icebox
icebreaker
ice cap
ice cream
indeed
indoor
inkwell
insight
instep
into
ironing board
jackrabbit
jawbone
jaw breaker
jaywalk
jellybean
jellyfish
jigsaw
kettledrum
keyboard
keyhole
keynote
kickoff
kneecap
knothole
ladybug
lady's slipper
lamplight
lamp post
landlady
landlord
landmark
landscape
landslide
lawbreaker
lawnmower
leapfrog
lemonade
lemon drop
lifeboat
lifeguard
lifelike
life-size
lifetime
lighthearted
lighthouse
lightweight
lipstick
livestock
lockjaw
log cabin
lookout
mailbox
mail carrier
mailman
make-believe
makeup
manpower
maybe
merry-go-round
midday
midnight
midway
milkmaid
milkman
milkshake
milkstool
milkweed
mincemeat
mockingbird
moonbeam
moonlight
morning glory
motorboat
motorcycle
motorman
mousetrap
mountainside
mushroom
namesake
necklace
necktie
neighborhood
nest egg
network
newsboy
newscast
newspaper
newsreel
nightfall
nighthawk
nightmare
nightshade
nightstand
noonday
nosebleed
nosegay
northeast
northwest
notebook
nutcracker
nuthatch
offspring
oilcloth
old-fashioned
one-sided
outcry
outdoors
outrage
outside
outwit
overboard
overcoat
overcome
overdue
overhead
overheard
overlap
overshoes
overtake
overturn
overweight
paintbox
pancake
paperback
paperhanger
paperweight
part-time
passageway
passkey
passport
password
pasteboard
patchwork
pathway
patrolman
paymaster
peacock
peephole
penknife
peppermint
quicksand
quicksilver
racehorse
racetrack
railroad
rainbow
raincoat
raindrop
rainstorm
rawhide
redhot
redwood
reindeer
ringleader
ringmaster
roadside
rollerskate
roommate
rosebud
rosebush
rosewood
roundhouse
roundup
rowboat
runway
safeguard
sagebrush
sailboat
saltshaker
sandbag
sandbar
sandman
sandpaper
sandstorm
saucepan
sawdust
sawhorse
sawmill
scarecrow
schoolhouse
schoolmaster
schoolmate
schoolroom
schoolyard
screendoor
scrub brush
seacoast
seagull
seahorse
searchlight
seashore
seaside
seaweed
secondhand
seesaw
sheepherder
shellfish
shipwreck
shipyard
shoelace
shoemaker
shoestring
shopkeeper
shoreline
shorthand
showcase
showdown
showroom
sidelight
sidetrack
sidewalk
silkworm
skylight
skyline
skyrocket
smashup
smokestack
snowball
snowbank
snowbird
snowbound
snowdrift
snowflake
snowman
snowshoe
snowstorm
soapsuds
softball
soft soap
softwood
somebody
someday
somehow
someone
something
sometime
somewhat
somewhere
sourdough
soybean
spaceship
spendthrift
sportsman
spotlight
springtime
stairsteps
stairway
standstill
starboard
stardust
starfish
starlight
steamboat
steam engine
steamship
stepladder
stepmother
stepping-stones
stonewall
storehouse
storeroom
streamline
streetcar
stronghold
suitcase
summertime
sunbeam
sunbonnet
sunflower
sunlight
sunrise
sunset
sunstroke
tablecloth
tablespoon
tableware
tailspin
tailwind
takeoff
teacart
teakettle
teaspoon
telltale
tenpins
textbook
thanksgiving
therefore
threadbare
throughout
thumbnail
thumbtack
thunderstorm
tiger lily
tightrope
timekeeper
timepiece
time table
tiptoe
toadstool
tomcat
tomtom
toolchest
toolroom
tongue-tied
toothache
toothbrush
toothpick
topcoat
topknot
topsoil
touchdown
trademark
underground
underhanded
updraft
uphill
upon
upside down
wagon wheel
wallpaper
warehouse
washcloth
washroom
wastebasket
wastepaper
watchdog
watchman
watermelon
waterway
wayside
weatherman
weekend
wheelbarrow
whenever
whetstone
whiplash
whirlwind
whitewash
wholesale
wholesome
widespread
wildcat
wildflower
windmill
windowpane
windshield
windstorm
wishbone
withheld
within
woodchuck
woodcutter
woodpecker
woodsman
woodwork
workbench
workman
workroom
workshop
yardstick
yourself

11. A Partial List of Homonyms

This list of homonyms is for the teacher's convenience. Homonyms are words that sound the same but do not mean the same and are not spelled alike. This list can be used for various activities for the children.

ad—add
aid—aide—ade
ail—ale
air—ere—heir
aisle—isle—I'll
alter—altar
ant—aunt
aught—ought
awl—all
arc—ark
bail—bale
ball—bawl
bare—bear
baron—barren
based—baste
bass—base

be–bee
beat–beet
beau–bow
beer–bier
belle–bell
berry–bury
berth–birth
blue–blew
boar–bore
board–bored
bolder–boulder
born–borne
bow–bough
boy–bouy
brake–break
bread–bred
breech–breach
bridle–bridal
brows–browse
build–billed
burro–burrow
but–butt
buy–by
cache–cash
calender–calendar
canvas–canvass
capital–capitol
carat–carrot
caries–carries
cart–carte
cast–caste
cause–caws
cede–seed
cell–sell
cellar–seller
cent–sent–scent
cents–sense
cereal–serial
chaste–chased
cheap–cheep
chews–choose
chili–chilly
choir–quire
chute–shoot
cite–site–sight
climb–clime
close–clothes
coarse–course
colonel–kernel
coral–choral
cord–chord
core–corps
counsel–council
coward–cowered
creak–creek
cue–queue
current–currant
dam–damn
days–daze
dear–deer
dew–do–due
die–dye
doe–dough
dual–duel
dun–done
earn–urn
eight–ate
ewe–you
eye–I
faint–feint
fair–fare
fairy–ferry
fate–fete
feat–feet
fir–fur
flare–flair
flea–flee
flew–flue
flower–flour
four–for–fore
fourth–forth
fowl–foul
freeze–frieze
gamble–gambol
gate–gait
gilt–guilt
grease–Greece
groan–grown
hail–hale
hair–hare
hart–heart
hay–hey
hear–here
heard–herd
heel–heal
hew–hue
him–hymn
hire–higher
hoard–horde
hoarse–horse
hole–whole
holy–wholly
hour–our
idle–idol
in–inn
its–it's
key–quay
knead–need
knew–new
knight–night
knit–nit
knot–not
know–no
knows–nose
laid–lade
lain–lane
lead–led
leaf–lief
leak–leek
lean–lien
leased–least
lesson–lessen
levy–levee
lie–lye
loan–lone
maid–made
mail–male
main–mane
mantel–mantle
marry–merry–Mary
mean–mien
meat–meet–mete
metal–mettle
might–mite
miner–minor
mold–mould
morn–mourn
morning–mourning
naval–navel
none–nun
one–won
ore–o'er–oar
ours–hours
owe–oh
pail–pale
pain–pane
pair–pear–pare
passed–past
pause–paws
peace–piece
peak–peek–pique
peal–peel
pearl–purl
peer–pier
plain–plane
pray–prey
presence–presents
pride–pried
principle–principal
prophet–profit
quarts–quartz
rain–reign–rein
raise–rays–raze
rap–wrap
read–red
read–reed
real–reel
right–write–rite
ring–wring
road–rode
roll–role
rose–rows
rote–wrote
sail–sale
scene–seen
sea–see
sealing–ceiling
seam–seem
seize–seas–sees
serf–surf
sew–so–sow
shear–sheer
shone–shown
sleigh–slay
soar–sore
sole–soul
some–sum
stare–stair
stationary–stationery
steak–stake
steal–steel
straight–strait
suit–soot
sun–son
sweet–suite
tail–tale
tea–tee
team–teem
tear–tare
tear–tier
there–their–they're
threw–through
throw–throe
time–thyme
to–too–two
toad–towed
tow–toe
tray–trey
vain–vein–vane
vale–veil
vial–vile
waist–waste
wait–weight
war–wore
way–weigh
weak–week
wear–ware–where
weather–whether
whirled–world
whose–who's
witch–which
would–wood
you–ewe
your–you're

7 Teaching the Bilingual Child

UNDERSTANDING THE BILINGUAL CHILD

A bilingual child comes from a different cultural background than the Anglo-American child, and his first days of school may be very terrifying for him. As in the case of all children, his first years have been extremely individualistic. He has learned to respond mainly to directions given to him as an individual. If he goes directly from this home environment to the first grade, the change from the individual to the group treatment may be drastic.

Many bilingual children must be taught American attitudes and habits, so firmly rooted in unfamiliar American living standards. They must learn to adjust to the school situation and to others in the classroom, to cooperate, to develop new personal habits, to follow directions, and to get and put away materials.

In teaching reading, the modern methods are based on the idea that learning is a process of discovering new meanings and developing knowledge in terms of the pupil's own experiences. This period is very important in the education of the child and should include training in visual and auditory discrimination, motor coordination, vocabulary development which may be quite limited, and in the social aspects of the classroom.

The bilingual child should, therefore, acquire wide experience along the lines of his interests which will enable him to understand stories and activities about which he will read. He should develop sufficient command of the simple English sentence, accuracy in enunciation and pronunciation, and a genuine desire to read.

The teacher may capitalize on experiences the child has outside of school. In teaching the bilingual child, it is best that the direct method be used by speaking English while teaching. Language is acquired by use, by associating verbal expressions with objects, ideas, or experiences. The translation method forces the child to associate one language form with another and he continues to think in his native tongue. This does not imply that it is not well for the teacher to know the foreign language, but she should avoid speaking it before the class in session.

VOCABULARY DEVELOPMENT

Activities of a nonreading type should be provided. These experiences should be in the form of contact with the other children socially. Since learning isolated words does not enable the child to speak a new language, the simple sentence is the unit structure of the teaching procedure. The direct association method between the object and the English word for it should be used.

Words are learned by showing the object, and saying, "This is an apple." In presenting the word *cow*, the child will grasp it more readily if the teacher says, "The cow says 'moo'." A game may be played by having the teacher or the child make the sound of the animal and another child give the name of the animal.

Example:

Teacher: "Moo-Moo."
Child: "It is a cow." If he gives the correct answer, he is *it*.

Names of objects in the schoolroom and the schoolyard should be taught by direct referrel to the objects themselves. Action words are taught by performing the action. The teacher should be careful not to introduce too many words or expressions of the same type in one day. The children should use the expressions they are learning over and over again.

Example:

Teacher: "I will roll the ball to Mary. Mary, please roll the ball to me."
Teacher: "What did Mary do?"
Child: "Mary rolled the ball to you."

Common action words such as *walk, run, stand, come, skip, hop* are taught by the teacher saying, "I walk," and then walking. "Can you walk?" and so on. Vocabulary cards, using 9-by-12-inch oak tags, should be made. A picture is pasted on each, and the name of the object is printed under it. These pictures can be obtained from magazines, or they can be drawn. Later the name of the object is covered and the children try to place a 3-by-9-inch cardboard with the name of the object under the correct picture.

To learn names of objects, 2-by-4-inch picture cards can be made. If a rubber-stamping set of pictures is not available, pictures can be cut from magazines and catalogs can be pasted on the cards. Make four or five cards for each object. Print the name of the object under the picture. Each child gets six cards and the remainder are placed face down on the table. The object of the game is to get sets of cards. After the child has laid down a set, he may draw six more cards. The children take turns, asking such questions as "Do you have a cat?"—or whatever object picture the child needs to make a set.

The child who has the most cards at the end of the game wins. A game similar to "Old Maid" can also be played with these cards.

There are many activities that will aid vocabulary-building. For further suggestions, please refer to the sections on Reading Readiness, Perceptual Awareness, Vocabulary, and First Grade Activities elsewhere in this book.

1. Poster and Chart Activities

Suggestions for charts are: pets, farm animals, birds, the zoo, colors, vegetables, fruits, food, furniture, family, toys, clothing, and so on. The children find pictures for these charts. They help paste them on the posters under the correct captions.

2. I Went—I Saw

The teacher says, "We shall play that you have taken a trip. When you come back tell us where you have been and what you saw. Because we want to make this make-believe, you may look at books for ideas, but you must tell us that it is make-believe. I have told you that you can always tell if a story I tell you or read to you is make-believe because it begins with "Once upon a time," or "Once there was." How can you tell us if it is make-believe?" (Have the children make suggestions.) Pictures may be used for this activity. The child goes to the front of the room and says, "I *went* to the store. I *saw* some oranges and bananas." The second child says, "I *went* to the river. I *saw* a boat," and so on.

3. Using the "ing" Endings

Use pictures of animals. The children each select a picture. Then each child tells about his picture.

Example:

"I *went* to the farm. I *saw* a horse. It was *running* and *galloping*. Then it was *drinking* water and *eating* hay." Keep a score to see how many times the child has used a word ending in *ing* correctly.

4. Names of Objects

In teaching the names of objects, the teacher first touches the object and gives its name, as, for example, "pencil." Later she says, "This is a pencil." As early as possible have the children take turns playing "teacher." Place four or five objects or pictures on the table or desk. The child playing "teacher" holds up an object and asks, "What is this?" A variation of this activity is to ask a child to leave the room. Someone removes an object, and when the child returns he is asked, "What did we take off the table?" If he guesses correctly, he may choose the next one to leave the room.

5. Vocabulary Drill

Teacher: "Carmen, you may go to the board and get the picture of the horn." Carmen gets the horn picture, and a card with the word *horn* printed on it. She says, "This is a horn." Later the children learn to say, "I went to the chalkboard. I got the picture of a horn." The teacher puts pictures of objects the children are learning to identify on the chalkboard ledge. The name of the object should be on the ledge, too. Words that cannot be illustrated can be used by means of a card with only the word on it.

6. Prepositions

The teacher holds a ball above her head and says, "The ball is over my head." After she has repeated this several times, she holds the ball behind her and says, "The ball is behind me." She puts the ball on the table, under the table, in front of the chair, and other positions, in each instance telling where the ball is.

7. Simon says, "Thumbs Up"

This is played like the old game "Simon Says." The children are to put their thumbs up only if the teacher has her thumbs up as she says, "Simon says, Thumbs up" and down if she says "down." If she does not have her thumbs up as she says "thumbs up," and the children follow her verbal instructions anyway, they are caught.

8. Right and Left

Use the singing game, "Looby Loo" for teaching right and left. The teacher uses other right and left hand activities such as holding up the right hand, holding down the left hand, stamping with the right foot, and so on. In this activity introduce the words *foot, hand,* and *arm.*

9. Use of Who and Whom

The children put their heads on the table or desk. One child is picked by the teacher to be "it." This child touches another child and says, "Who is it?" and the child replies, "Is it Marie?" and so on.

Another variation is have the children sit up, the child who is "it" touches another child and says, "Whom did I touch?" and the child who was touched replies, "It was I, Marie."—and so on.

10. Where?

An object is shown to the children who are told that after their intermission, when they come back to the room, the object will be hidden somewhere in the room. Children take turns trying to guess the location. A child says, "Where is the ball? Is it in your desk?" or the like. It is a good idea to use three or four objects that have been hidden, but the children concentrate on finding one object at a time.

11. See Saw

The teacher prepares a group of pictures which the children have not seen before. She pastes the pictures on cardboard to facilitate flashing them. The teacher flashes a picture and asks, "What did you see, Juan?" The child answers, "I saw a cat." The child flashes the next picture and asks another child, "What did you see?"—and so on.

12. Color Game

The teacher says, "I am thinking of something red. What is it?" The object should be in the room and in view of the children. The children guess by saying, "Is it a ball?"—and so on.

13. It Is I

One child gets under the teacher's desk. Another child raps on the desk. The child under the desk says, "Who is there?" "It is I," the child answers. "Is it Marie?" "No, it is not Marie." "Is it Rosa?"—and so on.

14. It Was I or Hide the Thimble

One child leaves the room and another child hides the thimble. The child who finds the thimble is to guess who hid it. The child asks, "Marie, did you hide the thimble?" "Yes, it was I," or "No, it was not I," she responds—and so on.

15. Spin the Platter

The child who spins the platter says, "Juan and I will play." Juan is to try to catch the platter before it drops. If he catches it, he spins the platter the next time.

16. Have or Haven't Any

The class is divided into two groups. Each correct answer gives a side a point. A child in the first group asks a question such as, "Have you any roses in your garden?" A child in the other group answers "I have some roses in my garden," or "No, I haven't any roses in my garden."

He in turn asks a question of the first group, such as "Do stars have wings?"—and so on.

17. Pronunciation of wh

Each child makes a pinwheel from colored paper and fastens it to a small stick or a pencil. His wheel will turn when he pronounces the *wh* sound correctly, as in *where, when, what,* and so on.

18. Don't and Doesn't

One child leaves the room and a small object is given to a child in the room. Upon his return to the room, he asks, "Does Marie have it?" A child answers, "No, Maria doesn't have it."—and so on.

After the children have had practice with *don't,* ask a child to leave the room and give two children objects such as a piece of chalk, buttons, or any small item. When the child returns to the room, he asks, "Do Marie and Anna have it?" They answer, "No, Marie and Anna don't have it," and so on.

19. Is and Are

Have pictures of various objects such as two apples, one ball, three chicks. The teacher asks a child to select a picture without letting the others see which one she has picked. The children ask, "Is it a ball?" or "Are there two apples?" The child who guesses correctly and uses the words correctly may hold the card. The child having the most pictures wins the game.

20. A Penny, A Penny

To play this game, a pupil who is "it" stands at the front of the room. The other pupils are seated before him. Two pennies are passed around among the pupils. All the players make motions of passing pennies whether they actually have one or not. The one who is "it" tries to guess who has one of the pennies. When ready to make a guess, he points at someone and says, "A penny, a penny." If the one pointed out hasn't a penny, he holds up his hands and says, "I haven't any," but if he has one of the pennies, he says, "a penny, too many," and he becomes "it."

Other small objects such as buttons, safety pins, and the like may be passed around to help the children become familiar with the names of those objects.

21. Have You Seen?

The children form a circle. One child walks around the outside of the circle, taps someone on the back, and asks, "Have you seen my friend?" The one tapped asks, "How was he dressed?" The clothing worn by the child is described: "He has a blue shirt." The child who recognizes the person described is "it."

22. Occupations

Pictures representing butcher, fireman, grocer, teacher, policeman, doctor, dentist, nurse, are placed for the children to see. One child says, "I see a grocer." The teacher or a designated child says, "Where do you see him?" The child answers, "In the grocery store." The child is then asked, "What is he doing?" and answers, "He is selling groceries."

Use the past tense, after the children have mastered the present tense. "I saw a postman." "Where did you see him?" "I saw him on the street." "What was he doing?" "He was delivering mail," and so on.

23. It Is I

The teacher or a child describes one of the pupils, who, when he recognizes himself, stands and says, "It is I."

24. Took and Taken

Some toy is placed on the table. One child goes from the room and another takes the toy from the table. When the child returns, he asks, "Has Billy taken the ball?" Billy answers, "Yes, I have taken the ball," or "I took the ball." If Billy was not the one, the pupil may have two more guesses. If he guesses correctly, he may continue going out. If he doesn't, he sits down after choosing another child to leave the room.

25. Grab Bag

Place pictures of objects in a box. Each child removes a picture from the box. The children guess what each of the others has. "Do you have a ball?" "Yes, I have a ball," and so on.

26. Doesn't and Don't

The teacher explains that *doesn't* stands for *does not.* She may write the words on the blackboard. Then she uses the word in sentences. She presents the word *don't* in the same manner. The teacher starts the game. Pretending to sew, she says, "My mother doesn't like to sew." Each child makes a similar type of statement, referring to some other activity while pretending to act out the word. *Father, sister, brother, baby, cat, dog,* and the like, can be substituted for the word *mother,* while *read, work, jump,* or some other verb can be used for the word *sew.* After the children use *doesn't* correctly, the word *don't* is introduced. "Mary and Rose don't like to jump," and so on.

27. Ate and Eaten

Pictures of food are given to each child. They pretend to eat the food. The teacher says, "Mary, what have you eaten?" Mary replies, "I ate an apple."

28. Did and Have Done

Each child is asked to tell what he did at home, and then dramatize it. Marie would say, "I did some dusting." Juan would say, "I did some cutting of grass." Each child dramatizes what was done while telling about it. The teacher then asks, "Marie, have you done some dusting?" and Marie answers, "Yes, I have done some dusting," and so on.

29. How the Animals Talk

Show a picture of a cat. "What does the cat say?" The child answers, "The cat says, 'meow, meow.' " Do the same with other animal pictures. Give an animal or bird picture to each child, who does not let the others know which animal or bird he has. He says what the animal would say, and pantomimes the action of the animal. The children might say, for example, "Was that a horse?"—and so on.

30. Scrap Books

Children can make scrap books about themselves. The pictures can be cut from magazines, or drawn. They can show the family, the house, the rooms in the house, the pets, the meals, the time they get up in the morning, the time they go to bed, and so on. Scrap books about their activities can be interesting. Other suggestions are scrap books about various foods, pets, transportation, and the like.

31. Toy Store

If the actual toys are not available, pictures may be used. Also the children can make delightful felt and papier mâché objects. Another project is to ask the children to bring toys from home. These are not to be handled except by consent of the owner. Toy shops have been known to loan toys and games to the classroom.

32. Grocery Store

Again, if the actual groceries are available it is more exciting for the children, but they can make vegetables and fruit from clay and gourds. Empty boxes and tin cans can be brought from home. The children construct the store from boxes, make their money, arrange their goods on the shelves, place the price tags on them, and then they are ready to play store.

33. Color

Collect pieces of paper and cloth of different colors. Place them in a large box and have smaller boxes labeled *green, red, blue,* and other colors. The children sort the bits of cloth and paper and place them in the correct boxes.

34. Coloring Pictures

Duplicate pictures similar to the ones in figure 8.2. Show how to color correctly. Hold up the red crayon and ask, "What picture shall we color red?" A child will say, "the apple." "What do you think the word under the apple is?" "It says apple." Allow sufficient time for the coloring of the apple. "Now what shall we color yellow?" "The pear." "What is the word under the pear?" "What shall we color brown?" "The hen." "What shall we color green?" "Yes, there are two things we can color green." "Now what shall we color blue?" "Yes it is a little bluebird." "What color haven't we used yet?" "What color shall we use to color the orange?" "You may color the balloon your favorite color."

35. Learning the Alphabet

Ask the children to follow the letters and dots in alphabetical order with the pencil and so make various animals and objects. As for example figure 8.1.

36. Learning Colors

Duplicate sheets similar to figure 8.3 below and help the children color the objects correctly. A color chart in front of the room will help them identify the right colors.

37. How Many? How Much?

Charts similar to the ones shown in figure 8.4 below can be made and placed on the bulletin board. Discuss the charts with the children. Ask them to make up some charts to be placed on the board, also.

38. Flannel Board Numbers

A flannel board is very useful in helping the children learn the numbers and the number facts. Various figures and objects are cut from flannel or felt and used in counting, in encouraging conversation, and in learning number facts. Figure 8.5 below is labeled "Which are not Mrs. 10's children?"

Figure 7.1 Follow the Letters

Figure 7.2 Coloring

READING INSTRUCTION

Keen interest in reading develops from a series of activities in the course of which the children discover that reading contributes to their pleasure and satisfaction. The children will like reading as long as they achieve a marked success. This can never be accomplished without the teacher giving careful study and preparation to her lessons. From the very beginning vigorous emphasis should be placed on the thought-producing process and the subordination of the mechanics of reading to thoughtful interpretation.

Reading for the bilingual child is very likely to be characterized by word-calling, rather than by rhythmic comprehensive units. The best procedures to use in overcoming word-calling is to have the reading material in short, easy units, each with a limited vocabulary of easy words. The contents should come from fields that fall within the social interests of these children. Care must be taken not to make the reading lesson too long and tiresome. It is far better to have many short periods for reading during the day than to have one or two long periods.

Principles in teaching oral reading are:

1. Oral reading other than sight-reading should follow rather than precede discussion.

Figure 7.3 Coloring

Please turn to the section on color for first grade for further teaching color suggestions.

2. Sight-reading should be so simple that it can be read intelligently without hesitation.
3. There should always be an attentive audience, which is, after all, the only motive for reading aloud. The reader faces the audience who listen attentively with closed books.
4. The teacher should not give directions in the mechanics of reading, such as "let your voice drop after a period," and the like. Such instructions should be given individually and at a special instructive period.
5. There should be no interruption for correction of errors.
6. The teacher should read aloud often to the children to set a good example.
7. Point out to the child the difficult word at once, "The first word in this line is *now*."
8. Give an opportunity for the repetition of new words in connection with additional interesting pictures, games, and other activities.
9. Make special observations regarding vague expressions for which a definite vocabulary should be substituted.
10. Teach as sight-words a preliminary list of words already in the child's speaking vocabulary.
11. The important words should be emphasized by having the pupils find them on the page in response to thought questions, such as "Find the words which tell where he is taking the cows."
12. It is advisable to put the phrase or the entire sentence on the chalkboard, placing the word to one side. In this way the child sees the word in context rather than as an isolated word.

For example:

cool, dark, quiet forest	*forest*
found some honey	*honey*

Ability to think can be developed by the use of such questions as:

What words would you use to describe *quiet?*
What was the most important happening in the story?

Are there more white dogs than black ones?
How many more?
How many black dogs are on the top row?
Are there fewer black dogs than white ones? Etc.

How many children are holding up their right hands?
Are there more holding up their left hands than right hands? Etc.

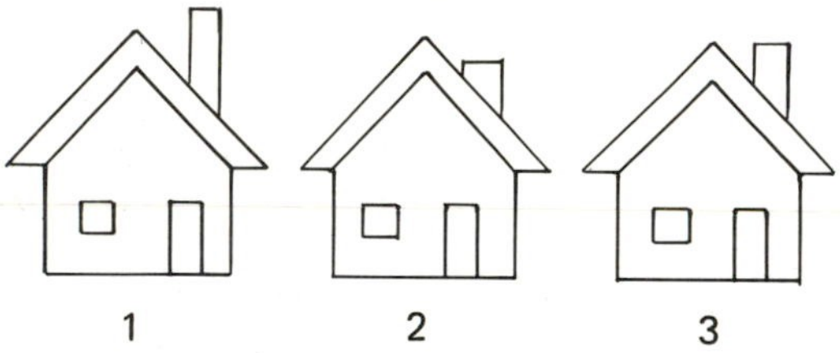

Which house has the tallest chimney?
Is the second chimney taller than the third?
Which chimney is shortest? Etc.

Whose rod is longest?
Whose line is longest?
Whose rod is shortest?
Is Bill's line short? Etc.

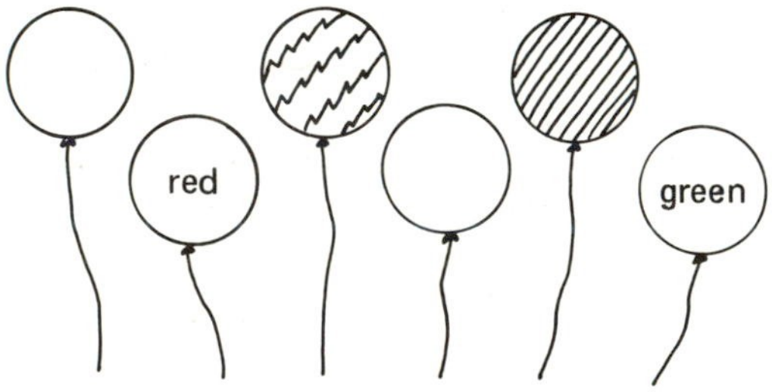

How many striped balloons are there?
Are there more red than white ballons?
How many white ones are there? Etc.

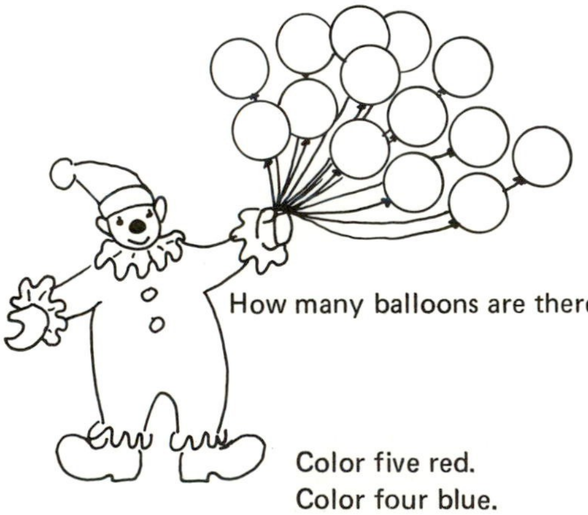

How many balloons are there?

Color five red.
Color four blue.
Color one green.
Color four yellow. Etc.

Figure 7.4 How Many? How Much?

Figure 7.5 Which are not Mrs. 10's children?

To stimulate interest in reading, a reading table should have an important place in the classroom. Every effort should be made to provide as many as possible of the really superior children's books in well-illustrated editions. Not all of the books will be ones that the children can read, but they will learn by perusing the pictures and having the teacher read to them. Books that are badly worn and dirty should be discarded and used for illustrations, charts, and so on. It is impossible to teach children to love books and care for them when the books on the table are in worn-out condition.

The bulletin board may also play a prominent part in the development of reading interests. The board should be placed on the level with the children's eyes. The value of the bulletin board depends upon its attractiveness, its timeliness, its relation to class activities, and the skill used by the teacher in making the interest stimulated by the bulletin board carry over into other reading activities.

The pictures should be changed frequently so that the children's first thought upon entering the room will be to look at the bulletin board and find what is new. Items about the weather or the day's activities may be posted there. A little serial story with a new picture and a new reading unit for each day may find a place on the board.

WORD RECOGNITION

Reading must begin with the learning of sight words. Some general contour is perceived with certain dominating letters or parts rising out of it. The ascending letters seem to play an important part and the alternation of vertical and curved letters may also help in structuralizing the form. Words that call up pleasant associations seem to be recognized more easily.

Word recognition to be made a meaningful process must be developed by introducing words, phrases, and sentences within the child's range of meaningful concepts and vocabulary. It is easier to remember meaningful words than those that recall no meaningful concepts. Also it is easier to remember terms commonly used in the child's oral expression than unfamiliar terms or those not commonly used.

Difficulties centering around word recognition often are eliminated by extensive reading of easy material, flash-card activities, word games, keeping word lists, and charts. Learning the isolated word does not enable the child to speak a new language, therefore the sentence should be the unit of procedure.

The children recognize a word when assisted by a recollection of the story, the context, and the appearance of the word. In addition, they have to start sounding the word, but usually only a partial sounding is required.

Many teachers tell the child to "look hard" at a word, yet they do not tell or teach him where to focus the eye. Merely looking hard without knowing what to *look at hard,* is of little help. Attention should be called to some specific feature of the word.

In order to develop independent and accurate recognition of words and word groups, the following suggestions may be helpful:

1. Having the children listen while the teacher reads. When she omits a word, the children supply it.
2. The teacher asks the children to find words, phrases, and sentences which she designates.
3. The children are asked to find how many times a specific word appears on a certain page.
4. The children make their own dictionaries and storybooks.
5. The children keep a word file. They go through these in their free periods.
6. Making words from phonograms.
7. Finding and discussing unfamiliar words.
8. Finding phrases that will answer the teacher's questions.
9. Finding words that have a given ending or prefix.
10. Reading directions and following them.

EXPERIENCE CHARTS

Please see chapter 2 for specific directions in preparing these charts. The charts are to be developed by the children, using as a basis some experience they have had. The following group activity was developed by a group of bilingual children. The student-teacher* took the children to visit a farm. Before making the trip, the teacher and children discussed what they would want to know and what they would look for. The children's questions were printed on the chart.

1. What is on the farm?
2. What buildings are on the farm?
3. What animals are on the farm?
4. How do they help the farmer?
5. What do they do for us?
6. How does the farmer care for them?
7. What machinery or tools are on the farm?
8. What is grown on the farm?
9. What does the farmer do for us?

After the trip, the children talked about their day at the farm. They began answering the questions they themselves had formulated. The children thought it would be a good idea if they made charts about their experiences and they wanted to make a farm book. The teacher went with the children to the library, where they found the farm books and took out all they could find. Some of the children wanted to make a miniature farm and offered to bring toys from home. Others said they could make animals from clay and other media.

The first experience chart, dictated by the children was printed as follows:

The Farm

We went to the farm.
We saw a white house.
We saw a red barn.
There was a big, round silo.
There were many other buildings, too.
We saw some horses.
There were many cows and calves.
There were pigs and chickens.
We saw a big tractor.
The farmer was nice to us.

Flash and phrase cards

to the farm	farm
a white house	white
a red barn	house
round silo	barn
other buildings	silo
some horses	other buildings
there were	horses
cows and calves	cows
pigs and chickens	calves
a big tractor	pigs
the farmer	chickens
was nice to us	tractor
	farmer
	nice

The procedures discussed for experience charts in chapter 2 were followed. The children made drawings for each chart and the charts were displayed throughout the entire study of the farm. The children made scrapbooks, learned songs, and listened to stories about the farm and farm animals. The class made experience charts about the farm buildings, the farmer, the tractor, and the animals.

*Unit presented by Miss Theda Washburne, Laboratory School, Silver City, New Mexico.

The following activities were pursued:

1. Word charts.

Words we know

horse	barn	farmer
calf	tractor	sheep
lamb	cow	chicken
	—and so on	

2. Pictures about the farm were drawn by the children.
3. Farm and animal pictures were cut from magazines.
4. The children listened to stories about the farm.
5. A farm scene, using cardboard boxes, was built.
6. Various kinds of grain grown on the farm were collected.
7. Corn and beans were planted, and their growth watched, by the children.
8. Pictures of farm products were collected.
9. Butter was churned by the children.
10. A vegetable garden was grown.
11. Charts showing what each animal eats were made.
12. Charts showing farm tools were made by the children, who also labeled them.
13. Farm songs were learned.
14. Clay animals and vegetables were modeled.

PHONICS

Nearly all authorities in reading now agree that children will benefit from practice in phonetic training. Teachers of bilingual children, in particular, feel that phonics aid this particular group in their pronunciation of words. Today, phonic readiness is recognizable, just as reading readiness is. As the child becomes aware of the phonic elements in the words he is using, he becomes ready for phonics. This usually takes place after the first few months of school after he has acquired a sight vocabulary of about one hundred words.

Children of low intelligence have more difficulty in using phonics, because the blending is a generalization, an ability which children in this category seem to lack.

No work in phonics should be given until the child thoroughly understands what it means to read and has established the correct eye habits. When phonics have been introduced before this stage, the children frequently tend to assume that certain phonemes are actual words and they become extremely confused. Phonics play a very useful part in reading after the correct reading habits have been established. It must be remembered, however, that phonetics will help the child sound out the word, but it does not mean that it will teach him the meaning of the word.

The phonetic training that makes the child feel that he masters a word by pronouncing it, and that correspondingly causes the teacher to accept the pronunciation as recognition, is positively detrimental to reading. The same phonetic ability that will connect the printed symbols and the oral symbols for the familiarly spoken and relatively small vocabulary of the child, will make similar connections for the large vocabulary which means nothing to him. Phonics should be considered a tool—not an end in itself. Phonics, when taught correctly, has the following values:

1. Helps the child in the identification of new words.
2. Is good training and assists in enunciation and pronunciation.
3. Helps in the development of speech coordination.
4. Helps materially in making the child an independent reader.
5. Trains the child to hear words correctly.
6. Is an aid to the teaching of spelling.

The teacher should first develop ear training but she should be careful not to distort the consonant sounds. Some pairs of phonemes that are frequently heard inaccurately are:

th and *f*	the short *i* and long *e*
t and *d*	*z* and *s*
t and *th*	*p* and *b*
long *a* and short *e*	*s* and soft *c*
k and *g*	*f* and *v*
v and *b*	short *a* and short *e*

Phonics should never be taught during the reading period. If during that period the child does not know the word, help him over it quickly but do not comment on the sounds. The phonic lessons should be short and snappy with the drills that are keenly interesting. Please refer to the section on phonics in chapter 6.

The first written phonic work can be taught by the following procedure: The teacher writes on the blackboard: *book, boy, ball, big,* and other words which he knows that begin with the letter *b*. The teacher pronounces the words and then asks, "What do you hear that is the same in all these words?" "What do you see that is the same in all these words?" Call attention to the letter *b*. Underline it with colored chalk. Write the letter *b* on the chalkboard. "What does this letter say?" Ask the children, "Whose name begins with this sound?" Write the name on the chalkboard. "Can you think of other words that begin with this sound?"

Phonetics badly taught are more harmful than none at all. Overemphasis on phonetic analysis encourages the development of word-callers. The teacher should give attention to individual needs. Chorus work seldom aids the child as much as individual recitation in the class. She must help the child avoid the habit of breaking words into separate sounds, as *c-an* or *cuh-an*. These are a few suggestions for games in phonic drill:

1. Beginning Sounds

The teacher says, "Today, we will have good ears. I am thinking of something that begins with the sound of *b*." (Write *b* on the blackboard.) As the children give the words, the teacher writes them on the board. The teacher and children later go over the words, using them in sentences, and should some not begin with the letter *b*, ask them why the word does not belong. Use other beginning sounds in the same way.

2. Yes or No

The teacher says, "I am thinking of the *m* sound. Tell me if all these words begin with the sound of m? . . . *mother . . . my . . . end . . . more . . . cook . . . mama.*" The children say "yes" when all the words begin with the letter sound designated by the teacher. They say "no" if they do not.

3. Follow the Leader

The teacher says a word and the children give words that begin with the same initial sound. The teacher says, "Chair." The children say, "Child, chicken, chili," and so on. The teacher writes the words on the chalkboard. The teacher then selects a child to give the first word while she puts the words on the board.

4. Rhymes

"Tell me the word I am going to leave out. Jack and Jill went up the ...." Ask the children to give as many words as they can that end the same as *hill*. Explain that these are called rhyming words.

5. Recognizing Initial Sounds

The teacher writes eight words on the chalkboard, such as: *girl, hen, cat, doll, sit, sing, dog, man, good.* "Let us put all the words that start with this sound in this row. Tell me which words to write here."

H	G	M	S
hen has	good girl	man make	sit sing

Apply final consonant sounds to the same type of exercise.

6. Finding Words in the Book

The teacher writes the letter *m* on the chalkboard. "Please turn to page 20 in your book and find the words that begin with *m*." Write the words on the chalkboard. Use other initial sounds.

7. Finding Initial Sounds

Write a list of known words on the chalkboard. Point to a word. "Mary can you find another word that begins like this one?" Erase the word if the answer is correct.

8. Recognizing Endings

Duplicate a list of familiar words and ask the children to draw a circle around those in each column that have the same endings.

see	room	card	can
seed	moon	hard	pan
car	need	root	make
dare	seed	soon	take

—and so on

9. Finding All the Things that Begin with "B"

Give the children pictures and ask each child to find in his picture all the things that begin with the sound of *b*. A picture with many details can be duplicated and all the children can work on the same picture, or each child could receive a different picture and explain to the class what he sees. Use the other initial sounds, too.

10. How Many Times Do You Hear the Sound?

Make up various sentences and ask the children to count the number of times they hear a word that begins with this particular letter.

Examples:

How many times do you hear the *n* sound in this sentence? "No, No, Ned, do not take the new egg." or How many times do you hear the *qu* sound in this sentence? "The quick, queer duck quickly said, 'Quack, quack.' "

11. Listening for Pairs of Words

Tell the children that you are going to say words in pairs. When both words are alike, like tap-tap, he is to nod his head yes. If they are not the same, he is to shake his head no.

tip . . . tip	sit . . . sit	lad . . . dad	make . . . bake
hit . . . hat	see . . . saw	my . . . my	pin . . . pin

—and so on

Points to be kept in mind in teaching phonics:

1. Do not begin with eye-training too soon.
2. Ear-training must precede eye-training.
3. The teacher should enunciate distinctly and with accuracy.
4. The child must hear and use the word in context many times to make it his own.
5. Acquiring a vocabulary is not the primary function.
6. Understanding and comprehension are the most important factors.
7. The direct method usually works most effectively.
8. Visual materials are very important. Pictures are good, but the actual object is better.
9. Make use of tapes and records.
10. When speaking, don't slow down your speech. However, avoid talking too rapidly.
11. Use the aural-oral method, which places emphasis on hearing and speaking.
12. Teach sentence patterns.
13. The teacher should become acquainted with the cultural background of the children.
14. Keep the materials at a level that the child can understand.
15. Remember, our way of life may be completely foreign to the child.
16. The first days can be very terrifying to the child.
17. The child should understand that phonetic training will not make him an independent reader.
18. Phonics can help in enunciation.
19. Phonics should be taught in a period apart from reading.
20. Attention should be given to individual needs. Some children do not need as much phonetic training as others.
21. Never allow the child to break up the words into separate sounds.
22. No concert or chorus work should be used.
23. Remember the child may be able to pronounce a word and yet not know its meaning.
24. The child is taught to identify phonetic elements in word symbols.
25. Help the children understand the multiple meanings of words whenever they appear, as in *run, bank, down, bill,* and so on.
26. Idioms and figures of speech can be very confusing to the children. When they appear, explain their meanings.

PERCEPTUAL AWARENESS

Being able to see and hear what is going on in our environment is especially important to the bilingual child. This is an essential part of the training for the foreign child. Accuracy in hearing can be developed through activities that will interest him.

At the beginning, ask the children to close their eyes and listen to sounds around them. Tell them that when you ask them to open their eyes, you will ask them to tell you what they heard. At first environmental sounds can be used, then the teacher adds additional sounds such as sharpening a pencil, closing a door, dropping a book, or writing on the chalkboard.

Other listening activities are listening to tapes, records, Mother Goose rhymes, poems, stories, and music. A complete set of listening tapes, workbooks, and teachers' handbook is put out by I-Med, 1520 Cotner Avenue, Los Angeles 90025. This set can be invaluable to the teacher of the bilingual child.

Visual awareness and acuity is most important in learning to read. If the child seems to have difficulty in seeing, recommendation for a visual examination should be made. However, there are those that *see,* but *see not.* They have never become aware of the things around them. Simple activities to help the child develop greater awareness include having them tell what they saw on the way to school, or placing objects about the classroom and asking the children to look for them. Showing the children partially completed pictures and asking them to name the complete object is helpful. An example is shown in figure 8.6. Showing parts of words can be used after the child is familiar with the word.

The teacher must remember that the bilingual child may have heard little English spoken in his home and that may not have been well-spoken. The child may have a much more limited background than the Anglo child. Frequently an emotional situation is involved. His inability to understand and be understood can produce feelings of inferiority.

With the teacher's encouragement and understanding, the bilingual child soon blossoms and shows great eagerness to learn. One of the biggest rewards that

Figure 7.6 Name the Object

a teacher can have is to see the child develop and become confident of his ability.

WORD LIST

Since there are many thousands of words in every language, and since some are needed much more than others, care must be taken to select those which will be most needed. Isolated words can have several meanings and therefore the words should be used in context in order to make it easier for the children to understand the meanings.

The following list will serve as a guide in vocabulary building. The variants of the words are not listed.

about
above
accident
ache
across
after
afternoon
afraid
again
against
air
airplane
all
almost
along
always
am
America
American
an
and
animal
any
apple
apron
are
arm
around
as
ask
asleep

at
ate
automobile
away
baby
back
bad
bake
ball
banana
bank
bark
barn
basket
be
beans
because
bed
been
before
began
begin
behind
bell
belong
below
best
better
bird
bit
bite

black
blanket
blue
book
both
bought
bowl
boy
bread
break
breakfast
bright
bring
brother
brought
brown
build
busy
but
butter
buy
by
cactus
cake
calf
call
came
can
candle
candy
can't

cap
car
card
care
careful
carrot
carry
cat
catch
caught
cent
chair
change
chase
cheese
chew
chicken
child
children
chocolate
church
circle
city
clay
clean
clear
climb
clock
close
clothes
cloud

coat
cocoa
cold
color
colt
comb
come
corner
could
country
cover
cow
crawl
crayon
cream
cried
cry
cup
cut
Daddy
dance
dark
day
dear
decide
desk
did
different
dig
dime
dinner
dirty
dish
do
doctor
does
dog
doll
dollar
done
don't
door
down
draw
dress
drink
drive
drop
dry
duck
each
earl
early
earn
earth
east
easy
eat
egg
eight
else
empty
end
enough
ever
every
eyes

face
fall
family
fan
far
farm
fast
fat
father
fed
feed
feel
feet
fell
felt
few
fight
fill
find
fine
finger
fire
first
fit
five
flag
floor
flour
flower
fold
follow
food
foot
for
fork
found
four
fresh
friend
from
fruit
fry
fun
funny
game
garage
garden
gate
gather
gave
geese
get
girl
give
glad
glass
go
goat
gone
good
goodby
got
grade
grandfather
grandmother
grass
great

green
grew
ground
grow
had
hair
half
hand
hang
happen
happy
hard
has
hat
have
he
head
hear
heard
heart
help
hen
her
here
hid
hide
high
him
his
hit
hold
home
hope
horse
hot
house
how
hungry
hunt
hurry
hurt
I
ice
ice cream
if
I'll
in
Indian
inside
into
iron
is
it
its
jam
janitor
jay
job
jump
just
keep
kind
kitchen
kitten
knee
knew
knife

know
laid
lamb
lamp
large
last
late
laugh
laundry
lay
learn
left
leg
lemon
let
letter
lie
light
like
little
live
long
look
lose
lost
lot
love
low
made
mailman
make
mama
man
many
market
may
me
meal
mean
meat
meet
men
middle
might
milk
mine
money
more
morning
most
mother
mouth
move
Mr.
Mrs.
much
my
myself
nail
name
near
need
needle
neighbor
never
new
newspaper

next	pail	potato	rubbers	sleep	talk	too	were
nice	pain	pretty	run	slow	teacher	took	wet
nickel	paint	pull	said	small	telephone	tooth	what
night	pan	put	same	smell	tell	toward	when
nine	pancake	quarter	sand	so	ten	town	where
no	paper	quick	sang	soft	than	toy	which
not	part	quiet	sat	some	thank	tree	while
nothing	party	quilt	saw	something	that	try	white
now	past	quit	say	soon	the	turn	who
number	paste	quite	see	sorry	their	two	whole
nut	pay	rabbit	seed	speak	them	under	whose
of	peach	race	seem	spoon	then	until	why
off	pear	rag	seen	stand	there	up	will
office	peas	rain	sell	start	these	upon	window
often	pen	ran	send	stay	they	us	winter
old	pencil	raw	sent	still	thing	use	with
on	penny	read	seven	stockings	think	vegetables	woke
once	people	ready	sew	stop	this	very	woman
one	pick	really	shall	stove	those	wait	word
onion	picture	recess	she	street	thought	wake	wore
only	pie	red	sheep	strong	three	walk	work
open	piece	rest	shoes	such	through	want	would
or	pig	rice	short	summer	throw	was	write
orange	pillow	ride	should	suppose	tie	wash	year
other	place	right	show	sure	time	water	yellow
out	plane	ring	side	surprise	to	way	yes
outside	plate	river	sing	sweet	today	we	yesterday
over	play	rode	sister	swing	together	wear	you
own	please	room	sit	table	told	well	your
paid	point	round	six	take	tomorrow	went	yours

8 Sensory Acuity and Emotional Reactions

Man gains all his knowledge and information through his five senses. The degree to which his perceptual awareness is developed depends upon his training and his own alertness and his desire and curiosity. Some individuals are far more aware of their surroundings and have developed far greater insight than others. This is due to the difference in their environmental background.

Training in developing perceptual acuity need take only a few minutes a day, and the period can be a time for relaxation when the pupils seem restless or lack concentration in what they are doing. Experiences in listening, feeling, smelling, visualization, imagery, and tasting will enrich learning as well as developing more meaningful concepts in all school subjects. This training will enhance their knowledge and understanding in every experience.

LISTENING AND REMEMBERING

Listening is more than letting sound waves enter the ear. Most of our learning is done by seeing and by listening. When the child first learns to talk, he learns the language he hears. Good listening begins at home, and good listening habits can be instilled by the parents. The parents' inattention to the young child's talk may lead to a feeling of insecurity and develop into poor listening habits. This, of course, is just as true for the teacher who hasn't time to listen to the youngster's enthusiastic discourse about his experiences.

An individual can think four to ten times faster than the average person can talk. Therefore we have about 400 to 1,000 concepts or ideas in thinking time to spare for every minute a person talks to us. What do we do with our extra time? Our minds won't wait. The thoughts race along ahead of the speaker, and while we are waiting for the words to come, our thoughts tend to go off on a tangent and sometimes they remain away too long.

Poor listeners are easily distracted and find it difficult to concentrate. Many people have fallen into careless habits of half listening. They are thinking about other things while the individual talks to them. When two people come together, they usually have something to say. Ordinarily, they must be listeners as well as talkers, and listening requires attention.

Aduts listen carefully to their automobile engines to see if they are running smoothly, but they usually listen less carefully to other people's conversation. If the other person stops listening, it is useless to talk, unless one finds the sound of one's own voice intriguing.

Most people remember only about half of what they hear, and often they will repeat this inaccurately. Poor listening habits may be due to lack of interest, poor concentration, or poor health. Bright people are not always the best listeners, nor do they necessarily have better memories. Hearing acuity is not always a measure of ability to retain information. However, to retain information, the individual must hear it accurately.

We all like to talk better than to listen, but it makes it more desirable if there is someone to listen with interest. We must avoid being the kind of listener who mishears and misquotes. It is rather difficult to learn without listening, and we can learn to listen.

How many times have you told the students to listen carefully? Did you tell them how to do it? Listening is a very important form of communication. Only one person can talk at a time and the others are expected to listen. At least, it is only polite for one person to talk at one time. The others must listen, or at least they should keep still, if they want to be polite. Of course, you cannot force anyone to listen unless he wants to. That is why it is important to say what you have to say in a convincing manner so that others will want to hear what you have to say. It is easier to talk than to listen, usually.

Listening is the act of receiving communication and information from others and from things. Most of the directions we receive are oral. People explain things to you, and if you want the correct information, you must be able to understand and remember what has been said. Or is it easier for you to read the directions? It is easier for most people to read the directions, because if they do not understand, they can reread the information until they do. Many times people do not completely understand oral directions and they don't want to bother to ask the informant to repeat the directive.

People listen for enjoyment, too. They listen to music, songs, plays, speeches, the song of birds, the sound of pets, and the sounds of nature. They are listening with appreciation and enjoyment and receive emotional satisfaction from this perceptual stimulation.

The students should learn to make mental pictures while listening to someone talk. This will help them remember.

Listening is a special skill. Too often we listen only half-heartedly to what is said, and as a result really do not understand everything. Good listening habits can be improved only if one makes an effort to listen thoughtfully.

There are many sounds that are not words, but they bring messages to us. The striking of the clock tells us the time, the ringing of the telephone tells us something, the hum of the bee, or the blowing of the wind brings a message. We can get ideas from the many sounds about us.

To increase listening ability, ask the pupils to make mental outlines and remember the important details as you read a descriptive paragraph. Ask them to close their eyes and listen for a minute, then tell what they have heard. The I-Med Publishers, Los Angeles, have a complete series for developing perceptual awareness in the form of workbooks and tapes. This material is for preschool through college level, and could prove helpful in the developing of students' listening abilities.

In 1938, several million Americans heard from their radios, "The Columbia Broadcasting System presents Orson Wells and the Mercury Theater of the Air in *The War of the Worlds* by H. G. Wells."

A few moments of silence followed that announcement, then an unexpected weather report, and then dance music. Suddenly an announcer broke in with a report that a series of explosions had been noted on the planet Mars, and that a meteor had landed in New Jersey.

The story was continued for twenty minutes, though the network and the individual stations interrupted three or four times to inform the listeners that the story they were hearing was fiction.

Hundreds of thousands of listeners ignored these interruptions and really believed that people from Mars were invading the earth. The explanation given for this reaction was that the people got excited and didn't listen perceptively. This is what happens in so many cases in our daily life. Some emotional reaction triggers off our "nonlistening" device, *and we hear not what we hear.*

Listening is a specific skill, and good listening habits help in remembering, too. We listen for names, addresses, instructions, directions, and announcements. It is easier to remember things if we understand them. Poor listeners are easily distracted and cannot concentrate. Students frequently fall into this category. It is rather difficult to learn without listening, but we can learn to listen.

One person cannot coerce another into listening, but he can make the information interesting enough so that the other person will want to listen. The first-grader is a better listener than a reader. He gains most of his knowledge from hearing others speak.

What, then, is memory, and how does it work? Your amazing "filing system" can store six hundred memories a second for lifetime and still feel no strain. These memories are printed indelibly upon the brain. Throughout life, each of us carries a fantastic "unwritten diary" tucked away in the brain. Here our experiences of what we saw, heard, touched, smelled, and tasted are safely filed and stored. Scientists have found that one item of memory is likely to be stored in several parts of the brain. So if one part of the brain should be destroyed, a copy of the memory may be retained elsewhere in the brain.

Intelligence has nothing to do with good memory. Sometimes people who are below average in intelligence can remember better than people who may be very bright. People who have a great deal on their minds may sometimes be forgetful. They can remember certain things very well, but tend to forget what they consider at the time to be the unimportant or uninteresting things.

The secret of remembering is to remember. If you are trying to remember something you are hearing, it is necessary to listen with concentrated effort. One must concentrate on certain details that are to be remembered. In studying, explain to your students that it is usually an aid to memory to go over the material a second or a third time. Making mental pictures of what is to be remembered is helpful.

Anyone can develop a better memory. One is not born with a superior memory. To remember something, one must have a reason or incentive for remembering it. Being tired can be a reason for forgetting, and tension and worry too can be causes for not remembering. The most important factor in developing a good memory is to make a point of wanting to remember. Spaced practice for recalling certain facts is important.

(Refer to activities listed under Preschool and First Grade for suggestions for listening.)

Too often students are unaware of the beauty of the sounds about them. They should become aware of the symphony of nature. We learn to relax when we hear good music and stories. We learn to thrill at the soft stirring of the leaves, the chirp of the cricket, the wind in the treetops, and the glorious song of the birds.

We also listen with our eyes. We let our imagination make sounds and pictures for us when we read a poem, a novel, or look at a picture. As the pupils become more aware of their surroundings, they will be able to express their reactions to their environment. They will learn that one can be awed into silence by a walk under the stars on a clear night. Almost everyone has seen the moon hanging in the pine tree, or has seen a ribbon of light through an almost closed door. Almost everyone has learned to listen and to see certain things that have given him a lifelong pleasure. He has learned to listen to the little sounds of life; the bee buzzing among the flowers, the grasses whispering in the breeze, and the tattoo of the raindrops. Nature has much to tell us.

The listening training may be presented in several ways. The teacher may wish to divide the class and work with small groups of six or eight. Those not working with the teacher may work on assigned activities.

Too frequently children are unaware of the beauty of the sounds about them. Listening to records of birds, farm sounds, musical instruments, and stories which have good elements of sound in them will aid in developing auditory acuity.

Sometimes the children may close their eyes and listen to the classroom sounds. This not only aids acuity of hearing but helps in developing the memory span. One child can be "it," while some other child speaks, using any intonation he wishes, and the "it" child, who has been blindfolded, guesses the speaker.

The teacher, or a pupil, can make sounds such as wrinkling paper, erasing the board, using the pencil sharpener, closing a desk drawer, and so on. The children place their heads on their desks or tables and close their eyes. The children then name the sound. Make several sounds in sequence and ask what sound was first heard, then what sound was made, and what was the last sound they heard.

A screen can be made by cutting the sides from a large cardboard box, or a large chart can be used. The screen will be used to hide from view what you are doing while you are using various objects for making different noises. Place the screen on a desk or table between you and the class.

In presenting these lessons, the teacher has an excellent opportunity for developing word concepts and for increasing the children's vocabulary. The first listening exercises should be devoted to developing an awareness of the sounds in their environment. The children are asked to close their eyes and listen to the sounds about them. "What was the first sound you heard?" "What was the loudest sound you heard?"

Explain that sounds may be used as danger signals, some are used to give information, and other sounds are used for enjoyment. Tell them that it is important to listen carefully so that we can carry out directions in school, in the home, and in our environment.

For listening activities, a few things are needed. A ball is used for counting the number of times it is bounced. A clock, whistle, hammer, bell, coins, and any thing from the home, such as an egg beater, can be used.

These activities can be oral or if the teacher wishes to have the children use pencil and paper, names of the objects or their pictures can be put on duplicated forms.

1. Listening for Directions

Grades one and two

Listening to simple directives can be helpful. Ask the children to respond to various directions. Such as:

1. Those who are wearing something blue may go to the back of the room.
2. Those whose birthdays are in March may clap their hands.
3. Those whose first names begin with A, B, or C may raise their right hands.
4. Those having an older brother may nod their heads.
5. Everyone with bright eyes may sit up straight and tall.

2. Learning to Remember

Grades one, two, three, and four

A small booklet is made for each child, with a picture on one page and questions about the picture on the other. The children look at their picture for a designated period of time, and then without referring to it again, answer the questions, such as, "Was there a dog in the picture?" "Did the girl wear a red dress?" "How many birds did you see?" After the child has answered the questions and checked them with the key, he puts his initial on the back of the booklet so that he will not get this particular book the next time this activity is presented.

3. Remembering What Is in the Picture

Grades one, two, three, and four

The children look at a picture and try to visualize it. Then without referring to it again, they underline the words that name objects in the picture. These words have been duplicated on sheets of paper. For example, if the picture is of a farm, the following list of words may be used:

barn	goat	bus	street	factory	farmer
house	tree	pig	door	school	park
cat	duck	chick	gate	rabbit	colt

4. Listening to Nursery Rhymes

Grade one

Prepare a page of pictures of the things that are mentioned in the nursery rhymes you are going to use. Give each child a duplicated copy. The children close their eyes while the rhymes are repeated and then they mark each item that was mentioned in the rhymes. Perhaps it would be even better to distribute the worksheets after the rhymes have been said to avoid any peeping.

5. Learning to Listen

Grades one, two, three, four, five, and six

Discuss the importance of listening, with the students. Listening is a specific skill, and good listening habits can help the student remember things better. A minute or two a day devoted to listening exercises can do a great deal for the students. In the lower grades, listening for specific sounds or simple words can be used. In upper grades, the students may be asked to listen for certain words as the teacher reads a selection. For further suggestions in developing listening, see *Developing Auditory Awareness and Insight,* I-MED Publishing Company, 1415 Westwood Boulevard, Los Angeles, California.

6. Learning About America Through Music

Grades two, three, four, five, and six

There are many songs written about various sections of the United States such as Carry Me Back to Old Virginy, Wabash, Bluebonnets of Texas, California Here We Come, Listen to the Mockingbird, Covered Wagon, Old Chisholm Trail, America, the Beautiful, and on and on. A map of the United States should be displayed and each child should have his own map. The children find the area on their maps when they listen to the recordings. This should not be the end of it—they will become interested in the section of the country and correlate it with their social studies.

This activity can be continued into the study of other countries as well.

FEELING

At times children are not aware of the meaning of words that pertain to the sense of touch. Children of all ages enjoy making or looking at the *Feel Book*. In the lower grades, the teacher can make the booklet, either with the children's help or by herself. In upper grades, the children can develop some excellent science materials. Children in the primary grades like to touch things; psychologically, there is a sense of security in this feeling process. While a booklet is usually the most desirable, the materials can be pasted or stapled to 9-by-12-inch cardboards and used individually. Games can be played by touching the material and guessing what it is, then mentioning something else that has the same feel.

The children should also have experiences in warm and cold, warm and warmer, large and small, large and larger, wet and dry, and so on. Weight can also be used here.

The children can close their eyes and listen and try to feel the story the teacher is telling.

1. Know Your Lemon

Grades one, two, three, four, five, six, and adults

This is a fun thing that is enjoyed by all ages and is an amusing activity for parties.

Each individual is blindfolded and given a lemon that he becomes acquainted with by felling and smelling it. After two or three minutes each lemon is placed on a sheet of paper which has squares marked off (and numbered). Only the teacher knows the code. Plastic lids or small paper plates really work better. The individuals now come up and look for their own personal lemon. This time the lemon must be recognized by sight only. Naturally the ones who recognize their lemons get to keep them.

Apples, nuts, oranges, or vegetables can be used, too.

2. Finding Out By Touch

Grades one and two

Objects are examined and touched by the children. Then these objects are listed in their correct categories.

Example:

Sticky	*Not Sticky*
paste	wood
scotch tape	glass
wet clay	dry clay

Smooth	*Rough*
glass	sandpaper
chalk	wood
silk	woolen cloth

Categories, such as wet and dry, long and short, dark and light, soft and hard, heavy and light, provide good experience.

3. The Feel Box

Grades one, two, three, and four

Use a box that has a hole cut in the lid for the child to place the hand in the box. The lid may need to be tied onto the box. Place various objects in the box, just a few for the younger children and more for the older pupils. The pupil places the hand in the box and is given a definite period of time to feel the objects. He may then either tell what he had felt, or he may draw a picture of the objects. A cloth bag also works very well. Questions like how many things, what did they feel like—soft or hard, etc., are helpful in developing awareness.

4. Longest, Shortest, Biggest, or Smallest

Grades one, two, three, and four

This exercise is similar to the one above but various lengths of pencils, chalk, or wooden dowels can be used for length. Balls of different sizes can be used and the teacher can ask how many small balls are in the box,etc.

5. Recognizing Weight

Grades one, two, three, four, five, and six

Wrap five or six boxes of different sizes. Place various items such as rice, pebbles, seeds, chalk, balls, etc., in each box. The children lift and shake the boxes and then each one writes on a piece of paper which box is heaviest, which one is next, down to the lightest one. These boxes can be weighed so the children can check their estimates.

SMELLING

Discuss the importance of the sense of smell. We can become aware of danger by the sense of smell, and we can experience many pleasant memories from smell. Why do we like some food. Really, it is our sense of smell that enhances our food. We remember past experiences when we smell certain things.

There are many easily attainable items than can be used in developing acuity in smell. Wet paper toweling, wet woolen cloth, fruit, vegetables, colognes, spices, and the fragrances of flowers and herbs can make enjoyable experiences. Care must be taken if any of the children are allergic to some things.

Older children can classify the objects or words that are listed as pungent, bitter, acid, sweet, or bland.

TASTING

If perceptual training is given in tasting, care must be taken that the materials are kept sanitary, and no food that could be harmful to the child should be used. Also, a child who is allergic to some food should not try tasting it.

Actually, the tongue is sensitive only to sweet, sour, salt, and bitter. Our olfactory glands, our sense of smell, have a great deal to do with the enjoyment of food. For older students, they should refer to their physiology or health books for further information. However, experiences in tasting bitter chocolate, some spices, lemon, orange peel, a slice of apple, or any other food or liquids illustrates the sense of taste to the pupil.

A cooking center in the classroom can combine the awareness to the five sense and mathematics as well. This center can promote the development of motor, language, and cognitive skills.

In mathematics, children can convert recipes to the metric system. They may wish to write their own cookbook. Some classrooms have been known to put out their own cook book and make a little money on it, as well as learning to estimate cost of production.

If cooking is out, at least the children can do such things as make punch and sandwishes for their parties. They should estimate the amounts needed and the costs.

Younger children can draw pictures of the ingredients needed for their refreshments.

VISUALIZATION

Visual acuity is of great importance to the attainment of success in reading. Inability to differentiate and discriminate can lead to ineffective understandings. In the beginning reading, the small child is led to note differences and similarities in small objects; in cutting, painting, and drawing, he begins to see line and contour and by looking at pictures he learns to look for detail.

Another simple experience for developing visual acuity is to place a few objects on the desk, and cover them with a box. The teacher lifts the box and covers the objects quickly again. The children tell what they saw. The number of objects can be increased as the children develop greater skill in observation. The teacher may also make a peep box, which is opened very quickly for a quick look, and the child names the objects in the box. Placing a designated number of objects about the room in the morning, the children can quickly look for them as they come in and whisper to the teacher what they found.

Jigsaw puzzles, colorful pictures, and toys are also helpful in developing visual awareness.

For older children more advanced exercises are used. If a tachistoscope is available, this is a satisfactory means for developing rapid and accurate visual discrimination.

The use of visual imagery should be encouraged in all grades. The teacher reads a short paragraph or a sentence and asks the chidren to make a mental picture of what she has read. Sometimes she can ask the children to describe the picture that they *made.*

Experiences with colors should not be overlooked. In lower grades the children use the primary and secondary colors, but older children can make charts and booklets, showing the many shades and hues of various fabrics, papers, and paints.

It is important that the child be guided by the teacher into an abundance of rich, direct sensory experiences. There are many wonderful learning experiences in the home and in the school that can be used in helping the child appreciate and understand his environment more effectively, and we cannot afford to overlook these opportunities.

Training in visualization is important in helping children have a more meaningful experience in reading. This type of activity also helps them in learning to remember. Some suggestions for developing this skill are given below.

1. Visual Imagery

Grades one and two

The teacher may say, "Close your eyes and listen while I say some words. Try to make a picture in your mind when I say the words. A *red ball.* Could you see a red ball? How big was it? What was it made of?" Continue with objects until all the children are able to visualize them; then action words may be introduced.

2. Recognizing Sound Words

Grades three, four, and five

Phrases which are to be matched to sound words are printed on strips of cardboard and a child works with them individually. The material may be either on the chalkboard or duplicated for a group project.

Example:

Match the phrases and the words:

stepping on a dry branch	patter
falling rain	sizzle
frying bacon	snap

3. Imagining in Your Mind

Grades three and four

The teacher says, "Think of many people out on the beach on a sunny summer day. Now think of the same place if a sudden storm came up. Write *B* in front of the phrases that tell what you might have seen before the storm and *A* in front of the phrases that tell what you might have seen after the storm."

........children picking up shells
........waves dashing over the sand
........bright umbrellas on the sand
........people eating lunch
........people rushing to cars
........dark clouds

4. Forming Sensory Images

Grades two, three, and four

Directions:

Read the words in each group and think how they make you feel:

bed darkness woolen blankets soft pillows
Do you feel: ....joyful? ....afraid? ....sleepy?

5. Forming Sensory Images and Making Judgments

Grades one, two, and three

Exercises similar to those given below can be helpful.

What can be sticky?	What can be flat?
wet paint	a round log
honey	a bus ticket
dry sand	pancakes—and so on

6. Strengthening Sensory Imagery

Grades one and two

The children listen to sounds and guess what they are. Then they close their eyes and guess what they are touching. After stories and poems are read they tell how it makes them feel.

7. See, Hear, Smell, Taste, or Feel

Grades two, three, and four

Directions:

Write S in front of the words that name things you can see, *H* in front of those that you can hear, *N* in front of those you can smell, *T* for taste and *F* for feel. You may be able to do more than one thing with some of the things listed.

........soft music	........furry kitten
........red apple	........white snow
........red rose	........white cake

8. Getting Imagery from Reading

Grades one, two, and three

After the children have read short paragraphs, they draw what they *saw* in the story without looking at the story again.

Example:

The two black horses ran swiftly down the lane. Jack stood under the apple tree and tried to catch them as they passed.

9. Using Pantomime

Grades two, three, and four

Directions:

Read this story carefully and act out what you have read.
She hugged her cat close to her heart and began singing a little song as she rocked back and forth.
The reader acts out the story and the others guess what the child is doing.

10. Using Riddles

Grades one, two, and three

Short riddles are developed about animals, objects, flowers and the like. The children guess what is being described. They may make up riddles for the others to guess and may make Riddle Books to take home.

11. Pantomiming Selections from the Reading Lesson

Grades two, three, and four

Selections are taken from the reading lesson. Each child draws a slip, reads the selections, and pantomimes it. The other children write the page and paragraph number that was acted out.

Example: Mary: page 75, paragraph 4

12. Telling What We Think About

Grades one, two, and three

Exercises similar to the example below are duplicated, and correct phrases are checked by pupils.

Example:

a. When we think of Christmas we think about
   ....nuts and candy
   ....gifts tied with ribbon
   ....spring flowers
   ....black cats
   ....keeping secrets

b. When we think of birthdays we think about
   ....buying tickets
   ....a pretty cake
   ....ice cream and cake, and so on

13. Making Mental Pictures

Ask the students to listen to short paragraphs read by the teacher. They are to try to visualize what is being read. Another procedure may be used, that of asking the students to read the paragraphs and visualize what they are reading. Suggestions for paragraphs are given below.

Examples:

a. *Read the selection below, then write the things that tell you spring is here.*

   As spring came everything seemed to blossom out. The old tree, which had been bare all winter, had tiny little green buds mixed in among the ugly brown branches. The flower bed, which had been just plain brown dirt or mud all winter long, had little fingers of green coming out of it. On the very top peak of the old, white, frame house sat a robin redbreast singing as loud as he could. Just at this moment the sun came into view from behind the grassy green hill in the distance, and it was the start of the first day of spring.

b. *Read the following selection and then, without referring to it again, draw a diagram on a separate piece of paper of the route Mr. Doe follows to work every morning.*

   Mr. Doe is a bookkeeper and the only exercise he gets is walking to and from the building in which he works. He takes the same route every morning as follows: two blocks east to Laurel Park, where he takes the path diagonally across the park to the southeast. After leaving the park, he walks three blocks south, then turns east and crosses a bridge. One block north of the bridge is the office building in which Mr. Doe works.

c. *Read this selection and then list the things mentioned.*

In the attic, the small child had his first intimation that there was much of this strange new world in which he had no part. As he opened the door, the light from a small window on the opposite wall outlined a dusty trunk to the left of where he stood. On the right side, the walls were lined with bookshelves groaning under a load of boxes, books, old phonograph records, a typewriter, and, near the floor, three old dolls covered with cobwebs. He stepped around a metal chest as he walked over to inspect the dolls more closely.

EMOTIONAL REACTIONS

Children should learn to identify the emotional reactions of each character in the story, to understand what kind of a person he is and why he acts as he does in a given situation. Through these experiences, children can learn to direct their own behavior and reactions into the right channels. In the lower grades, children can dramatize parts of the story to portray the emotional reactions of the characters. Suggestions for activities in helping the children discern these emotional reactions are given below. These exercises may be modified according to the grade level and the needs.

1. Identifying Emotional Reactions

Grades one, two, three, and four

After a story has been read, the children may complete sentences by selecting words which pertain to each character's reaction. The exercise may be duplicated or written on the board.

Example:

a. John felt ....
(happy, sad, angry)
b. Mary felt ....
(proud, embarrassed, sad)

2. Interpreting Behavior of Characters

Grades two, three, four, five, and six

After reading a story, the children answer questions similar to the examples given below.

Example:

a. Why do you think Mary wanted to wait for Jane?
b. Why did Mary have so many friends?

3. Interpreting Feeling

Grades two, three, four, five, and six

Sentences from the reading assignment are duplicated, and the children choose the word that best describes the feeling expressed in each.

Example:

a. His *startled* leap almost frightened the boy.
........sedate ....awed ....surprised
b. His heart beat *wildly*.
........excitedly ....proudly ....drowsily
—and so on

4. Discovering Attitudes and Moods

Grades two, three, four, five, and six

After reading a story in the reader, the children complete sentences which have been prepared.

Example:

a. A little boy waited .... for his mother.
b. The .... deer stood in the shadows.

5. Forming Associations

Grades three, four, five, and six

Lists of words are prepared and the children write what the words in each list make them think of.

Directions:

What do these words make you think of?

a. white........ storm........ snow........ chill........ frosty
....
....
b. pound........ smash........ crash........ bang........ jar
....
....
c. damp........ mud........ swish........ rain........ wet
....
....

6. Identifying Self with Character

Grades four, five, and six

Questions similar to those below are asked about a story in the reader. These may be duplicated or written on the chalkboard.

Example:

a. If you had been in Jane's place, what would you have done?
b. If you had seen the bear, what would you have done?

7. Describing Feelings

Grades three, four, five, and six

A list of words is prepared that could be used to answer questions about a story from a supplementary reader.

Directions:

Choose the correct word to write after each sentence.
attentive friendly surprised naughty
a. Page 56. The dog wagged his little tail, but he didn't bark. ....
b. Page 57. The children wanted to do something they shouldn't do. ....
c. Page 57. The children did not expect a package. ....
....
d. Page 58. They listened while the man talked. ....
....

8. Describing Characters

Grades four, five, and six

Descriptions of characters from the reading lesson are duplicated or written on the chalkboard and given to the pupils to identify.

Example:

Who are these characters in the story of Robin Hood?
a. Sworn to capture Robin Hood
b. An outlaw
c. He gave Robin a blow on the head
d. His motto was "rob the rich and help the needy."
—and so on

9. Emotional Reactions

Grades one, two, three, four, five, and six

In reading, the student should learn to identify the emotional reactions of the character and try to understand why the character reacts as he does in a given situation. Draw small ovals about an inch high to represent faces. Place dots to show where the eyes, nose and mouth should be. For the lower levels, the teacher reads a short story to the children, and they put in the facial expressions to show how the character feels. For further activities in showing emotional reactions, read sentences or phrases to the children. At upper levels, the teacher can write words on the blackboard and the students illustrate the facial expression.

Example for lower grades:
a. Mary was very excited.
b. June was sick today.
c. Peggy was very lonesome.
d. Mother was shocked at the news.
—and so on

Example for upper grades:
a. amazed
b. terrified
c. astonished
d. worried
—and so on

10. How Did Each Person Feel?

Grades three, four, five, and six

Have the students draw small ovals about an inch high. As the teacher reads the word, they draw the facial expressions on the ovals. Discuss illustrations. Suggestions for expressions:

amazed	delighted	happy	queer
amused	determined	haughty	satisfied
annoyed	disappointed	humble	scared
ashamed	displeased	impatient	self
astonished	distressed	impressed	shocked
bashful	embarrassed	jolly	shy
boastful	envious	lazy	sorrowful
bored	excited	lonesome	surprised
businesslike	flattered	mad	terrified
calm	frightened	merry	timid
cautious	furious	modest	tongue-tied
comfortable	gay	naughty	unhappy
contented	glad	overjoyed	vexed
curious	greedy	pleased	worried
dazzled	guilty	proud	

11. Reading About a Character

Grades four, five, and six

Mimeograph stories or ask the pupils to read designated paragraphs in the reading books. They are to answer questions designated by the teacher.

9 Diagnosis of Reading Problems

Causes for Reading Disabilities

No isolated factor can be designated as the sole cause of reading disability, but if the student is to overcome his problems, his deficiencies must be recognized.

The roots of the difficulties may go back to preschool years. Sometimes the importance of this period is overlooked by parents, and it is possible that some traumatic experience has contributed to the student's problems. Emotional factors such as fear, anxiety, rivalry, jealousy, hostility, and the feeling of inferiority can create problems. Frustrations and unhappiness can play havoc with the student's development, and his resistance to learning may come from a sense of failure and insecurity.

The entire teaching approach to the student who is retarded in reading must be one of understanding and caution. The student who has felt that he is a failure usually is extremely sensitive and discouraged, and he will hesitate to attempt some new work because he usually thinks that it will mean only another failure. He may have a distaste for reading and thus be inhibited and easily distracted. Unlimited patience and consideration therefore are important for successful reading training. Tensions must be relaxed, and the student must be able to gain confidence in himself.

Every student has certain capacities and limitations. He will learn some things quickly and well, and others may not be learned so readily. Being able to read as well as other students can affect the individual's entire personality.

To improve the student's reading ability, it is necessary to identify the causes of his problem and then remove them if possible. Diagnosis is a matter of studying the symptoms, finding the cause of the problem, and then planning the remedial and corrective procedures.

A thorough analysis of an individual's reading problems will usually take several sessions, depending upon the seriousness of the case, the cooperation of the subject, and the accessibility of the subject's records. Unless the adult has a great many problems, the time for required analysis is much shorter than that needed for the younger student.

For the child, an initial interview with the parents is advisable. At this time routine information is obtained. The parents fill out the application forms, and they can be asked to make a personal rating of the child.

The parent should be informed that little improvement will be noticed during the first few weeks of training, and that it is impossibe to predict the length of time required for complete retraining. An average period of time can be quoted, and the parents should be told that cooperation from the home and the child will to some extent help determine the period of instruction.

The school reports on academic ability, health, and the anecdotal records are valuable to the director of the reading program, and they can save much time in making the diagnosis. Conferences with the school counselor, teacher, supervisor, and physician are helpful.

Too frequently, little importance is given to the sociological area, or the child's background. The frustrations generic to his position in the family, the place of the family in the community, and the economic status are all factors influencing the child's behavior and his ability to concentrate and to learn. There may be many unrecognizable disturbances that can produce strong emotional reactions in an individual. Sometimes the child's place in a group, the characteristics of his gang activities, his relationships in the home, his closeness or lack of closeness to members of his family, and even pets may affect a boy or girl.

Information about a student can be obtained through observation and conversation. In working with the student, a good rapport is necessary. In a student conference, the room should be comfortable and attractive, with good lighting and ventilation. There should be no distractions, such as people interrupting the conference or telephone conversations.

The primary grade child may be asked to draw a picture of the family and home. Some psychologists ask the child to do this: "If you had to erase one, which one would you erase?" Some children are quite sophisticated and realize why the question has been asked. Tommy, an eight-year-old, explained to the director of a reading clinic that he had been asked to draw the members of his family and was then told to erase one of them. He said that the paper was quite small, but "I knew what they were after, so I drew myself real small, and then I erased myself."

It is possible to learn about the child from such activities as making booklets about himself or his family, completing an interest inventory, doing finger painting, or by observing the child in projective play. A one-way glass is excellent for observation if it is possible to have one installed in the clinic.

Sentence completion can be used for older children, but it must be remembered that some students will be very cautious about what they write. An autobiography may be illuminating in gaining insight into some students' problems. Illustrations of an autobiography sentence completion forms can be found in chapter 3.

A student's interest in books, how many he reads, the books found in the home, and the time he spends with reading material—all may help in diagnosing his problems.

CAUSES FOR READING DISABILITIES

Some of the major causes for reading disabilities are listed and briefly explained below.

A. PHYSICAL FACTORS

1. Neurological

Inability to read may be due to congenital defects in the brain in some few cases. Much research needs to be done in this area in order to come to a more definite conclusion.

The question of word-blindness has been controversial, but it is generally agreed that there are two types:

a. There may be inability to recognize words as a result of a brain injury.
b. There may be a congenital word-blindness, which is the inability to learn to read when there are no other factors involved.

2. Endocrine Disturbances

Endocrine disturbances, which affect reading ability, are limited to a few cases. These, together with neurological factors, should be the findings of a physician and should be treated by him. He may be able to make suggestions to the teacher and help her in working more effectively with the student.

A small number of students have a chronic nervous disease characterized by seizures, at irregular intervals, in which there is loss of consciousness. In some instances, the trace is very small, but it could be a cause of ineffective school performance. Only a physician should make such a diagnosis, but a teacher should be informed of such a condition, since the student may be under some form of medication.

3. Vision

Some students have 20/20 vision when tested on the Snellen chart, but this does not give an indication of what the student sees at near-point. The student who squints or frowns, holds his head at an angle, or holds his book too far from or too close to his eyes, should be given a visual examination.

The student who becomes fatigued quickly may have a visual problem. If he finds the printed page fuzzy or distorted, it is very possible that he will form a dislike for reading. The teacher should arrange for rest periods, better lighting, large print, and sight-saving activities for the student.

4. Auditory Disability

Some students may appear sullen and inattentive to the teacher, but in reality they are unable to hear well. If a student does not respond to questions, or if he holds his head to one side when he is listening, he may not be hearing distinctly. A hearing test should be arranged for him.

5. Dominance

There are several theories on dominance and preference, but none of them has proven completely satisfactory. Dominance should be given some consideration in studying a student, however, but the diagnosis should come from a physician.

6. Coordination

Poor muscular coordination may be an indication of some other factor which hinders the student in his school performance. The student who moves slowly may be slow in all performances, whether physical or mental. It must not be assumed, however, that because the student has poor coordination he will be poor in reading.

7. Fatigue

A student who is tired cannot perform as efficiently as if he has average or above-average energy. Some of the causes of tiredness may be lack of rest and insufficient sleep, malnutrition, poor vision, and illnesses.

8. Physical Handicaps

Physical handicaps can be a problem if the student does not accept his difficulty. Most difficulties resulting from handicaps can be overcome to a large extent through proper counseling and guidance.

9. Absence from School Due to Health Problems

It is natural to expect a student who is absent from school frequently to find it difficult to keep up his work, because he will miss many class discussions and directions which will help in preparation for class.

10. Split-Growth Concept

The split-growth technique may be useful in determining those pupils who are retarded in reading due to a retarded physical growth pattern. Research in this area has been done by W. C. Olson and B. O. Hughes.[1] They studied the development of height, weight, strength of grip, ossification of wrist bones, teeth, mental growth, and school progress. They believed that reading was as much a part of growth as physical development. The criticism that might be made of this technique is that the psychological aspects were not

1. Willard C. Olson and B. O. Hughes, "Concepts of Growth—Their Significance to Teachers," *Childhood Education* 21 (October 1944):53-63.

assigned an important role in the development of the student.

11. Speech Defects

Speech defects should be studied carefully with the assistance of a speech consultant. Some students who have speech difficulties find it difficult to read in lower grades, and when they get into upper grades they have a mind-set or mental block against reading.

B. PSYCHOLOGICAL FACTORS

1. Intellectual Capacity

The student's mental capacity is not always *the* factor in learning to read, but an inferior mental or learning capacity can make the process slower. Some students are able to grasp directions and instruction more quickly and have better insight, but some students with a high mental capacity are unable to read well. In the case of the brighter student, frequently the class pace and materials were boring to him when he started to learn to read, and he was inattentive. Later, he continued to be disinterested in reading and class instruction because of this early experience.

2. Emotional Factors

Causes for emotional stress can be one or more of the following:

a. Pressures from home and community.
b. Emotional instability—worries easily.
c. Emotional factors unrelated to reading.
d. Short memory span.
e. Extrinsic rather than intrinsic motivation.
f. Lack of interest.
g. Unfavorable reading attitudes.
h. Mental immaturity.
i. Environmental distractions.
j. Social immaturity.
k. Uses failure to read as a means of compensation.
l. Feeling of insecurity and incompetence.
m. Overdependence on teachers and parents.
n. Nagging from parents and teachers.
o. Withdrawing behavior—shyness, timidity, daydreaming.
p. Sensitiveness to criticism, feelings easily hurt.
q. Fearfulness.
r. Inability to carry responsibility.
s. Temper outbursts, quarrelsomeness.
t. Boasting.

C. EDUCATIONAL FACTORS

1. Poor Instruction

In this category, inadequate materials and equipment, distracting environment, inadequate reading readiness program, and promotional policies should also be considered.

2. Poor Study Habits

The student who has no curiosity will not be as alert to learning as the one who has an innate appetite for learning about things. Poor students usually cannot apply themselves to the assigned work, and they do not seem to care whether or not they complete the work. Ineffective study skills usually result in poor study habits. Some students guess rather than study to find out.

Some students are very good in memorizing, and the teacher is not aware of their inability to read because they are able to perform during the class discussions. Many first-grade children have learned to memorize the stories, and the teacher thinks they are reading and therefore fails to help them as she would otherwise.

3. Inadequate Vocabulary

The student may have difficulty in using word analysis and context clues in helping him learn new words. If he has a good stock of sight words and can apply his phonetic and structural word analysis skills, there should be no problem in developing a good vocabulary.

4. Too Low Rate of Reading

If the student does not read words in groups or thought units, he will have a low reading speed. Physical factors such as lip movement, inner vocalization, head movement, and pointing with a pencil or finger will retard reading rate. Other factors to be considered are material that is too difficult, inadequate vocabulary, lack of interest in the material read, poor concentration, and emotional blocking.

5. Poor Comprehension

Inability to retain what has been read may be due to any of the foregoing factors, together with insufficient instruction in the skills of reading.

D. ENVIRONMENTAL FACTORS

Unsatisfactory lighting and ventilation, poor seating, and distractions all may be reasons for ineffective reading. The environment outside of the classroom also may be part of the difficulty. The home environment, a place to study, home and social activities, and the socioeconomic status of the family will influence many students.

As noted earlier, a thorough analysis of an individual's reading problems will take time, depending upon the severity of the case, the cooperation of the subject, and the accessibility of the subject's records.

The charts that follow are designed to help the teacher discover and correct the student's difficulties. The numbers that follow each of the Problems in the first part of each table refer to the numbers of those specific items enumerated under Diagnosis, Causes, and Corrective Procedures (part 2 of each table).

VISUAL DISABILITIES

TABLE 1

DEFECTIVE VISION

(Part 1)

Problems	Diagnosis	Causes	Corrective Procedures
1. Astigmatism.	1, 2, 3, 6, 9-10	1, 2, 5, 10	1-8
2. Hyperopia.	3, 4, 6	1, 2, 3, 5, 10	1-8
3. Improper fusion.	1-4, 9-15	2-8, 10	1-8
4. Muscular imbalance.	2, 9, 14, 15	2, 3, 4, 5, 8	1-8
5. Myopia.	2, 3, 9, 14, 15	1-5, 7, 8, 10	1-8
6. Stereopsis.	3, 6	2-5, 7, 8, 10	1-8
7. Strabismus.	1-3, 6, 9-13	2, 3, 4, 5	1, 2, 3, 4, 8
8. Suppressions.	1, 2, 3, 9-13	2, 10	1, 3, 6, 7, 8
9. Mirror imagery.	16, See reversals	9, 10	1, 2, 3
10. Eye dominance.	2, 3	9, 10	1, 8

(Part 2)

Diagnosis	Causes	Corrective Procedures
1. Blurred vision.	1. Structural deviation.	1. Examination by eye specialist.
2. Headaches.	2. Improper focus.	2. Rest periods.
3. Frowning.	3. Muscular imbalance.	3. Improved lighting.
4. Bloodshot eyes.	4. Injuries, accidents.	4. Short work periods.
5. Discharge from eyes.	5. Diseases, illnesses.	5. Larger size type.
6. Awkwardness.	6. Inadequate lighting.	6. Dull-finished paper.
7. Inflamed eyes.	7. Emotional factors.	7. Sight-saving activities.
8. Sleepiness.	8. Malnutrition.	8. If glasses are prescribed pupil must wear them.
9. Fatigue.	9. Hemispherical dominance.	
10. Dizziness.	10. Poor nerve reception.	
11. Blinking.		
12. Squinting.		
13. Book too near or far from eyes.		
14. Excessive head movement.		
15. Reads and writes words in reverse.		

TABLE 2

POOR VISUAL ACUITY

(Part 1)

Problems	Diagnosis	Causes	Corrective Procedures
1. Lacks visual discrimination.	1, 2, 3, 4, 5	1, 2, 3, 4	1, 2, 3, 4, 5, 6, 7, 8, 9, 10
2. Fails to recognize words.	1, 2, 3, 4, 5	1, 2, 3, 4	1, 2, 3, 4, 5, 6, 7, 8, 9, 10
3. Functional blindness.	1, 3, 6	1	10

(Part 2)

Diagnosis	Causes	Corrective Procedures
1. Telebinocular Survey.	1. Emotional disturbances.	1. Note similarities and differences in pictures and objects.
2. Cannot see clearly.	2. Defective vision.	2. Constructing picture dictionaries.
3. Does not associate meaning with symbols.	3. Lack of mental maturity.	3. Demonstrate left-to-right progression.
4. Slow in making discrimination.	4. Inadequate training in visual discrimination.	4. Increase sight vocabulary.
5. Does not analyze words.		5. Finding missing parts of pictures.
6. Printed page indistinct.		6. Jigsaw puzzles.
		7. Matching activities.
		8. Art activities.
		9. Games with visual experiences.
		10. Remove emotional block.

Serious defects in vision may be responsible for the students' reading disabilities. It is estimated by the American Optometric Association that twenty-three percent of all children between the ages of five to fifteen years need to wear glasses, and the number increases as individuals become older. Probably fifty percent of all reading difficulties are to some extent due to poor vision.

TABLE 3

NARROW PERCEPTUAL SPAN

(Part 1)

Problems	Diagnosis	Causes	Corrective Procedures
1. Word by word reader.	1, 2, 3, 4, 7, 8	1, 2, 3, 4	1-18
2. Slow reading rate.	1, 2, 3, 4, 5, 6, 7, 8	1, 2, 3, 4, 5	1-18
3. Reads with hesitancy.	1, 2, 3, 4, 5, 6, 7, 8	1, 2, 3, 4, 5	1-18
4. Has reversals.	1, 2, 3, 6, 7	1, 2, 4	1, 2, 3, 4, 6, 7, 8, 9
5. Makes regressions.	1, 2, 3, 4, 5, 7	1, 2, 3, 4	1, 2, 3, 6, 7, 8
6. Poor eye movement.	1, 2, 3, 4, 5, 6, 7	1, 2, 3, 4, 5	1-18
7. Lacks comprehension.	1, 2, 3, 4, 5, 6, 7	1, 2, 3, 4, 5	1-18

TABLE 3 (Continued)

TABLE 3 (Continued)

(Part 2)

Diagnosis	Causes	Corrective Procedures
1. Observe eye movement with mirror or pin hole test. 2. Does not comprehend. 3. Slow reading rate. 4. Too many fixations per line (five or more). 5. Regressions. 6. Reversals. 7. Inability to hold place. 8. Word by word reader.	1. Visual deficiency. 2. Inadequate first grade teaching. 3. Material too difficult. 4. Insufficient number of sight words. 5. Fatigue. 6. Habit. 7. Has not learned to read in thought unit.	1.Teach left to right progression. 2. Read easier meaningful material. 3. Always read silently before reading orally. 4. Write word on blackboard in context. 5. Give multiple choice tests with choice of phrases. 6. Use phrases on flashcards. 7. Use phrases on filmstrips. 8. With both hands, frame phrases in book that teacher has read orally. 9. Have shorter reading periods. 10. Watch for fatigue. 11. Stress reading for thought. 12. Utilize marks of punctuation in word groupings. 13. Place emphasis on thought element. 14. Book held at proper distance from eyes and at right angles. 15. If child hesitates, tell him the word, later analyze if necessary. 16. See how much child can see on either side of a dot in center of line. 17. Cut a 1/2 x 3 inch slit in a 2 1/2 x 5 inch card. Slide down page. Read as many words as possible. 18. Open book quickly. Try to see as many words as possible.

TABLE 4

REGRESSIONS

(Part 1)

Problems	Diagnosis	Causes	Corrective Procedures
1. Moves eyes right to left over material read.	1, 2, 3, 4, 5, 6	1, 2, 3, 4, 5	1, 2, 3, 4, 5, 6

(Part 2)

Diagnosis	Causes	Corrective Procedures
1. Right to left movement of eyes during reading. 2. Use pinhole test. 3. Failure to recognize words. 4. Inaccurate reading of word. 5. Confusion of meaning. 6. Inadequate perception.	1. Incorrect eye movement. 2. Deficiencies and inaccuracy in word recognition. 3. Lack of phonetic training. 4. Materials too difficult. 5. Vocabulary low.	1. Training in left to right progression. 2. Increase vocabulary. 3. Easier material. 4. Teach student to make use of context clues. 5. Train in reading for thought units. 6. Urge student to stop indulging himself by looking back.

Many students form reversal tendencies because their beginning reading was too difficult and they formed the habit of moving the eyes back and forth because they could not recognize the words nor understand what they were reading. Giving the student confidence in his reading through the use of easy and interesting material is very helpful.

TABLE 5

FAULTY EYE MOVEMENT

(Part 1)

Problems	Diagnosis	Causes	Corrective Procedures
1. Too many fixations.	1, 2, 3, 7, 8, 9, 10, 11, 12, 13	1, 3, 4, 5, 6, 7, 9, 10, 11, 12	1, 2, 3, 5, 6, 7, 8, 9, 12
2. Regressions.	1, 2, 3, 5, 7, 8, 10	1, 4, 5, 7	1, 2, 3, 4, 6, 7, 9
3. Reversals.	1, 2, 3, 6, 10	1, 4, 7, 8	3. 6, 9, 10
4. Improper fixations.	1, 2, 3, 7, 8, 9, 10, 11, 12, 13	1, 3, 4, 5, 6, 7, 9, 10, 11	1, 2, 3, 5, 6, 7, 8, 9, 12
5. Lacks rhythm.	1, 2, 3, 7, 8, 9, 10, 13	1, 2, 3, 4, 5, 6, 7, 9	1, 2, 3, 4, 6, 7, 9, 11
6. Return sweep faulty.	4, 10	1, 7	1, 2, 3, 9

(Part 2)

Diagnosis	Causes	Corrective Procedures
1. Reads slowly.	1. Faulty vision.	1. Use pin-hole test. Small hole in center of printed page. Observe subject through this hole while he works.
2. Reads hesitantly.	2. Points to words.	2. Mirror observation for eye movement.
3. Lacks rhythm.	3. Overemphasis on oral reading.	3. Read easier material.
4. Has faulty return sweep.	4. Inadequate vocabulary.	4. Resist impulse to look back and make regressions. Read to end of sentence or paragraph.
5. Makes regressions.	5. Word by word reader.	5. Indent fixation at least 1/2 inch at beginning of each line.
6. Has reversals.	6. Overemphasis on phonics.	6. Learn to read in thought units.
7. Is a word by word reader.	7. Lack of training in rhythmic eye movement.	7. Use phrases in filmstrips.
8. Has narrow perceptual span.	8. Too little phonetic training.	8. Place rubber bands vertically over page at suitable distances to widen perceptual span.
9. Makes too many fixations.	9. Material too difficult.	9. Check for faulty vision.
10. Lacks binocular coordination.	10. Print too small.	10. Phonetic analysis.
11. Fixates on first letter at the beginning of each line.	11. Lines too long.	11. Train in left to right progression.
12. Lip movement.	12. Lip movement.	12. Eliminate lip movement.
13. Head movement.		

TABLE 6

STREPHOSYMBOLIA (reversals)

(Part 1)

Problems	Diagnosis	Causes	Corrective Procedures
1. Confuses one word with another.	1, 2, 3, 6, 7, 8, 9, 10	1, 2, 3, 4, 5, 6, 7, 8, 9, 11, 12, 13, 15	1, 2, 3, 4, 5, 6, 7, 8, 9
2. Writes words backward.	1, 2, 3, 4, 5, 9	1, 2, 3, 4, 5, 7, 9, 11, 12, 13, 14	1, 2, 3, 5, 6, 7, 8, 9
3. Extreme reversals	1, 2, 3, 4, 5, 6, 7, 8, 9, 10	1, 2, 3, 4, 5, 6, 7, 8, 9, 10, 11, 12, 13, 14	1-14

(Part 2)

Diagnosis	Causes	Corrective Procedures
1. Lack of eye coordination. 2. Mispronunciation. 3. Confuses one word with another. 4. Writes letter and words in reverse. 5. Faulty motor control in writing. 6. Word by word reader. 7. Lack of interest in reading. 8. Poor comprehension. 9. Guessing. 10. Substitutions.	1. Mental immaturity. 2. Faulty vision or hearing. 3. Lack of phonetic training. 4. Use of inappropriate material. 5. Vocabulary too difficult. 6. Makes regressions. 7. Has not been trained in left to right progression. 8. Inability to read for meaning. 9. Poor eye coordination. 10. Cerebral dominance. 11. Incomplete or mixed dominance. 12. Various learning disorders. 13. Carelessness. 14. Fails to notice the beginning letters of words. 15. Lighting and glare.	1. Note how word begins. 2. Use phonetic skills. 3. Train in left to right progression. 4. Use easy, interesting reading material. 5. Student prints words. 6. Student learns to type. 7. Learn a sufficient number of sight words. 8. Give definite motor clue to direction. 9. Compare reversed words with correct spelling. 10. Draw arrow pointing to right, under word reversed. 11. Underline first letter of word in green and last letter in red. 12. Tracing and sounding out words. 13. Show correct form. 14. Study initial sound of words.

AUDITORY AND SPEECH DISABILITIES

TABLE 7

LACK OF AUDITORY ACUITY

(Part 1)

Problems	Diagnosis	Causes	Corrective Procedures
1. Low acuity.	1, 2, 4, 5, 6, 7, 8, 9 10, 11, 12, 13, 14, 15	1, 2, 3, 4, 5, 6, 7, 8, 9, 10, 11, 12	1-19
2. Poor sound discrimination.	1, 2, 3, 4, 5, 6, 7, 8, 9, 11, 13, 14, 15	1, 2, 3, 4, 5, 6, 7, 8, 9, 12	1-19
3. Hearing loss.	1, 3, 4, 5, 6, 7, 8, 9, 10, 11, 12, 13, 14, 15	1, 2, 3, 4, 5, 6, 7, 8, 9, 10, 11, 12	1-19 1, 3, 8, 9, 10, 11, 12
4. Limited range of pitch.	1, 2, 4	1, 2, 3, 4, 6	2, 3, 4, 5, 6, 7, 8, 9,
5. Poor auditory memory.	4, 5, 6, 7, 8, 9	2, 3, 4, 6, 11	10, 11, 12, 13, 14, 15, 16, 17
6. Defective speech.	1, 2, 4, 6, 7, 8, 9, 11, 13, 14	1, 2, 3, 4, 6, 10, 12	1-19
7. Inattention.	1,2, 3, 9, 10,12, 14, 15	1 2, 3, 4, 6, 10, 11, 12	1-19

(Part 2)

Diagnosis	Causes	Corrective Procedures
1. Audiometer test. 2. Whisper and watch test. 3. Poor hearing, but passes on audiometer test. 4. Speech indistinct or defective. 5. Cannot recognize rhymes. 6. Insenitive to similarities in word endings and beginnings. 7. Errors in vowel and consonant sounds. 8. Omissions and substitutions. 9. Inattention. 10. Cannot understand directions. 11. Poor spelling. 12. Boredom. 13. Oral reading filled with errors. 14. Head noises. 15. Earache.	1. Hearing impairment. a. hereditary. b. injury. c. illnesses. d. adenoids, sinuses. 2. Perceptual disability. 3. Lack of experience. 4. Immaturity. 5. Has difficulty in associating meaning with spoken symbol. 6. Poor memory span. 7. Meager vocabulary. 8. Frequent colds. 9. Wax or foreign body in ear. 10. Inattentiveness due to adults talking and making no point. 11. Disinterest in material. 12. Emotional block.	1. Have hearing tested by physicians. 2. Encourage accurate pronunciation. 3. Use rhymes, jingles, poems, songs. 4. Provide good model of speech. 5. Call attention to difference in two words which are confused. 7. Learn to detect differences in words as *boat, boot – house, mouse.* 8. Distinguish between high and low tones. 9. Tap rhythm. Student imitates it. 10. Listen and reproduce sequence of sounds. 11. Tap loudly and softly – distinguish. 12. Recognize individual voices. 13. Close eyes, listen to sounds. 14. Keep hands and book from face while speaking. 15. Do not turn back to students while speaking. 16. Speak naturally. 17. Stand still while speaking. 18. Write key vocabulary on blackboard. 19. Place hard of hearing in front.

TABLE 8

SPEECH DIFFICULTIES

(Part 1)

Problems	Diagnosis	Causes	Corrective Procedures
1. Stammering.	1, 3, 4, 7, 8, 9	6, 9, 11-15	3, 4, 6, 7
2. Stuttering.	1, 3, 4, 7, 8	6, 9, 11-15	3, 4, 6, 7
3. Lisping.	1, 2, 4, 6, 7	1-9, 11, 12	1-7
4. Faulty articulation.	1, 7, 9	1-11	1-7
5. Monotonous voice.	1, 4, 5, 6, 7, 8	1, 2, 5, 6, 8, 9	4, 5, 6
6. Too much or too little volume.	1, 4-8	1, 2, 6, 8, 9, 15, 16	4, 5, 6
7. High-pitched voice.	1-9	1, 2, 6, 6, 8, 9, 14-16	4, 5, 6

(Part 2)

Diagnosis	Causes	Corrective Procedures
1. Poor auditory acuity.	1. Incorrect speech in home.	1. Audiometer test.
2. Lisping.	2. Faulty hearing.	2. Show student how to place tongue for correct articulation.
3. Stuttering, stammering.	3. Parents' speech.	3. Put student at ease.
4. Faulty breath control.	4. Poor teeth.	4. Show student how to breathe properly.
5. Monotonous tone.	5. Oral malformation.	6. Use correct speech.
6. Hearing test.	6. Emotional instability.	7. When student stutters, do not correct him then but help him later.
7. Poor articulation.	7. Dysphonia	
8. Nervousness, tenseness.	8. Poor sound discrimination.	
9. Difficulty in pronunciation.	9. Frustration.	
10. Foreign accent.	10. Injuries to speech areas of brain.	
11. Nasal tones.	11. Hand dominance forcibly changed.	
12. Speaks too rapidly.	12. Nagging at home or school.	
	13. Foreign language in home.	
	14. Speaks too rapidly.	
	15. Self-consciousness.	
	16. Poor muscular coordination.	

HANDEDNESS

TABLE 9

HANDEDNESS

(Part 1)

Problems	Diagnosis	Causes	Corrective Procedures
1. Use of left hand.	1, 2, 3, 4	1	1, 2
2. Difficulty in writing.	2, 3	1, 2, 3	1, 2
3. Right to left progression.	2, 3	2	1, 2

TABLE 9 (Continued)

TABLE 9 (Continued)

(Part 2)

Diagnosis	Causes	Corrective Procedures
1. Use of left hand. 2. Reversal errors. 3. Right to left progression. 4. May have left eye preference, which can be checked by holding pencil at arm length, focusing at tip, bringing to eye. If left-eyed, it will be directed to left eye.	1. Nerve organization of student. 2. Incorrect instruction. 3. Trying to change to right hand.	1. Use of preferred hand. 2. Teach left to right progression.

Generally the correlation between abnormalities and reading disabilities is not close but occasionally a connection is found that affects the diagnosis and the remedial procedures.

Theoretically the left-handed and left-eyed person or one of mixed laterality (right hand/left eye or vice versa) is apt to have difficulty with the left to right eye movements required in reading. This difficulty is greater in early grades than at college level.

Hand preference is well established before the age of five. Eye dominance seems to be established at age of three. Sixty to seventy percent of the population are right-eyed, and ninety percent are right-handed.

PSYCHOLOGICAL FACTORS

TABLE 10

EMOTIONAL INSTABILITY

(Part 1)

Problems	Diagnosis	Causes	Corrective Procedures
1. Lacks poise.	1, 2, 3, 11, 12, 17, 22, 23, 24	1, 2, 3, 4, 5, 6, 7, 8, 10, 11, 12, 14-19	1, 2, 3, 4, 5, 6, 7, 8, 9, 10, 11, 12, 13
2. Nervous, excitable.	1, 2, 3, 7, 9, 10, 11 12, 13, 14, 16, 21, 22, 23, 24	1, 2, 3, 4, 5, 6, 7, 8, 9, 10, 11, 12, 13, 14, 15 16, 17, 18, 19	1-13
3. Self-conscious, shy.	1-7, 9, 10-14, 16, 18	1-19	1-13
4. Aggressive.	3, 4, 5, 6, 8, 15, 19	1, 2, 3, 4, 5, 6, 8, 12	1-13
5. Stubborn.	2, 3, 4, 5, 6, 7, 10, 19	1-19	1-13
6. Unable to adjust to school environment.	1-24	1-19	1-13
7. Lacks independent work habits.	1-24	1-19	1-13
8. Easily annoyed.	1-24	1-19	1-13
9. Unable to complete task.	1-15	1-19	1-13
10. Narrow recognition span.	1-14, 18	1-19	1-13
11. Short memory span.	1-14, 18	1-19	1-13

TABLE 10 (Continued)

TABLE 10 (Continued)

(Part 2)

Diagnosis	Causes	Corrective Procedures
1. Tires easily. 2. Passive, shy. 3. Restless, tense. 4. Will not share or take turns. 5. Uncooperative. 6. Stubborn. 7. Fails to adjust. 8. Cannot work alone. 9. Unable to resume responsibility. 10. Tendency to be jealous. 11. Feels uncomfortable with others. 12. Irritable 13. Inattentive. 14. Short memory span. 15. Aggressive. 16. Over-dependence on teacher. 17. Repeats grade. 18. Daydreaming. 19. Truancy. 20. Defeatism. 21. Hypertension. 22. Nail biting. 23. Scratching. 24. Constant body movement.	1. Feeling of insecurity. 2. Home difficulties. 3. Overly protected. 4. Antagonism between student and parents or teacher. 5. Dissension and quarreling in environment. 6. Nagging at home. 7. Feeling of inferiority. 8. Parents make comparison with other children's abilities. 9. Overly systematic methods. 10. Feeling of failure. 11. Too much pressure and coercion. 12. Mental immaturity. 13. Being made to read before he is ready. 14. Work too difficult. 15. Reading at frustration level. 16. Dependence on mother. 17. Deficiency in readiness. 18. Overstrict parents. 19. Compensations.	1. Development of correct study skills. 2. Harmonize factors which cause emotional conflict. 3. Avoid antagonism. 4. Eliminate undue pressure. 5. Visit home. 6. Avoid rushing student into group activities or reading. 7. Discover his special abilities. 8. Find his interests. 9. Read at instructional level. 10. Give praise and encouragement. 11. Let student know that you are his friend. 12. Provide for quiet individual activity for period. 13. Remove causes of tension. 14. Conference with parents.

TABLE 11

SHORT MEMORY SPAN

(Part 1)

Problems	Diagnosis	Causes	Corrective Procedures
1. Cannot remember words.	1, 2, 3, 4, 5, 7, 10, 11	1, 2, 3, 4, 5, 6, 7	1-14
2. Forgets instructions.	1-11	1-7	1-14
3. Inability to recall events of story.	1-11	1-7	1-14
4. Poor response to school work.	1-11	1-7	1-14
5. Inattention.	1-11	1-7	1-14

TABLE 11 (Continued)

TABLE 11 (Continued)

(Part 2)

Diagnosis	Causes	Corrective Procedures
1. Forgets what he has read. 2. Lacks in comprehension. 3. Inability to remember words. 4. Poor memory for visual materials. 5. Give intelligence test. 6. Can remember only short sequences. 7. Sometimes daydreams. 8. Cannot follow instructions. 9. Disinterested in work. 10. Failure to use picture clues. 11. Failure to use structural analysis.	1. Immaturity. 2. Low intelligence. 3. Lack of visual imagery. 4 Material too difficult. 5. Poor instruction. 6. Lack of motivation. 7. Emotional instability.	1. Motivation in need for remembering. 2. Listening to recordings and then reporting what has been heard. 3. Summarize stories. 4. Answer multiple choice questions. 5. Look at detailed picture and list objects. 6. Learn to read in thought units. 7. Read a selection and then make a mental outline. 8. Memorize short poems. 9. Use spaced recall in practicing retention. 10. List things seen on way to school. 11. Trying to remember things that occurred previous day. 12. Activities such as "Minister's Cat." 13. Repeat sentence spoken by another student or teacher. 14. Make use of association in learning to remember.

TABLE 12

EXTRINSIC INSTEAD OF INTRINSIC MOTIVATION

(Part 1)

Problems	Diagnosis	Causes	Corrective Procedures
1. Disinterested in school.	1-6	1-14	1-21
2. Nonpromotion.	1-6	1-14	1-21
3. Poor attitude.	1-6	1-14	1-21
4. Frustrations.	1-6	1-14	1-21
5. Emotional instability.	1-6	1-14	1-21
6. Dislike for reading.	1-6	1-14	1-21

TABLE 12 (Continued)

TABLE 12 (Continued)

(Part 2)

Diagnosis	Causes	Corrective Procedures
1. Ineffective reading. 2. Dislike for reading. 3. Inattentive. 4. Lack of interest and enthusiasm. 5. Inferior learning capacity. 6. Discover pupil's interest.	1. Teacher insists on subject matter only. 2. Teacher suppresses student. 3. Inadequate past experiences. 4. Material too difficult. 5. Material too meager. 6. Uninteresting material 7. Goals directed entirely by teacher. 8. Teacher regards course of study as a prescription rather than as a guide. 9. No preparation for reading lesson. 10. No clear-cut purpose. 11. Inefficient reading instruction. 12. Lack of motivation from within. 13. Lack of well developed readiness program. 14. Poor home environment.	1. Student should be aware of his progress. 2. Material should be sufficiently easy but challenging. 3. Start with student's interests. 4. Provide guidance. 5. Be encouraging. 6. Balance recreational and informational reading program. 7. Establish harmonious working relationships. 8. Present motivating work. 9. Prepare activities related to reading material. 10. Have study or guide questions on reading material. 11. Give student adequate background of experience and information before reading a selection. 12. Use textbook illustrations. 13. Follow the teacher's manual. 14. Use related materials with reading lessons. 15. Audio-visual materials. 16. Vary lessons. 17. Use reading materials within student's abilities. 18. Do not introduce too much material at one time. 19. Use games and exercises. 20. Use filmstrips. 21. Let student browse among books.

TABLE 13

LACK OF INTEREST

(Part 1)

Problems	Diagnosis	Causes	Corrective Procedures
1. Inattention.	1, 2, 4, 7	1-15	1-13
2. Unsatisfactory school work.	1, 2, 3, 4, 5, 6, 7	1-15	1-13
3. Discipline.	1-7	1-15	1-13
4. Nonpromotion	1-7	1-15	1-13
5. Inadequate concepts.	1, 3, 4	1-15	1-13
6. Lacks imagination.	1	1-15	1-13

TABLE 13 (Continued)

TABLE 13 (Continued)

(Part 2)

Diagnosis	Causes	Corrective Procedures
1. Inattentive.	1. Lack of previous success.	1. Vary teaching techniques.
2. Daydreaming.	2. Material too difficult.	2. Consider individual needs.
3. Carelessness.	3. Lack of experience or background.	3. Group students according to performance levels.
4. Fails to complete assignment.	4. Unobserving teacher.	4. Use suitable materials.
5. Irritable, easily annoyed.	5. Ineffective instruction.	5. Discover interests.
6. Causes class disturbance.	6. Insufficient materials and equipment.	6. Encourage and praise student.
7. Test hearing and vision.	7. Lack of visual acuity.	7. Develop activities related to reading lesson.
	8. Low auditory acuity.	8. Present new experiences.
	9. Physical disabilities.	9. Broaden student's conceptual background.
	10. Uninteresting material.	10. Use filmstrips and pictures.
	11. Mental immaturity.	11. Adapt material to present reading level.
	12. Meager vocabulary.	12. Have interesting books available.
	13. Inadequate concepts.	13. Encourage research.
	14. Material too easy.	
	15. Overemphasis on word calling.	

TABLE 14

UNFAVORABLE READING ATTITUDES

(Part 1)

Problems	Diagnosis	Causes	Corrective Procedures
1. Inattention.	1-10	1-16	1-12
2. Ineffective reading.	1-10	1-16	1-12
3. Dislikes reading.	1-10	1-16	1-12
4. Lacks reading skills.	1-10	1-16	1-12

(Part 2)

Diagnosis	Causes	Corrective Procedures
1. Withdraws from reading.	1. Attitude of other members of family.	1. Vary material and instruction.
2. Meager experiences.	2. Previous experience with reading.	2. Create interest.
3. Faulty reading habits.	3. Started formal reading before ready.	3. Develop charts, utilizing child's experience.
4. Reading skills not developed.	4. Nagged at home or school.	4. Read books to students.
5. Daydreams.	5. Criticism without constructive help.	5. Praise generously.
6. Easily distracted.	6. Older child used as example.	6. Provide interesting books and pictures.
7. Inattention.	7. Material too difficult.	7. Motivate work.
8. Lacks concentration.	8. Inadequate vocabulary.	8. Check physical health and health habits.
9. Rationalization.	9. Lacks ability in word analysis.	9. Provide interesting activities that correlate with reading.
10. Weak vocabulary.	10. Material uninteresting.	10. Student keeps progress chart.
	11. May be working at frustration level.	11. Student works at instructional level.
	12. Poor instruction.	12. Give short assignments, increase length gradually.
	13. Inability to read.	
	14. Home attitude against school.	
	15. Rationalization.	
	16. Lacks experiential background.	

TABLE 15

MENTAL IMMATURITY

(Part 1)

Problems	Diagnosis	Causes	Corrective Procedures
1. Immature mentally.	1, 2, 3, 4, 5, 6, 7, 9 11-17	1-13	1-11
2. Lacks muscular coordination.	4, 5, 8, 13, 16	1, 3, 4, 5, 9, 12, 13	2, 5, 6, 9
3. Speech difficulties.	1-17	1-13	1-11
4. Short memory span.	1, 2, 3, 8, 9, 11, 12, 14, 15, 16, 17	1, 3, 5, 9, 10, 11, 12, 13	1-11
5. Inattentive.	1-17	1-13	1-11
6. Meager vocabulary.	1, 2, 3, 5, 6, 7, 8, 11, 12, 14, 15, 16, 17	1-13	1-11
7. Inferior learning capacity.	1-17	1-13	1-11
8. Failure to recognize words.	1-17	1-13	1-11

(Part 2)

Diagnosis	Causes	Corrective Procedures
1. Intelligence tests.	1. Low intelligence.	1. Student should work at ability and instructional level.
2. Reading tests.	2. Started reading before ready.	2. Provide rich and varied experiences.
3. Visual and auditory tests.	3. Visual or auditory disability.	3. Use visual materials.
4. Lacks muscular coordination.	4. Lacks muscular coordination.	4. Create pride in achievement.
5. Eye and hand dominance.	5. Limited background and experience.	5. Develop ability to take responsibilities.
6. Speech problems.	6. Foreign language in home.	6. Provide strong motivation.
7. Inadequate vocabulary.	7. Eagerness of parents.	7. Encourage student.
8. Lacks physical vitality.	8. Teacher did not know when child was ready to read.	8. Help student see problems and learn how to overcome them.
9. Poor memory and attention span.	9. Physical handicaps.	9. Develop self-confidence.
10. Lacks initiative.	10. Mental immaturity.	10. Group discussions.
11. Over-dependence on teacher.	11. Poor school attendance.	11. Develop ability to evaluate.
12. Emotional immaturity.	12. Emotional instability.	
13. Chronological immaturity.	13. Reprimanded for failure.	
14. Timidity.		
15. Social immaturity.		
16. Feeling of insecurity.		
17. Language immaturity.		

TABLE 16

ENVIRONMENTAL DISTRACTIONS

(Part 1)

Problems	Diagnosis	Causes	Corrective Procedures
1. Unable to adjust.	1-5	1-13	1-7
2. Unattentive.	1-5	1-13	1-7
3. Nervous, tense.	1-5	1-13	1-7
4. Aggressive or shy.	1-5	1-13	1-7
5. Truancy.	1-5	1-13	1-7

TABLE 16 (Continued)

TABLE 16 (Continued)

(Part 2)

Diagnosis	Causes	Corrective Procedures
1. Nervousness. 2. Lack of interest. 3. Emotional instability. 4. Feels insecure. 5. Poor school work.	1. Family influence. 2. Lack of magazines and books in home. 3. Personal anxieties. 4. Playground disturbances. 5. Reaction to storms. 6. Poor lighting in home and school. 7. Poor schoolroom seating. 8. Ventilation in home and school. 9. Economic insecurity. 10. Illiteracy, foreign language. 11. Ignorance. 12. Inconsiderate parents. 13. Overly affectionate parents.	1. Give feeling of security. 2. Discuss problems. 3. Participation in happy classroom situations. 4. Interest patrons in school and home environment. 5. Help student develop sense of well-being 6. Give praise. 7. Adult education.

TABLE 17

SOCIAL MALADJUSTMENT

(Part 1)

Problem	Diagnosis	Causes	Corrective Procedures
1. Lack of school adjustment.	1-8	1-7	1-5
2. Cannot share.	1-8	1-7	1-5
3. Prefers to work alone.	1-8	1-7	1-5
4. Shy or aggressive.	1-8	1-7	1-5
5. Lack of poise.	1-8	1-7	1-5
6. Emotional stress.	1-8	1-7	1-5

(Part 2)

Diagnosis	Causes	Corrective Procedures
1. Withdrawal. 2. Physical handicap. 3. Poor home environment. 4. Unwilling to share. 5. Emotionally unstable. 6. Lacks initiative. 7. Unaccustomed to responsibility. 8. Student tearful, nervous.	1. Broken homes. 2. Quarreling in home. 3. Unhappiness in home. 4. Economic status. 5. Parents inattentive or overprotective. 6. Poor neighborhood. 7. Dislike of classmates.	1. Visit home and help parents. 2. Give student security in school. 3. Build up confidence. 4. Give responsibility to student. 5. Praise student.

A student with reading difficulties has undue emotional tensions because he is involved in a triangle of emotions. His parents show their unhappiness in his failure, the teacher is disappointed, and he is the most unhappy of them all because not only does he think that he is a failure, but he feels that he has let his parents and teacher down. Since emotional instability plays such havoc in school situations, it is important that the teacher learn to diagnose cases of emotional stress effectively and help the student overcome his fears and unhappiness.

Many factors are enmeshed in the problem of emotions. The teacher must give the child a feeling of security and build up his confidence in himself. Since emotional problems cause reading disability, and reading disabilities can cause emotional disturbances, it is difficult to overcome the pressure. When the inability to read has been the cause of the emotional stress, it usually disappears as soon as the student learns to read.

WORD ANALYSIS

TABLE 18

INADEQUATE VOCABULARY

(Part 1)

Problems	Diagnosis	Causes	Corrective Procedures
1. Lacks comprehension.	1-9	1-12	1-19
2. Dislikes reading.	1-9	1-12	1-19
3. Difficulty in expressing himself.	1-9	1-12	1-19
4. Inability to interpret implications.	1-9	1-12	1-19
5. Fails to understand specific word meanings.	1-9	1-12	1-19
6. Reads slowly.	1-9	1-12	1-19

(Part 2)

Diagnosis	Causes	Corrective Procedures
1. Inability to understand obvious facts stated in text.	1. Lack of experience.	1. Varied experiences.
2. Slow silent reading.	2. Home environment.	2. Visual materials.
3. Hesitancy in oral reading.	3. Foreign language in home.	3. Dramatization of words.
4. Limited comprehension.	4. Defective vision.	4. Have students list words they know.
5. Fails to express himself satisfactorily.	5. Mental immaturity.	5. Provide simple, interesting material.
6. Lack of vocabulary sequence.	6. Intellectual inability.	6. Anticipate vocabulary needs of daily assignments. Present in other context.
7. Disinterested in reading.	7. Difficulty in word recognition techniques.	7. Develop interest in increasing vocabulary.
8. Mental immaturity.	8. Reading material too difficult.	8. Keep word book for new or troublesome words.
9. Low intelligence.	9. Does not know how to use dictionary.	9. Make use of current school experiences, seasonal interests and units of teaching.
	10. Habit of guessing.	10. Problems which require informational answers.
	11. Refusal to try word.	11. Oral discussion periods.
	12. Inadequate word attack.	12. Use dictionary.
		13. Make charts and booklets.
		14. Give descriptions and tell experiences.
		15. Attempt to have a carry-over of vocabulary from one book to another by using closely related series.
		16. Become aware of new words.
		17. Get words from contextual and picture clues.
		18. Train in structural and phonetic analysis.
		19. Encourage wider reading.

TABLE 19

DIFFICULTY IN WORD RECOGNITION

(Part 1)

Problems	Diagnosis	Causes	Corrective Procedures
1. Reads slowly.	1-10	1-13	1-14
2. Meager vocabulary.	1-10	1-13	1-14
3. Comprehension low.	1-10	1-13	1-14
4. Has difficulty in recognizing words.	1-10	3, 5, 9, 11, 12, 13	1-14
5. Dislikes reading.	1-10	1-13	1-14

(Part 2)

Diagnosis	Causes	Corrective Procedures
1. Fails to recognize abstract sight words.	1. Fails to make use of clues.	1. Use of phrases.
2. Hesitates in oral reading.	2. Immaturity.	2. Exercises in building compound words.
3. Fails to make use of contextual clues.	3. Low mental capacity.	3. Learn to utilize context clues.
4. Has low stock of sight words.	4. Lack of experience.	4. Make use of configurations.
5. No power of word analysis.	5. Poor visual analysis.	5. Use picture clues.
6. Numerous requests for help with words.	6. Lack of training in word analysis.	6. Phonetic analysis.
7. Depends on parents or teacher.	7. Inadequate phonics.	7. Word analysis.
8. Makes substitution, omission, additions.	8. Poor vocabulary.	8. Provide incentive.
9. Has reversals and regressions.	9. Inappropriate methods of perceiving and learning new words.	9. Build picture dictionaries.
10. Reads hesitantly.	10. No motivation.	10. Training in vocabulary development.
	11. Visual inefficiency.	11. Workbooks.
	12. Inability to use context clues.	12. Study roots, stems, prefixes, suffixes, and base words.
	13. Dislike of reading.	13. Give visual tests.
		14. Give easier, interesting material.

TABLE 20

FAILURE TO MAKE USE OF CONTEXT CLUES

(Part 1)

Problems	Diagnosis	Causes	Corrective Procedures
1. Limited vocabulary.	1, 2, 3, 4, 5	1-9	1-8
2. Comprehension low.	1, 2, 3, 4, 5	1-9	1-8
3. Poor reader.	1, 2, 3, 4, 5	1-9	1-8

TABLE 20 (Continued)

TABLE 20 (Continued)

(Part 2)

Diagnosis	Causes	Corrective Procedures
1. Test vision. 2. Makes word substitution. 3. Perfunctory vocabulary. 4. Comprehension unsatisfactory. 5. Indifference to reading.	1. Limited vocabulary. 2. Carelessness in word recognition. 3. Not trained to use context clues. 4. Teacher does not make use of contextual instruction. 5. Mental immaturity. 6. Lack of experience. 7. Material too difficult. 8. Lack of motivation. 9. Lacks phonetic ability.	1. Student should read to end of sentence or paragraph to try to recognize the word. 2. Ask questions and make suggestions to guide student to recognize word. 3. Sentence completion exercises. 4. While telling a story, pause and have students supply the missing word. 5. Rearrange sentences or paragraphs in a story and have students arrange sequence. 6. Vocabulary building. 7. Easier reading material. 8. Phonics.

TABLE 21

INABILITY TO PERCEIVE WORD BEGINNINGS OR ENDINGS

(Part 1)

Problems	Diagnosis	Causes	Corrective Procedures
1. Fails to recognize words.	1-6	1-7	1-13
2. Incorrect pronunciation.	1-6	1-7	1-13
3. Hesitancy in reading.	1-6	1-7	1-13
4. Weak in comprehension.	2, 4, 5, 6	1, 5, 6, 7	3, 5, 8, 9, 12

(Part 2)

Diagnosis	Causes	Corrective Procedures
1. Often associated with reversal tendencies. 2. Failure to note or discriminate beginnings as *s* in see, saw. 3. Pronounces words incorrectly. 4. Cannot analyze words phonetically. 5. Auditory tests. 6. Visual tests.	1. Carelessness. 2. Phonics presented too soon. 3. Defective hearing. 4. Defective vision. 5. Poor instruction. 6. Lack of word analysis. 7. Inadequate phonetic training.	1. Pronounce initial consonant sound until student begins to recognize sound. 2. Write words on chalkboard. Student underlines first letter. 3. Place emphasis on noticing word endings and beginnings. 4. Build word families. 5. Use dictionaries. 6. Exercises in alphabetizing. 7. Use large wall charts with: s b — — sat big sang boy 8. Students fill in blanks. (S—— likes to run). 9. Draw pictures to complete sentences. (I sleep in a b——.) 10. Pictures from magazines. Student names objects beginning with designated sound. 11. Riddles: I am thinking of a word that begins like the word *sat*. 12. Select words used in context (Alice has a new h——.) 13. Write initial sound as teacher says word.

TABLE 22

DIFFICULTY IN SYLLABICATION

(Part 1)

Problems	Diagnosis	Causes	Corrective Procedures
1. Inability to pronounce words correctly.	1-4	1, 2	1-5
2. Poor spelling.	1-4	1, 2	1-5
3. Incorrect division of words in writing.	1-4	1, 2	1-5

(Part 2)

Diagnosis	Causes	Corrective Procedures
1. Cannot pronounce longer words. 2. Spelling poor. 3. Fails to divide words correctly at end of line. 4. Limited in structural analysis.	1. Poor or no instruction in syllabication. 2. Poor auditory acuity.	1. Use dictionary. 2. Ear training. 3. Learn to use diacritical markings. 4. Practice dividing words into syllables. 5. Learn the following study helps: a. If the first vowel letter in a word is followed by two consonants, the first syllable usually ends with the first of the two consonants. In other words, divide between the consonants. However, do not separate letters representing a single sound, such as proph-et, or math-ematics. b. If the first vowel letter in a word is followed by a single consonant, that consonant usually begins the second syllable. c. If the last syllable of a word ends in *le*, the consonant just before *le* usually begins the last syllable. d. Do not separate a final *ed* from the rest of the word unless it is itself a syllable, as joined, not join-ed; walked, not walk-ed; but lift-ed, or point-ed.

SPEED AND COMPREHENSION

TABLE 23

INEFFECTIVE COMPREHENSION

(Part 1)

Problems	Diagnosis	Causes	Corrective Procedures
1. Lack of interest.	1-10	1-13	1-19
2. Inability to answer question satisfactorily.	1-10	1-13	1-19
3. Poor concentration.	1-7, 9, 10	1-13	1-19
4. Inexpressive oral reading.	1, 2, 5-10	1-13	1-19
5. Cannot follow continuity of story.	1, 2, 4-10	1-13	1-19

TABLE 23 (Continued)

TABLE 23 (Continued)

(Part 2)

Diagnosis	Causes	Corrective Procedures
1. Passive reading. 2. Does not understand what has been read. 3. Cannot answer questions. 4. Lack of interest. 5. Mental test in severe cases. 6. Tense and inattentive. 7. Pronouncing words but not getting thought. 8. Cannot organize what he reads. 9. Slow word recognition. 10. Overemphasis on mechanics of word recognition.	1. Inadequate experience. 2. Immaturity. 3. Low intelligence. 4. Poor eye movement. 5. Inadequate vocabulary. 6. Vagrant thoughts disturb child. 7. Lack of motivation. 8. Poor instruction. 9. Material too difficult. 10. Reading at frustration level. 11. Fails to have a plan for working. 12. Mechanical inaccuracies in reading. 13. Overemphasis on oral reading.	1. Student begins at instructional level. 2. Provide interesting material. 3. Have variety in instruction. 4. Learn to organize material. 5. Give sequence of events. 6. Provide study guides and problems. 7. Present purpose for reading. 8. Learn to concentrate. 9. Develop vocabulary. 10. Motivate work. 11. Widen perceptual span. 12. Phrase or unit reading. 13. Filmstrips and other materials pertaining to lesson. 14. Read with expression. 15. Outline material read. 16. Provide easy but challenging material. 17. Give shorter assignments. 18. Discussions promoting the understanding of: a. Figures of speech, b. Words, c. Idiosyncrasies. 19. Teach use of punctuation marks.

TABLE 24

UNSATISFACTORY SILENT READING RATE

(Part 1)

Problems	Diagnosis	Causes	Corrective Procedures
1. Reads below average rate of speed.	1-13	1-20	1-12
2. Cannot complete assignments.	1-13	1-20	1-13
3. Improper eye movement.	1-13	1-20	1-12
4. Word by word reader.	1-13	1-20	1-12
5. Lacks comprehension.	1-13	1-20	1-13
6. Fails to enjoy reading.	1-13	1-20	1-12
7. Lip movement.	1, 2, 4, 7, 8, 10, 11	2, 3, 5, 9, 12, 16, 17	1, 2, 3, 4, 6, 7, 10, 11,
8. Inner vocalization.	1, 2, 3, 5, 7, 8, 10, 11	1, 2, 3, 5, 9, 12, 16-20	1, 2, 3, 4, 6, 7, 10, 11,
9. Inefficient in word analysis.	2, 4, 5, 6, 9, 11-13	3, 4, 5, 12, 13, 15, 16 18, 19, 20	1, 2, 3, 7-13
10. Reads too fast for comprehension.	12, 13	16	1, 8, 12, 13

TABLE 24 (Continued)

TABLE 24 (Continued)

(Part 2)

Diagnosis	Causes	Corrective Procedures
1. Lip movement. 2. Hesitancy. 3. Inner vocalization. 4. Poor eye movement. 5. Word by word reader. 6. Comprehension low. 7. Reads below average rate for silent rate reading. Average words per minute 1st........-80-100 2nd........-100-140 3rd........-120-160 4th........-140-180 5th........-160-200 6th........-180-280 7th........-180-300 8th through college— -180-1,000 8. Lacks ability in word analysis. 9. Narrow perceptual span. 10. Short memory span. 11. Reads too fast and sacrifices understanding. 12. Reads too slowly but comprehends well. 13. Omissions and substitutions.	1. Inner speech. 2. Lip movement. 3. Word by word reader. 4. Cannot syllabicate. 5. Emotional instability. 6. Material uninteresting. 7. Defective vision. 8. Narrow perceptual span. 9. Lack of interest. 10. Poor attitude. 11. Faulty eye movement. 12. Inadequate vocabulary. 13. Lack of practice in reading. 14. Head movement. 15. Unable to analyze words. 16. Poor instruction. 17. Short memory span. 18. Overemphasis on word analysis. 19. Material too difficult. 20. General slowness in all responses.	1. Choose material that has good carry-over vocabulary. 2. Limit amount of reading. 3. Rereading of known material for a definite purpose. 4. Eliminate head, throat, finger and lip movement. 5. Read under time pressure. 6. Read to music and rhythm. 7. Keep progress chart. 8. Do not sacrifice speed for comprehension. 9. Practice on mechanical equipment. 10. Provide interesting material. 11. Motivate reading. 12. A good reader adjusts his reading speed to three levels according to his purpose. 13. Give exercises on comprehension.

TABLE 25

INEFFECTIVE ORAL READING

(Part 1)

Problems	Diagnosis	Causes	Corrective Procedures
1. Reads in an inaudible voice.	1, 2, 3, 8	1, 2, 3, 4, 6, 8, 9, 10	1, 2, 3, 4, 5, 6, 7, 12
2. Reads in high-pitched voice.	1, 2, 3, 8	1, 2, 3, 4, 6, 8, 9, 10	1, 2, 3, 4, 5, 6, 7, 12
3. Lack of breath control.	1, 2, 3, 8	1, 2, 3, 4, 6, 7, 8, 9, 10	1, 2, 3, 4, 5, 6, 7, 9, 10, 12
4. Poor enunciation and articulation.	1, 2, 3	1, 2, 3, 4, 5, 6, 7, 8, 9, 10	1, 2, 3, 4, 5, 6, 7, 8, 9 10, 12
5. Insertions and substitutions.	2, 4, 6	1, 2, 3, 4, 5, 7, 8, 9, 10	1, 3, 5, 6, 7, 8, 10, 11, 12
6. Repetitions.	2, 4, 6	1, 2, 3, 4, 5, 7, 8, 9, 10	1, 3, 5, 6, 7, 8, 10, 11, 12
7. Does not remember what has been read.	2, 4, 6	1, 2, 3, 4, 5, 7, 8, 9, 10	3, 5, 6, 7, 10, 11, 12
8. Reads too slowly or too rapidly.	1-8	1-10	1-12

TABLE 25 (Continued)

TABLE 25 (Continued)
(Part 2)

Diagnosis	Causes	Corrective Procedures
1. Poor voice control. 2. Nervous and tense. 3. Poor articulation. 4. Short memory span. 5. Unsatisfactory reading rate. 6. Dislikes reading. 7. Holds book too near or too far from eyes. 8. Inexpressive oral reading.	1. Immaturity. 2. Poor instruction. 3. Emotional instability. 4. Oral reading before silent reading. 5. Inadequate vocabulary. 6. Adenoids, tonsils. 7. Poor vision. 8. Lack of fluency. 9. Faulty word recognition. 10. Lack of voice control.	1. Have student sit some distance away and read correctly pointing out how to read effectively. 2. Read in dramatization. 3. Help him become conscious of his difficulty. 4. Emphasize conversational voice. 5. Provide easier material. 6. NEVER read orally until selection has been read silently. 7. Relieve embarrassment and self-consciousness. 8. Apply phonics. 9. Practice in clear enunciation. 10. Insist on accurate reading. 11. Give written or oral exercises on comprehension. 12. Choral reading.

TABLE 26
REPETITIONS
(Part 1)

Problems		Diagnosis	Causes	Corrective Procedures
1. Repeats words read orally or silently.	1-3		1-9	1-8
2. Lacks comprehension.	1-3		1-9	1-8
3. Lack of rhythm in reading.	1-3		1-9	1-8

(Part 2)

Diagnosis	Causes	Corrective Procedures
1. Slow reading. 2. Repeats words. 3. Lacks fluency in reading.	1. Slowness in word recognition. 2. Faulty eye movement. 3. Nervousness or self-consciousness. 4. Failure to comprehend reading material. 5. Habitual. 6. Occur with reversals. 7. Slow word recognition. 8. Poor comprehension. 9. Material too difficult.	1. Use of phrase cards. 2. Use of questions requiring reorganization of context. 3. Remove distractions. 4. Choral reading. 5. Larger stock of sight words. 6. Provide training in word analysis. 7. Provide easier material. 8. Check handedness and eyedness.

TABLE 27

POOR PRONUNCIATION

(Part 1)

Problem	Diagnosis	Causes	Corrective Procedures
1. Language handicap.	1, 2, 3, 4, 5, 6, 7, 8	1, 2, 3, 4, 5, 6, 7, 8, 9, 10, 11 12, 13, 14, 15	1-19
2. Speech difficulty.	1, 2, 4, 5, 7, 8	1, 2, 4, 5, 6, 7, 9, 10-15	1-19
3. Incorrect pronunciation.	1, 2, 3, 4, 5, 6, 7, 8	1, 2, 3, 4, 5, 6, 7, 8, 9, 10-15	1-19
4. Substitutions.	1, 4, 5, 7, 8	1, 2, 4, 5, 6, 7, 9, 10-15	1-19

(Part 2)

Diagnosis	Causes	Corrective Procedures
1. Inaccurate speech.	1. Carelessness.	1. Test for auditory and visual acuity.
2. Limited vocabulary.	2. Reads too rapidly.	2. Give training which requires accurate perception.
3. Inattention to meaning.	3. Limited experience.	3. Training in word analysis.
4. Unable to say certain letters.	4. Lack of phonics.	4. Syllabication.
5. Audiometer test.	5. Material too difficult.	5. Phonetic analysis.
6. Telebinocular Survey test.	6. Hearing loss.	6. Attack new word through initial sounds.
7. Check student's home environment.	7. Inattention.	7. Teach long and short vowel sounds.
8. Physical defect should be determined by specialist.	8. Faulty vision.	8. Learn prefixes and suffixes.
	9. Inadequate vocabulary.	9. Drill on common sight words.
	10. Foreign background.	10. Decrease rate of oral reading.
	11. Defective formation of speech organs.	11. Illustrate and dramatize new words.
	12. Inability to perceive differences in sounds even though hearing is normal.	12. Drill on words that are easily confused.
	13. Nervousness.	13. Practice on internal vowels.
	14. Habit.	14. Give easier reading material.
	15. Imitation of another individual.	15. Choral reading.
		16. Teacher must be a good example.
		17. Learn and repeat rhymes and jingles correctly.
		18. Dramatization which call for different types of voices as baby with a medium voice, and father with a big deep voice.
		19. Help each student with the particular sounds he cannot say. Show him the position of lips and tongue if necessary. Have him listen to the sound in rhymes and jingles. Have him try to say the sound using easy words with one consonant and a vowel as in "key"or "cow."

TABLE 28

WORD BY WORD READING

(Part 1)

Problems	Diagnosis		Causes	Corrective Procedures
1. Poor comprehension.	1, 2, 5	1-14		1-12
2. Slow reader.	1-5	1-14		1-12
3. Reads word by word.	1-5	1-14		1-12
4. Finds reading uninteresting.	1-5	1-14		1-12
5. Inadequate phrase reading.	1-5	1-14		1-12

(Part 2)

Diagnosis	Causes	Corrective Procedures
1. Student reads word by word.	1. Poor instruction.	1. Silent reading before oral reading.
2. Weak in comprehension.	2. Immaturity.	2. Place emphasis on thought getting.
3. Inner vocalization.	3. Fails to recognize that the *idea* is the important factor in reading.	3. Work for reading in thought units.
4. Lip movement.	4. Material too difficult.	4. Tachistoscopic exercises, using phrases.
5. Indifferent to reading.	5. Lack of interest in material.	5. Give interesting but easy material.
	6. Sentences too long.	6. Use phrases on filmstrips and flash cards.
	7. Lacks background.	7. Learning games involving thought units.
	8. Has not been taught to read in thought units.	8. Stories with suspense.
	9. Lacks basic vocabulary.	9. Student answers questions pertaining to materials read.
	10. Overemphasis on word recognition and phonics.	10. Workbooks.
	11. Lack of attention to punctuation.	11. Avoid finger pointing.
	12. Lack of attention to thought.	12. Avoid lip movement and inner vocalization.
	13. No motivation.	
	14. Inability to associate ideas and to perceive relationships.	

TABLE 29

LIP MOVEMENT AND INNER VOCALIZATION

(Part 1)

Problems		Diagnosis	Causes	Corrective Procedures
1. Slow reading.	1-5		1-13	1-9
2. Moves lips or has inner oral movement.	1-5		1-13	1-9
3. Word by word reader.	1-5		1-13	1-9
4. Individual usually is unaware of problem.	1-5		1-13	1-9

TABLE 29 (Continued)

TABLE 29 (Continued)

(Part 2)

Diagnosis	Causes	Corrective Procedures
1. Reads slowly. 2. Poor comprehension. 3. Moves lips. 4. Inner speech. 5. Points with finger.	1. Tries to sound out word he does not recognize. 2. Overemphasis on oral reading. 3. Insufficient emphasis on meaning. 4. Too much stress on reading with expression. 5. Instruction has not stressed phrase units. 6. Slow reader. 7. Auditory learner. 8. Lacks sufficient vocabulary. 9. Early instruction stressed auditory phrases. 10. Too much phonetic training. 11. Lacks visual imagery. 12. Weak in vocabulary development. 13. Material too difficult.	1. Have student become aware of his habit. 2. Reduce amount of oral reading. 3. Increase silent reading. 4. Use tachistoscopic phrase reading. 5. Give easier and more meaningful material. 6. Place finger over lip. 7. Stress more speed in reading. 8. Speeded reading and comprehension exercises. 9. Press thumb on soft part of under-jaw.

INSTRUCTIONAL CAUSES

TABLE 30

INSTRUCTIONAL

(Part 1)

Problems	Diagnosis	Causes	Corrective Procedures
1. Introduction to reading before child is ready.	1-5	1-21	1-11
2. Interruptions in training.	1-5	1-21	1-11
3. Skipping grades.	1-5	1-21	1-11
4. Repeating grades.	1-5	1-21	1-11

TABLE 30 (Continued)

TABLE 30 (Continued)

(Part 2)

Diagnosis	Causes	Corrective Procedures
1. Student dislikes reading. 2. Student lacks perserverance. 3. Tendency to retreat from responsibility. 4. Tendency to engage in daydreaming. 5. Lack of interest in work.	1. Illness. 2. Irregular attendance. 3. Transferring from school to school. 4. Physical defects. 5. Incorrect grouping. 6. Poor seating. 7. Begins reading before ready. 8. Emotional instability. 9. Inadequate or incorrect teaching techniques. 10. Teacher's attitude. 11. Too much or too little drill. 12. Too little or too much oral reading. 13. Overstress on one skill. 14. Purposeless reading. 15. Failure to check on development of basic skill. 16. Format of book. 17. Failure to create enthusiasm. 18. Difficulty locating information. 19. Inadequate developmental experience. 20. Lack of reading readiness. 21. Insufficient reading materials.	1. Improve instruction. 2. Teacher enthusiasm. 3. Make reading meaningful. 4. Evaluate instruction. 5. Improve specific skills. 6. Arouse student's curiosity. 7. Have sufficient reading materials available. 8. Create a need for reading. 9. Have flexible and workable groupings. 10. Analyze student's needs and abilities. 11. Make frequent check on student's progress.

TABLE 31

IMPROPER GROUPING IN CLASSROOM

(Part 1)

Problem	Diagnosis	Cause	Corrective Procedures
1. Child unable to progress at his own rate of achievement.	1-7	1-7	1-7
2. Child given feeling of failure.	1-7	1-7	1-7
3. Child not working at his instructional level.	1-7	1-7	1-7

(Part 2)

Diagnosis	Causes	Corrective Procedures
1. Basis of results of intelligence and achievement tests. 2. Teacher's observation. 3. Pupil is restless and not making proper progress. 4. Lack of interest. 5. Different pupil interests. 6. Different rates of learning. 7. Visual and auditory tests.	1. Failure to give standardized tests. 2. Lack of check on child's progress. 3. Failure to consider the child's social level. 4. Failure to regroup child. 5. Teacher assumes all children's needs are similar. 6. Failure to note individual differences. 7. Lack of detection of physical handicaps.	1. Observe student's behavior. 2. Give standardized tests. 3. Make grouping flexible. 4. Group according to activities. 5. Plan reading program so it will provide for individualization. 6. Give student material at his instructional level. 7. Develop maximum power of each student.

TABLE 32

UNSUITABLE READING MATERIALS

(Part 1)

Problems	Diagnosis	Causes	Corrective Procedures
1. Insufficient material.	1-3	1-4	1-6
2. Unsuitable material.	1-3	1-4	1-6
3. Uninteresting material.	1-3	1-4	1-6
4. Materials worn and dirty.	1-3	1-4	1-6

(Part 2)

Diagnosis	Causes	Corrective Procedures
1. Student is not interested in reading. 2. Student is tired of reading same type story over and over. 3. Material too difficult.	1. Economic status of board. 2. Teacher not informed as to suitable material. 3. Disinterest of parent and local officials. 4. Failure to read brings same book to child second year.	1. Make charts, scrapbooks. 2. Develop contracts in reading. 3. Inform administrative office of needs. 4. Inform parents. 5. Have stories with action. 6. Discover student's interests.

Various kinds of diagnostic procedures can be employed in learning more about the student. As mentioned previously, autobiographies, sentence completion, and check sheets can be developed for this purpose.

10 Instruments and Equipment as Teaching Aids

Equipment for Diagnostic Procedures
Reading Training Materials
Reading Materials

There are a great many auto-instructional devices available, and there are various points of view regarding the value and use of such material in the teaching of reading.

Well-trained reading teachers realize that reading instruction must be sound and valid, and that students must develop the correct skills if they are to be efficient readers.

There is disagreement as to the effectiveness of mechanical devices. Some educators believe that the students will do as well or better without the mechanical devices. There are others who believe that these machines have a special interest for the students and serve as a motivating factor. The mechanical equipment may hold the students' interest and so help break down the resistance to reading instruction. The teacher's enthusiasm about the machines reflects in the students' attitude.

Whereas teachers should not expect audiovisual devices to replace personal instruction in the classroom, they should use them in conjunction with their own instruction. But many reading rooms are heavily mechanized and over-machined. The teacher must bear in mind that the instruments are a means to an end, but their value should be determined by the extent to which they help achieve certain goals.

EQUIPMENT FOR DIAGNOSTIC PROCEDURES

Equipment is virtually a necessity for some diagnoses. In visual screening, although the teacher may be aware of some difficulty because a student has difficulty in seeing or hearing, she will want to have a more objective test made to confirm her thinking.

In the case of auditory acuity, the teacher can give the watch or whisper test, and if a student fails to respond, she will want a more objective diagnosis made.

Various machines are available which can be used by the reading teacher. Some parents hesitate in taking their children for an eye examination or a hearing test, but if the teacher will screen these students, the parents usually will be glad to take them to a specialist for a thorough examination.

Machines used for screening and diagnosis include the following:

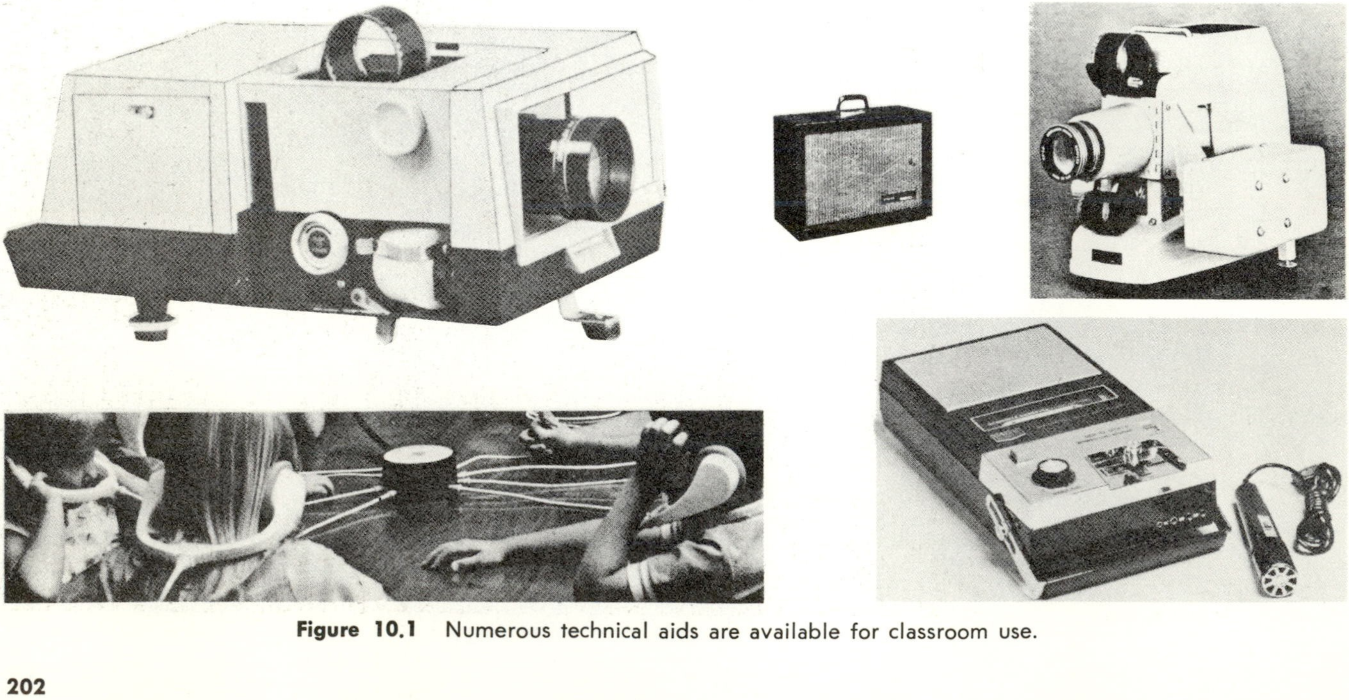

Figure 10.1 Numerous technical aids are available for classroom use.

1. Keystone Telebinocular Visual Survey (Keystone Company)
2. Orthorator (Bausch and Lomb Optical Company)
3. The Reading Eye (Educational Development Laboratories)
4. Beltone Audiometer (Beltone Electronic Corporation)

If teachers plan to use any of the above equipment, they should take special training in giving diagnostic tests and interpreting the results.

Teachers should be aware of the inherent limitations of the Snellen Chart tests for vision. Many students tell the teacher that they have 20/20 vision. This means that they can see what they are supposed to see normally at twenty feet, but the test does not take into consideration the near-point vision. A student may have good farsighted vision and not see at all clearly at sixteen inches from the eye.

READING TRAINING MATERIALS

Under this heading falls the use of semiautomated audiovisual materials such as filmstrips, slides, records, cassettes, tape recorders, television, radio, films, and opaque and overhead projectors.

The audiovisual materials make it possible to instruct more students with fewer teachers, but they may not be able to provide the personal touch that can be given to smaller groups.

A second media group instructs simultaneously and is referred to as teaching machines. Today there are many machines and many types of training materials available to the schools. It would require an entire book to list all the media on the market. If a teacher is interested in these instruments she should consult the catalogs in the administrative offices. Representatives from the audiovisual companies are glad to come and demonstrate their equipment. Complete information may also be obtained by writing to the following:

1. National Audio-Visual Equipment Directory, Fairfax, Virginia.
2. Audio-Instructional Devices, AID, Box 4456, Lubbock, Texas.
3. Instructional Materials and Equipment Distributors, 1520 Cotner Avenue, Los Angeles.
4. A Guide of Programmed Instructional Materials, by the Center for Programmed Instruction, Inc. U.S. Dept. of Health, Education and Welfare, Office of Education, Washington, D. C.

FILMSTRIPS AND SLIDES

Filmstrips are easy to use and provide an enriching experience for students. The strips may be shown on individual viewers or on the screen. Filmstrips are available on almost every subject and are reasonably priced. Cassette commentaries accompany many of the filmstrips or the teacher can make the cassettes to accompany the strips.

Slides can be used at every grade level. They can be purchased commercially or they can be student-produced. Cassettes can accompany the slides. Slides are available in almost every drug store and in camera shops. Some students prepare slides for their special reports. An adaptive lens on a camera makes it possible to reproduce pages from books for use as slides.

CASSETTES AND TAPE RECORDERS

The teacher and students are able to record their work as an aid to making presentations on all subjects. For lower grades, exercises for following directions and for listening are very helpful. The cassette recorder is a compact machine that is easy to use. Some students

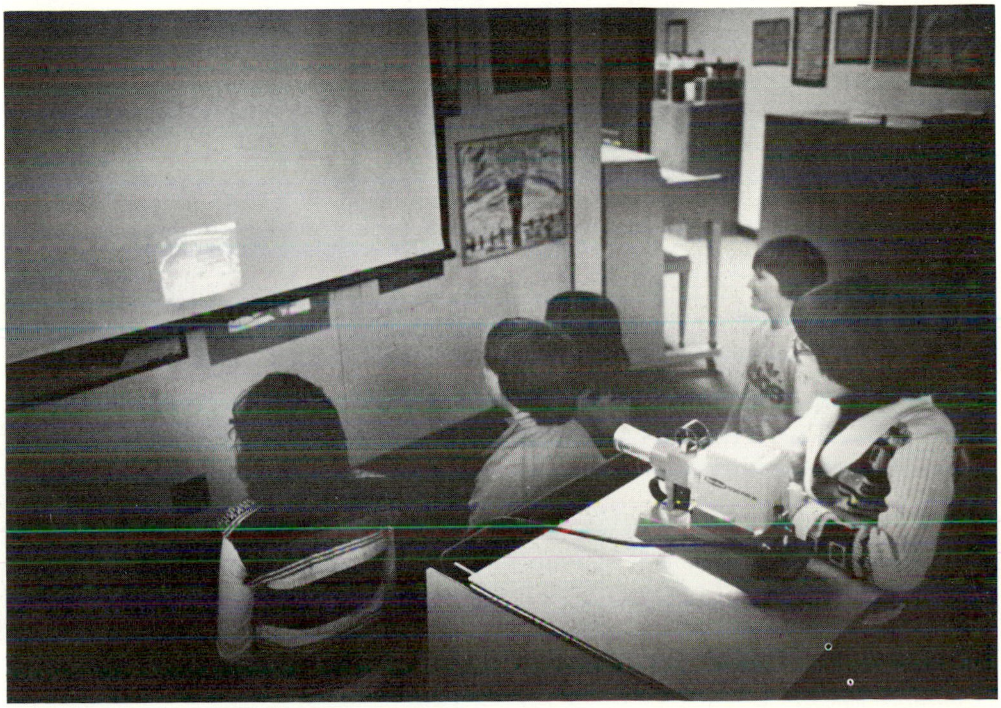

Figure 10.2 Filmstrips are valuable learning aids.

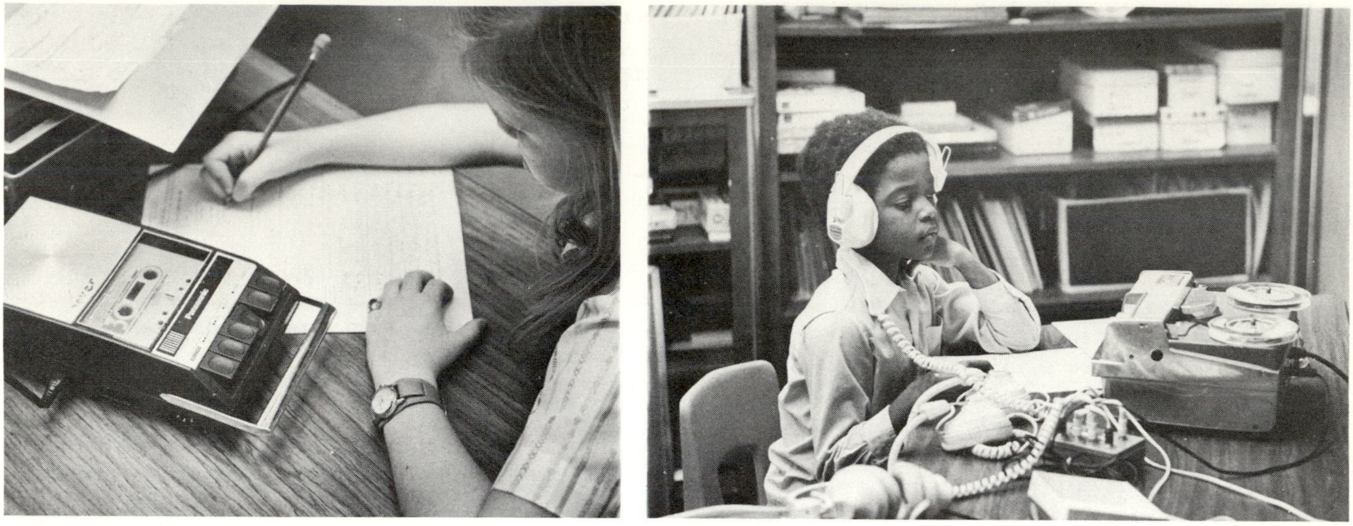

Figure 10.3 Students can readily follow taped instructions.

in fourth, fifth, and sixth grade like to have their own recorders with which they can record class discussions, as well as music which they may present to the class. Commercially-made cassettes can be purchased from school service stores.

OVERHEAD PROJECTOR

The overhead projector is used for group discussions. The teachers and students can make their own transparencies for projector use by photographing pictures from books, or they can make them by drawing their own illustrations. The image is projected on a wall or screen for class discussion. In using this machine, the teacher or the student giving the demonstration faces the audience. In explaining specific features or items, the teacher or student can point to the specifics under discussion.

OPAQUE PROJECTOR

Almost anything can be shown on this projector, including pictures in books, magazines, postcards, live specimens, and students' work. The object is reflected by a mirror in the projector. The one objection to this piece of equipment is that it is bulky and heavy to move about.

READING MACHINES

There are many reading machines on the market today. If the machines serve as motivation for the students, they will have answered some purpose. However, the teacher should not expect the machine to replace his personal interest and instruction in the classroom.

STUDY CARRELS

If individualized instruction is to be presented, study carrels are available. The portable type carrel is especially convenient because it can be moved about the room and stored when not in use. Permanent carrels may be built for the instruments that are not easily movable.

Figure 10.4 The overhead projector is used for group discussions.

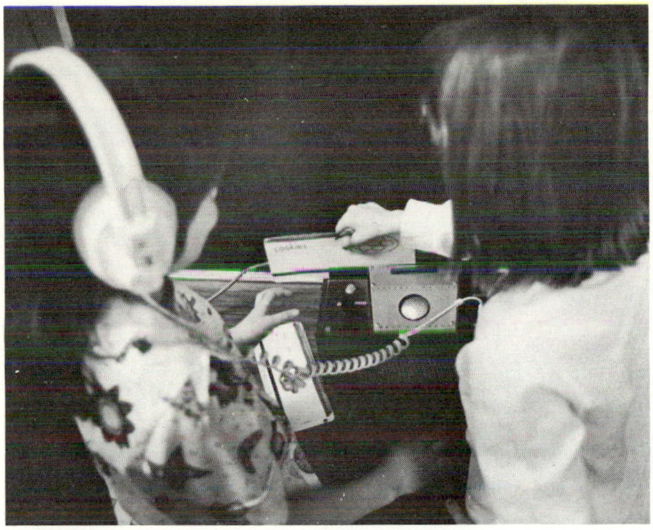

Figure 10.5 Reading machines serve as motivation for the students.

Figure 10.6 Carrels are available for individualized instruction.

LISTENING CENTERS

Listening centers are useful for self-directed study. The head phones are connected to a jack and can accommodate up to eight students at a time. Cassettes, tapes, and records can be used for this type of directed learning. If tapes or cassettes are used, the tapes can be commercial or made by the teacher.

READING MATERIALS

A large variety of reading materials suited to the needs and interests of the individuals should be accessible at all times. Books should be placed so that the students will be able to examine them and read them. Magazines, picture files, and clipping files should be also a part of the classroom.

Games and various activities are described in this book. It it hoped that the teacher will enlist the help of parents and older students in making the games.

Workbooks may be used, but with caution. Some students have experienced too many failures already, and they have had many workbooks assigned to them in the hope that those workbooks would do the trick in helping to make good readers of them. Workbooks can be very useful if they are properly motivated and properly used.

A reading program, to be successful, must be flexible and fitted to the needs of each student. No one technique or program can be designated as the only successful means for teaching reading. The reading training must center in students rather than books, and it must adjust to the individual needs and interests of each student.

The flexibility of the program and the teacher's willingness to persist in her efforts are the important ingredients in a successful reading program. In teaching reading, the teacher must take a step-by-step approach and accept the student for the person he is rather than as a norm or statistic. It is of greatest importance that the instruction begin at the level where the student can perform with confidence and not in the grade where he is supposed to be in school. The teacher must be encouraging and have an unwavering belief in the student's ability to read successfully.

Figure 10.7 Listening centers are useful for self-directed study.

Index